THEY LIED
TO US IN
SUNDAY SCHOOL

UNCOVERING THE LIES, FRAUD AND DIVINE
CLAIMS OF ORGANIZED RELIGION

IAN ROSS VAYRO

Joshua Books

JoshuaBooks.com

All correspondence to the publisher
Joshua Books
PO Box 1668
Buddina 4575
Queensland Australia

First Printing 2006

Category: Author: Religious & Theology: History: Ancient Mysteries

ISBN 0 9756878 6 7

Cover artwork from a fourteenth Century painting of the Crucifixion on an altar screen at Dorchester Abbey in Oxfordshire UK.

Dedicated to Doug Turner, who was an enduring source
of inspiration with the unique ability of reducing
the most complex ideas and religious principles
down to simple bush logic.

Also to Jim Christian for his selfless assistance
and consideration. Thank you!

No Disputes

Because some people may find themselves at odds with conclusions reached in this book, the author, publisher and associates of this publication will **not** engage in time-consuming written religious argument with readers who hold different opinions.

Those who doubt what is revealed in this book should conduct their own research to verify that the knowledge recorded is supportable in historical records and church archives.

The author has no dispute with Christians who are sincere and whose practice coincides with an ethical sensibility. The intention of *They Lied to us in Sunday School* is to expose doctrines and dogma wrongly proclaimed by ecclesiastical authority as true and factual. This book is published for the benefit, wisdom, instruction and spiritual enlightenment of modern humanity.

They Lied to Us

"Traditional beliefs are like sacred cows grazing in the northern paddock of ones mind. The time has come to open the gate ...

This is well researched information. You may well wonder why the defenders of the modern Christian religions have not asked these questions. Ian Ross Vayro confronts his readers with questions begging the asking and provides answers for serious consideration.

During many years of my ministry I could not reconcile the tribal, jealous, angry, vengeful god of the Old Testament with the One who is unconditional love and who Jesus claimed to be his father. Until I realised that my faith was indeed blind I never began to question. So, one question leads to another and another. You will find many of the answers within these covers if you are prepared for confrontation. Anyone seeking truth must be personally responsible to begin the search.

If you are courageous enough to admit the questions and open enough to receive the answers, then read this book."

Jim Christian

Former minister of charismatic full gospel church - Gold Coast, Australia

The unbelievable success of Books like 'The Da Vinci Code' has indicated that most of the inhabitants of this planet are starved for intellectual stimulation and sensible discussion about the spiritual aspects of their lives. Science has still not agreed on precisely where mankind originated and the Church has never successfully answered the big questions of their genesis and faith. Despite a myriad of new cults and religions, the complete under-standing of our Godhead has advanced little in the past 2000 years. The excesses and accusations published almost daily about the clergy and the Church are both unsettling and confusing to many of us.

Ian Ross Vayro is trained in Ancient History and Archaeology and has made a lifetime study of Theology. In this work, he delves deeply into times BCE and around the Christian era to take the reader on a most interesting journey. **He covers an impressive array of topics and shares with us precisely where he believes we came from; backing it up with scientific collaboration.** This book took him six years to write and displays an encyclopedic knowledge of the Bible and contemporary documentation. In a non-invasive style he opens our eyes to many Biblical anomalies within the prevailing historical context and shows us things the clergy never would, and supplies reliable references for each and every conclusion. Using archaeological detective work, he pulls meaning from the Biblical Scriptures. Sometimes they got it wrong but Vayro does not point the finger at anyone and mostly just reports the facts his research has uncovered. Apart from obvious conclusions, in many cases he leaves the final interpretation to you. It becomes quite apparent however, that our 'mind pictures' from our childhood are way out of focus and that we have been fed on untruths in our learning process. This resulted in the provocative title of this book.

This book is destined to become a classic and is 'required reading' for the parent, schoolteacher or clergyman who wants to source accurate Scriptural knowledge within the contemporary historical context, in order to answer the difficult questions. It is a 'must read' for the Christian or non-Christian who wants to locate a lifetime of research between the covers of just one book.

About the Author

Ian Ross Vayro was born in Townsville, North Queensland, Australia. He was raised in a farming community near Dalby and attended a one teacher primary school. On leaving 'the bush' he was educated in Brisbane then served in the Royal Australian Air Force which allowed him to travel extensively and instilled the discipline he has utilised in most endeavours since. Ian studied Electronic Engineering then Classical Ancient History and Archaeology a somewhat unusual mix and tempered this with a lifelong interest and personal research in Theology. He actively created a successful business life, becoming the best in his business field, culminating in his own hugely successful Outdoor Advertising Company. Ian achieved greatly through a commitment and focus and somewhat perfectionist attitude which he has transferred to his research and work as an author. He is continually spurred on by his numerous collisions with religion in his own search for spiritual truth.

Early in his life Ian observed how people accepted the most implausible data without question when it came as part of one's religious education. His concern was that the Christian message has mostly survived in an uneducated environ and that the teachers of this dogma always restricted their research to just the one Book with no consideration for the contemporary historical context. In his research over the years Ian discovered repeatedly that the supposedly ineffable 'Word of God' will not withstand much scrutiny at all and its conclusions are not only unsubstantiated but are also at variance with recorded history. His decision to make his findings public was motivated by a simple event. When flooding occured in the western Queensland town of Charleville, his own children were told in religious education classes that the people in this town must be evil and that God was punishing them. This was the last straw for someone from the 'bush'. The fact that unqualified and unsuitable people were allowed to teach this nonsense to young children when they were at their most vulnerable, concerned Ian greatly. He commenced his work at that point. His high energy and intelligent questioning resulted in heavy research over several years yielding the discoveries within these covers. He causes his readers to ask some long withheld questions about the 'truths' taught to each and every one of us in our childhood. This is a good read and compels us to confirm, that like Ian, we were all lied to!

CONTENTS

PARTY TRICKS

Let's Play – Twenty Questions

Many books make promises and then don't really deliver; I hope this book is not like that; and I believe that it just may contain things that surprise you. It may outline new things you haven't heard before and show you things that you were never told. It may even change the way you view your Bible. You don't think so? OK; before you commence this book, please try these simple questions; then see if you agree with your answers at the end of your read. This may demonstrate that like me, you were lied to, and that what we were both taught in Sunday School is not necessarily the truth or in some cases what the Bible says anyhow.

(I'll leave the scoring to you, allocate five points for each fully correct answer and mark yourself out of 100.)

1. Was Adam the first man and Eve then created to be his mate? Were they created as babies and cared for, or created fully grown? Was Eve the only wife of Adam?

2. Does the Bible say that Adam, Eve or both of them ate the forbidden apple? Who sinned, Adam or Eve? In the Garden of Eden, what did Adam and Eve use to cover their nakedness?

3. According to Genesis, how many of each animal did Noah take into the ark? Was he rescuing them to preserve the species or were they a food source for his family?

4. How long did the waters prevail? What birds did Noah release to see if there was dry land? Where did the ark land?

5. Was Jesus born in a stable in Bethlehem? Was Jesus' birthday 25 December 0001?

6. What is a manger? How many Wise men visited the baby Jesus?

7. Was Jesus' mother Mary described in the Bible as a 'virgin'? How is it that she had a sister also called Mary?

8. Was Mary in fact the "Queen of Heaven"? Was it the same 'virgin' Mary who made contact with the shepherd children at Fatima, Portugal in 1917, the event classed as a miracle by the Vatican?

9. What is a 'messiah'; does this title mean 'Saviour'; 'Son of God'; King of the Jews or something else? Was Jesus actually the King of the Holy land, the so called "King of the Jews"? Why did the scriptures say he was to be called Immanuel, yet we call him Jesus?

10. What is an angel? Are they white robed sons of God, flying with magnificent wings from the 'Heavenly Host' of God to assist mankind and intercede, on his behalf? Who comprise the Heavenly Host? If Lucifer was a son of God and Jesus was a son of God does this mean they were brothers?

11. What is it that the Bible says will send us to Hell?
    (a)   The rejection of Jesus
    (b)   Lack of faith
    (c)   Sin
    (d)   Lying
    (e)   Breaking the Ten Commandments
    (f)   Not doing good deeds
    (g)   All the above

12. Did both Joseph and Jesus work as carpenters? What was the occupation of Mary Magdalene? What was the occupation of Jesus' mother Mary?

13. When God gave his only begotten Son to die as atonement for the sins of mankind; was this sacrifice of Jesus the 'Son of God' a totally unique event that sets Christianity apart from other religions? Had this sort of sacrifice ever occurred before? Do other religions follow a similar theme or is this what makes Christianity unique? Why does Christianity require the sacrifice of the 'innocent' to redeem the 'guilty'?

14. Where does God reside and is it 'off limits to mankind'? Can a man gaze on the face of God and live?

15. Could we someday locate God, perhaps on another planet? From the Bible, does he dwell in darkness or in the light? Is he accessible, or hidden?

16. The Catholic Church gave specific, stern warnings about one of the following describing it as 'dangerous'; which do you think? (a) rock & roll music (b) motor racing (c) eating chocolate (d) martial arts.

17. What can you recall about the god Ba`al? Was he a 'pagan' entity? Why was he so hated by the Old Testament Hebrew scribes? Was he ever worshipped by the Hebrew people?

18. Why was Jesus called, 'Jesus of Nazareth' if he was born in Bethlehem, sojourned in Egypt and lived in various parts of Galilee? Did Jesus ever marry?

19. Since the <u>Jewish</u> religion rejects Jesus Christ as the Messiah, how is it that the <u>Christian</u> religion still embraces the Jewish Torah in the form of the Old Testament and retains the early Jewish history and its patriarchs like Adam, Noah, Abraham, Moses, and King David as its

own? Are the Christians telling the <u>Jews</u> who wrote the Bible that they got it wrong?

20. How many Disciples did Jesus recruit and how were they selected? Did Jesus previously know them or did he select them at random? Who replaced Judas Iscariot?

Just jot down your answers, and then read on!

CHAPTER ONE

INTRODUCTION: THEY LIED TO US

"You believe Adam was made of the dust of this earth. This I do not believe, though it is supposed that it is so written in the Bible; but it is not to my understanding.... I do not believe that portion of the Bible as the Christian world do. I never did, and I never want to. What is the reason that I do not? Because I have come to understanding, and banished from my mind all the baby stories my mother taught me when I was a child."

Brigham Young, Journal of Discourses, Vol.2, p.6

I believe this book, *'They Lied To Us In Sunday School'* was crying out to be written and I am still somewhat surprised that I am the one who finally wrote it. Someone unshackled by indoctrination, needed to seek out the truth, and to address the errors, contradictions and absurdities in the Bible in its historical context, to honestly and fairly compare other sources to the Biblical view, where possible, and outline what may have occurred in reality, and to seek out the Godhead behind the Christian dogma. I hope and believe that to a fair degree, I have been successful in this endeavour. The final say is however always up to you the reader and it is you who will analyze and do the final summation on whether we got it right. You must then decide whether you believe the direction our research takes us, or not. This is however not a "tearing down" exercise and should never be considered as such. What we are seeing this century is a full paradigm shift in the world religions that are based on the original Jewish texts. This encompasses the **Jewish, Christian** and **Islamic** faiths and accounts for an enormous number of today's believers. Professor Kuhn explained that a 'paradigm' represents;

"The entire constelllation of beliefs, values and techniques shared by the members of a given community or discipline." [1]

The professor goes on to state the prevailing situation that once paradigms are set, recipients seem totally blocked to contrary suggestions. In other words, 'There is nothing as permanent as proved error". Change will only come with education and in this age of information technology, the laity is becoming educated. Accordingly that which was held as unequivocal Christian dogma is now becoming intellectually rejected as quaint mystic hangovers from the past. I am certainly not the first to come up with much of this information and have to believe that the learned among the clergy are quite aware of these things and are simply keeping them from the laity. This has of course been the situation for millennium.

Had this book been called "They Lied to **Me** in Sunday School", the reader might reasonably assume that as a result of the lies told to me in my youth, I now have some axe to grind, which is actually far from the truth. I certainly have no personal vendetta against one of my now aging Sunday School teachers. It just happened that my studies have uncovered a wide-spread deception that has changed the course of history, a deception of such mammoth proportions, that I felt it should be shared. I discovered that most of us had been taught large doses of palpable nonsense and although this was not necessarily restricted to Sunday School; was certainly most prevalent there. It is an interesting story and an interesting journey and I am really glad you are along for the ride.

The first part of the discovery is that the whole Christian package taught to us from Sunday School was not the truth and both you and I accepted things in good faith that are simply not true. Collectively it has affected our thinking, our culture and our lives. Our society en masse rarely questions anything to do with religion, or if they do, inertia ensures that no one does much about it. This applies particularly to spiritual things and results in a "lock on/lock out" mentality with an inbuilt refusal to act, to evaluate, to actually question, or even for a minute, to stop and THINK.

The enormity of the whole fraudulent religious philosophy became more apparent as I progressed. The imparting of untruths (whether or not it is done intentionally) is still called lying, so this, along with the realization that a large portion of church attendees the world over have been lied to, resulted in this book. The generic nature of the misinformation makes it certain that you, like me, were lied to, and that resulted in the title in its present form. The deception is however even bigger than that, gaining the proportions of a global scotoma (blind spot) throughout Christendom. The broad "They" in the title could cover anyone and everyone from the original Hebrew scribes, the early Roman Church, the later Church hierarchy, the myriad translators and clergy right down to the individual Sunday School teachers. The conversion of the original Jewish message for a Roman audience and the resulting Church "system" was heavily biased, firstly because the Romans occupied the Holy Land in the time of Jesus and secondly because the resulting Christian religion was "manufactured" initially by the emperor Constantine to bring stability to the various sects within the Byzantine Empire and later as 'big business' by the Vatican. The deception however started even earlier than this.

In the preliminary days of Christianity, it was actually considered fair game to stretch the truth about the acts of Almighty God and the deeds of the not yet deified Jesus. Saint Paul chose to spread the esoteric message at all costs devoid of any historical context. He could not believe that lying could be construed as a sin if it were lies to promote the glory of God. It seems that it was accepted practice within the prevailing culture, to use any means, fair or foul to promote a particular Saviour or God and tell of his deeds. People of those times thought differently than we do today and quite genuinely saw no harm in this practice.

Romans 3 : 4, 5 & 7 *God forbid; yea let God be true and man a liar; as it is written that thou mightest be justified in thy sayings and mightest overcome when thou art judged. For if the truth of God hath more abounded through my lie unto his glory; why yet am I also judged as a sinner?* Saint Paul in the KJV. (King James version)

2 Corinthians 12 : 16 *But be it so, I did not burden you; nevertheless, being crafty, I caught you with guile.* Saint Paul in the KJV.

In fact we get an each way bet on this one from St Paul, in 2 Corinthians 12

: 16 he admits that he does use trickery or guile to obtain converts then in 1 Timothy 2 : 3 Paul claims that he does not use trickery or guile.

Even the most astute Church fathers like Eusebius felt lying for God was certainly excusable;

> *"It is an act of virtue to deceive and lie, when by such means the interest of the Church might be promoted... I have repeated whatever may redound to the glory (of the Christian religion) and suppressed all that could tend to the disgrace of our religion."* [2]

Echoing Eusebius, Mosheim states;

> *"...it was an almost universally adopted maxim, that it was an act of virtue to deceive and lie, when by so doing they could promote the interest of the church."* [3]

If we reference the Bible, there are indications in the Gospels that Jesus himself engaged in this deceptive practice. In the Gospel of John, we read where Jesus tells his disciples that he is not going to Jerusalem for the Feast of the Tabernacles, and then later goes secretly by himself. (Note: Some versions have Jesus saying he is 'not yet' going but this is an obvious alteration from the original.) There is no real reason for the deception since Jesus doesn't simply change his mind; he actively chooses to lie about not attending, and then attends in secret.

> **John 7 : 2** *Now the Jew's feast of tabernacles was at hand.*
>
> **John 7 : 8** *Go ye up unto this feast: I go not up unto this feast: for my time is not yet come.*
>
> **John 7 : 10** *But when his brethren were gone up, then went he also up unto the feast, not openly, but as it were in secret.*

Kersey Graves believed that various religions, including Christianity, commonly committed frauds and regularly told lies and accordingly became particularly adept at imparting falsehoods;

> *"Great numbers, of every age and of every religion, have been guilty of systematic frauds and falsehoods to support their religions, to an extent of which we have no conception. They not only practiced it, but they reduced it to system. They avowed it and they justified it by declaring it to be meritorious to lie in a good cause."* [4]

In like manner, the Roman Church had no qualms about editing the scriptures and basing the selection of books for inclusion in the Bible on the vested interests of the Bishops and the Church. Books of integrity with widespread usage were voted out, whilst lesser-known works with lesser credentials were included, simply selected because the wording happened to assist in building a church ideal or promoting a church power base; or simply because they followed the selected proto-orthodoxy that was required. The stalwart Christian Bishop, **Clement of Alexandria** even wrote the fraudulent, *'Epistle of Barnabas to the Church at Corinth'* sometime before 200 AD expressly to secure a new market for the Jesus message among the Gentiles and establish and condone separation from the Jews. He fought vehemently, but unsuccessfully, to have his 'fake' scripture included in the New Testament canon. If it had been successful we would probably accept it today, never knowing this background story. This demonstrates the depths to which an 'honorable' and learned Bishop was prepared to stoop to gain and promote the required message of the Church. Regarding the modification of dogma by the Roman Church and the Papal Fathers, Martin Luther had this to say:

> *"I am reading the decrees of the pontiffs, and… I do not know whether the Pope is the antichrist himself, or his apostle, so greatly is Christ misrepresented and crucified in them."* [5]

Luther then recorded at a later time on his excommunication;

> *"Already I feel greater liberty in my heart; for at last I know that the Pope is the antichrist, and that his throne is that of Satan himself."* [6]

For some four hundred years after the time of Christ, we find that Christianity comprised a number of rival groups with competing theologies; each one struggling to see their own particular 'orthodoxy' triumph over the others 'heresy'. The problem is that each and every one of the heretics believed that his or her doctrine was orthodox, regardless of whether it encompassed truth or not. For example Christ was considered divine, he was also considered human. For some he was a God, others considered him a man with God in him, for others he was God made into a man. The debate raged on and got fairly untidy. Writings from early Christian advocates, Clement of Alexandria and Origen *(Origenes Adamantius)* suggested that Jesus' heavenly body was able to change its appearance at will - a decidedly juvenile notion – with Clement actually claiming that Jesus ingested no food for nourishment but ate simply to convince his followers that he actually had a body. [7]

These were considered church leaders and astute writers and were included as part of the 'intelligentsia' of the day. The reality is that the yardstick for what eventually became 'orthodox' (and is today called the ineffable word of God) was never 'TRUTH' in any guise. It was in fact based on 'POWER' with the victorious group classifying the losing party's doctrine as heresy.

In those times it was Rome that had the power to gain dominance and accordingly it also gained orthodoxy for its edited doctrine and was able to classify any contrary view, and even those from primary sources, as heretical. For example it defies logic that Rome adopted the original Jewish Scriptures and now teaches Roman orthodoxy in the face of the 'heretical Jewish religion' that denies Jesus as the Messiah? We can study the spirited intolerance of any contrary view, demonstrated by Rome in the inquisition and in the ferocity of the campaign to totally wipe out groups like the Cathars and the Bogomils. The bottom line is that with various disparate groups, each with vested interests, deliberately altering texts, it is fairly apparent that there is little chance whatever that even fragments of our Bibles today, are of divine emanation.

Ehrman put it this way;

"...theological disputes, specifically disputes over Christology, prompted Christian scribes to alter the words of Scripture in order to make them more serviceable for the polemical task. Scribes modified their manuscripts to make them patently "orthodox" and less susceptible to "abuse" by the opponents of orthodoxy." [8]

I believe that there may be readers of this book who are suffering because they simply cannot accept, or come to terms with the message being imparted by their religion or church. This is not uncommon and can lead to enormous frustration. I was in that situation once, myself. The Bible is not tolerant of unbelievers.

Mark 16 : 16 *He that believeth not, shall be damned.*

In fact the American Archbishop of St Louis stated:

"Heresy and unbelief are crimes; and in Christian countries, as in Italy and Spain, for instance, where all the people are Catholics, and where the Catholic religion is an essential part of the law of the land, they are punished as other crimes"

So an Archbishop of the Catholic Church actually went on record as saying that unbelief of a contradictory, distorted message that is really quite implausible, (virgins having babies, men walking on water and Jesus being the only son of God and literally raising the dead) should be treated as criminals and evoke severe punishment. This alone validates the decision in many countries (not including Italy and Spain) for the 'separation of powers' of Church and State. Of course the benchmark here is the Church's own interpretation, and any deviation by their definition can be classed as heresy and accordingly as a crime. What happened to Jesus' message of 'love, tolerance and understanding'? St. Augustine, the stalwart Father of the Christian faith must have recognized this in his astute quotation;

Christianity is "a religion of threats and bribes, unworthy of wise men." [9]

Actually the Christian religion's requirement of 'Belief' rather than 'Works', as recorded in the Bible, to achieve everlasting life, simply defies logic. It is not rational more particularly since the human thought process is to evaluate present data against previously stored experience and conclude the truth or not, of the subject ideal. Only a ridiculously staunch dictatorship could command what a person is to think and to believe. Non-acceptance of this strange and edited message is actually totally founded, completely warranted and entirely natural in this situation for an educated, thinking person, unshackled by indoctrination. There is an interesting story about the native American Indian Chief 'Red Jacket' that illustrates this point. When the Christian missionaries told his people the Bible story of the redemption for the sins of man to be found in the crucifixion of Jesus Christ, the Son of God; the Chief listened respectfully and intently, and then showed that he had entirely missed the point, when he replied;

"Brothers, if you white men killed the son of the 'Great Spirit', be it on your heads, we Indians had nothing to do with it. If he had come among us, we would not have killed him; we would have treated him well. You must make amends for that crime yourselves." [10]

My intent here is certainly not to promote anarchy; it is simply to remove the lies so we can view the subject fairly, assess it and move on. We are only in search of the truth and will consider all possibilities. In some cases we may be killing a few sacred cows and removing a crutch or two but only if in fact those cows are sick or the crutches faulty. At the very least the reader will discover new ways of looking at some Bible stories and end up with a far deeper knowledge and appreciation of the Christian religion. Hopefully we may also pick up some neat little anecdotes our research has dug up. For example did you know that the Catholic Church struggled hard for many years to block the eating of **chocolate**? They saw it as a 'dangerous' food they said. The real reason was however that the early inhabitants of Central America had dedicated the chocolate plant to their pagan Gods. They ceremoniously fed massive amounts of chocolate to persons selected for sacrifice so the blood would be enriched by chocolate and thus more appealing to the Gods. The Bishops of the early church knew about the dedication of chocolate to pagan Gods, and accordingly still had a problem with this food, until quite recent times.

Some bits we will cover are lighthearted and fun whilst other parts are really shocking and disgusting. That's just the way it is. The time is now right since there is not much the Church can do about it. They can no longer brand us as heretics and burn us at the stake. Even excommunication is a bit out of style. I have to believe that in most cases, these discoveries we make are things already known to the Church hierarchy but certainly things that they don't share with the congregation. Now with children of my own I feel quite strongly when they come home from school with plainly ridiculous stories from Religious Education. The Church has had its way for too long with no accountability. I think it is sad that Sunday School is one of the few places where totally unsuitable, unqualified and ill-equipped persons can be selected to teach what is sometimes simply quaint myth but other times actually quite harmful nonsense; all with total immunity. Tragically, the students have no redress whatsoever. Some of the current Christian teachers are just plain ignorant and perpetrate un-truths through lack of knowledge, others because they found no other way to protect a principle that is inherently flawed. Some want to impress their God, to store up jewels in heaven for their works and others simply regurgitate their indoctrination no longer able to distinguish between lies and truth. Many are motivated to tell people how great their God is, simply because they so much want him to be, and view this "play acting" as a requirement and a Christian duty. There is also a definite thrust at taking things allegoric and making them historical fact; perhaps they are still establishing their orthodoxy!

I have watched so many truly ridiculous documentaries on video and TV, where fundamentalist Christians with a total lack of evidence use untruths to support their belief that if they can for example, prove evolution wrong, this would by default prove their form of creationism right. Unfortunately they seem to believe that this is somehow the will and requirement of their God. In this book we will unravel this mystery and bring it to a believable conclusion. Despite all this, I repeat that I am genuinely not on any sort of vendetta against anyone, or their specific religion or their Church, not even those who actually lied to me. I am not intending to single out Romans or creationists, fundamentalists or charismatic believers; there is just no point. They have a different way of viewing things. Bultmann made this cogent observation;

> *"The whole conception of the world which is presupposed in the teaching of Jesus in the New Testament, generally is mythological, i.e., the conception of the world as structured in three stories, heaven, earth, and hell; the conception of the intervention of supernatural powers in the course of events; and the conception of miracles, especially the conception of the intervention of supernatural powers in the inner life of the soul, the conception that men can be tempted and corrupted by the devil and possessed by evil spirits. This conception of the world we call mythological because it is different from the conception of the world which has been formed and developed by science since its inception in ancient Greece and which has been accepted by all modern men."* [11]

In a desire to gain more followers, the Church has for centuries (perhaps unwittingly) promoted overpopulation of the Earth, particularly in third world countries. This is a fault that is set to haunt us for generations to come. Because it has been such an impediment to the advancement and development of mankind, I view serious thought about religion and the sensible study of same as a particularly worthwhile endeavor. I find it interesting and even amusing that most Christians do neither. Have you noticed how some people "find Jesus" or "get religion" or become "born again" and instantly jump in, boots and all, with no investigation period? Those same people may purchase a new car, a suit of clothes, or a gym membership and appear to put more investigation and consideration into that purchase, than to this new lifestyle they are choosing. A lifestyle that is about to change their entire lives forever. I find this somewhat strange.

An advertising executive today, for example, must have a good all round knowledge of the industry across a broad spectrum of media; a builder would usually know quite a bit about his sub-contractors trades and a plumber would have some knowledge of the ways his trade differs in other countries. Not so teachers of the Bible message. In most cases their information is extremely biased and prejudiced and their minds firmly closed. Their study is limited to one book without even a basic knowledge of the contemporary historical context or the alternate opinions prevailing. I cannot argue with people who believe Jesus lives within their heart as their personal Saviour, nor is that my aim. If you wish to devote your life to your religion, church or personal Saviour, feel free, go right ahead. Please, don't let me interfere with you. We'll just accept that this book is not for you; most particularly if you mean to make this kind of commitment, as most Christians seem to do, without researching the facts to the utmost of your ability and circumstance. In fact in most cases without any research at all. For those readers who really do seek the truth though; understand that the Bible actually supports our stance:

Hosea 4 : 6 *My people are destroyed for lack of knowledge.*

2 Peter 1 : 5 *"For this very reason, make every effort to add to your faith, virtue; and to virtue, knowledge."*

You may choose to reject the extensive research we go through and the conclusions we draw. If however you find that this research causes you to stop and think, even for a moment, then it is worth the effort to me. I am committed to the search.

I recall it was Albert Schweitzer who said something like, *"Man's biggest problem is that he just doesn't think."*

With reference to his religion, it is not just that man doesn't think, he must now actively UNLEARN all the nonsense he has absorbed since childhood, start to THINK even if for the very first time and then RELEARN virtually everything. This has proved to be a major challenge for man as he seems particularly reticent to embrace other possibilities and the hitherto unexpected. Perhaps Henry Wheeler Shaw's character Uncle Josh Billings had it more correct when he said;

> *"Man's ignorance ain't cause he ain't ever learned nutten; It's cause he learned too many things that jes' ain't so."*

Perhaps that is too simplistic as well because in addition there appears to be a 'play acting' element within the Christian churches where the social aspect is sufficiently attractive to allow otherwise astute and reasonable people to apparently accept the most implausible aspects of the religion, within a herd mentality. I think maybe Professor Martin Buber had it right when he stated;

> *"Mundus vult decipi"* (the world wants to be deceived). [12]

Most lies from Sunday School are naturally associated with the Bible in its various translations and interpretations. I have noted teachers who regularly manipulate passages to squeeze out a bit more intrigue. Often a totally earthly, mundane message is made to look esoteric or made to take the form of a miracle. This is only exacerbating the modifications that have already been made by the scribes. A simple example of this came to light with the 'vision' that Ezekiel described, *"the heavens were opened and I saw visions of God"*. The hybrid beasts he went on to describe by the river Chebar, with the faces of lions, eagles and men, have been analyzed down through time and have been given the most fantastic interpretations. In fact some 2500 years after the time of Ezekiel, archaeologists en-earthed the very stone statues at that actual location by the Chebar canal in Nippur. They were representations of ancient Babylonian Gods, and Ezekiel was describing precisely what he saw there (visions of Gods) but this is certainly not the message the Bible imparts. As a further example we can observe the fairly uncommon Hebrew word *'khiydah'* that is not translated fairly or consistently through the Old Testament. It is altered across various passages to bias each situation in our English Bible. Some translation examples include;

'*riddle*' in **Judges 14 : 12–17** and **Ezekiel 17 : 2**; as '*hard question*' in **1 Kings 10 : 1** as '*dark saying*' in **Psalm 49 : 5** and **Proverbs 1 : 6** and as '*dark sentence*' in **Daniel 8 : 23**. [13]

Now the word was never meant to be this flexible or adaptable, the translators have simply manipulated the meaning in each case to suit their requirement. We find that today various sects will interpret verses to their particular liking and then ignore others that don't suit. This leads to such situations where groups insist that Saturday must be observed as the true Sabbath and others say assembling on Sunday is fine. It goes even further than that, because misunderstandings can occur even where there is no hidden agenda or subterfuge intended; like the huge discrepancies between different versions of the Bible. The interpretation can also be totally subjective.

Vendyl Jones stated;

> "*The Jew and the Christian have many identical words in their vocabulary of faith, such as God, Messiah, Bible, Salvation, Redemption, Sin and Kingdom. Yet the definition, connotation and denotation of each by the Jew and Christian are variant and sometimes even opposite in meaning. At the same time, both the Jew and the Christian have many words which are totally alien to each other and yet may have the same meaning...*" [14]

Jones goes further to state that Jewish and Christian differences will likely remain because Christians fail to recognize that the Hebrew language used in the scriptures is, *Leshon ha-Qodesh*, "the Holy Tongue". A lesson for all of us is that similar boundaries exist between most language and cultural differences. To suggest that an English translation of the Bible in this 21st. Century holds rigid fidelity to the original Jewish manuscript is to be simply quite naïve.

We will also see how the Jews of the captivity, recorded partly understood Sumerian and Babylonian stories into the books of the Old Testament. We will follow myth as it became recorded as historical fact and vice versa. We will look at how the Emperor Constantine, himself a Sol Invictus, Sun worshiper, realized that he could utilize the Hebrew religion and went on to use a manipulated, Romanized Bible to unite his unravelling Byzantine Empire. This meant that, translation became flexible, and only selected scripture, which carried the required message, was introduced; after other orthodox scripture was omitted. We will see Roman alterations, on top of perpetuated Hebrew misunderstandings, set out in the Bible that are now somewhat ludicrously claimed to be the inerrant Word of God. The early translators actually admitted that at times they were so appalled with the message that they modified or left out the parts that offended:

Jeremiah 8 : 8 *How can you say, "We are wise, for we have the law of the Lord," when actually the lying pen of the scribes has handled it falsely?*

The Bible actually tells us that the scribes have lied and tampered with the message; and this in a Bible that also carries the following assertion;

Proverbs 30 : 5 *'Every word of God is flawless'*

If we choose to believe that the Bible is in fact the Word of God, and its message 'flawless', we will soon see abundant evidence that this is simply not true. It seems that the Lord too has not been entirely truthful, with Jeremiah in this case;

Jeremiah 20 : 7 *O Lord, you deceived me, and I was deceived; you overpowered me and prevailed. I am ridiculed all day long; everyone mocks me.*

We can see too, an example where tampering with the message is obvious;

Exodus 4 : 24-26 *And it came to pass by the way in the inn, that the Lord met him* (Moses) *and sought to kill him.*

This now reads like nonsense whereas it originally recorded the aborted attempt by God to kill Moses and then the eventual killing of Moses' son instead. This was not considered suitable behavior from Almighty God so was heavily censored. Modern Bibles also simply omit the sick parts in **Job 42 : 13-15** where God allows Satan to kill Job's 7 sons and 3 daughters and then replaces them with more beautiful ones.

To be a prophet in Biblical times would not have been an easy billet. If you got it right it was down to God. If you got it wrong you had to die and possibly because it was God himself who was deceiving you all the time:

Jeremiah 23 : 26-27 *How long shall this be in the heart of the prophets that prophesy lies? Yea, they are prophets of the deceit of their own heart.*

Luke 24 : 25 *Then he (Jesus) said unto them, O fools, and slow of heart, to believe all that the prophets have spoken:*

Deuteronomy 18 : 20 *But the prophet, which shall presume to speak a word in my name, which I have not commanded him to speak..... that prophet shall die.*

Ezekiel 14 : 9 *And if the prophet be deceived when he hath spoken a thing, I the Lord have deceived that prophet, and I will stretch out my hand upon him, and will destroy him from the midst of my people Israel.*

The Lord says that he will destroy a prophet of Israel for uttering a prophecy after he has 'enticed' that prophesy himself. Can we appreciate that this is madness?

So if by the end of this book we agree we were 'sold a pup' we must look for a replacement philosophy. Man is still a spiritual being and cannot function as a 'total unit' without exercising and feeding his spirit. As we progress in this book, the journey may become rocky for some, and start to stretch credibility to the limit. Remember that not much of this is new to the clergy; it is only members of the laity who have been kept from any enlightenment. We will be looking at hard evidence where possible and showing various things recorded about each event. It is for you to decide which you believe is the most plausible. We will be introduced to ancient documents that show a different Jesus to our mind picture. We will see a Jesus of Royal birth, with powerful affiliations, with rich and influential friends working within a dynasty to regain the Jewish Kingdom. The Book of Thomas has Jesus married to Salome who may be his sister or is actually another name for Queen Helene. Dr. Barbara Theiring of Sydney University states that there is considerable evidence that Jesus was born in "the Queens House" outside Qumran and not in Bethlehem at all. (15) This is probably correct and we will show that the Bethlehem story occurred not at Jesus' birth but at the time of a documented census of Governor Quirinius, when Jesus went through his 'born again' (bar mitzvah) ceremony, at 12 years of age. Governor Quirinius was a real person and the census he held and its timeframe, documented fact. If it doesn't support our 'mind picture' or our Bibles, guess which one is wrong!

Even when the orthodox Bible was loosely established; further corruption of the message was ensured right up to the 18th. Century, when clergymen 'decided' which passages they should share with the laity and which passages shouldn't be read. For example, **Porteus** was an 18th century English Bishop who with the Church's blessing made an index of what should and shouldn't be read in the Bible. Whether the 'Word of God' needed this extreme censorship or not, the Porteus index was utilized for many, many years to come. Even prior to this index, only the Church hierarchy had access to scripture and then only in a dialect of Western Rome known as Church Latin. The first, second and third century Greek and Semitic languages had been translated into Church Latin in about the fourth century. Even people who could read Latin had trouble with this, since it became a specialized Church Latin, understood only by the clergy. This is the way things were for many hundreds of years to come; with the church hierarchy telling the laity what it thought should be known.

In October 1536, **William Tyndale** was executed as a heretic by strangulation and burning for his crimes against the Church. What had he done? William Tyndale had attempted the first translation of the Bible into English. Nothing more! His assistant and supporter **Miles Coverdale** was eventually able to complete an English version amid cries from the Catholic Church that it was a Protestant heresy and equally strong criticism from the Protestant community that it was a sell out to the Catholics. Trying to complete this project without being classified a heretic, whilst trying to appease the warring Catholic – Protestant factions must have necessitated that Coverdale make many concessions in his translations. What he achieved was pretty remarkable even though his translation has now proven to fall down on many points. This persecution of scholars was not a quickly passing phase in Church development and almost eighty years later the Dean of London's St. Paul's Cathedral, **John Colet**, was suspended for simply translating the Lord's Prayer into English for the enlightenment of his parishioners. To fully grasp the mentality of the Church we must appreciate that clergy reading out the more uplifting parts of the Bible in totally incomprehensible "Church Latin" was fully acceptable yet sharing these things in the local vernacular was vehemently avoided and ultimately punishable. This sounds like a Church that did not want its dogma scrutinized. In the

UK, a decree called the *'Constitution of Oxford'* actually made it illegal to translate any part of the Bible into English.

It was the Stuart King, **James IV of Scotland** (and James I of England) the only child of Mary, Queen of Scots, who arranged the first acceptable English translation in the early 17th century. He used a team of around 50 translators for three years who also came up against the Catholic-Protestant infighting over translation. Their work was then submitted to the editing of **Sir Francis Bacon** who spent an additional eighteen months in this task. Bacon was a lawyer and a genius of the English language. He was a master of 'cryptography' the art of writing secret codes in cipher and a practicing member of several secret societies. In addition both the King and Francis Bacon were Freemasons and it is likely that to some degree, this also influenced their translation. Some of Bacon's private agenda was certainly added and likewise, the King himself, had his own schema which Bacon was obliged to add. It was in fact King James who had the words *'authorised version'* and *'authorised to be read in the Church's of England'* added to this version to empower and promote his kingship within the church and establish his version's orthodoxy. In the words of Dr. Macknight;

> *"It was made a little too complaisant to the king in favoring his notions of predestination, election, witchcraft, familiar spirits, and kingly rights, and these, it is probable, were also the translators' opinions. Their translation is partial, speaking the language of and giving authority to one sect."* [16]

The translators however complained that they were not allowed to trust their own judgment in translation but their work was censored for "reasons of state." The king was apparently quite a sick individual and certainly did have vested interests. King James is said to have been a notorious 'closet' Christian homosexual who murdered his young lovers and cruelly victimized countless heretics and certainly enjoyed persecuting women. [17] He enjoyed hunting and once he killed an animal, it is reported that he would literally roll about in its blood. Some believe that he practiced bestiality while the animal lay dying. No matter how bad the accusations, he justified his actions by the 'divine right' of kings. While King of Scotland in 1591, he personally supervised the torture of poor wretches caught up in the witchcraft trials of Scotland. James would even suggest new tortures to the examiners. One 'witch', Barbara Napier, was acquitted through lack of evidence. That event so infuriated James that he personally wrote to the court on 10 May 1551, ordering a sentence of death, and actually had the jury called into custody. The King himself presided at a new trial and only released them without punishment when they reversed their verdict on poor Barbara Napier. [18]

On the death of King James in 1625, his son King Charles ascended the throne. He was married to Henrietta Maria a French princess who was also a Catholic. Concerns that he would oppose the use of the King James Bible in favour of the Catholic Vulgate were however unfounded. Charles promoted the KJV as he very much enjoyed the 'divine right of kings' promoted by his fathers translation and had an agenda to wipe out the 'Geneva' English translation that was becoming popular, because its margin notes (designed to aid translation) specifically warned against excesses by the monarchy. King Charles continued to promote the King James Version, favoured by evangelic Christians and still in use today. Today's version however differs in a number of details from the KJV of 1611. There are even considerable differences between the KJV published by Oxford, Cambridge, and Nelson publishers. In addition we find numerous printing errors in different editions. **William Kilburne** in 1659 found a total of **20,000 errors** in six different KJV's [19] In addition there is the collectable "Wicked Bible" edition of the KJV where **'not'** is omitted from the seventh commandment stating, **'thou shalt commit adultery.'**

In 1701 **Bishop Lloyd** endorsed the chronology of Ireland's Archbishop, **James Ussher** who in 1658 after studying the family histories contained in the Bible, simply guessed at a date of 2348 BCE for the flood, and used Biblical generations to interpolate that Adam and Eve were created in 4004 BCE. In 1779 the Church approved book, *'Universal History'* actually stated that God commenced the Creation at the random timeframe of **9 am on the 23 October 4004 BCE** by the Julian calendar. (Perhaps the Godhead union specifies deities should work precisely nine to five.) Somewhat ironically, the Vatican decreed that any contradiction of this date amounted to heresy, resulting in excommunication by the church. It was Pope Pius XII who finally relaxed this patently ludicrous decree as recently as 1952.

If somehow God's hand miraculously guided the Christian message to this point and regardless of the translation, if the Bible is really the work of an in-errant, perfect and loving God, we would not unreasonably expect it to be a pretty remarkable document, totally free of error and misunderstanding. The Bible itself states in **Deuteronomy 2 : 3-4** "His works are perfect." I think we'd agree that it should be superlative literature in every respect, when compared to anything that could be conceived by the mind of mortal man. Whether written by the hand of God, or religious scribe inspired of God, it should be cogent, accurate, clear, concise, and with a consistent motif, throughout. In short it should be something pretty special. Check it for yourself in **2 Timothy 3 : 16** *"All scripture is the work of God."*

This book will show that unfortunately Timothy got it wrong. In reality the Bible falls far short of this ideal, and clearly reveals itself as an errant and very inconsistent, totally contradictory group of works that is unreliable as prose, as literature, as philosophy, as history and most particularly as religion. The Christian writer **Adamantius Origen** (185 – 251 AD) commented on the 'God given' Ten Commandments;

> *"If we hold to the letter, and must understand what stands written in the Torah after the manner of the Jews and common people, then I should blush to confess aloud that if he is God who has give these laws; then the laws of men actually appear more excellent and reasonable."* [20]

In addition we must ask, why for example, is the story of King David's lust for Bathsheba, (the daughter of Eliam, the wife of Uriah the Hittite) included in a religious book. It features voyeurism, adultery, seduction and bastardry plus uncontrolled lust to a stage where David arranges for the murder of Bathsheba's husband, so he can possess her. Read it for yourself in: **2 Samuel 11** and appreciate that these are the forbears of Jesus Christ. Without this union Jesus would not have been born. Continue on to **2 Samuel 2 : 13** for the rape of David's daughter Tamar by her half brother or back to **Genesis 35 : 22** for the seduction of Jacobs concubine Bilhah by his oldest son Reuben. We will study Bible passages of almost unbelievable cruelty and deceit by both Almighty God and patriarchal church fathers, and we will read passages of obvious, palpable nonsense written by the early church Bishops.

Some Christians may argue that the Bible does meet their criteria as a wonderful recording of the word of God or the acts of Jesus. They are living in 'Fantasyland'. These indoctrinated souls emphatically state, that because the Bible is the word of God, it simply must be without error or inconsistency. They then believe every word must be factual and taken literally, because it is the word of God. It matters not which proposition comes first, the other is deemed to follow. There are actually a number of real problems contained within the Bible that have only survived the centuries because of an un-enlightened audience. Quite a few Biblical precepts are both unreasonable and unlikely since they are in obvious disagreement with common sense as well as the somewhat perfect qualities one would reasonably expect of an all powerful God. Some assertions are demonstrably wrong. Even the overall religious motif is neither consistent nor harmonious and is not in line with God's supposed omniscience. The Christian apologist **Tertullian** once wrote;

> "'Our faith is certain because it is impossible' in other words, the whole Christian faith is so completely at variance with the world of common sense that we think it is unlikely to be based upon invention; anyone who wanted to tell lies would make statements more intrinsically believable than those enunciated in the Christian creeds." [21]

On this point, Laurence Gardner had this to say:

> "Large sectors of the working population could neither read nor write, and so they admired, respected and trusted those who were more scholarly.... Throughout the twentieth century, however, things changed and by way of obligatory schooling, people became both literate and investigative. Now they are able to read for themselves and can form their own opinions and beliefs. This however, has not changed the medieval dogma of the stalwart clerics, who are content to see their congregations dwindle rather than rejoice in the educated age of enlightenment." [22]

In fact, any form of education originally meant power and even in those early days, the initiates were given the 'real' knowledge whilst the rest became but tools in the hands of the rich and knowledgeable. This has been the case down through the ages and largely accounts for the ongoing pompous attitudes of the Church over its congregation. This attitude is not so different today; however a far greater percentage of the population is now educated. Early Christianity was divested of any doctrines which empowered the individual and these were replaced by doctrines of fear and threats. Astrology and reincarnation are but two doctrines totally removed from the scriptures for these reasons, though they are still found on the spiritual level of Christianity, Judaism and Islam. Only Christianity however replaced them with a living burning hellfire and a doctrine of threats and punishments. No longer is it reasonable to hold on to the ludicrous sacred cows of the past, nor is it any longer necessary to trust the 'educated' clergy to translate for us and intercede on our behalf. In total disregard of those who postulated a flat earth, the Earth remained round; and aero planes still fly today despite those who held the belief that 'heavier than air' craft could never get off the ground.

There is some pretty weird stuff to uncover in the Bible and at times we will locate some lesser known passages. Many Christians would not believe that this following classic is actually recorded in their Bible:

Numbers 22 : 21 – 30 *"And God came unto Balaam at night, and said to him, if the men come to call thee, rise up, and go with them; but yet the word which I will say unto thee, that shall thou do. And Balaam rose up in the morning and saddled his ass, and went with the princes of Moab. And God's anger was kindled because he went; and the angel of the Lord stood in the way for an adversary against him."*

It doesn't make much sense but to be reasonable, in context God had apparently told Balaam to go with the Princes of Balak, and when he went with the princes of Moab, well God's anger was kindled. This is odd, but wait there's more;

"Now he was riding upon his ass, and his two servants were with him. And the ass saw an angel of the Lord standing in the way, and his sword drawn in his hand; (in reality, how could the writer possibly know what the ass saw or felt) *and the ass turned aside out of the way, and went into the field; and Balaam smote the ass, to turn her into the way. But the angel of the Lord stood in a path of the vineyards, a wall being on this side, and a wall being on that side. And when the ass saw the angel of the Lord, she*

36

thrust herself into the wall, and crushed Balaam's foot against the wall; and he smote her again. And the angel of the Lord went further, and stood in a narrow place where was no way to turn either to the right hand or to the left. And when the ass saw the angel of the Lord she fell down under Balaam; and Balaam's anger was kindled and he smote the ass with his staff. (Quite obviously Balaam is not report-ing this and it doesn't sound like the word of God) *And the Lord opened the mouth of the ass and she said unto Balaam, What have I done unto thee, that thou hast smitten me these three times?"* (Poor old Balaam it seems, wasn't even slightly surprised when his ass suddenly did a 'Mr. Ed' impersonation, he answered right back.) *"And Balaam said to the ass, because you have mocked me; I would there were a sword in mine hand, for now would I kill thee."* (This is some paranoia trip; do I have this correct, Balaam wants to kill the ass for mocking him.) *"And the ass said unto Balaam, Am not I thine ass, upon which thou hast ridden ever since I was thine unto this day? Was I ever wont to do so unto thee?* (In other words; did I ever mock you before?) *And Balaam said Nay."* (That's Nay! not Neigh!)

By the end of this book you may not believe that the Bible records the sacrosanct and inviolable word of God, including the talking donkey that supposedly mocked Balaam. You may find difficulty justifying some of the contradictory and ridiculous statements, the sexist inequality, the human sacrifice, the wholesale slaughter of men, women and children and the needless, senseless, cruelty we uncover. You may object to the warfare fought through the ages even to this day in the various names of God. If you are fully at ease worshipping a Saviour who was literally born of a virgin, walked on water, died and rose again and now lives immortally in Heaven which just happens to be "up" from anyplace one resides on this Earth, don't bother reading further. If your prayers are heard and answered and the ancient tribal Storm God of Israel is the universal God you worship today, please stop now. This book is not for you.

From here we will start by intelligently exploring the Bible, with its odd stories and contradictions, look at the etymology of the words used, hopefully in the contemporary context in which it was written and re-examine some blatantly incorrect translations. We will also look at many forms of supporting and conflicting documentation. We will look at it as religion, as history and as philosophy. I wish to make it clear however that this book I have written is not really finished and can probably never be finished. We should never say *"I have found the truth"* because infinite truth is, indeed, infinite. So vehemently believing that we have found the total truth, could simply mean we have stopped looking.

As new evidence comes to light and as older evidence becomes more widely understood, things here will need to be updated, revised and some things changed. For example if I had written this book before the Dead Sea Scrolls or say the Nag Hammadi documents were available for study, this book would now be in need of an update. That is the basic difference between a scientific approach, where new information can upgrade old, in an open, objective forum, as opposed to the fundamentalist type Christian approach, where only selected information, aimed at supporting a pre-ordained conclusion is introduced and where investigation is entirely restricted to just one book. This is not far removed from the reported attitude of the Muslims under the Arab General Amru, who justified the burning of the priceless remnants of the great library at Alexandria, by saying *"if it is not in the Koran we don't want to read it; if it is in the Koran we already have it"*. Sad as that is, it is worth noting that contrary to popular belief, it was a mob led by the Christian Bishop Theophilus who did the initial burning of the priceless ancient contents of that library.

I have tried hard to be fair and quote the most learned scholars, in many cases the professors of philosophy, theology and religion at the major universities in the world. These I hopefully believe are honest people and learned in their fields, searching only for truth without the pre-ordained 'wish list' and hidden agendas of some of the Christian manipulators who right from Sunday School, were so adept at using unlikely answers to explain to me the insurmountable inconsistencies, contradictions and absurdities found in my Bible. The Church has never fully come to grips with Education or Science always remaining in a 'cold war' situation with them. It has always relied on simple folk, the uneducated, naive and gullible who constituted the mass of its power base. Religion has always been by nature a threat to scientific progress and only now is that threat diminishing. Now of course it is Education and Science that are blowing the whistle on the flawed doctrine the Church teaches and this is finally shackling Church power. Back in the mid 16ᵗʰ. Century, however the situation was quite different when the church was all-powerful and Science was in its infancy. The Church taught then that the earth was the center of the universe and the Sun revolved around it and no matter how incorrect this was it was the Church opinion that held sway.

Galileo Galilei was born in 1564 in Pisa and initially studied Medicine and later Physics, Philosophy and Mathematics at the University of Pisa. In 1585 Galileo became a lecturer in Mathematics at Padua University near Venice and amazed his peers as probably the most gifted thinker of his time. He traveled to Rome in 1611 armed with the telescope he had made and met with high-ranking clergymen in an attempt to show them his discoveries and prove to them that the Copernican model of the Earth revolving around the sun was true and correct. Even though Galileo made it quite clear that this did not threaten their tenets, the Church did not want to listen. Galileo found himself thereafter under official scrutiny. Pope Urban VIII rigidly insisted that Galileo refrain from undermining the centuries old church teaching. Ironically this was not even a literal Bible teaching. The church had actually adapted it from the works of the Greek philosopher, Aristotle, not from the scriptures at all. Since they had based their teachings on his model (and they were infallible) the Church hierarchy now claimed it as the immutable word of God. Over the next few years this led to harassment, questioning, humiliation, imprisonment, torture, and finally a trial for heresy for the unfortunate Galileo. In modern times, this unfair trial has been classified as one of the greatest miscarriages of justice of all time, even rivaling the trial of Jesus. Today we can read a letter that Galileo wrote to a student;

> *"Even though scripture cannot err, its interpreters and expositors certainly can, in various ways. One of these, very serious and very frequent, would be when they always want to stop at the purely literal sense."* [23]

Particularly since he knew for a fact that they were totally wrong, Galileo could hardly have been gentler on the arrogant Church. The doctrine of papal infallibility has been under attack by theologians since its proclamation in 1870, by Pope Pius IX and the First Vatican Council. Catholic theologian, Hans Kung, in something of an understatement recorded that;

> *"Numerous and indisputable errors of the ecclesiastical teaching office including the condemnation of Galileo have brought the dogma of infallibility into question".* [24]

In 1979 Pope John Paul II went on record stating that Galileo *"had to suffer a great deal…at the hands of men and organizations of the Church"* and made attempts to achieve a review of the Galileo case. Some 13 years later an insipid statement was issued from the Church to the effect that *'certain theologians; contemporaries of Galileo, had failed to grasp the non-literal meaning of the scriptures, when describing the physical structure of the universe'.* That is pretty close to what Galileo himself had documented; and remained as close to an admission of guilt and public apology that the Church ever came. In recent times it is said that a dilapidated copy of Galileo's original notebook writings came apart to expose under the cover lining, his terse handwritten statement that, *'even if the Church were to burn me as a heretic it would not alter the fact that the Earth revolves around the sun'.* This shows that despite the cruel harassment of an old and sick gentleman, one of the greatest scientists and thinkers of all time, despite the full force of the inquisition, and despite his death, while still under house arrest in Florence in 1642, Galileo made a fool of the Catholic Church and its dogma of infallibility. Not much of a 'last laugh' but a laugh just the same.

Matthew 24: 4 records the words of Jesus, *"Take heed that no man deceives you."* I have a concern that those who told us lies in Sunday School, all too often foisted on us when we were most vulnerable or naïve, were actually fairly ignorant themselves of the Bibles' contents. They were allowed into the job by clergy who fully understood their collective short-comings, and that of the syllabus they taught. The apostle Paul continually warns us against these false teachers and false prophets.

1 Timothy 1 : 7, *" Desiring to be teachers of the (Jewish) law; understanding neither what they say nor whereof they affirm."*

1 Thessalonians 5 : 19–21 *"Do not quench the Spirit; do not despise prophetic utterances. But examine everything carefully; hold fast to that which is good;"*

1 John 4 : 1 *"Dear friends, do not believe every spirit, but test the spirits to see* *whether they are from God, because many false prophets have gone out into the world."*

Whilst man has been incredibly negligent in heeding these warnings and in protecting his doctrine from vandalism; the Christian message has been corrupted to a point where it is now unrecognizable from the original, and has become, as a religious tool of salvation, perfectly valueless.

My experience has been that many teachers, despite having committed their lives to the Bible, have little knowledge of its origins, development and the context in which it was assembled and could not even recognise the shortcomings of their Holy Book today. Many of them were led to indoctrination by a friend and immediately chose to accept and promote the Bible's factuality without an investigation period and again their reading of the scriptures was entirely divorced from any historical context. It is now time to grow up.

The Bible states *"Come as little children"*. It does not state *"Stay as little children"*. The apostle Paul took this further when he said;

1 Corinthians 13 : 11 *"When I was a child, I spake as a child, I understood as a child, I thought as a child: but when I became a man, I put away childish things."*

It is now too late to be vigilant, the damage is done. In most cases Sunday School teachers are, in my opinion, in no way competent to teach the Christian message to others. They claim only the trust in their friend and a newfound personal experience with Jesus as their qualification. And yet, they remain totally ill equipped and unqualified, and in their ignorance, or in their quest to find new converts for their God and with no accountability at all, cease to even consider truth and reason as they regurgitate their indoctrination. They quite simply lie to us.

"The fact that true faith doesn't need evidence is held up as its greatest virtue; but it is capable of driving people to such dangerous folly that faith seems to me to qualify as a kind of mental illness."

Richard Dawkins, Professor of Public Understanding of Science at Oxford University.

CHAPTER TWO

SOMETHING IS WRONG HERE

'The Word of God must be enveloped in discrete mysteries far from the reach of the common man'

Cardinal Jimenez de Cisneros; spiritual advisor to Queen Isabella of Spain in 1502.

The Initial Realization

"I owe Christianity a debt, and so, I believe does the world we have lived in for the last 2000 years."

These are the opening thoughts in the foreword of; *'Two Thousand Years - The First Millennium: The Birth of Christianity to the Crusades'* by the English broadcaster and writer Melvyn Bragg. He continues;

"Christianity also owes me an explanation for the bigotry, the wickedness, the inhumanity and the wilful ignorance which has also characterized much of its 'history'." [1]

Now Bragg is probably echoing the thoughts of many of us who grew up in the 20th. Century carrying an inherent respect for Christianity and things of God; who only now have started to question the less pleasant aspects of this religion like those things quoted above. As we become wiser and more educated it becomes more difficult daily to overlook things that are plainly not right.

As a young person, I first studied religion as part of a congregation. I believed then that the church took itself far too seriously, with a consistent focus on the church and its platform, rather than the needs of the people and the impact of the message it was imparting. These were the tail end of the days of fire and brimstone and there were obvious problems reconciling the wrathful, jealous God of the Old Testament with the benevolent, forgiving God of the New Testament. The first was a threat with a big stick and the second a friend offering love and kindness and these entities were used alternatively 'as required' with appropriate readings selected from the Bible. The church required a subservient congregation, and to be called "God fearing" was the Christian's ultimate personal compliment. Regardless of these difficulties, I could never understand why the dedicated followers of the great King Jesus didn't act like winners especially if they truly believed and accepted that their salvation had conferred on them everlasting life in paradise. The motivational trainer, Zig Ziglar used to say;

"The Lord didn't put the diamonds on the Earth for the devils crowd, now did he?"

And hey, I believed him. Lack of self-esteem is the very thing Jesus tried to address in supporting the poor, the commoner, the sick and the meek. *"You can do it!"* was his message; *"If you have faith as a grain of mustard, greater things will ye do".*

Philippians 4 : 4 *"May you always be joyful in your union with the Lord. I say it again rejoice! "*

Ephesians 2 : 19 *"Now therefore ye are no more strangers and foreigners but fellow citizens with the saints, and the household of God."*

I thought to myself, if you truly believe this you would rejoice! Yet despite this, I saw Christians who acted like anything but winners and despite having supposedly attained the gift of salvation, they held no thought of an abundant life on Earth no matter how temporary they considered it to be. They tried to 'work off' the gift of salvation they had been given, trusting more in pity than acceptance, in compassion more than justice. There are said to be over **300 laws** and **667 sins** mentioned in the Bible, I guess, one for every human frailty. I now understand that the Christian doctrine, particularly the adopted Old Testament, promotes a miserable religion based on the harsh Jewish dogma, originally recorded for austere desert dwellers, which was cast in a spirit of retribution, unworthiness, fear of punishment and inadequacy.

This is obvious in passages like:

Romans 3 : 23 *For all have sinned, and come short of the glory of God.*

Exodus 9 : 27 *The Lord is righteous, and I and my people are wicked.*

Isaiah 64 : 6 *We are all as an unclean thing, and all our righteousness's are as filthy rags.*

Joshua 24 : 19 *He will <u>not</u> forgive your transgressions or your sins.*

The point I am making was apparently understood well by Henri Frankfort of Chicago University who wrote:

> 'In Hebrew religion, and in Hebrew religion alone, the ancient bond between man and nature was destroyed. Those who served Jehovah must forgo the richness, the fulfilment, and the consolation of a life which moves in tune with the great rhythms of the earth and sky'. [2]

The Dead Sea Scrolls left by the ascetic community at Qumran contained The Manual of Discipline, which emphasises this point in their own words;

> "The rules include having a daily sacred meal of bread and wine; community of property; and being subject to penances such as exclusion from the sacred meals for periods of ten days up to two years for offences such as laughing loudly… " [3]

The other religions based on the Jewish scriptures also illuminate man's unworthiness. From the Hebrew Bible;

> **Obadiah 51 : 1** *"Though thou exalt thyself as an eagle, and though thou set thy nest among the stars, thence will I bring thee down saith the Lord."*

This theme is continued in the Koran;

> **Qur'an 18 : 8** *And verily we shall make all that is on the Earth a bare dry soil (without vegetation or trees).*

Certainly, the Old Testament is based on the hard and inflexible code of a tent dwelling, desert people, and was of necessity harsh and austere. On the other hand, we were told of the love, rewards and great joy our God has in store for us but no one actually practiced it. We read that David danced before the Lord and yet if one was happy and enjoying one's Christian walk, in my congregation it was somehow construed as an abomination to the Lord. As well as being confused by these mixed messages, we were ground down and taught to be firmly in the "victim" business. The Bible predicted persecution and ridicule for God's elite and we were indoctrinated that persecution and ridicule are part of a Christian's lot. We were held in high esteem if we brought this abuse upon ourselves in acts of self-fulfilling prophecy. God was a hard taskmaster who demanded unswerving obedience. Meanwhile we praised him and spoke of his love and care for us, it was quite confusing. We thanked him for displaying such love when he sent his only begotten son to die for us all, as the ultimate blood sacrifice. We encountered a kind of hypocrisy in the clergy with a role for play-acting that I could not fathom. Today, I see that the way they guide their flock is contrary to all best practice productivity and management styles. Now, with children of my own, and a lot of study behind me, I can also see that we were taught palpable nonsense.

I recall at the time, a bumper sticker, sold to parishioners at our church:

"GOD SAID IT, I BELIEVE IT, THAT SETTLES IT"

Many bought this sticker and displayed it on their cars; never once pausing to reflect on just how narrow-minded that statement really is. But then the Christian walk decreed to some extent that successful Christians be fairly narrow minded.

I like to visualize given situations and in this case was not able to separate the religion from its contemporary historical component, as others seemed able to. In fact I knew Christians who practised their religion quite easily whilst avoiding the historical facts entirely. There were plenty of sacred cows in our Church paddock, and I recall being nearly crucified myself, on occasions for questioning things that weren't to be questioned, regardless of how interested I may have been in solving a scriptural riddle or how highly implausible an interpretation might have seemed. This started at a young age with simple Biblical errors like the following:

1 Kings 16 : 6-8 *Bashaw died in the 26ᵗʰ year of King Asa's reign*

2 Chronicles 16 : 1 *Bashaw built a city in the 36ᵗʰ year of King Asa's reign.*

How did he do that?

1 Kings 16 : 23 *Omri became king in the 31ˢᵗ year of Asa's reign and he reigned for a total of 12 years.* (or up to the **43ʳᵈ** year of Asa's reign)

1 Kings 16 : 28-29 *Omri died, and his son Ahab became king in the 38ᵗʰ year of Asa's reign.*

How was that possible?

1 Chronicles 3 : 19 *Pedaiah was the father of Zerubbabel.*

Ezra 3 : 2 & 3 : 8 *Shealtiel was the father of Zerubbabel.*

2 Kings 9 : 27 *Jehu shot Ahaziah near Ibleam. Ahaziah fled to Meggido and died there.*

2 Chronicles 22 : 9 *Ahaziah was found hiding in Samaria, brought to Jehu, and put to death.*

What do these errors mean; the Bible is not the perfect word of God? With this sort of contradiction it is fairly apparent that it could not be the work of just one writer. At the very least it seems the editors were asleep at the wheel! If God was 'almighty' and actually devised and wrote the Bible it could not be beyond him to get it to the people without errors. So as I continued questioning and encountered more hostility, I discovered to my amazement that the Bible actually supported my stance:

1 Thessalonians 5 : 21 *"Prove all things; hold fast to that which is good."*

Isaiah 1 : 18 *"Come now and let us reason together, saith the Lord."*

Not in our congregation though; God, the Bible and their doctrine were taught as being quite infallible, you believed it and anything wrong in a person's Christian walk was definitely their fault alone. Inside the cover of my first Bible I wrote from **Mark 9 : 24** *"Lord I believe; help thou mine unbelief."* I prayed this prayer feverishly, daily, before my studies showed just how normal disbelief of the Bibles convoluted message really is. I learned that the questioning and non-acceptance of much of the doctrine by a thinking individual, was perfectly understandable. I found in the Bible, a bigoted, chauvinistic and condoning religion of justification. Many, many passages relate "God ordained" atrocities; such passages reflected the macho, warlike, Hebrew tribal psyche of the writers in those times. What these scribes wrote must certainly be considered unworthy of an almighty, benevolent, loving God and quite inconsistent with God's supposed omniscience. It would take more conviction than I could muster to believe that the scribes were writing this on behalf of any God.

The Church has had a full 2000 years to prepare its opposition to critiques like this book that discloses conflict in Bible passages. Of course they cannot risk their livelihood by admitting that these errors exist. They always bring out the old failsafe arguments, *"you are looking at it too literally; the Bible contains mysteries that only we are privy to. Some parts are allegory."* If they are reading the same passages with a deeper understanding of the hidden meanings, fine, but in many years of study I have never been convinced that the clergy have any keys to hidden passages whatsoever. In fact today, my knowledge of History and Archaeology usually gives me the edge in understanding passages within the contemporary historical context. If it is a fact that they have this wisdom and enlightenment on tap, why is it that in their role as teachers, they are not passing it on to the laity? St. Athanasius of Alexandria was not only aware of the allegorical nature of many Bible texts; he suggests that, *"Should we understand sacred writ according to the letter, we should fall into the most enormous blasphemies."* The learned Christian writer Origen stated that the body of the scriptures is made up of history and stories that are not literally true, but are for the instruction of ignorant and simple minded folk. He claimed that glaring contradictions stirred people into investigating the real meaning of these impossible edicts. What absolute nonsense. Do we worship a God of the 'particularly learned' or did Jesus preach to simple folk? If we encounter a Bible that gives us passages of palpable nonsense, we direct our search elsewhere. To pretend to dig hidden meaning out of obviously erroneous Bible passages is simply building parachutes. This argument cuts both ways and we will discover passages taken literally by the clergy; that are quite apparently veiled allegory. After all, the Church still teaches the Genesis creation of Adam and Eve in the Garden of Eden, don't they?

Rev. Kythera Ann Grunge got it correct when she cogently observed;

"Allegorical interpretations arise spontaneously whenever a conflict between new ideas and those expressed in a sacred book necessitate some form of compromise." (4)

Accordingly we are not simply taking the Bible too literally. The Church simply retreats to this argument whenever we disclose conflict in Bible passages.

The Who's Who of the Plural Godhead

Let's commence with a search for Almighty God himself. He certainly seems to differ from the Old to New Testament displaying an entirely different persona. In addition, just how does one locate and identify the one true God within the Trinity? Scholars can confirm that this question is not nearly as simple as Christians now claim. The ancient Egyptians used a book they called; *"Reu nu poert em hru"* which translates as *'The Chapters of coming forth by day'*. It is an illustrated collection of very ancient scripture and funeral rites that includes magic spells and formulas written on papyrus. We know this work today as the *'Egyptian Book of the Dead'*. Written in ancient times, some considerable time before the Bible, the *'Egyptian Book of the Dead'*, tells us that the great God **Atem** (not Aten) created the God **Shu** and the Goddess **Tefnut** from his own body. He then declared he had become three rather than one God. It seems that this was the very first Holy Trinity within a Godhead. Some time after this but still well before Christianity the ancient Indian religion had a trinity of **Brahman**, **Krishna** and **Shiva**. Pagan religions too had triumvirate Godheads and there is no question that the idea of a Trinity existed long before the event of the Christian religion.

In Babylon around 1400 BCE the **Sun**, **Moon** and **Venus** were worshipped as a triad. In that relationship, the planet Venus was noted as the 'Queen of Heaven'. [5] We can find recorded in the Bible several examples of the Hebrew people worshipping the Queen of Heaven some five centuries before the time of Christ and it is thus not surprising to find this Goddess included in early Christian trinities. (For examples see **Jeremiah 7 : 18** and **Jeremiah 44 : 17-25**). Not commonly known is that the Christians in fact adopted several versions of a trinity before settling on the current choice as late as 325 AD at the council of Nicea. Even then there was confusion, with the followers of St. Aurorius Augustine (354 – 430 AD) of the Alexandria school believing that just as man has **Knowledge, Will** and **Conscience**, then God holds the form of **Father, Son** and **Holy Ghost**. Taking a somewhat contrary position, three Greek Orthodox Bishops saw this as making God too much like man and saw the **Father**, the **Word** and the **Holy Spirit** as being differing manifestations of the one God. So by mere fluke, Christianity ended up as a **monotheistic** religion yet somehow it has a triumvirate Godhead. **The Father, the Word and Holy Ghost**.

1 John 5 : 7& 8 *for there are three that bear record in heaven, the Father, the Word, and the Holy Ghost; and these three are one. And there are three that bear witness in earth, the Spirit, and the Water and the Blood; and these three agree in one.*

Now this is despite other scripture stating;

Deuteronomy 6 : 4 *Hear, O Israel: The lord our God is one Lord.*

Isaiah 43 : 10 *" ... before me there was no God formed, neither shall there be after me."*

Isaiah 45 : 7 *"I am the Lord and there is none else*

Isaiah 45 : 6 *...so that from the rising of the sun to the place of its setting men may know there is none besides me. I am the Lord, and there is no other.*

Then we find in;

Colossians 2 : 9 *For in him (Christ) dwelleth the fullness of the Godhead bodily.*

So now we are told the Godhead dwells 'bodily' within Christ. Scripture tells us that there is one God, and then we are told there are three Gods. Well I'm confused!

This brings to mind the old saying about 'not one *iota* of difference'; that saying came about from a controversy in the Byzantine Empire when sorting out this very question about the personalities within the Godhead. The orthodox Catholics believed that God the Father incorporated God the Son, whilst the Arian sect thought that they were separate personalities within the same Godhead. Now the Father and Son combined in Greek is recorded as *Homo-ousion* and the Father and Son separate is *Homoi-ousion* with just one Greek letter iota being the difference. The Arian doctrine was declared heretical in 325 AD and the Catholic doctrine prevailed even though there was just one iota of difference.

We should now look briefly at another Bible mystery that indicates the Heavenly Host actually resides with God; the same God who says he acts alone;

Luke 2:13 *"And suddenly there was with the angel a multitude of the heavenly host praising God"*

Who were the 'host' of heaven? Etymology tells us that the word 'host' was a previously non-existent English word, created by the Bible translators. For a long time to come it was not a word in the vernacular of Bible readers. My Sunday School teachers assumed that the host must have been Angels although there was no evidence to support this. (At other times the 'heavenly host' appear to be the stars and planets). The passage above states that the 'host' were 'with the angel', indicating that they were not the same beings. This stance is also supported by the learned Rabbi ben Jochai who after a lifetime of study stated that they were certainly not the same. In fact the real English translation from the original texts that offended the translators, should have been *'heavenly army'*, not *'heavenly host'* at all, so it is unlikely angels are meant. This is confirmed when the same Hebrew word is used in the following:

> **Exodus 14:17** *I will harden the hearts of the Egyptians, and they shall follow them: and I will get me honour upon Pharaoh, and upon all his host, upon his chariots, and upon his horsemen.* (It is not difficult to see that this refers to Pharaoh's Army)

Thus we can accept that the Heavenly Host is really an army. Now an early name of God was **Jehovah-Sabaoth** (YHWH-Sabaoth) and this confirms Almighty God as a God of war since 'Sabaoth' is the very word translated as *'host'* and accordingly **Jehovah-Sabaoth** means 'God of armies'. So whom do a heavenly army fight? It gets more confusing. For example, what is meant in the following?

> **Isaiah 24 : 21** *And it shall come to pass in that day, that the Lord shall punish the host of the high ones that are on high, and the kings of the earth upon the earth.* (Can we at least ask who and why?)

When God is mentioned in the Hebrew Bible, in many cases, the Canaanite word 'Elohim' (or Eloheem) is used which is the plural form of Eloh, meaning 'Gods'. This is quite wrongly translated as God (singular) in the KJV Bible and most other versions, but there is no doubt whatever that, plural Gods were originally intended. This is scary stuff for Christians. How do we possibly reconcile this as a monotheistic religion? Apparently, with an awful lot of smoke and mirrors and a fair bit of confusion! It gets worse, the Christian writer **Adamantius Origen** (185 – 251 AD) wrote;

"… the Gospel of the Hebrews, in which the Saviour says; 'Just now my mother the holy spirit, took me by one of my hairs and brought me to Tabor, the great mountain.' "

Is Jesus actually nominating his Mother Mary as the Holy Spirit in this passage? If so, this would indicate that the early Hebrews included Mary in the Godhead not as the 'Queen of Heaven' in this case, but as 'The Holy Spirit'. Part of this quotation, *"Just now my mother, the Holy Spirit, took me by one of my hairs,"* was also quoted by none less than Bishop St. Jerome, who compiled the Catholic Vulgate Bible.

My studies showed that to appease the Pagan worshipers of the virgin goddess **Astarte** (Ishtar) the Byzantine Emperor Constantine had the Roman Church also include the Virgin Mary in the Godhead for a time, as a mother figure, to gradually replace Astarte. This of course left one deity over so apparently Mary was said for a time to be the same as the Holy Spirit. This was a fraudulent manipulation of the already fraudulent Trinity. Let's look at an interesting verse from the Koran, which mentions the beliefs of those who still consider Jesus and Mary to be part of the Trinity, and choose to worship them.

Al Qur'an 5 : 119: *And behold! God will say, "O Jesus the son of Mary! Didst thou say unto men, worship me and my mother as gods in derogation of God?" He will say: "Glory be to Thee! Never could I say that which I had no right (to say). Should I have said such a thing, Thou wouldst indeed have known it."*

We must note that although we may not agree with their religion, the Koran writers were intelligent people who believed they were writing absolute fact and obviously had a problem with the inclusion of both Mary and Jesus in the Godhead, which must have been a prevailing occurrence at that time, to warrant the mention. It is worth noting an unusual passage recorded by Joseph Smith, the founder of the Church of Jesus Christ of Latter Day Saints which states;

"I will teach on the plurality of Gods. I have selected this text for that express purpose. I wish to declare I have always and in all congregations when I have preached on the subject of the Deity, it has been the plurality of Gods. It has been preached by the Elders for fifteen years." [6]

In addition other Church fathers of the Mormon Church taught plural

Gods.

> *"How many Gods there are, I do not know. But there never was a time when there were no Gods and worlds …"* [7]

Where does this leave us? Well we find that Gods (plural) were originally used in the scriptures and that the concept of a trinity within the Godhead predates the Bible by a very long time. We can then follow the evolution of the trinity throughout various members and see that the final Biblical choice was merely a random selection by the Catholic Church. God is somehow singular but nevertheless plural at the same time and a manufactured word 'host' was used to hide his heavenly 'army'. We even found a Bible passage that intimated that the plural godhead dwelt within Jesus. This doesn't instil much confidence that we have located God within our Holy Books. Something appears to be wrong here.

Mastema in the Godhead?

In early Bibles the passages: **Exodus 4 : 24 & 25** tell us that God the Father turned on his servant Moses and tried to kill him. This same story is also included in the non-canonical Hebrew *'Book of Jubilees'* that was previously called *"The Apocalypse of Moses"* and is even claimed by some Jews to be the book, dictated to Moses by an Angel on Mount Sinai. The attack on Moses in the 'Book of Jubilees' however, is blamed on a "bad" spirit of the Godhead called **Mastema**. This means that the bad side of God was sufficiently defined that it was actually given a separate name and identity. This evil identity it states, was actually a personage included in the Godhead. Does this then mean that we have God the Father, Jesus the Son also known as the Word, the Holy Spirit, Mary the Queen of Heaven plus Mastema the Evil Spirit somehow force fitted into a Trinity, all within a monotheistic religion? This is starting to get a bit silly! The actual derivation indicates that Mastema is a word that meant 'the dark or warlike' side of YHWH. This dark side is branded with the name 'Mastema' and these following passages show additional evil intent that doesn't look good for a benevolent Father God;

> **Exodus 32 : 14** *And the Lord repented of the evil which he thought to do unto his people.*

Isaiah 30 : 26 ... *when the Lord binds up the bruises of his people and heals the wounds he inflicted.*

Isaiah 45 : 6-7 *I am the Lord and there is none else. I form the light and create the darkness, I make peace and create evil, I the Lord do all these things.*

1 Samuel 16 : 23 *And it came to pass, when the evil spirit from God was upon Saul, that David took an harp, and played with his hand: so Saul was refreshed, and was well, and the evil spirit departed from him.*

Numbers 31 : 17-18, Deuteronomy 20 : 16-17, Joshua 10 40-42, Ezekiel 9 :4-8 *The Spirit of God promotes slaughter.*

Judges 14 : 19 *And the Spirit of the Lord came upon him, and he went down to Ashkelon, and slew thirty men of them, and took their spoil,*

1 Samuel 18 : 10 *And it came to pass on the morrow, that the evil spirit from God came upon Saul.*

Now these quotes may not necessarily refer to Mastema, although several specifically refer to 'the evil spirit from God' and we are led to believe that this is Mastema. How then does the Christian hierarchy explain this?

"When discussing the story of Noah and the flood, author Karen Armstrong (A History of God, 1993), as a panelist on Moyers' program, asserted that God is "not some nice, cozy daddy in the sky," but rather a being who decidedly behaves frequently "in an evil way." With his actions in connection with the flood, Armstrong said, God originated the idea of justifiable genocide. Hitler and Stalin, one might deduce, acted on the instruction of such stories as that of the flood and of Sodom and Gomorrah when instituting the holocaust and the camps of the Gulag. Had the panelists called on Gnostic scriptures, they could have quoted many precedents for Armstrong's criticism of the vengeful God of the Old Testament". (8)

Christians would audibly gasp at this, however Karen Armstrong is an ex-nun, an educated and astute student and a capable writer and the reality is that The Old Testament God is depicted as a cruel and ruthless warmonger and no dictator in history has outstripped him for deceit, wrath and senseless killing. There are plenty of passages we will encounter later that show this macho, warlike, ruthless side that again confirms his origins as a

Hebrew tribal war God.

Still searching for the Trinity, the Bible actually confuses the Godhead issue even further;

John 1 : 1 Jesus and God are one.

John 1 : 14 Jesus is God incarnate.

Mark 1 : 1 Jesus is the Son of God.

Acts 2 : 22 Jesus was a man approved by God.

John 10 : 30 Jesus and the Father are one.

John 14 : 28 The Father is greater than Jesus.

John 3 : 17 Jesus does not judge or condemn.

John 5 : 27& 30, Acts 10 : 42, 2 Corinthians 5 : 10 God the Father has passed it to Jesus to judge.

John 8 : 15 Jesus does not judge mankind but God the Father does.

John : 9 : 39 Jesus came into the world to judge

John 12 : 47 Jesus did not come into the world to judge

John 5 : 22 God does not judge.

Romans 2 : 2-5, 1 Peter 1 : 17, Revelation 20 : 12-13 God does judge.

Jude 1 : 14-15 God judges with ten thousand of his saints

John 5 : 24 Believers do not come into judgment.

Matthew 12 : 36-37, 2 Corinthians 5 : 10 , Hebrews 9 : 27, 2 Timothy 4 : 1 All persons (believers along with non believers) come into judgment.

John 5 : 31 Jesus says that if he bears witness to himself, his testimony is not true.

John 8 : 14 Jesus says that even if he bears witness to himself, his testimony is true.

John 6 : 44 No one can come to Jesus unless he is drawn by the Father.

John 10 : 27-29 None of Jesus' followers will be lost.

1 Timothy 4 : 1 Some of them will be lost.

The Biblical writers apparently did not work in harmony at all and with this lack of harmony comes unbelievable confusion. Questions too, must be asked about the actual selection of the works included in the Bible against the works left out. Some non-canonical works put an altogether different slant on Biblical themes and one can but wonder on the position of doctrine today, had they been included. From the Bible writings it is not even possible to conclude with any certainty, if there is or is not a trinity. Accordingly a vote at the Council of Nicea in 325 AD decided this matter for the Church and their decision became part of the infallible word of God. I sure hope they prayed about it first!

The Garden of Eden

The word '**Eden**' in Hebrew means *'delight'*, *'pleasure'*, or loosely, *'paradise'*; however, '**E.DIN**' in Sumerian means *'plain'*, like the river flat between rivers, perhaps indicating the location of this Biblical garden. There are suggestions of Garden of Eden sights around the world; however the serious scholars seem to agree on two probable locations. One now inundated in the Persian Gulf at the mouth of the Tigris and Euphrates Rivers and the other nearer their source in the foothills of modern day Turkey. The Bible is not a good source as here we see a major geographical flaw. The Bible makes it clear we are looking in the area of the Euphrates River, with the mention of an additional three rivers; and then by a translation error locates one of these rivers in **Ethiopia.** This is just plain nonsense as with some research, all four rivers can be identified. None are in Ethiopia, which is some 1000 kilometres away.

Let's look at the offending verses:

Genesis 2 : 10-14 *Now a river went out of Eden to water the garden, and from there it parted and became four riverheads. The name of the first is Pishon; it is the one which skirts the whole land of Havilah, where there is gold. And the gold of that land is good. Bdellium and the onyx stone are there. The name of the second river is Gihon; it is the one, which goes around the whole land of Ethiopia. The name of the third river is Hiddekel; it is the one, which goes toward the east of Assyria. The fourth river is the Euphrates.*

The Rivers listed are:

1. **Pishon** that skirts the land of Havilah
2. **Gihon** that winds around the land of Ethiopia (Cush)

3.   **Hiddekel** that goes towards the east of Assyria

4.   **Euphrates** still known as such to this day

1. The **Pishon** was a tributary of the Euphrates that has dried up today and the land of Havilah; according to **Genesis 10 : 7** was inhabited by a known Biblical people descended from Havilah the son of Cush (the son of Ham, the son of Noah) and that a later descendent of Shem (the son of Noah) was also called Havilah the son of Joktan in **Genesis 10 : 29**. This does not entirely remove the confusion.

2. The **Gihon** is a main tributary of the Tigris and winds through the land of '**Kash**' east of Babylon, and known today as Al'Uhaimir. The incorrect translation of '**Kash**' to '**Ethiopia**' is nonsense based on a misunderstanding of the language of both the Greeks and Egyptians who used the name '**Cush**' for the Ethiopian part of Africa known today as Sudan. Laurence Gardner called this the Land of Kish. [9]

To exacerbate this confusion, as shown above, Cush was recorded as the father of Havilah, and in addition Kish was the father of King Saul. When we consider that Hebrew was recorded without the vowels it is not hard to see how these misunderstandings occur.

3. The name **Hiddekel** indicates the river Tigris, which does flow as stated. The name 'Tigris' in Greek is recorded as 'Hiddeqel' in Hebrew and in the Bible is recorded as Hiddekel. [10]

4. The Euphrates is well known to this day and flows into the Persian Gulf. [11]

In support of the Biblical verse; '**Bdellium**' was a fragrant resin, tapped from trees in Arabia, and various types of precious and semiprecious stones were also found here. Farouk El-Baz, a scientist from Boston University, claims an ancient river can be spotted on satellite photos of the Arabian Peninsula. He believes this river, which he called The Kuwait River, once joined the Tigris and the Euphrates where they join at the head of the Persian Gulf and corresponds with the Pishon. El-Baz believes it dried up around 3000 years ago. The archaeologist and former curator of the Harvard Semitic Museum, James A. Sauer, supports him in his book, '*The River Runs Dry*', [12] Sauer documents that the so-called Kuwait River may well be the

Biblical, Pishon River. Laurence Gardner states:

"The four 'Rivers of Eden' (Genesis 2 : 10-14) have caused any amount of theological confusion, with researchers questing far and wide for rivers that might fit the Old Testament depictions. There is no mystery to unravel, though, for the conventional English version of the Genesis text has been fully mistranslated in this regard." [13]

The Jewish historian Flavius Josephus (37 AD – 100 AD) originally had the Jewish name of **Joseph ben Matthias** but took Roman citizenship and changed his name to **Titus Flavius Josephus** and his works *'The Jewish War', 'Antiquities of the Jews'* and *'Against Apion'* plus his autobiography *'The Life'* are invaluable eye-witness accounts of the momentous turning point in Judaism, Christianity, and Western civilization. For much of the first century history of the Holy Land, Josephus is our only real source of knowledge. For a completely different 'global' perspective on the Garden of Eden, Josephus had this to say;

"Now the garden was watered by one river, which ran round about the whole earth, and was parted into four parts. And Phison, which denotes a multitude, running into India, makes its exit into the sea, and is by the Greeks called Ganges. Euphrates also, as well as Tigris, goes down into the Red Sea. Now the name Euphrates, or Phrath, denotes either a dispersion, or a flower: by Tigris, or Diglath, is signified what is swift, with narrowness; and Geon runs through Egypt, and denotes what arises from the east, which the Greeks call Nile." [14]

The 'Mormons' believe that the Garden of Eden was in North America and the Mississippi and Missouri Rivers were nick-named the Euphrates and Tigris; and thus they locate the 'Garden of Eden' on the American continent. This theory does not hold much support outside their church.

Adam and Eve and the Tree of Knowledge

Regardless of the location of the Garden of Eden, we have all heard about Adam and Eve covering themselves by wearing a **fig leaf.** Despite its widespread acceptance this is not entirely scriptural. Take your pick. In **Genesis 3 : 7** Adam and Eve cover themselves with **aprons** made out of fig leaves, and then in **Genesis 3 : 21** The Lord made **coats of skins** for them. Translators vary in the rendering of the Hebrew word that is recorded correctly as 'aprons', with the Geneva Bible of 1560 documenting it as 'breeches' a word for trousers that is little used today. Displaying someone's marvellous sense of humour, this version became known as the "Breeches Bible".

In reality what the scribes are recording here is that it was traditional for Sumerian servants or slaves to go naked and this identified their subservient position. The gaining of knowledge meant that Adam and Eve were no longer servants, no longer created only 'to till the ground'. They were no longer subservient and accordingly couldn't wait to cover themselves with aprons to show this new status. The Lord acknowledged this when he gave them coats to wear. Let's look at the situation in the Garden of Eden, where the serpent actually speaks human language, presumably Sumerian or Hebrew, and has quite a conversation with Eve.

Genesis 3 : 1 – 6 *Now the serpent was more crafty than any of the wild animals the Lord God had made. He said to the woman, "Did God really say, 'You must not eat from any tree in the garden?'" The woman said to the serpent, "We may eat fruit from the trees in the garden, but God did say, 'You must not eat fruit from the tree that is in the middle of the garden, and you must not touch it, or you will surely die.'" "You will not surely die," the serpent said to the woman. For God knows that when you eat of it your eyes will be opened, and you will be like Gods, knowing good and evil." And when the woman saw that the tree was good for food, and that it was pleasant to the eyes, and a tree to be desired to make one wise, she took of the fruit thereof, and did eat and gave also unto her husband with her; and he did eat.*

The Bible tells us in **Genesis 2 : 17** that God told Adam if he ate the fruit of the tree of knowledge, then that day he would surely die. As described above, Eve gave him the fruit and Adam ate it. Just a bit later in **Genesis 5 : 5** it tells us that Adam lived for 930 years and then died.

No room for misinterpretation, no half measures. **Eat the fruit … you die.** Yet Adam ate the fruit and he didn't die. Is God a liar? See **Hebrews 6 : 18, Psalms 19 : 7** and **Titus 1 : 2** They all say, *"God cannot lie."* **Numbers 23 : 19, Proverbs 12 : 22, Titus 1 : 2** *God never lies and cannot lie. He hates lying and finds it an abomination.* You must agree that this is pretty fatal to either the Bible's or Almighty God's inerrancy. I pondered then if a spiritual death or a loss of eternal life was meant, since this could make perfect sense. Christians often argue that this is where man lost immortality. Not so, the Hebrew language makes distinctions between normal death, murder, execution and spiritual death with a separate word for each;

Muth to die a physical death.

Tirtzach (tear - tzach): the murder of an innocent person

Mahvet (mah - vet): the execution of a person deemed guilty of a transgression. As in stoning, for breaches of Jewish law.

Karet (kar - et): To be cut off; implies a spiritual death and the eradication of the entire soul (neshamah) and accordingly terminates any chance of resurrection. The death can also be physical but it is the heavenly eradication of the soul that prevents resurrection.

The souls (nefashot) of people are also graded '**neshamah,**' being of the higher order soul as opposed to '**nefesh**' a person with a soul similar to an animal's, indicating that if the body is killed, then the soul will be cut off from heaven. Now when we search the case of Adam in Genesis (Beresheet) in the Hebrew Torah we find the word used is *'Muth'*...meaning, *'to die a physical death'* and this of course is the word for actual death. I have even had clergy say that a day with God is a thousand years and accordingly Adam died before he was a thousand years old so therefore 'that day' he surely died. This is really grasping at straws!

It is just a tad sexist, yet the Bible says in the New Testament;

1 Timothy 2 : 14 *And Adam was not the one deceived; it was the woman who was deceived and became a sinner.*

OK this is the kind of verse the early Church (and several other groups) used to grind down women and it's all a lie. Sorry! The writer of Timothy, you got it wrong! How does one account for the actions of Adam if he was not **himself**, deceived and why in **Genesis 3 : 17 – 24** does it detail the punishments metered out by God, **specifically to Adam** for his sin. It seems that the writers of Timothy had never read the letters to the Corinthians either:

1 Corinthians 15 : 22 *For as in Adam all die…Death is passed to all men by the*

sin of Adam.

See also:

Romans 5 : 12 *Therefore, just as sin entered the world through one man, and death through sin, and in this way death came to all men, because all sinned -*

Furthermore what was the purpose of the banishment from the Garden after their sin, and the positioning of the *"flaming sword that turned every way to keep the way of the tree of life"* in **Genesis 3 : 24**? Wasn't the damage already done, or didn't the fruit that helped Adam and Eve distinguish between good and evil really have that power at all? Why lock them out once they had eaten the forbidden fruit; why shut the gate after the horse has bolted? It doesn't make much sense!

The next point for consideration is that we were taught to hate the serpent that encouraged Eve to sin; we were told he represented the Devil. Remember the serpent told Eve, "No you won't die". This proved to be the absolute truth, yet he is supposed to be the devil, **John 8 : 44** *"the father of liars, with no truth in him"*. Meanwhile our righteous, truthful God apparently told porkies. This section alone goes a long way towards scuttling the Bibles credibility. For an infallible God who cannot lie, something is very wrong here!

Lastly on the Adam and Eve issue, we were always told that the 'forbidden fruit' was an **apple** however there is nothing whatever in any scripture to indicate that it was in fact an apple. Primary industries professionals today will confirm that the apple did not exist in those times and they can trace its development to a much later timeframe. So was it a fig? Actually there is nothing to indicate that it was an actual fruit at all. The apple tree however has vestiges of *'immortality through Wisdom'* (the gaining of knowledge) and has been identified as a symbol of consummation. Interesting too is that from early times the Bible records a huge percentage of 'barren' women and in ancient times from **Genesis 30 : 14-17** the 'mandrake plant' was highly valued as a sex stimulant to overcome supposed problems in this area. The Hebrew word rooted in the ancient Ugaritic term for mandrake literally means "love giver". Its Aramaic rendering stresses its power to disperse the demons trying to rob woman of her fertility. The Revised English Version of the Bible rather sadly translates the 'mandrake' in the above passage as 'love apple'.

Lying

So back to God telling lies. Apart from this case, is it actually a fact that God can't lie? Are the Bible writers unanimous on God's inability to lie?

1 Kings 22 : 23 *Behold the Lord hath put a lying spirit in the mouths of all these thy prophets and the Lord has spoken evil concerning thee.* (Check it yourself!)

2 Thessalonians 2 : 11 *God shall send them strong delusion, that they should believe a lie.* (Is this the same God you worship?)

Jeremiah wasn't convinced about God's credibility; he asks God, **Jeremiah 15 : 8** *"Wilt though be to me as a liar".*

Proverbs 12 : 22 *Lying lips are an abomination to the Lord.* (Really? Do as I say not as I do.)

This confuses the lying matter further but we must consider that another part of the Adam and Eve concept is also flawed. How can God require (in fact demand) good from his creations, who could not yet distinguish good from evil? Think about it! In addition God has a problem with persons desiring the ability to distinguish between right and wrong. This desire is apparently sufficiently sinful to be punishable by death.

Read it verbatim from the King James Bible;

Genesis 2 : 17, *"But of the tree of the knowledge of good and evil, thou shall not eat of it; for in that day that thou eatest thereof, thou shalt surely die."*

So God is demanding that without the ability to distinguish good from evil; you will do only good! This is not logical. The New Testament then does a bit of a back-flip on this in **Hebrews 5 : 13-14** by saying that only babes on milk are unskilful in righteousness, but those of full age are expected to discern good from evil. This is quite confusing!

Jesus Was Born in a Stable

The familiar Nativity scene always shows baby Jesus in a stable with donkeys, sheep and cattle in the background and is found to be quite false.

In fact it is totally pagan. The Dead Sea Scrolls indicate that Jesus was born in "the Queen's house" outside Qumran. [15]

If he really was of the Royal House of David this makes a lot more sense than a future King being born in a stable. **Luke 2 : 7** says *"And she brought forth her first born son, and wrapped him in swaddling clothes, and laid him in a manger; (because there was no room for them in the inn.")*

The "inn" bit in parenthesis is not included in early Bibles and was added to this scripture much later. At the time of Jesus there was no such thing as an 'inn'. People stayed with friends or family. Smith's Bible Dictionary does not confirm that the bit in parenthesis was added later despite the fact that we have available older Bibles that feature its exclusion. Smith's Dictionary nevertheless admits that bit is in error but claims it is because of a faulty translation, which should read, *"(because there was no place in the room.)"* The Bible's report on the visit of the wise men, has something different to say **Matthew 2 : 11** *"And when they were come into the house, they saw the young child with Mary his mother…"*

So they were in a house; the Bible says so. A **'manger'** was a kind of feed basket or frame to hold hay or straw for livestock to eat. The word 'manger' in French means *'to eat'* and there is likely a connection. It was quite common practice in those times to place one inside a house to use as a baby crib. Saint Francis of Assisi in 1224 AD introduced a manger into his church likely creating the first Nativity scene. Why are we taught that Jesus was born in a stable when this is not what is stated in the Bible? The reason is due to concessions made to the pagan religions when Constantine introduced Christianity as the official Byzantine religion. The Roman worshippers of **Mithra** had no problem identifying with the Nativity scene. Their god **Zoroaster** was born of a virgin, in a grotto housing animals, and was attended by shepherds. Somehow a 'stable' became a 'grotto', became a 'cave' and in Bethlehem today guides show the tourists the **"actual cave"** where Jesus was born, without a thought for just how anti-scriptural this is. It is advertised in tourist brochures. Despite this being total rubbish all but the elect are fooled. There is not one shred of evidence in the Bible or elsewhere to indicate that the Hebrew prince Jesus was born in a stable, grotto or cave. It might scare some Christians to know that the entire

Nativity scene along with its annual 25 December ritual is also entirely pagan.

The Magi & Their Gifts

The word 'Magi' would usually refer to the 'wise men' or priests of the Zoroaster religion, and they believed Jesus was the next incarnation of their God. We were always taught that there were **three** wise men. Where this actually came from, I have no idea. The Bible covers the visit of the wise men in Matthew and in Luke, but not once mentions the number as three. The Persian version of this story is more specific. It clearly states that there were **five** Wise Men and coincidently this is the same number who attended the birth of Confucius according to the ancient Chinese texts. Still our Nativity scenes and our Christmas cards always show **three** wise men from the East. Perhaps there were five, perhaps ten, perhaps twenty, but the number is not recorded in the Bible. These men brought Gold, Frankincense and Myrrh, so the clergy must have just decided one gift apiece so there must have been three.

> **Matthew 2 : 11** *And when they were come into the house, they saw the young child with Mary his mother, and fell down, and worshipped him: and when they had opened their treasures, they presented unto him gifts; gold, and frankincense, and myrrh.*

A new born prince in the Holy Land where there was no Hebrew king on the throne, would promote a visit from the wise men of the East, only if he was of a very special dynasty. If in reality the wise men came from Persia or Anatolia, (Turkey) as is taught in that country to this day, then at that time they would certainly not have been followers of the God YHWH (Jehovah). This means that Jesus had to be of a much more important dynasty that would cross religious boundaries. We will search this more in a moment. We should firstly look to the gifts of the wise men.

Gold, is the first recorded royal gift, and was quite possibly not for monetary purposes. It may well refer to the 'white powder' form of gold that was ingested by the kingly dynasty to enrich the blood and to stimulate the pituitary gland to heighten awareness in similar fashion to meditation. This usage was practised by the Sumerians and the Egyptians and some scholars attribute the extreme longevity of the early patriarchs recorded in the Bible to the use of this powder. The Egyptian pharaohs used 'white powder gold' to attain a tranquil state (the opposite of chaos) that they called Ma`at.

Frankincense was derived from the sap of certain trees, and was highly prized by the ancient Egyptians and Hebrews. It was heated to produce a very strong and pleasant odour, richer than the incense used today. Because the trees were not plentiful, and the process long and arduous, it was extremely valuable and a fitting gift for royalty.

Myrrh, (*commiphora myrrha*) was a herb used by Egyptians in embalming and along with the white powder form of gold, was used in calming the mind in a form of meditation and to increase awareness and focus, to assist the Pharaoh to achieve the state of Ma`at. It was also used to make perfumes, and even insect repellent. Ancient Greek and Roman physicians used myrrh to treat wounds and as a digestive aid. Today myrrh is still utilised to strengthen the immune system by stimulating the production of white blood cells. It is also an herbal remedy for treating sore throats, colds, coughs, asthma, and chest congestion and to prevent tooth decay and gum disease. These things were fitting gifts for royalty.

Jesus of Nazareth

Why was this title given to Jesus when it was said he was born in Bethlehem and lived in Galilee? There is considerable information available that strongly suggests that **Nazareth** was not even a town at the time of Christ and when it finally became a town it was called **Natzrat**. A person from Natzrat was called a **Natzrati**. First settlement here was believed to have taken place some 67 years after the birth of Christ. It then took at least another 30 years to become a sizeable town. Why then does the Bible mention 'Jesus of Nazareth'?

Jesus and his brothers were associated with a Jewish sect called the Essenes and within this group was a sub group called the **Nazarenes**, which meant '*keepers*' or in full, '*keepers of the covenant*'. Some scholars say that the Nazarenes were in fact the military arm of the Essenes but if this is true, they were certainly not fanatically militant like the zealots. It is often claimed that

Jesus was the founder of this group however that is easily disproved since they are known to have existed in a similar format since 397 BCE. [16]

In an amazing twist the historians and writers Philo, Milman, Tytler and the more contemporary Kersey Graves record that the Essenes doctrine was a close parallel of Buddhism. In fact they claim that the Essenes held all the doctrines of Buddhism and yet the Essenes are fairly well accepted as the forerunners of the early Christian movement. We cannot dismiss this since there is definite exposure of the Essenes to the Buddhists doctrine. It is now widely understood that the Essenes doctrine and precepts sprang from the Buddhist School of **Pythagoras** in Alexandria, Egypt. For these reason many writers now conclude that Christianity actually came out of Buddhism.

There is a similar word **Nazoraeans** meaning *'fishers'*, which applied to the evangelic pre-Christian sect that despite its similarity is not to be confused with Nazarenes, although both appear to have become a generic term for early Christians. This group's symbol was the fish since they were **"fishers of men."** That alone is interesting, because it makes it apparent that the early Christian symbol even before Christ was a fish and it was a few hundred years later that it became a cross. A common illustration used by the early Christians was the acronym 'IXOUE' written within the body of a fish. It stood for a Greek phrase which translates as *Jesus Christ God's Son - Saviour'* and coincidently this assembled acronym spells out the Greek word for 'Fish'. **Epiphanies** mentions a pre Christian group in the Holy Land known as *'Nasaraioi' (Nazoraios)*. [17] That word too, appears to derive from the Egyptian word for 'fishes' but has a connotation of coming apart from the world. The Essenes sect wore white robes and the Nazarenes are thought to have had medical training. Who knows, this medical training in that day and age may even account for some supposed healing miracles of Jesus. Now whether it was 'Jesus the **Nazarene**' or 'Jesus the **Nazoraean**' this is still being wrongly translated as "Jesus of Nazareth", to wrongly indicate that he came from the town of Nazareth, a town that probably didn't exist at that time and even if it did was then called **Natzrat**. We can almost laugh at the inane Biblical mix up that follows:

Matthew 2 : 23 *"And he came and dwelt in a City called Nazareth; that it might be fulfilled which was spoken by the prophets, he shall be called a Nazarene".*

An interesting explanation of the pre Christian group 'Nasaraioi' (Nazoraios) mentioned by Epiphanies is explained by David Pratt:

> The Hebrew name for Christians has always been notzrim, and although modern Christians claim that Christianity only started in the 1st century CE, the 1st-century Christians in Israel considered themselves to be a continuation of the notzri movement, which had been in existence for about 150 years. In the rabbinical tradition, Jeshu ben Pandera is also called Jeshu ha-Notzri (Jesus the Nazar). The Greek equivalent of notzri is nazoraios (or nazaraios/naziraios). The stem of this word means 'to keep oneself separate' — an indication of the ascetic nature of this sect. The early Christians conjectured that nazoraios (variously rendered Nazar/Nazarite, Nazorean or Nazarene) meant a person from Nazareth and so it was assumed that Jesus lived in Nazareth.... The expression 'Jesus of Nazareth' is therefore a mistranslation of 'Jeshu ha-Notzri'. [18]

I think the final word on this subject should go to Knight and Lomas who make the impressive point;

> "It struck us as a painful contortion of logic to say that Jesus was duty-bound to go and live in a particular place because some long-gone soothsayer had said he would" [19]

What Does it Take to be Saved?

The aim of every Christian is to become "born again" or "saved" to achieve the gift of eternal life of perpetual bliss with their Lord. This is of prime importance to Christ's followers and its achievement has become the keystone to all Christian dogma. So, how does one obtain this gift; what does it take to be saved?

Matthew 10 : 22, Matthew 24 : 13 & Mark 13 : 13 *He that endures to the end will be saved.* (Assuming of course that he is a believer?)

Mark 16 : 16 *He that believes and is baptised will be saved.* (Even if he doesn't endure to the end?)

John 3 : 5 *Only he that is born of water and Spirit will be saved.* (So the above is wrong?)

Acts 16 : 31 *He that believes on the Lord Jesus will be saved.* (Even if he is not baptised of water and spirit?)

Acts 2 : 21 *He that calls upon the name of the Lord will be saved.* (Even if he doesn't endure to the end?)

Romans 10 : 9 *He who confesses with his mouth "Jesus is Lord" and believes in his heart that God raised him from the dead will be saved.* (Even if he is not baptised of water and spirit?)

1 John 4 : 7 *He who loves is born of God* (so now "love" is also a requirement)

John 12 : 32 *Jesus implies that all persons can be saved.* (With no further criteria required)

Timothy 2 : 3-4 & 2 Peter 3 : 9 *God wants all to be saved.* (OK can we count on that?)

Matthew 7 : 21 *Not everyone who calls on the name of the Lord will be saved.* (Why is that?)

Acts 2 : 21 & Romans 10 : 13 *Whoever calls on the name of the Lord will be saved.* (That's not what we just read)

Luke 13 :24 *Many will try to enter the Kingdom but will be unable.* (Why not?)

Acts 2 : 39 *Those God calls to himself will be saved.* (What about the others?)

John 12 : 40, Acts 2 : 21, Acts 2 : 39, Romans 9 : 27 & Romans 10 : 13 *Some will not be saved.*

Matthew 7 : 21, Luke 10 : 36-37, Romans 2 : 6, Romans 2 : 13 & James 2 : 24 *We are justified by works, not by faith.*

John 3 : 7, Romans 3 : 20-26, Ephesians 2 : 8-9 & Galatians 2 : 16 *We are justified by faith, not by works.*

I find this truly amazing. The primary purpose, the raison d'etre for Christians becoming "born again" is to become "saved" and yet the reality is that the Bible gives us no consistent or precise direction of what is required to achieve this. No wonder Christians begin to, 'feel things in their heart,' because it seems that is the most reliable guide, in this religion. I would think that the gaining of converts and guiding them to become 'saved' should be a major purpose of the religion and its Biblical record. One would expect the guidelines for the process to be made perfectly clear. This ceremony is not new, it has been around for thousands of years and one would expect the leaders to have a handle on this by now. Individual doctrines and individual clergy teach their versions of "the truth" in line with the passages they choose to adopt and promote. Individual Christians seem to become absolutely and totally committed that they have the correct formulae, even though there are so many choices and the Bible instructions are a totally ambiguous and inconsistent hotch-potch. Something is dreadfully wrong here!

Mary Magdalene the Scarlet Woman

Mary of Bethany or Mary the Magdalene was born in 3 AD. Her mother was Eucharia of the Royal House of Israel and her Father was Syrus (the Jairus) of Capernaum. Syrus was the Chief Priest, subordinate to the High Priest. Mary was of Royalty and herself a priestess. She was a very high profile person, held in the highest esteem and as such according to: **John 12 : 3** was the person selected from all the Holy Land to anoint the future King of Israel. Think about what this means!

Tony Bushby makes a good case for her father Syrus actually being the same 'Cyrus' recorded in The Book of James as being a descendant of the linage of Kings. Bushby states that this was another name for 'Caswallon the Second' and quotes an old record that has Caswallon as the father of Lazarus. Martha, Mary and Lazarus were brother and sisters in the Bible so this would of course make King Caswallon the father of Martha and Mary as well. [20] The Gospel of James states that Mary, Martha and Lazarus were *'born of right noble linage'* and the Bible also shows Lazarus to be a rich man; the Catholic Church would rather you didn't know this since for many years they have promoted Mary Magdalene as a prostitute. This *'noble linage'* may confirm Bushby's link to Caswallon who was the King of Britain, making Mary Magdalene a Celtic Princess and possibly a Druid Priestess. Whether this is true or not, Mary Magdalene was most certainly not a harlot or prostitute. The portrayal of Mary as such, commenced with an erroneous sermon preached in 591 AD by none other than **Pope Gregory the Great** and this lie is savagely continued by the Church to this day. The patriarchal Roman Church promoted this concept, in order to discredit Mary, because they feared the dynasty of the off-spring she might produce. Mary wore the scarlet robes, in that time depicting a Priestess and because of the Roman Church; "scarlet woman" still today depicts a harlot.

In early times the Pope even decreed by Papal bull that artists were not to paint Mary in red. Later still the church tried to limit painters to blue only. These Papal bulls are available today for you to read and grasp the iniquity of the Church system. The Roman doctrine effectively removed power from all Hebrew women of the Bible but Mary Magdalene especially concerned the Roman Church who set out to negate the Royal bloodline of Jesus. There is evidence that Jesus was married to Mary Magdalene and they did have children. Margaret Starbird an independent scholar and theologian has emerged as a senior advocate for this heretical idea of a marriage between Jesus and Mary Magdalene, commenced in her 1993 work, *The Woman with the Alabaster Jar*. Starbird maintains that the meaning of "The Magdalene" does not derive from the town of Magdala, a fishing village on the shores of Lake Kinnaret but rather from the Hebrew word *'magdala'* (migdol) meaning 'tower-stronghold' or simply 'elevated'. [21] The Catholic Church was terrified of descendants of Jesus since they had fraudulently usurped his power through the implementation of their own papal dynasty. Now that the Papal linage is firmly entrenched; now that there is little chance of the Papal dynasty being overthrown by members of the Desposyni of a Jesus bloodline, this stance of Pope Gregory's was officially repealed by the infallible Church in 1969, quietly admitting their error. No one even noticed!

Personally, I can't help but feel annoyance, that a woman priestess of the exceedingly high calibre of Mary Magdalene can be called a prostitute or harlot from so many pulpits every Sunday when very little research is required to totally dismiss this lie of the Roman Church. Like other gossip, the perpetrators believe that ignorance is an excuse, allowing them to do this nasty work with total immunity. If Jesus was to return, he just may take a multitude of the clergy to task for the way his wife has been so savagely defamed.

It is a well-documented fact that Bishop Clement removed a portion of Mark's gospel when he made his now well-known quote *"Not all true things are to be said to all men"*. He goes on to describe *"true truth"* and *"truth according to the faith"* maintaining that the faith option must always be chosen. The deleted section made it clear that Jesus and Mary Magdalene were man and wife. This should come as no surprise because on a number of occasions Jesus is addressed as Rabbi, and a requirement is that a Rabbi must be married. In fact Jewish tradition dictated that an unmarried man was 'incomplete' in that his state of not having a wife broke the commandment of God to, *"be fruitful and multiply"*. Thus religious perfection could only be attained in a married state. In fact in an unmarried state, the prayers of a high priest could not be completely efficacious and thus he was not permitted to conduct worship on the Day of Atonement, the most sacred day of the year. In addition, if Jesus was the legitimate King of the Jews it was also imperative that he be married with due haste in order to leave an heir to the throne. The following passages secretly acknowledge a relationship between Jesus and Mary Magdalene:

The Gospel of Thomas verse 114, has Simon Peter making a comment that certainly is demeaning to women. Simon Peter says to Jesus and the gathered disciples that Mary Magdalene should leave them;

"for women are not worthy of life." Jesus replies that he himself will *"lead her in order to make her male, so that she too may become a living spirit resembling you males. For every woman who will make herself male will enter the kingdom of heaven."*

This is a really enlightening religion!! It is Jesus however who states that he will personally lead her in order to make her male.

Gospel of Peter XII. 50 – 52 *Now early on the Lord's day Mary Magdalene, a disciple of the Lord - which, being afraid because of the Jews, for they were inflamed with anger, had not performed at the sepulcher of the Lord those things which women are accustomed to do unto them that die and are beloved of them - took with her the women her friends and came unto the tomb where he was laid.* This again links Mary Magdalene and Jesus.

Gospel of Mary of Bethany (Mary Magdalene) *Peter said to Mary, "Sister, we know that the Saviour loved you more than other women [cf. John 11:5, Luke 10:38-42]. Tell us the words of the Saviour which you have in mind since you know them; and we do not, nor have we heard of them."* This indicates that Jesus had a closer relationship with Mary than he had with his disciples.

Another interesting snippet can be found in **1 Corinthians 9 : 5** *"Have we not power to lead about a sister, a wife, as well as other apostles, as the brethren of the*

Lord and Cephas (Peter)". This KJV text looks a little clumsy so we should look further back to the first Sinai Bible, and here we find a subtle difference:

1 Corinthians 9 : 5 *"We have authority to lead about a sister as a wife, even as the followers and the Lord's brothers and Cephas, do we not"*.

This is interesting because a sister may simply mean a sister in the Lord or a fellow parishioner, but it would appear a little strange to select one at random to lead about as a wife. Cephas (Peter) was married to his actual sister Jotape who accompanied him. Bushby claims that Jesus' brothers were married to their sisters Martha and Salome and that Mary Magdalene was in fact Jesus' half sister. [22]

The *Mar Saba* document found in the Mar Saba Monastery near Jerusalem in 1958 by Morton Smith, Professor of Classical Ancient History at Columbia University, shows conclusively that the marriages of Jesus were in fact deliberately removed from the Gospels by Church decree at the Fifth Ecumenical Council held in Constantinople in 553 AD. [23]

This secret marriage was certainly known by the Church over the following years. It is claimed that later intelligentsia such as Leonardo da Vinci learned this directly from Pope Leo X. As reported in Time Magazine of October 4th. 1954, the proof of this came to light when his famous painting "The Last Supper" was cleaned and consolidated, revealing that the figure at the right hand side of Christ, was indeed a woman with flowing red hair. It seems that Leonardo da Vinci has left us an image of Mary Magdalene and cryptically revealed to us, the secret wife of Jesus. In addition there is a stained glass window within the Kilmore Church (Church of Mary) in the village of Dervaig on the Scottish, Isle of Mull. This window depicts Jesus with an obviously pregnant Mary Magdalene and features verse 42 from the following Bible passage.

Luke 10 : 38-42 *"Now it came to pass, as they went, that he entered into a certain village: and a certain woman named Martha received him into her house. And she had a sister called Mary, which also sat at Jesus' feet, and heard his word. But Martha was cumbered about much serving, and came to him, and said, Lord, dost thou not care that my sister hath left me to serve alone? bid her therefore that she help me. And Jesus answered and said unto her, Martha, Martha, thou art careful and troubled about many* *things: but one thing is needful: and <u>Mary hath chosen that good part, which shall not be taken away from her.</u>"*

We are discovering that things aren't exactly as we were told. The realization now is that we are no better off as adults than when we were in childhood. The scriptures are still problematic and the clergy still have no answers.

"Either God wants to abolish evil, and cannot; or he can, but does not want to; or he cannot and does not want to. If he wants to, but cannot, he is impotent. If he can, but does not want to, he is wicked. But, if God both can and wants to abolish evil, then how come evil is in the world?"

- Epicurus.

CHAPTER THREE

LIES & DECEPTION

"It is the nature of all religions based on fear and unchangeable dogmas, to deter and thus exclude its disciples from all knowledge adverse to their own creeds. And sometimes their own religious systems are magnified to such a magnified appreciation above all others as to lead them to destroy the evidence of the existence of the latter for fear of their ultimate rivalry".

Kersey Graves, *The Sixteen Crucified Saviours.*

The Anointing of Jesus

The anointing of a Rabbi or especially a Jewish King, is a very important ceremony indeed. Just how paramount was the anointing of Jesus the Messiah, the King of the Jews, and the saviour of the world. If we were to research this event there would be three initial questions;

    (i)   Where did it take place?

    (ii)   Who performed the ceremony?

    (iii)   What was the procedure involved?

Let's look to the Bible for the answers to these initial questions concerning this event:

Matthew 26 : 6–12, Mark 14 : 3 The anointing of Jesus takes place in Bethany at the house of Simon the leper.

Luke 7 : 36–38 It takes place at the house of a Pharisee in Capernaum.

John 12 : 1– 3 It takes place in the home of Lazarus, Martha & Mary.

Matthew 26 : 7, Mark 14 : 3, Luke 7 : 37 An unnamed woman does the anointing.

John 12 : 3 Mary Magdalene does the anointing.

Matthew 26 : 7, Mark 14 : 3, The anointing oil is correctly poured on Jesus' head.

Luke 7 : 38, John 12 : 3 It is used to anoint his feet.

How peculiar, the Bible is not clear on even one point about this major event leading to the supposed coronation of its Messiah. Forget the divinity of Jesus for a moment; even an historical record of the coronation of a king would have to be more accurately recorded than this.

A required role of the Messiah or "anointed one" at the time of Jesus was to be a strong ruler who could rid the Holy Land of the dreaded Romans. At that time the Romans ruled Israel through puppet kings, the Herods. Rome had taken control of the Holy Land in 63 BCE and by the time of Christ, the Children of Israel were fed up, and looking for a "priest-king" the descendant of David, the rightful King of the Jews to gain back the Jewish throne. His requirement was to fulfill supposed Old Testament prophesy of re-establishing the kingly line of David and securing the future of the Jewish people in a Messianic age, centered on the temple of Jerusalem. Jesus is not found on any list of Kings. He never ruled the Holy land and was unsuccessful at removing the Romans; therefore we must say that in achieving this primary objective, he was not successful and therefore must be considered a failure as a Jewish Messiah. The Jews reject Jesus and are still waiting for the Saviour.

Which Messiah?

In the Old Testament we find several Messianic entities, who cannot reasonably be nominated as a proto-type Jesus. Today the church claims these passages as prophesy of the coming Jesus; actually there is not much else they could say. Recall that the Jews who wrote this stuff reject Jesus as the true Messiah, yet rather strangely these prophesies supposedly crop up in their work;

> **Genesis 49 : 10** *The sceptre shall not depart from Judah, nor a lawgiver from between his feet, <u>until Shiloh come</u>; and unto him shall the gathering of the people be.*

> **Numbers 24 : 17-19** *I shall see him, but not now: I shall behold him, but not nigh: there shall come <u>a Star out of Jacob</u>, and a Sceptre shall rise out of Israel...*

> **Zechariah 6 : 12-13** *Thus speaketh the Lord of hosts, saying, "Behold <u>the man whose name is The Branch</u>; and he shall grow up out of his place, and he shall build*

the temple of the Lord: even he shall build the temple of the Lord; and he shall bear the glory, and shall sit and rule upon his throne; and he shall be a priest upon his throne: and the counsel of peace shall be between them both."

Isaiah   11 : 1- 3 *A shoot will come up from the stump of Jesse; from his roots <u>a Branch</u> will bear fruit. The Spirit of the Lord will rest on him -the Spirit of wisdom and of understanding, the Spirit of counsel and of power, the Spirit of knowledge and of the fear of the Lord - and he will delight in the fear of the Lord.*

Jeremiah   23 : 5-6 *Behold, the days come, saith the Lord, that I will raise unto David <u>a righteous Branch</u>, and a King shall reign and prosper, and shall execute judgment and justice in the earth. In his days Judah shall be saved, and Israel shall dwell safely: and this is his name whereby he shall be called, <u>The Lord our Righteousness</u>.*

Daniel 7 : 13 *I saw in the night visions, and, behold, <u>one like the Son of man</u> came with the clouds of heaven, and came to the Ancient of days, and they brought him near before him.*

Isaiah 9 : 6 *For unto us a child is born, unto us a son is given: and the government shall be upon his shoulder: <u>and his name shall be called Wonderful, Counselor, The Mighty God, The Everlasting Father, The Prince of Peace</u>.*

Hebrews 7 : 1 – 3 *For this Melchizedek ... Without father, without mother, without descent (or descendants), having neither beginning of days, nor end of life; but made <u>like unto the Son of God</u>; abideth a priest continually.*

So we find **Shiloh, a Star out of Jacob, the righteous Branch, Wonderful, Counselor, The Mighty God, The Everlasting Father, The Prince of Peace, One like the Son of Man** and finally **Melchizedek, like unto the Son of God.**

These titles do not refer to Jesus. All appear to be Kings and rulers, appropriately of the Royal tribe of Judah yet Jesus was supposedly the son of Mary, a Levite the Priestly class of Aaron. In addition, several groups like the Manicheans claimed the New Testament's, John the Baptist as the true Messiah and this makes the whole Messiah issue even more confusing. Ashford had this to say;

"It seems to follow logically... that Jesus Christ could not possibly be the same Saviour or Messiah as was anticipated in the writings of the Old Testament... And yet despite

this, the Church has maintained for two thousand years that the Old Testament was anticipating the future coming of Christ at the End of Days." [1]

The Old Testament was the property of the Jewish religion; they wrote the above passages, yet they reject outright any possibility that Jesus was the awaited Messiah. Who are we to now hijack their Old Testament, add to this a New Testament, and then claim the Jewish Old Testament contains a prophecy of the coming Jesus of the Christian religion. We are kidding ourselves! Let's give the Rabbi's and learned scribes credit for a few brains.

Peter – the First Pope?

This is a widely held fallacy and is entirely fraudulent. The Roman Church still promotes Simon Barjona or Simon called Peter as the first Pope. They hold him in awe and yet the scriptures state that the Romans martyred him in Rome apparently by upside down crucifixion. To this day Popes sit in the "Chair of St. Peter" in "St. Peters" Basilica in The Vatican. Incidently the word 'Basilica' comes from the root word 'basilisk' which depicts a mythical serpent or dragon. The whole association is based on lies and was used by the Church to create a false Papal dynasty from Peter (as Jesus' right hand man) to usurp the power of Jesus as head of the Christian religion and give it to the Roman Church. Another purpose was to create a mandate free from Jewish-ness and the Desposyni who carried the Holy Bloodline of Jesus. It is hard to reconcile that this same Peter was also executed for crimes against the Roman Empire. Paul was supposedly beheaded around the same time and the Jews certainly can't be blamed for these two. The following passage is the one the Church uses to 'prove' they descend from Peter;

In **Matthew 16 : 13 – 18** *When Jesus came into the coasts of Caesarea Philippi, he asked his disciples, saying, whom do men say that I the Son of man, am? And they said, some say that thou art John the Baptist: some, Elias; and others, Jeremiahs, or one of the prophets. He saith unto them, But whom say ye that I am? And Simon Peter answered and said; Thou art the Christ, the Son of the living God. And Jesus answered and said unto him, Blessed art thou, Simon Barjona: for flesh and blood hath not revealed it unto thee, but my Father, which is in heaven. And I say also unto* *thee, that thou art Peter, and upon this rock I will build my church; and the gates of hell shall not prevail against it.*

This loses a little in translation however; careful reading will confirm that this is not saying that the Church was based on Peter. Here Jesus colloquially said, "As sure as you are Peter, upon this foundation I will build my church." The "rock" or **foundation** on which Jesus wanted to build his Church was the belief that he was the Christ, the son of the living God. Not on a foundation of Peter. The proof of this is that flesh and blood had not made the revelation to Peter but God the Father. This confusion is exacerbated because Peter's name was really Simon. Remember he was Simon, called Peter. The Hebrew word Peter or 'petros' meant a stone or rock. His nickname meant roughly "Rocky". The similar word used for foundation was "petra" a solid rock; however they are not the same.

In **Mark 8 :27** we get a repeat of the Matthew story but look how it continues:

Verse 33 *But when he had turned about and looked on his disciples, he rebuked Peter, saying, Get thee behind me, Satan: for thou savorest not the things that be of God, but the things that be of men.*

Does this sound like dialogue with the man to whom he has just handed over all power.

Actually Peter was never Pope (officially or un-officially.) Peter was never even a Bishop of Rome. **Linus** the son of **King Caractacus the Pendragon** of Britain was the first Pope appointed by the apostle Paul in 58 AD during Peter's lifetime. [2] A work on the lives of the Popes called *"Liber Pontificalis"* wrongly asserts that Linus' home was in Tuscany and that his fathers name was Herculanus. Irenaeus stated (in *Adversus Haereses III*) that Peter and Paul put the Church in order in Rome and then handed over to Linus. This was likely true, however, many Catholics now utilize this statement to wrongly confirm that Peter was the first Pope and Linus the second. Rome claimed that in the above Bible passage, Jesus handed over power and the keys of heaven to Peter, who gave all power to their Roman Church and commenced a Roman, Papal dynasty. By saying Peter was the first Pope they got away with it, right to this very day, even though it is such an easily discounted fraud. Even when the Catholic Church announced that it had found the burial place of Linus next to that of St. Peter within the Vatican, complete with an appropriate inscription, it was found that there were additional faded letters preceding the name 'linus' indicating that it was most likely the sarcophagus of someone bearing another name like Anullinus or Aquilinus.

The Church still teaches that Peter received the keys to Heaven from Jesus and now does guard duty at the Pearly Gates admitting only the faithful. To show just how ridiculous this scenario actually is, we can easily source the Egyptian 'Book of the Dead' and see that it is plagiarised in its entirety. The doorkeeper to the gate of Heaven in the 'Egyptian Book of the Dead' is actually called PETR meaning 'the Rock'.

Leprosy and Contemporary Beliefs

Some Biblical statements, viewed in today's context, must be seen as simply absurd, in that they depict primitive beliefs. Many Biblical stories that remain crucial to the Christian religion are discredited by numerous inconsistencies. Look at God's thoughts on the disease leprosy in **Leviticus 13 & 14**. God dictates that the priest is to lock up sufferers for 7 days before pronouncing them clean or unclean.

> **Leviticus 14 : 3-7** *tells how two birds are to be taken and one killed in an earthen vessel over running water and the live one dipped in the blood of the other and used to sprinkle it over the patient 7 times. He then has to wash, shave off his beard, hair and eyebrows then sacrifice two lambs with oil and fine flour and have the priest dip in the blood and spread it on his right ear, right big toe and right thumb then pour the remaining oil over his head.*

Read it in your Bible, I'm not making this up.

Now Jesus was called the "Great Physician" but I'm quite sure that with this sort of bedside manner and a diagnosis resulting in this sort of 'witch doctor' treatment, God wouldn't get a lot of repeat business. It sounds like a weird, pagan blood ritual not the treatment of a skin disorder that doctors today will tell you, in contradiction of the Bible, is not even contagious. God is all knowing and infallible, the same yesterday, today and forever; but somehow his medical and scientific knowledge from around 300 BCE seems to track that of man exactly. This however didn't stop **Elisha** in **2 Kings 5 : 27** from cursing **Gehazi** and his descendants <u>forever</u> with leprosy and the Lord himself in **Numbers 12** from using the disease as a chastisement against **Miriam** when she was upset about Moses marrying the Ethiopian woman. It documents how the Lord inflicted Miriam with leprosy and for 7 days she was cast out of the camp. Miriam was probably Moses' sister/wife and accordingly it would be predictable, if not totally understandable, that she was a little miffed at Moses marrying the Ethiopian woman. Yet God demonstrated absolutely zero social skills and didn't understand or appreciate this fairly basic psychology that a woman could be a bit upset at her husband marrying another woman. She needed firm punishment!

Demons

Mental health has certainly come a long way in the past 2000 years, and particularly in the last 100. At the time of Jesus any mental illness and much physical illness was thought to be caused by demons and could be cured only by rituals and exorcism. Why, because the Bible is supposedly the inerrant "Word of God", and it tells us that demons cause mental illness, blindness, deafness, lameness and various other complaints. Today we know this is simply not true.

Examples:

Matthew 4: 24 *all sick people, those possessed with devils and those which were lunatic.*

Matthew 12 : 22 *blind and dumb possessed of a devil*

Matthew 17 :15–18 *Lunatic son has a devil cast out*

Mark 1 : 26 *the unclean spirit had torn him*

Mark 9 : 17 *Son with a dumb spirit who foams at the mouth is healed*

Luke 9 : 1 *Jesus gave disciples power and authority over devils and to cure diseases*

Luke 9 : 42 *Jesus rebuked the unclean spirit and healed the child*

Luke 11 : 14 *Cast out a spirit and the dumb spake*

Acts 8 : 7 *Those taken with palsies and the lame healed of possession with* *unclean spirits.*

All these examples are however, then contradicted by **Exodus 4 : 11** where God explains to Moses that **he alone decides** who will be dumb, deaf, blind, etc. It just doesn't work both ways. Well did God get it wrong, or did the scribes who wrote the Bible get it wrong. It really doesn't matter which, the Bible's plausibility is left pretty suspect. Of course we believe the scribes got it wrong but doesn't that also prove that the Bible is **not** the infallible word of God.

Remember poor Legion, In **Mark 5 : 9** he is living amongst the tombs and cutting himself with sharp stones. Jesus comes along and asks what his name is and he, or the demons, answer *"Legion, for we are many"*. The demons then rather strangely ask that they not be cast into the deep but instead, into a herd of 2,000 swine. The swine run down into the sea and are drowned. Does the death of the swine kill the demons or are they then cast into the deep anyway? It is a crazy story with little or no point, yet it is repeated in **Luke 8 : 30** in its entirety. A third version in **Matthew 8 : 28** however has <u>two</u> possessed men coming out of the tombs and there is no mention whatever of Legion just the same swine story. The uncertainty in the number involved in this story is fairly disconcerting. We also see a repeat of this confusion in the gospels; **Matthew 20 : 29-34** *Jesus heals two blind men on the way to Jericho.* The same story; **Mark 10 : 46-52** *Jesus heals one blind man.* If in reality 2,000 swine were involved in the Legion story as stated, regardless of the currency at the time a shepherd's weekly wage would buy no more than say 5 pigs. At a value of say 20 pigs a month, the equivalent of a bit over 8 year's wages were lost. Jesus was lucky not to end up in serious trouble, up for restitution of today's equivalent of something approaching a quarter of a million dollars. This is a very strange story and I would question if it was in fact poor Legion's behaviour that was the most odd.

Naked Men & Phallic Symbols

We have already spoken of the austere nature of the Hebrew lifestyle, the harsh laws and the low self esteem these things promoted. It is not surprising that in those times nakedness was considered particularly shameful. An example follows that shows the lengths to which sons would go, to avoid seeing their father naked.

Genesis 9: 23 *And Shem and Japheth took a garment, and laid it upon both their shoulders, and went backward, and covered the nakedness of their father; and their faces were backward, and they saw not their father's nakedness.*

They must have seen something to know that he was naked and required covering! We should look at these stories contained in the Bible, firstly because they seem quite strange, and one might wonder at their inclusion in such a work, and secondly, because the clergy do not teach them. It is also a little surprising to find the Bible spell out that during the Exodus, the priest Aaron made the children of Israel go naked and I can't help but wince at the thought of that desert sunburn on certain exposed body parts.

Exodus 32 :25 *And when Moses saw that the people were naked; (for Aaron had made them naked unto their shame among their enemies:)*

Further, we are assured that by the wish of God, Isaiah went naked and barefoot for three years.

Isaiah 20 : 2-3 *Go and loose the sackcloth from off thy loins, and put off thy shoe from thy foot. And he did so, <u>walking naked and barefoot</u>. And the Lord said, like as my servant <u>Isaiah hath walked naked and barefoot three years</u> for a sign and wonder upon Egypt and upon Ethiopia;*

If this author was to walk around naked and barefoot for three years, I am confident it would not adversely affect Ethiopia or Egypt but it would quite possibly upset my Dutch neighbors more than a little bit. Still Isaiah doing so was a sign and a wonder to that region. There is certainly an intrinsic awe and paranoia of nakedness and the 'rules of Leviticus' forbid seeing any family member unclothed. I see no reason for the inclusion of any of this in the Bible.

Leviticus 20 : 20 *And if a man shall lie with his uncle's wife, he hath uncovered his uncle's nakedness: they shall bear their sin; they shall die childless.*

Leviticus 20 : 13 *If a man also lies with mankind, as he lieth with a woman, both of them have committed an abomination: they shall surely be put to death.*

These rules expressly state that death is the punishment; for homosexuality, and cross dressing is prohibited in **Deuteronomy 22 : 5.** Despite this death sentence, if we were looking at any other book, I feel sure that the conclusion would be that homosexuality is described in some of the Bible passages. This was not a new concept with many pagan Gods showing homosexual tendencies. Even the Greek Zeus spoke of his love for Ganymede (Catamitus) whose ravishing beauty had roused his passion, and his son Apollo had his group of twenty male 'favourites'. Now in the Bible, David seems a little too expressive in the following;

> **2 Samuel 1 : 26** : *Jonathan: very pleasant hast thou been to me: thy love to me was wonderful, passing the love of women.*

> **Daniel 1 : 9** *Now God had brought Daniel into favour and tender love with the prince of the eunuchs.*

There was an obvious obsession to hide ones nakedness yet in contrast, the displaying of ones virility by way of male offspring is quite pronounced. Strange too is the mentality that led to the following passages:

> **Deuteronomy 23 : 1** *He that is wounded in the stones, or hath his privy member cut off, shall not enter into the congregation of the Lord.*

Leviticus records the unworthiness of certain members of a community to be chosen as priests or to make the offerings of the Lord;

> **Leviticus 21 : 17- 20** *For whatsoever man he be that hath a blemish, he shall not approach: a blind man, or a lame or he that has a flat nose, or anything superfluous, or a man that is broken footed or broken handed, or crookbackt, or a dwarf, or that hath a blemish in his eye, or be scurvy, or scabbed, or hath his stones broken;*

So a eunuch is not worthy to become a priest and make offerings to the Lord and a man with his 'stones broken' is not allowed into the congregation of the Lord. Apparently nobody told the disciple Philip because he baptised one into the kingdom of Heaven;

> **Acts 8 : 38-39** *And they went down both into the water, both Philip and the eunuch; and he baptised him. And when they were come up out of the water, the Spirit of the Lord caught away Philip, that the eunuch saw him no more: and he went on his way rejoicing.*

In total contradiction to Leviticus and Deuteronomy, not only are eunuchs allowed into the congregation; men are encouraged to make themselves eunuchs 'for the kingdom of heaven's sake';

Matthew 19 : 12 *For there are some eunuchs, which were so born from their mother's womb: and there are some eunuchs, which were made eunuchs of men: and there be eunuchs, which have made themselves eunuchs for the kingdom of heaven's sake.*

In this case there appears no rhyme or reason to the logic of God's word; we now see that the same Lord who in Leviticus and Deuteronomy claimed eunuchs could not join the congregation, rejoices in those who keep his Sabbath and covenants;

Isaiah 56 : 4 *For thus saith the Lord unto the eunuchs that keep my Sabbaths, and choose the things that please me, and take hold of my covenant;*

Moslem tradition tells of **Uthman** who asked Mohammed's permission to castrate himself to escape temptation. He was severely reprimanded by Mohammed who showed a more sensible approach with the following words, *"he who castrates himself or another does not belong to my followers."* We saw earlier that Bishop Clement of Alexandria removed part of the gospel of Mark to hide the marriage and offspring of Jesus. He removed other parts as well from the original record. **The Secret Gospel of Mark**, containing those missing parts is said by Clement to be in the custody of the Church in Alexandria, but whose existence must be publicly refuted, to counter the copies circulated by the infamous sect of the Carpocrations. The second missing portion originally followed **Mark 10 : 34** and contains the story of the raising of Lazarus and we will notice it gets a somewhat different treatment in 'The Secret Gospel of Mark' compared to the current altered KJV Bible;

Mark 14 : 51 *"And they come into Bethany. And a certain woman whose brother had died was there. And, coming, she prostrated herself before Jesus and says to him, "Son of David, have mercy on me". But the disciples rebuked her. And Jesus, being angered, went off with her into the garden where the tomb was, and straightway, going in where the youth was, he stretched forth his hand and raised him, seizing his hand. <u>But the youth, looking upon him, loved him and began to beseech him that he might be with him.</u> And going out of the tomb they came into the house of the youth, for he* *was rich. And after six days Jesus told him what to do and in the evening <u>the youth</u>* <u>*comes to him, wearing a linen cloth over his naked body. And he remained with him*</u> <u>*that night, for Jesus taught him the mystery of the Kingdom of God*</u>. *And thence, arising, he returned to the other side of the Jordan."* [3]

Compare this to the passage in our KJV today:

Mark 14 : 51-52 *And there followed him a certain young man, having a linen cloth cast about his naked body; and the young men laid hold on him: and he left the linen cloth, and fled from them naked.*

In a bit of a downplay, Clement's answering letter to his enquiring clergyman states:

"But 'naked man with naked man' and the other things, about which you wrote, are not found. And after the words, 'And he comes into Jericho,' the secret Gospel adds only, 'and the sister of the youth whom Jesus loved and his mother and Salome were there, and Jesus did not receive them.' But the many other things about which you wrote, both seem to be, and are, falsifications."

Perhaps they are and perhaps they are not. Look too, at these following verses and consider the purpose of their inclusion in the 'Word of God'.

Romans 1 : 24-32 *Wherefore God also gave them up to uncleanness through the lusts of their own hearts, to dishonour their own bodies between themselves... for even their women did change the natural use into that which is against nature ... And likewise also the men, leaving the natural use of the woman, burned in their lust one toward another; men with men working that which is unseemly ... Who knowing the judgment of God, that they which commit such things are worthy of death, not only do the same, but have pleasure in them that do them.*

We all heard the story of Jesus walking on water and coaxing Simon Peter to walk out to join him; however we weren't told Peter did this trick whilst naked;

John 21 : 7 *Therefore that disciple whom Jesus loved saith unto Peter, It is the Lord. Now when Simon Peter heard that it was the Lord, he girt his fisher's coat unto him, <u>for he was naked</u>, and did cast himself into the sea.*

This is absolutely crazy; seriously, who goes out with his mates in a fishing boat, buck-naked? This is a very silly book and it brings tears to my eyes just thinking about landing a stinger.

In fact the story of Jesus walking on water is absent from the early versions of the Bible which show it to be a later fraudulent addition. The oldest manuscripts state that Jesus walked <u>by</u> the water. This means that walking <u>on</u> water was considered to be worthy of adding as a specific Jesus 'miracle,' however, why the 'naked' embellishment was required for Peter, I can not say.

> **1 Samuel 19 : 24** *And he (Saul) stripped off his clothes also, and prophesied before Samuel in like manner, and <u>lay down naked</u> all that day and all that night. Wherefore they say, is Saul also among the prophets?*

So lying about naked qualifies one as a prophet?

> **Habakkuk 2 : 15** *Woe unto him that giveth his neighbour drink, that puttest thy bottle to him, and makest him drunken also, that thou mayest look on their nakedness!*

Really now, who would bother. I feel quite sure my neighbours would certainly agree.

> **2 Samuel 6 : 13** *"And David danced before the Lord with all his might; and David was girded with a linen ephod. ... And as the ark of the Lord came into the city of David, Michal, Saul's daughter looked through a window, and saw King David leaping and dancing before the Lord; and she despised him in her heart. ... And Michal the daughter of Saul came out to meet David, and said, "How glorious was the king of Israel to day, <u>who uncovered himself to day in the eyes of the handmaids of his servants, as one of the vain fellows shamelessly uncovereth himself</u>!"*

We view David as such a pious, dedicated man of God, but would we change our minds if he was part of our congregation and danced naked before the Lord in the sight of the handmaidens and servants. How would the papers report it if a King did this today?

Early Canaanite worship utilized the display of genitals and the naked body as a significant feature of worship and early Christian writings show deep concern at this practice. Despite this reluctance, phallic worship certainly existed in the early Christian Church. Statues of Christian saints have been found displayed in various churches, complete with oversized penises. In Southern France for instance, phallic worship took place within the confines of a Christian shrine. Women, who had been denied the joys of motherhood, invoked St Foutin, an ithyphallic saint, said to be originally the first Bishop of Lyons, in an attempt to rectify their situation. When Protestants captured the town of Embrum in 1585 and destroyed the local church they discovered relics of the saint's phallus. Its tip was red, said to be from the many libations of red wine poured over it by childless women. Perhaps this says something for the talents or prowess of that particular saint during his lifetime, however what we are clearly seeing, is that Christians certainly reverted to former pagan fertility practises. Professor Gregory Webb of Cambridge University and Secretary of the Royal Commission on Historical Monuments discovered that a staggering ninety per cent of all pre-Reformation churches in Britain hid pagan fertility symbols such as the stone image of a phallus within the Christian alter. [4]

We find that the Egyptian Pharaohs recorded their children as "fruit of my loins" or "those who came out of my thigh" and the Bible indicates that this was also common practice among the later Hebrew. There was also an ancient Hebrew practice where a man would make a promise or swear an oath with his hand on his penis, or (apparently without trepidation) on the genitals of the other party, simply because as an organ of reproduction it was considered his most sacred possession. In fact the word 'Testament' as a document of sacred oath comes from the same derivation as 'Testes'. We see in Genesis where Jacob asked Joseph to solemnly promise that his remains would be removed from Egypt and buried in the Holy Land. He was not satisfied until Joseph swore with his hand "under my thigh". Abraham also took an oath this way;

> **Genesis 47 : 29** *And the time drew nigh that Israel must die: and he called his son Joseph, and said unto him, If now I have found grace in thy sight, put, I pray thee, <u>thy hand under my thigh</u>, and deal kindly and truly with me; bury me not, I pray thee, in Egypt.*

> **Genesis 24 : 2** *And Abraham said unto his eldest servant of his house, that ruled over all that he had, Put, I pray thee, thy hand <u>under my thigh</u>:*

> **Genesis 24 : 9** *And the servant put his hand under <u>the thigh of Abraham his master</u>, and sware to him concerning that matter.*

I think maybe it would be appropriate to resurrect this practice today and swear all oaths with our hands on our 'willy'. That certainly would upset the pomp and austerity of taking an oath during a court session, now wouldn't it? It might brighten up the court appearance considerably!

Jesus Gets Around

We mentioned in the introduction how Christians seem to accept the Christian message with nary a thought for the prevailing situation or historical content. The following contradictory passages are documented to question how the congregation can still proclaim the Bible to be the infallible word of God despite these and other quite obvious errors. No education or special skills are required here to see that something is really amiss.

Matthew 4 : 1-11 and **Mark 1 : 12-13** Immediately following his Baptism, Jesus spent forty days in the wilderness resisting temptation by the Devil.

John 2 : 1-11 Three days after the Baptism, Jesus was at the wedding in Canna.

Matthew 4 : 5-8 The Devil took Jesus to the pinnacle of the temple in Jerusalem, then to the mountain top to view the worlds kingdoms.

Luke 4 : 5-9 First to the high place, then to the pinnacle of the temple in Jerusalem.

Matthew 5 : 1 Jesus delivers the famous 'Sermon on the Mount' and the people are amazed.

Luke 6 : 17-49 After coming down, he delivers this famous sermon while on "a level place" or on the plain.

Mark and **John** do not include the Sermon on the Mount or the Sermon on the Plain. From **Acts** and the various **Letters to the Apostles**, Paul doesn't seem familiar with either the Sermon on the Mount or the Sermon on the Plain.

Matthew 21 : 12-13 The cleansing of the temple and throwing out the money changers occurs at the end of Jesus' career.

John 2 : 13-16 It occurs near the beginning of his career.

Matthew 21 : 1-17 The sequence was: triumphal entry to Jerusalem, cleansing of the temple, stay at Bethany.

Mark 11 : 1–19 Triumphal entry, cleansing of the temple, leaving the City, cursing the Fig tree.

Luke 19 : 28–47 Triumphal entry, cleansing of the temple, daily teaching in the temple, leaders plot to kill him.

John 12 : 1–18 Cleansing of the temple (early in his career), Then Anointing and Supper with Lazarus, followed by triumphal entry.

If we search for an explanation, the discrepancies of time placement are likely due to the level of writing in each gospel or book telling the story. For example the Gospel of John does not say what it means or mean what it says because of the nature of the Kabbalistic writing used. Kabbalah is one of the most misunderstood parts of Judaism and many non-Jews (and even some Jews) think of Kabbalah as 'the dark side of Judaism'. Many of these misunderstandings arise largely from distortions of the teachings of Kabbalah by non-Jewish mystics and occultists. Kabbalah was popular among Christian intellectuals during the Renaissance and the Enlightenment periods, and they reinterpreted its doctrines to fit into their Christian dogma. The Kabbalah style however, means that we can never take literally what certain Books of the Bible say when it comes to time placement. This in no way diminishes our argument at all because very few of the clergy or the congregation would understand this concept or how to interpret it, nor does it hold much meaning today. It only serves to make any story less believable because we can not detect these mechanisms within its structure and simply see the contradictions.

Harold Bloom has become one of the most prominent voices calling attention to the creative character of the Gnostic alternative to mainstream religion. His writings have made a powerful case for the perennial value of the positions taken by Christian Gnostics, Jewish Kabbalists, and Sufi mystics, all of whom are inspired by a common gnosis. This is what he had to say:

"If you can accept a God who coexists with death camps, schizophrenia, and AIDS, yet remains all-powerful and somehow benign, then you have faith, and you have accepted the covenant with Yahweh.... If you know yourself as having an affinity with the alien or stranger God, cut off from this world, then you are a Gnostic, and perhaps the best and strongest moments still come to what is best and oldest in you, to a breath

or spark that long precedes this Creation." [5]

The story of Jesus riding on an ass and the foal of an ass was apparently recorded to fulfil prophesy from;

Zechariah 9 : 9 *Rejoice greatly, O daughter of Zion; shout, O daughter of Jerusalem: behold, thy King cometh unto thee: he is just, and having salvation; lowly, and riding upon an ass, and upon a colt the foal of an ass.*

Let's see that;

Matthew 21 : 2-7 Two disciples follow Jesus instructions and bring him an ass and her colt and Jesus rides both in his triumphal entry.

Mark 11 : 2-7 Two disciples find a colt only and bring it for Jesus to ride

Luke 19 : 30-35 An undisclosed number of disciples obtained an un broken colt for Jesus.

John 12 :14-15 Jesus himself finds an ass's colt to sit on. Somebody could have edited this into a coordinated story at the very least. Continuing on;

Mark 4 : 11, Mark 11 : 25 Jesus says that he uses parables so that the meaning of some of his teachings will remain secret to at least some persons. He explains the meanings of the parables only to his disciples. He thanks God for hiding some things from the wise while revealing them to 'babes'.

John 18 : 20 Jesus says that he always taught openly, never secretly. The 'Feeding of the Multitude' with the loaves and fishes was performed by Jesus according to Bible scriptures. Ancient records claim that it was a trick in the repertoire of the Egyptian magicians long before Jesus was born. It is supposed that Jesus learned the trick when he was in Egypt. Today's clergy, who have not seen the Egyptian records, claim it is an analogy for spreading the Christian message to the vast multitude using just a few evangelists. Worth noting too is that in **John** the food was from a little boy's lunch; whilst **Matthew, Mark** and **Luke** claim the disciples brought the food.

Mark 6 : 52 The people were so unimpressed with the 'Feeding of the Multitude' that they did not even understand the event.

John 6 : 14-15 They were so impressed that they tried to convince Jesus to be their king.

Check this one;

John 13 : 36 Peter asks Jesus where he is going.

John 14 : 5 Thomas does the same.

John 16: 5 Jesus says that none of them have asked him where he is going.

Shady Dealings

We have all heard of primitive tribes calling on their pagan Gods for good hunting, good harvests, for rain, fertility, victory in battle etc. Many records of early man state that most cultures believed sickness, disease pestilence and famine happened when the Gods were displeased. Few of our clergy dwell on, or teach the evolution over the past 2,500 years of the Hebrew tribal, "Storm God" El Elyon into the global God YHWH we worship today. In the early times the Hebrews would expect nasty little "dummy spits" from their warlike, storm God. This God is said to be the same yesterday, today and forever, however a few embarrassing primitive leftovers crop up in the Bible and can't be explained away. Firstly the Bible hedges its bets with the following;

Numbers 11 : 33 *God inflicts sickness.*

Job 2 : 7 *Satan inflicts sickness.*

The Bible tells us that, Almighty God offered a health insurance scheme to the Israelites where one could purchase protection against plague; others it seems gained free indemnity:

Exodus 30 : 12 *When you take a census of the Israelites to count them, each one must pay the Lord a ransom for his life at the time he is counted. Then no plague will come on them when you number them.*

By all appearances and in passages like this it appears that God is unaccustomed to his kingly role with the Hebrew people. Did anyone wonder or ever question in the above passage just what God would do with the ransom? If it was to be cash money, do you think He would get in some groceries or perhaps He could go shopping and buy a new crown and a new robe, maybe a DVD player? This is a pretty silly verse! For that matter why do we always view God in out-dated clothing? It made sense for the Hebrew to view their God in robes; however why do we still view him this way today? Why wouldn't he wear a comfortable suit today? Incidentally; where would he shop for his robes?

> **Numbers 8 : 19** *Of all the Israelites, I have given the Levites as gifts to Aaron and his sons to do the work at the Tent of Meeting on behalf of the Israelites and to make atonement for them so that no plague will strike the Israelites when they go near the sanctuary."*

Here God arranges atonement for the Israelites to protect against plague. So whether or not the ransom was paid, we read that soon after, Moses relayed a quite specific promise that the Lord would protect the Hebrews from all sickness. This is a definite Biblical covenant and no doubt the Hebrew people believed it and took comfort that their Almighty God had favoured them in this way.

> **Deuteronomy 7 : 5** *The Lord will keep you free from every disease. He will not inflict on you the horrible diseases you knew in Egypt, but he will inflict them on all who hate you.*

Ooops! This one didn't come off and there was epidemic plague to follow. We can see too that the prophets specifically predicted that the Hebrew people would never serve Nebuchadnezzar the king of Babylon:

> **Jeremiah 27 : 9** *So do not listen to your prophets, your diviners, your interpreters of dreams, your mediums or your sorcerers who tell you, 'You will not serve the king of Babylon'.*

Ooops! What about the captivity in Babylon that followed. In addition we find threats against any people who attack the city of Jerusalem:

> **Zechariah 14 : 12** *This is the plague with which the Lord will strike all the nations that fought against Jerusalem: Their flesh will rot while they are still standing on their feet, their eyes will rot in their sockets, and their tongues will rot in their mouths.*

Ooops! Despite these threats God in fact did an 'about face' and supported Nebuchadnezzar when he sacked Jerusalem and took the children of Israel into captivity; totally negating his covenant and going back on his word. The clergy must know this; I can't be the only one who cross references this stuff.

Jeremiah 21 : 6 *I will strike down those who live in this city (Jerusalem) - both men and animals—and they will die of a terrible plague.*

Jeremiah 21 : 9 *Whoever stays in this city will die by the sword, famine or plague. But whoever goes out and surrenders to the Babylonians who are besieging you will live; he will escape with his life.*

Ooops! God reneged on the deal. This is in direct contradiction to his covenant! Did the Hebrew get their insurance premiums refunded? I don't think so.

But wait God did another about face at the end of the Babylonian captivity and resolved to take revenge upon Babylon for all the sufferings it had inflicted on Israel. Although they were heathens, he chose Cyrus, the king of Persia, and his father-in-law Darius, the king of Media, to achieve his vengeance and together they went up against Belshazzar, the ruler of the Chaldeans. The war lasted a considerable time, and fortune favoured first one side, then the other, until finally the Chaldeans won a decisive victory. God's team resumed the war against Babylonia with even more energy, and God vouchsafed them victory. They finally conquered the whole of Belshazzar's realm, and took possession of the City of Babylon. The subjugated lands were then divided between Cyrus and Darius, the latter King receiving Babylon and Media, the former Chaldea, Persia, and Assyria and at this time the Hebrew were freed and allowed to go home to the Holy Land.

However, back to God's covenant. It would be a little tedious to read all the examples of God, contrary to his word, punishing His people with plague, pestilence and the sword so we have just listed a few as examples. Take a moment to be grateful that we don't seem to suffer God's fits of wrath today. Nevertheless, perhaps he became a role model for current politicians who blatantly say one thing then do another. It certainly seems that He was less than truthful with the children of Israel but at least he seems to have mellowed over the years because we don't seem to see this brattish behaviour from God today.

Exodus 32 : 35 *And the Lord struck the people with a plague because of what they did with the calf Aaron had made.*

Leviticus 26 : 25 *And I will bring the sword upon you to avenge the breaking of the covenant. When you withdraw into your cities, I will send a plague among you, and you will be given into enemy hands.*

Numbers 14 : 37 *these men responsible for spreading the bad report about the land were struck down and died of a plague before the Lord.*

Numbers 25 : 9 *Then the plague against the Israelites was stopped; those who died in the plague numbered 24,000.*

Deuteronomy 28 : 59 *the Lord will send fearful plagues on you and your descendants, harsh and prolonged disasters, and severe and lingering illnesses.*

1 Chronicles 21 : 14 *So the Lord sent a plague on Israel, and seventy thousand men of Israel fell dead.*

Ezekiel 28 : 23 *I will send a plague upon her and make blood flow in her streets. The slain will fall within her, with the sword against her on every side. Then they will know that I am the Lord.*

Zechariah 14 : 15 *A similar plague will strike the horses and mules, the camels and donkeys, and all the animals in those camps.* (Why kill the animals?)

It appears God has still more plagues, in the planning stage for the last days:

Revelation 15 : 6 *Out of the temple came the seven angels with the seven plagues. They were dressed in clean, shining linen and wore golden sashes around their chests.* (If you're going out to dispatch a plague to kill thousands of people, at least be sure to look your best.)

Revelation 16 : 21 *From the sky huge hailstones <u>of about a hundred pounds each</u> fell upon men. And they cursed God on account of the plague of hail, because the plague was so terrible.* No real surprises here, I think I'd curse too if hit by a one hundred pound hail stone. (One hundred pound hailstones – really?)

I can see no way that these passages don't prove a series of broken promises by Almighty God. In addition, there is obviously some obsession of the writers with God ordained atrocities. I think I'd choose the other loving God we learned about.

The Promised Land

The Old Testament relates how YHWH God orchestrated the Exodus of the Children of Israel, with Moses, out of Egypt to the Promised Land. This land flowing with milk and honey was specifically prepared just for them although we had been told it had already been given to Abraham by a much earlier covenant with God. Recall the selected texts we learned at Sunday School and how God supplied the manna to sustain them on their journey.

We were never really encouraged to read the full story. Try it now in your Bible. Here by stealth and wile (with God on their side) the Hebrew people murder innocent men, women and children and commit unspeakable atrocities against the indigenous tribes, in a bloody massacre to steal their land. It is all graphically detailed. It is also pre-ordained since, in **Genesis 34 :10-11** God admits he is about to do terrible things, and advises that **Amorites, Canaanites, Hittites, Perizzites, Hivites and Jebusites** are to be driven out of their lands. He goes further in Exodus telling Moses he will send an 'angel' to achieve this.

> **Exodus 33 : 1-5** *Then the Lord said to Moses, "Leave this place, you and the people you brought up out of Egypt, and go up to the land I promised on oath to Abraham, Isaac and Jacob, saying, 'I will give it to your descendants.'* <u>*I will send an angel before you and drive out the Canaanites, Amorites, Hittites, Perizzites, Hivites and Jebusites.*</u> *Go up to the land flowing with milk and honey.*

The justification for the slaughter of the indigenous peoples to gain their land is that they were uncircumcised heathens who worshiped other Gods. This is despite the children of Israel being in an identical situation themselves, a few short years before. Did they now act as missionaries to the people they came in contact with, spreading the good news about this wonderful God they had recently found? No they did not! They killed these people for being heathens and stole their land. **Genesis 34 & 35** shows that Jacob and his sons, of the children of Israel, were liars and con men of little integrity and that their God fully condones and even promotes their trickery and killing. I actually wouldn't want any of them for a friend. These unsavory characters became the heroes and mighty men of God, the scribes recorded their deeds, and justified their actions, simply because they believed that the land was really theirs as promised by God. They still believe that today. Just look at this example set by Almighty God;

> **Deuteronomy 20 :16** *"But of the cities of these people, which the Lord thy God does give you for an inheritance, thou shall save alive nothing that breatheth".*

This is a contradiction of the very inheritance contained in God's covenant, yet no matter how gross the actions, the justification was that they were just performing the will of God. Earlier in **Exodus 15 : 3** Moses was so proud to sing about the Lord saying, *"The Lord is a man of war; YHWH is his name".*

Think of the situation that exists in the land of Israel today. I really fail to see how the Promised Land could possibly be called the inheritance or gift from God, if in fact the children of Israel had to kill everyone in it, to steal it. The above passages and the whole concept are non-sequitur. The way the Bible stories are written, they are quite apparently a tool, after the event, to justify the cruelty, cold-blooded murder, ethnic cleansing or plain genocide that occurred in the overthrow of the so-called Promised Land. They have absolutely no value as scripture to promote good living or a Godly lifestyle. In fact they have nothing whatever to do with religion apart from the old macho, *"my God is stronger than your God".* Imagine if this same God of Israel was running the land rights for the Australian Aborigines, the American Indians, or sorting out the situation in Kosavo or Timor. Could it really be that Hebrew <u>man</u> actually created <u>God</u> in his own image to <u>justify</u> these atrocities he perpetrated? The Old Testament is certainly a document of justification. If not, how does one reconcile the following?

Justification for Destruction and Killing

Moses couldn't help but notice from the Ten Commandments, that God forbids killing. **Exodus 20 : 13** *Thou shalt not kill.* Very plain and very definite with little room for error. By **Exodus 32 : 27** however, this is totally contradicted as God commands killing, telling the children of Israel to take swords and each man slay his brother, his companion and his neighbour. In reality nothing has changed to this day with the Jewish Nation still struggling for acceptance and ready, willing and able to take up arms against her neighbouring Arab, Moslem states, should they pose any threat. There's no other interpretation, it seems the Children of Israel created a megalomaniac, contradictory, vengeful, petulant and quite whacko, tribal God who could be melded to justify any crime. If he was a real God he would be a role model for later killers like Vlad the Impaler, Josef Stalin, Adolph Hitler, Idi Amin, Pol Pot, and Sadam Hussein. The message is not one of tolerance; it says, *"kill anyone who doesn't think like you do"*. It is possible that this is the first time you realized that the Christian Bible contains all this disgusting and unpalatable cruelty and war-mongery? Very little from these Biblical passages is passed on to the congregation because it does not promote God or the Church fathers in a very good light. In fact it hi-lights the cruelty within the Hebrew Genesis and hi-lights just what a macho religion this is. These passages become very difficult to reconcile with the loving God of Peace and Mercy promoted by the Christians. One could wonder if the Hebrew tribal God could really be the same God of the New Testament. This does not fit with what we were taught does it?

I just can't fathom how Christians can read in the New Testament **James 5 : 11** *The Lord is full of compassion and mercy*, and then explain away the Old Testament reports of God's bursts of wrath and anger, by saying man's inadequacies provoked him. I would defy any Christian to reconcile their benevolent, loving God with the following examples of bigotry, cruelty, senseless killing and sickening, macho, warmongering. An amazing consideration as you read, is that the Lord claims to have actually "hardened the hearts" of the enemies in order to orchestrate a battle with Israel.

> **Joshua 11 : 20** *"For it was of the Lord <u>to harden their hearts</u>, that they should come against Israel in battle, <u>that he might destroy them utterly</u>, and that they might have no favour, but that he might destroy them, as the Lord commanded Moses."*

Recall this as you read on of immeasurable deceit and unimaginable suffering, to realize that it is just a game of tin soldiers to Almighty God;

> **Deuteronomy 7 : 2** *and when the Lord your God has delivered them over to you and you have defeated them, then <u>you must destroy them totally</u>. Make no treaty with*

them, and <u>show them no mercy</u>.

Numbers 25 : 4 *The Lord said to Moses, "Take all the leaders of these people, <u>kill them and expose them in broad daylight</u> before the Lord, so that the Lord's fierce anger may turn away from Israel."*

Exodus 32 : 27 - 29 *Then he said to them, This is what the Lord, the God of Israel, says: Each man strap a sword to his side. Go back and forth through the camp from one end to the other, each <u>killing his brother and friend and neighbour</u>. The Levites did as Moses commanded, and that day about three thousand of the people died. Then Moses said, you have been set apart to the Lord today, for you were against your own sons and brothers, <u>and He has blessed you this day</u>.*

Numbers 31 : 17-18 *Now kill all the boys. And <u>kill every woman who has slept with a man, but save for yourselves every girl who has never slept with a man</u>.*

Hello!!!

Is this the same God who commanded, **Thou shalt not kill**. This appears to be a God without compassion, scruples, morals or ethics!

"I was already biscop of Hippo when I went into Ethiopia with some servants of Christ.... In this country we saw men and women without heads, who had two great eyes in their breasts; and in countries still more southly, we saw people who had but one eye in their foreheads."

St. Augustine (Syntagma page 52 – Taylor).

CHAPTER FOUR

THE JESUS PEDIGREE

Matthew 13 : 13 *"They seeing, see not; and hearing, they hear not,
neither do they understand."*

Rabbi Jesus Christ

Jesus in the Bible

We need to recognize that Christianity is based on the hijacked history and
scriptures of the Jewish religion and utilizes that religion's patriarchs, with
the glaring difference that the Jews do not recognize Jesus as the Messiah.
We would be arrogant in the extreme to believe that the original Jewish
doctrine is wrong and yet the Christians who copied from it got it right. As
children, we were taught that the Christian religion ultimately revolves around
Emmanuel, Jesus Christ the Messiah, the King of the Jews, the son of 'God
the Most High', the descendant of King David, born of the virgin Mary,
with his (step) father Joseph, a humble carpenter. Jesus supposedly died for
our sins on the cross as the ultimate sacrifice. This is pretty central to one's
Christian walk and yet it is at best, allegory and wishful thinking, and at
worst, easily dismissed as total rubbish. Let's take it a step at a time.

The word **Christ** (from the Greek, *Khristos* and Latin, *Christus*) simply
meant, 'King' with no religious connotations whatsoever and was used
regularly as a kingly title. Thus "Christ" is not a name but a title. Its derivation however originally comes from an Indian (Hindi) root meaning
'Anointed' as a king was anointed. This too is ironical because Jesus was a
religious leader or Rabbi but never actually ruled the Holy Land and is not
shown on any list of Jewish Kings. Neither is 'Christ' original, with the
Indian God, **Lord Krishna** (originally Chrishna) having an identical

derivation, which certainly precedes the Bible by some considerable time. Jesus was appropriately anointed in the Bible by Mary Magdalene (who was a priestess and of a royal linage) and accordingly adopted the title of Christ, however no evidence for this exists outside the Bible.

The word **Messiah** didn't mean saviour at all, it too meant, "Anointed one". All kings and most priests were in fact anointed ones and potential Messiahs. At the time of Christ, the Jews were looking out for a special Messiah who would overthrow the cursed Romans and remove them from their land. It had nothing whatever to do with the Son of God or any religious precept. The word **Messiah** comes from the Hebrew *Mesheach* "to anoint" but the original derivation comes from the Egyptian "messeh" which means crocodile. The Egyptian crocodile God of fertility was "Sobek" and as a result great reverence was given to crocodiles. The word "messiah" resulted when initiates were "anointed" with crocodile fat in their wedding ceremony before they became Pharaoh. Although it is not quite correct, the Bible indicates that the words, *Christ* and *Messiah* were pretty much interchangeable when the disciple Andrew had this to say in **John 1 : 41** *We have found the Messiah, which is, being interpreted, the Christ.*

Now the Old Testament prophets said the Messiah was to be called **Emmanuel**, yet his parents called him **Yahshua** (or Yehoshua) which is similar to the English 'Joshua', yet to this day he is known the World over by the Greek rendering of 'Jesus'. 'Yah' is a diminutive of YHWH and 'shua' is to do with salvation; hence the name means roughly *'YHWH gives salvation'* or simply *'YHWH saves'*. In the time of Jesus, pronouncing the name of God, YHWH was quite restricted and when used inappropriately could even result in a death sentence; so Jesus' name, *Yahshua*, was commonly pronounced 'Yeshua' or 'Yehoshua' to avoid pronouncing the *Yah*.

Even today Jewish believers call Jesus, 'Yeshua' or 'Yehoshua' instead of *Yahshua.* The name **Emmanuel** derives from the ancient Egyptian, *"Amun u El"* which means, *"the hidden one is God"* from the Egyptian *Amun – "the hidden one"* and *El –* a generic term for God. In the same vein we have all heard God referred to as the *"Most High."* This title was a standard Canaanite title for Ba`al adopted later for Almighty God; however it dates back to Ancient Egypt where the Sun God Ra (Re) was always worshipped at precisely high noon, when he was *"the most high"* above the Earth. Ra, was referred to in Egyptian prayer as *"God – the most high."* Even the supposed Biblical terms *"King of Kings"* and *"Lord of Lords"* are not original; they are present in the Hymn to Osiris in the Egyptian, 'Book of the Dead' and were also titles used by the Persian King Darius to describe himself.

Mary the mother of Jesus was said to be the daughter of the High Priest, Matthias. Mary was born just before 25 BCE, when Matthias was listed as the priest of the Capernaum synagogue. Around 6 BCE, he became the high priest of the Jerusalem temple; probably the most important religious figure in the Holy Land at the time and was later killed for his part in removing the offensive Golden Eagle of Rome that Herod had erected in the Jerusalem Temple. We find something strange in the Biblical account of the crucifixion of Jesus; the Bible reports there are three "Mary's" present and two of them are sisters (both called Mary):

> **John 19 : 25** *Now there stood by the cross of Jesus, his mother Mary, and his mother's sister Mary, the wife of Cleophas, and Mary Magdalene.* Check it in your own Bible!

So are we to think that Jesus' mother **Mary** had a sister also called **Mary** who became the wife of Cleophas? No! Not exactly! Jesus' mother was actually **Miriam** called Mary. Both **Mary** and **Miriam** were titles of servitude so these could be hiding yet another given name. The name '**Mary**' by which Miriam is known in the Bible was actually more a Royal title than a name, related to Davidian descendency. This title was gained when she became betrothed to 'the Joseph' who was of the tribe of Judah and the kingly descendent of King David. Likewise Miriam's sister also was called Mary once she joined the dynasty of Cleophas, by marriage. The Bible confirms that Miriam-Mary's husband Joseph was of such a Davidian dynasty:

> **Luke 2 : 4** *Joseph also went up from Galilee, into Judea, to the city of David, which is called Bethlehem, because he was of the house and lineage of David.* Mary-Miriam herself was a descendant of Aaron, of the priestly tribe of Levi and only became 'Mary' when betrothed to Joseph.

There is a dynasty at work here, Jesus' disciples were mostly related, some being his cousins; two actually being the sons of Cleophas and Mary. Today, we have enormous problems with fixing precise history due to changes introduced during the copying of scriptures. This was done in ancient times, by various sects, each with their own agenda, and each adding their own brand of propaganda resulting in perpetuated errors and untruths. Each Gospel was written on a different level of understanding. Mark was written in the plain language of the day; Luke used metaphors, similes and other mechanisms to tell it, but actually not tell it. Matthew was written in the vernacular of nobility, which was judicial and employed the use of parables specifically to bring out special meanings. John was written in the language of the 'mystic' which employed the 32 laws of the Kabala and is pretty much valueless to the uninitiated. Now translate all this into Greek then into English to a point where the mechanisms are convoluted and confused and the result is a fairly vague replication of the original. There are also many suppressed scriptural works that, despite considerable usage in ancient times, were not included in the Bible, presumedly because of their content. In fact the Bible could have been a vastly different book with some of them included. This of course also means that the worshippers who used those works had a doctrine that was vastly different to the Christian religion of today. Theology professor Burton Mack, for example, goes as far as to describe the present day gospels' portrayal of Jesus as;

"fantastic"; "the result of a layered history of imaginative embellishments of a founder figure". [1]

The four canonical Gospels; Matthew, Mark, Luke and John, suffered most from apocryphal mimicry, but in addition there were alternate works, including alternate Gospels, containing Gnostic, Kabbalistic, heretical or invented material. To actually find an historical Jesus in this maze is virtually impossible.

'The Jesus Seminar', an association of progressive Biblical scholars based in California, was formed in the 1980s and has played an important role in exposing the unreliability of the early Christian record. Its members believe that Jesus was primarily a sage who taught that the kingdom of heaven is within. They dismiss the gospel stories of him working miracles, and regard him as too enlightened to have threatened his opponents with damnation on Judgement Day. This is just a typical dualistic mechanism that follows on from the intimidating Old Testament format and was certainly added later. In fact, the members of The Jesus Seminar reject as inauthentic, some three quarters of the sayings actually attributed to Jesus in the gospels. (2)

The Talmud and other sources ascribe supernatural activities to many great Rabbis of which Jesus was but one. In fact it is documented that some Rabbis actually pronounced a name of God and ascended into heaven to consult with the Gods and the angels on issues of great public concern. Absolutely ludicrous Infancy Gospels, purporting to give details of Jesus' early life, were very popular, including the **Infancy Gospel of Thomas**; with stories of Jesus as a child working miracles, making clay birds and bringing them to life and striking a playmate dead in a squabble. **The Proto-evangelium of James** gives details of Miriam-Mary's early life and strangely names her parents as Joachim and Anna. There becomes no way of identifying which story is the correct one. It is considered that this Anna just could be the prophetess mentioned in **Luke 2 : 36-37** as a widow aged 84 still living in the temple but if it were true, why would she not be cared for by Joseph and Mary when the care of elderly parents was a Hebrew commandment.

The "Virgin" Mary

Strangely - the concept that Mary was a virgin is not original Christian dogma at all, and stems from the beliefs of various pagan cults, where a mother figure produces a God, in each case born of a virgin. (3) Nowhere! Repeat, nowhere, in the original Hebrew Bible or in the original New Testament does it state that Mary was a virgin. This was mistranslated in the English versions. It is actually easy to see how this happened. In the Latin translations of the Roman Church, Mary was described as "**virgo**" but in Latin this simply means a young woman. To describe a virgin they would use "**virgo intacta**" which they did not. Now the Latin translation "virgo" came from the Hebrew "**almah**" which again meant a young woman. To denote "virgo intacta" (if this was any of their business) they would have to use, "**bethula**" which they did not. It should be remembered that early society was not entirely aware of the biological part man played in conception and accordingly strange ancient myths existed. There were quaint carry overs of this mythology for many years to come. The concept of the "immaculate conception" and that Mary was "ever virgin" (and this despite having a number of children after Jesus) came some 700 years later, from the Catholic Council of Trullo in AD 692. The Catholic hierarchy 'decided' that Mary was "ever virgin" then claimed, contrary to the Bible, that the brothers and sisters of Jesus were really his cousins. There is some truth that the Jewish term for cousins and brothers was not as well defined as it is in today's English, however this is a silly statement by the Catholics since the same Bible certainly indicates that Joseph only put off sex with his wife until after the birth:

> **Matthew 1 : 24 – 25:** *Then Joseph being raised from sleep did as the angel of the Lord had bidden him, and took unto him his wife: And knew her not till she had brought forth her firstborn son: and he called his name Jesus.*

There is a ridiculous passage in the Gnostic, **Infancy of James; 19 : 18 to 20 : 12** which refers to **Salome**, the supposed sister of Miriam-Mary. It records that Salome cannot believe the 'virgin birth' and must "*insert her finger*" (in a similar fashion to 'doubting Thomas') to be assured that the post-pardum Mary was still virginal. Only the most ignorant or indoctrinated audience would even suffer reading this rot. About here Mary would have coined that cry of women the world over, *"Does God really love me or is he just using me for sex."*

Perhaps the patriarchs had a problem with the actual meaning of the word 'virgin'. Remember the search for a wife for Abraham's son Isaac. This is what the Bible says verbatim about his intended wife Rebekka;

> **Genesis 24 : 16** *And the damsel was very fair to look upon, a virgin, neither had any man known her.*

So clearly Rebekka was; (i) a virgin and (ii) neither had any man known her. (in the Biblical fashion.)

I always thought that the two were mutually inclusive so perhaps there is some associated confusion of meaning with translation from the Hebrew.

Another thought on the virgin birth is that the Sun-God entities dating from very ancient times in Egypt were believed to have reproduced with only one parent, in this case a father. It seems that this concept was adapted in ignorance to the personage of Jesus. Alvin Kuhn makes the point:

"Had the early Christian Fathers known of the inner meaning of the symbolism of the Egyptian Ptah, as Khepr-Ra, who was typed by the male beetle that incubated in the ground and without union with the female transformed and regenerated himself after twenty-eight days (exactly a moon cycle) in the form of the young scarab, symbol of the new-born sun in the moon, they would have been intelligent enough to have avoided the great schisms that divided the Church into Roman and Greek Catholic bodies over the abstrusities of this very origin of the persons of the Trinity." [4]

In other words the whole 'one parent' concept in Godheads was likely allegoric and plainly pagan and dated from the most ancient times. We will see later that many Gods were supposedly born of virgins.

For well over a millennium there remained controversy over the Immaculate Conception and in 1854 Pope Pius IX declared that *"This doctrine must be believed firmly and constantly by all the faithful."* The Church further promoted that somehow original sin was present in the soul of all mortal men since Adam, with the solitary exception of Miram-Mary whose soul *"was clothed in sanctifying grace"*. From the time of Miriam-Mary however, the Nazarene sect, at one stage led by Jesus' brothers James and Joses, denied the virgin birth, and who would be in a better position to know than they would? As "Ebionites" (a sect called 'the poor') they are strongly denounced for denying the virgin birth, in the writings of both the Bishop Irenaeus and the writer Eusibius. They were also denounced for rejecting totally scriptures containing the thoughts and teachings of St Paul, whom they correctly considered a heretic. Note too that when Jesus went missing in the Bible story and was found in the temple by Joseph and Mary another hint of his real parentage is given. Miriam-Mary had this to say, **Luke 2 : 48** *"I and thy father have sought thee sorrowing."* It seems unlikely that Miriam-Mary would phrase it that way if it were not so, particularly if as recorded, the angel had enlightened her about the virgin birth.

Nevertheless, in a Bible created for a Roman audience, we were taught the unlikely story that Jesus was the child of Mary and the Holy Spirit with Joseph taking no part. This does not make any sense because at the very introduction of the New Testament, the Bible goes to great pains to show the Kingly descent of Jesus from King David, through the pedigree of his 'father' Joseph, to prove his legitimacy as the rightful King of the Jews. Yet in the same breath it says he was born of a virgin, negating this descent. Mary is described as a Levite and as such was not of the Royal House of David, the tribe of Judah (and accordingly the ruling class). Thus if Jesus resulted from virgin birth, then he could not be the King or Messiah. One has to be wrong! If the mother of Jesus was to be a virgin hand picked by the Holy Spirit, he would have certainly chosen a woman of the tribe of Judah.

In like manner we read crucial information in **Jeremiah 22 : 30** where God decrees that no man of the seed of **Jechoniah** shall ever prosper or sit upon the throne of David; and yet **Matthew 1 : 11-12** traces the pedigree of Joseph back to this same Jechoniah, again negating any chance of Kingship for Jesus, through the linage of Joseph. Damned if you do, damned if you don't, but there is yet another consideration! The Law of Moses included the principle of separation of powers of Church and State. Accordingly the king was not allowed by Jewish Law to take on the role of a priest or engage in priestly duties, and vice versa. This is made clear with King Uzziah;

> **2 Chronicles 26 : 16-18** *But when he was strong, his heart was lifted up to his destruction: for he transgressed against the Lord his God, and went into the temple of the Lord to burn incense upon the altar of incense. And Azariah the priest went in after him, and with him fourscore priests of the Lord, that were valiant men: And they withstood Uzziah the king, and said unto him, It appertaineth not unto thee, Uzziah, to burn incense unto the Lord, but to the priests the sons of Aaron, that are consecrated to burn incense: go out of the sanctuary; for thou hast trespassed; neither shall it be for thine honour from the Lord God.*

So those who want to view Jesus as a potential King of the Jews must negate the virgin birth to trace his descent from King David through Joseph. Those who wish to view him as a spiritual leader require the virgin birth to trace his descent from Aaron through Miriam-Mary. The Jechoniah curse then negates the former and tenders it inoperative. Soon we will see that the 'Panthera' story also negates the latter and makes it too, totally untenable. This is a tough one for Christians.

The Herods

The story of Mary as Miriam starts earlier than the time of Christ and is linked to the ruling Herods. The Herods were **Nabatean Arabs** and Herod the Great was an Idumean, half Jew (some scholars call them Greek Jews). His mother was **Cypros**, a Nabatean of the Royal line of Petra and his father was the Idumean, **Antipater I**. Herod the Great was of Edomite stock. These were the descendants of the Biblical Esau and populated an area of land south of Bethlehem and Jerusalem. The Herod family ruled Idumea at the time that the popular **Maccabean** (Hasmonean) dynasty ruled Palestine. Through a series of family misfortunes, jealousy and deceit, the Hasmonean Jews became vulnerable to a Roman takeover. The Herodians took advantage of the weakness and confusion within the Maccabean family and eventually, with the aid of Rome, conquered the Hasmoneans. Antipater I the father of Herod the Great, was made governor of Judea, while Herod himself became governor of Galilee. After Antipater's death, it was Marc Antony, who ruled the eastern provinces of the Roman Empire and eventually made Herod a tetrarch of Judea.

This is a crucial point! The popular Hasmonean leader **Antigonus** regained control of the Holy Land in 40 BCE and ousted Herod from power, claiming himself to be **King of the Jews**. Herod then approached Marc Antony for help, who, along with Octavian, convinced the Roman senate to appoint Herod as King of the Jews. This declaration was in name only, as it still took Herod (at age 35) three more years of fighting to fully reclaim Jerusalem in 37 BCE and with the sanction of Rome to finally administer the Holy Land. We will look soon at how Marc Antony had Antigonus killed and the possible effect this had on the Christian religion to this day.

After ousting the Hasmonean Jews, this placed the Arab, Herod, as a Roman puppet on the Jewish throne and partly explains the Jewish hatred of the Herods. [5] By the time of the birth of Christ the aging Herod the

Great was nearing death, resulting in considerable conspiracy within the palace, as the various heirs jockeyed for positions. Herod had ten wives (Josephus wrongly says 9) and many sons and daughters. [6] Various factions formed in support of each son becoming King. The true heir was the first son **Antipater III** of the first wife **Doris** and this was endorsed by Rome. In fact Antipater III had spent considerable time in Rome and had become a friend of Augustus Caesar after lavishing expensive gifts on the Emperor. A decree was sent out from Rome by Caesar supporting Antipater, and according to Josephus, his father Herod had also listed Antipater as his heir.

The Herod palace in Jerusalem has an amazing history and was the scene of quite incredible happenings. Earlier the famous Cleopatra lived in this palace complex while Marc Antony was campaigning in the area of eastern Turkey. According to Josephus, Cleopatra so loved this palace that Mark Antony gave it to her as a gift. Later, after Antony and Cleopatra were defeated by Octavian/Caesar Augustus at the Battle of Actium in 31 BCE, Herod the Great got this palace back. It was in one of the swimming pools of this palace complex that Herod had the last Hasmonean male heir to the Jewish throne, who was the brother of his wife, "accidentally" drowned by his soldiers. Not long after, Herod had this wife, the Hasmonean princess Mariamne (Greek for Miriam) the granddaughter of Hyrcanus II and daughter of Alexander the Hasmonean, murdered here in 29 BCE. Herod was so paranoid and jealous of the Hasmoneans' popularity with the Jewish people that he even accused **Aristobulus** and **Alexander**, his two sons by Mariamne, of treason, and had them both murdered in 6 or 7 BCE. Herod got rid of anyone who may wish to take power from him including his own heirs. This is a possible link to the Biblical 'slaughter of the innocents' as there is no evidence apart from the Bible on the killing of all male children under 2 years of age.

Herod's sister Salome did not like Herod's son Antipater III, supporting instead a younger son called Herod Philip, whom she could manipulate. It is believed that she stirred up King Herod to a point of madness. He called an audience with his son and heir Antipater III who returned from Rome, in 4 BCE. Herod mad with power and paranoia, just before his death, had Antipater III murdered in the prison in this same palace. This prompted Augustus

Caesar to state, *"It is better to be Herod's hog (Greek, hus) than his son (Greek, huios)."*

In his book *"The Marian Conspiracy"*; Graham Phillips states that the Jewish historian Flavius Josephus recorded;

> *"Antipater was appointed to be Herod's successor; and that if Antipater should die first, then his first son by the high priest's daughter should succeed."*

Phillips draws on *"The Laws of the Jews"* by Joseph Schreiber who states that the wife of Antipater III was Miriam (Marianne in Greek) and if in fact she was the High Priest's daughter, this could make her the same Miriam (virgin Mary) daughter of the high priest Matthias soon to become mother of Jesus. This hypothesis would have us believe that Jesus was the grandson of Herod. This certainly gave me some trouble; however Phillips again drawing on Joseph Schreiber makes an excellent point to support the paternity of Jesus;

> *"When Jesus was tried around AD 33, (by Pontius Pilate) there was only one person that Roman law would have recognized as king of the Jews - a surviving son of Antipater."*

This was the law passed down from Augustus Caesar in Rome, which Pilate would conscientiously administer. He continues;

> *"In John's gospel Pilate asks Jesus, 'Art thou the King of the Jews?' Jesus' eventual answer is 'To this end was I born.' If this referred to his claim to be a descendant of David, then Pilate would have ordered him crucified immediately. On the contrary, Pilate's deliberation to the Jewish elders is, 'I find no fault at all.' For the episode to fit into any kind of historical context, Pilate finding no fault in Jesus' claim to be the King of the Jews means that Jesus must have been claiming to be the only person Rome would have recognized to hold the title - the son of Antipater."*

This is a nice, tidy hypothesis if in fact Jesus was actually crucified for being the 'King of the Jews'. The only problem being that it is based totally on Phillip's unreferenced statement from Josephus and on checking we find that in fact, <u>Josephus said no such thing!</u> In 'Antiquities of the Jews' - Book XVII - chapter 3; verse 2, Josephus records:

> *"Antipater was appointed to be his successor; and that if Antipater should die first, his (Herod's) son, Herod Philip, by the high priest's daughter (Mariamne), should succeed.* [7]

There is no question that here Josephus means the first successor is **Antipater III,** and the second successor is Herod the Great's next living son **Herod Philip,** the son supported by Salome. The mention of the high priest's daughter certainly refers to Herod the Great's own wife Mariamne II the mother of Herod Philip (*daughter of the Egyptian, Simon Boethus, appointed as high priest by Herod*) and I believe that this totally ruins Phillip's theory and the chance of Jesus being the son of Antipater and grandson of Herod. Actually Herod had two wives called Mariamne the first being the daughter of Alexander the Hasmonean and the second being the daughter of Simon Boethus, who Herod appointed High Priest. We need now to look a little further and a more likely scenario will be revealed. There is a very good reason why Pontius Pilate sat up and took notice of Jesus' claims and we will look at that now.

Panthera

The ancient Jewish Talmud (on which the Bible is based) confirms that Miriam-Mary was the mother of Jesus and that Joseph played no part. The Talmud is not however, an advocate of virgin birth. This ancient source states unequivocally that Jesus' father was a Roman army officer called **Panthera** (Panther) through adultery or rape. We must understand that the devotees of the Jewish faith believe their Holy book, which certainly predates the Bible, to be inerrant, and hold this to be recorded historical fact. Jesus is referred to as **Yeshu'a ben Panthera** in several places and the belief that his physical father was a Roman soldier called Julius Tiberius Panthera is also contained in various other ancient documents and was a fairly widespread belief. In addition, there are differing reports in ancient documents including the Talmud, calling Jesus '**Yeshu'a ben Stada**'. Now '*stada*' was a Jewish term for infidelity meaning '*strayed one*', used to brand a woman who was unfaithful to her husband. It seems that the earlier writers judged Miriam-Mary as having been unfaithful to her betrothed Joseph, and accordingly they recorded Jesus as a bastard son. Even if she had been the victim of rape it would change nothing, in those times. The astute scholar Gustav Dalman states in his 1894 work, "*Jesus Christ in the Talmud, Midrash, and the Zohar*":

"Jesus is commonly referred to in the Talmud and in Talmudic literature by the expressions "Son of Stada", and "Son of Pandera" These are so accepted that they appear constantly in the Babylonian Talmud (cp. the Targum Sheni on Esther VII 9) even without the name Jesus. It might seem to be a question as to who it is that is to be understood by these. But in the Jerusalem Talmud (Avodah Zarah II. 40d), the full name is given as Yeshu ben Pandera (for which Shabbath XIV 14d has more briefly, Yeshu Pandera); and in the Tosephta on Hullin II, the full name is given as Yeshu ben Pantera and Yeshu ben Pantere. So then Ben Pandera or ben Pantere also bears the name Yeshu. Further, the Jesus the Nazarene who is "hanged on the evening before Passover" (Sanhedrin 43a) is on the other hand (Sanhedrin 67a) also called the "son of Stada". It is evident that in both these places the same person is spoken of. Here these two passages may be considered conclusive, since they repeat each other using the similar language, and in a section of the text which is chiefly concerned about Jesus; and so we see that Jesus was also referred to as Ben Stada". [8]

Now this comes from the very source of the Bibles scriptures and its omission from today's Christian Bible must have been deliberate since it is inconceivable that it could have been overlooked. Here we see ben Panthera and ben Stada clearly identified with Jesus in the very works that became the Bible. This is confirmed in the book, *'Yehoshua, Yeshua or Yeshu; Which One is the Name of Jesus in Hebrew?'* by Dr. James D. Price who was Professor of Hebrew and Old Testament studies at Temple Baptist Seminary in Chattanooga, TN;

"The editor's footnote reads: 'In the uncensored editions of the Talmud there follows this important passage "And this they did to Ben Stada in Lydda (. . .), and they hung him on the eve of Passover. Ben Stada was Ben Padira. Hisda said: 'The husband was Stada, the paramour Pandira. But was nor the husband Pappos b. Judah? - His mother's name was Stada. But his mother was Miriam, a dresser of women's hair? (. . . megaddela neshayia): - As they say in Pumbaditha, this woman has turned away (. . .) from her husband, (i.e., committed adultery)' [9]

The mention that the capital punishment of Jesus took place in the ancient city of Lydda (Lud or Lod) in Palestine, reminds us that Saint George, the Patron Saint of England was a third century martyr from Lydda. This city on the coastal plain of Israel, 10 miles southeast of Tel Aviv-Jaffa and about 25 miles from Jerusalem, was the location for the revolt of the Jews against the Romans in the first century AD. It was then officially called Diospolis by the Romans, but the popular name always remained Lydda or Lod. A few scholars have identified this City with London, UK and that is incorrect. Actually the Emperor Constantine stated that Diocletian (284 – 305 AD) martyred St. George in Lydda in Palestine on 23 April (coinciding with the Roman shepherd festival of Parilia) for refusing to worship the old pagan Gods. Stuart Nettleton claims that it was Constantine who actually invented an allegoric Saint George to represent the sacrifice of Jesus in this precise location. [10] This could even have been to blur the personage of Jesus and dilute this Jewish-ness in the Catholic Bible.

Now St. Epiphanies implies in his writings that Jesus lived around 100 BCE. We must proceed through his work with caution since we find some fairly curious and contradictory statements. Epiphanies actually gives us a genealogy in which **Panthera** is recorded as the grandfather of Jesus, yet he also intimates that he is his father. Further confusion creeps in when he says that Jesus lived in the time of King Alexander Jannaeus (who reigned from c. 103 to 76 BCE) but then goes on to say that Jesus was born some 70 years after Jannaeus' death. All this in the same account. The writer St. Epiphanies is hardly likely to have been that inconsistent so it appears that he had a hidden agenda or there has been some modification and editing, or we could put it down to errors in copying or translating his work. Quite confusing!

There are in fact several other writers who align Jesus with the time of King Alexander Jannaeus. The confusion comes from the belief that Jesus was the character called, *'The Teacher of Righteousness'* within the Dead Sea Scrolls. It is almost certain that he was not, with opinion split as to whether John the Baptist, James the Just, or someone else, is referred to and whether or not the timeframe is actually accurate. Herein lies the rub, it is possible that the Christ figure is entirely allegoric and a composite of many people of stature. Professor Alvar Ellegard has suggested that the main prototype for a mythical Jesus was indeed the 'Teacher of Righteousness' and argues that this figure was the founder of the Judaic reform movement known as the Essenes, and that he actually died around 100 BCE. Now this theory has a lot of merit, however we know that the Essenes have existed in a similar format since 397 BCE, so accordingly this sect could not have been actually formed by this character. There were actually four main Zaddoki groups known as (i) **Essenes** (ii) **Zealots** (iii) **Sicarii** and (iv) **Nazoraens** with significant inter-sectarian differences, usually to do with how militant a stance should be taken against the Roman infidels. The Professor of Semitic Language and Civilization at the Sorbonne, **Andre Dupont-Sommer**, presented a paper in 1950 on findings from of the newly translated Dead Sea Scrolls from Qumran. He lectured on the sect called the *'Sect of the New Covenant'* who's leader was 'The Teacher of Righteousness' who was held to be the Messiah, was persecuted by the Romans, tortured and finally martyred. His followers believed they were living in the last days and that the end of the world was imminent. Even Dupont-Sommer concluded that this was an exact proto-type of Jesus. Rabbi's generally believed that Jesus was actually the Messianic hopeful Y'shua ha Meshiach, a Nozri born around 100 BCE, the son of Judas of Gamalas, and who lived with the Essenes. [11] The Knights Templar called those initiated into the Johannite mysteries, 'Knights of Palestine'. The Nazarenes in Basra in Persia still hold a tradition that their brothers in Malta and Europe will eventually restore the doctrine of their prophet *Iohanan* (Saint John), the son of Lord Jordan, and eliminate from the hearts of humanity each and every other false teaching. [12] We certainly wish them well.

Even though by convention the four Gospels are always placed first in the New Testament, a little known fact is that the letters of Paul were actually written before any of them and are commonly dated as early as c. 50 AD. This shows that Paul did not hear of Jesus through the New Testament Gospels and did not have these scriptures to aid his preaching about Jesus. He possibly carried the Jewish Torah but taught the Jewish law and the story of Jesus; actually formulated from very scant sources indeed. In fact the Bible tells us that Saul who became St. Paul came from Tarsus which just happened to be the centre of Mithras worship in Asia Minor. It would certainly make sense that it was St. Paul who took the existing Persian legend of Mithras, 'the son of God' and wove it around the Jesus story. According to the Bible, St. Paul was also a Roman citizen, so in his position as a great orator would likely have been up with Roman politics; he would certainly have known about the crucifixion of Antigonus, the King of the Jews and the martyrdom of 'The Teacher of Righteousness' and was in the perfect position to add this to the Jesus myth. Recall that Paul claimed to know nothing except, *"Christ Jesus and him crucified"*. According to Ellegard, St. Paul and his colleagues were the first to refer to this allegoric, Christ figure in the Greek term of **'Jesus'**, and it was they who introduced the idea that he was the Messiah and Saviour. He acknowledges that the Teacher of Righteousness from the pages of the Scrolls differs in many ways from the Jesus of the Gospels, but stresses that the latter is largely a composite, fictional figure;

> *"I think that the Teacher of Righteousness of the Essenes was in fact the figure — either historical or not—behind the Jesus of Paul and his contemporaries. The main question of this stage is why the second century Christians substituted another, fictional Jesus, and how they managed to convince their communities on this point, and how they succeeded in obliterating virtually all evidence about the original, Essene Jesus".* [13]

If this is correct it immediately alleviates all the problems we have been encountering. It explains why the records are contradictory, why the Bible is a lone source on most of the life of Jesus and why Jesus is so often confused with other characters with similar motifs. In his book, *Who Was The Real Jesus*, author David Pratt draws on the work of Michael Wise to further clarify this point;

> *In a highly speculative reconstruction of the life of the Teacher of Righteousness (who may have been called Judah), Michael Wise argues that he was a priestly prophet, a member of the elite, and rose to pre-eminence around 105 BCE as a leader of the political coalition that supported King Alexander Jannaeus (who reigned from c. 103 to 76 BCE). Alexander was supported by the Sadducees and oppressed the Pharisees, but when his wife, Alexandra, became queen, she did an about-face and embraced the Pharisees. Judah, who came to regard himself as the messiah, defied the new regime, labelling it Satan's dominion. He was arrested, charged with false prophecy, and exiled around 74 BCE, and within a few years he had been killed. Wise does not specifically link the Teacher with the Essenes.* [14]

Despite this confusion surrounding the life of Jesus, it seems that unwittingly St. Epiphanies confirms the Panthera story;

> "*The traditional church writings of St Epiphanies, the Bishop of Salamis (315-403) again confirmed the Panthera story and his information was of a startling nature. This champion of Christian orthodoxy and saint of Roman Catholicism frankly stated; 'Jesus was the son of a certain Julius whose surname was Pantera.'*" (15)

Let's follow up another confirmation;

> "*Ben Stada was ben Pantera, Rabbi Chisda said; the husband was Stada the lover Pantera. Another said, the husband was <u>Paphos ben Jehuda</u>; Stada was his mother … and she was unfaithful to her husband.*" (16)

Paphos ben Jehuda is a character thought to have lived a century after Jesus, however Paphos was also the name of a town visited by the apostle St. Paul, where he blinded the false prophet;

> **Acts 13 : 6-10** *They travelled through the whole island until they came to Paphos. There they met a Jewish sorcerer and false prophet named Bar-Jesus, who was an attendant of the proconsul, Sergius Paulus. The proconsul, an intelligent man, sent for Barnabas and Saul because he wanted to hear the word of God. But Elymas the sorcerer (for that is what his name means) opposed them and tried to turn the proconsul from the faith. Then Saul, who was also called Paul, filled with the Holy Spirit, looked straight at Elymas and said, "You are a child of the devil and an enemy of everything that is right! You are full of all kinds of deceit and trickery. Will you never stop perverting the right ways of the Lord? Now the hand of the Lord is against you. You are going to be blind, and for a time you will be unable to see the light of the sun."*

Do you agree that this is strange? Ironically the false prophet here is called **bar Jesus** (son of Jesus?) or **Elymas** which apparently means 'sorcerer' and strangely the time frame is right for him to be a descendant of Jesus. Elymas was initially recorded as a Jewish spiritual man capable of performing wondrous acts of power. The magic powers Jesus supposedly learned in Egypt were sometimes described in similar fashion. Bar Jesus was certainly accepted in the upper crust of Cyprian society and his services were initially greatly sought by the Roman proconsul. The coming of Paul and Barnabas however saw him relegated to the role of 'sorcerer' and 'false prophet'.

An article from 1944 by Jeremi Wasiutynsky on the net (in a European language that could be bad Danish) accuses Jesus of being called ben Stada the son of a prostitute, and traces this scenario back to an ancient (pagan) Mesopotamian tradition that the Saviour must be born of a 'holy prostitute'. He has Jesus going to Egypt in 87 BCE when King Jannaeus commenced tracking down the 'farisserner' and actually crucified 800 of them. Although he states that it comes from the Church father's original scribbles, much of the Wasiutynsky work appears to be based on the work of Celsus and he has a Jew saying to Jesus;

> *"Your mother was a poor woman who worked as a prostitute. You moved to Egypt where you learned magic which you later used to fool your own people."* [17]

He correctly documents that the Egyptian magicians could fight devils, heal the sick, raise the dead, and use magic to feed a multitude with little or no food. In other words they were versed in the very miracles later attributed to Jesus. These things are confirmed in ancient Egyptian literature. Wasiutynsky also noted that these magicians were called **"God's Sons"** which is obviously the same as the Sons of God. This certainly gives us something to think about.

The Hebrew Records

The Jewish Talmud was written between the 1st. and 6th. Centuries AD; compiled from earlier verbal and written traditions of ancient Jewish commentary. It is divided into two sections, the *Mishnah* and *Gemara*. The Mishnah concentrates on material up to AD. 220, while the Gemara contains commentaries on the Mishnah and covers material up to the fifth or sixth century. It is believed that the Gemara actually contains older Mishnahic statements. The material covered within the Talmud ranges from issues relating to such things as legal disputes and questions known as the *Halakah*. The legends, anecdotes and other sayings used to illustrate the traditional laws are called the *Haggadah*. There are essentially two Talmuds. The first is known as *Talmud Yerushalmi* or The Talmud of Jerusalem, compiled around AD 400 in the Holy Land. The Talmud of Jerusalem was the last product of Palestinian Rabbinic Judaism. The second, called *Talmud Babli* or the Talmud of Babylon was compiled sometime during the sixth century AD. [18] This fact assists our hypothesis that an abundance of Sumerian records from Babylon (and records from Egypt) found their way into the Christian Bible.

Many years later the various passages in the Talmud, specifically referring to Jesus, were amalgamated with other material to create the *'Sepher Toldoth Jeshu'* (Book of the Generations of Jesus). This work also places Jesus as a contemporary of **Alexander Janneus** the Sadducee, King of Judea, who reigned from 106 to 79 BCE and also of Simeon ben Shetach who lived in 90 BCE. The *Sepher Toldoth Jeshu* even tells us that Jeshu (Jesus) outlived Jannaeus, who is known to have died in 79 BCE (at 86 years of age). The Talmud also mentions a man, **ben Perachiah** who it says fled to Egypt with Jeshu to escape being killed by King Jannaeus, (and not by King Herod). As stated previously, this Jeshu (Jesus is the Greek form of Jeshu) is possibly confused with 'The Teacher of Righteousness' found in the Dead Sea Scrolls, and could be an entirely different character. The Talmud however contains the historical record of a character we saw earlier, who seems to mirror the life of the Biblical Jesus.

We should seek some clarification on this;

Jeshu is said to have been the disciple of Joshua ben Perachiah, who was certainly a historical figure, being one of the most prominent rabbis of the time. During the persecution of the Pharisees by Alexander Jannaeus, which began around 94 BCE, Joshua ben Perachiah fled with Jeshu to Alexandria in Egypt, where Jeshu is said to have learned magic. Described as a learned man, Jeshu was expelled for heretical tendencies from the school over which Joshua presided. He became a religious teacher, had several disciples, and preached to ordinary people. He was accused of practising sorcery, deceiving Israel and estranging people from God. After being tried and convicted, he was stoned to death and his body was then hung up as a warning to others. [19]

It is thought by serious scholars that the mother of Jesus Miriam-Mary, had a brother called Joshua, and there is a high possibility that it is this same Rabbi Joshua ben Perachiah. In other words Jesus was a disciple of his own Uncle Joshua. Miriam-Mary is shown in the Bible to have had a sister called Salome. The *Sepher Toldoth Jeshu* indicates that Miriam-Mary is also related to Queen Helene, who is one and the same as Salome, whose brother was Rabbi Simeon ben Shetach. Here we see a close relationship of Jesus with Royalty and two of the most distinguished Rabbis, however if it is true, then the time frame we were taught for the life of Jesus is seriously out of whack. [20]

St. Paul makes no mention of the birth of Jesus, of his ministry in Galilee or Jerusalem, his miracles and teachings, or the details of his passion. He claims he knows naught but *"Christ and him crucified"*. We already noted that the letters of Paul were actually written before any of the Gospels so we can safely assume that Paul was not familiar with the Gospels when he commenced preaching about Jesus as the Messiah. What makes this difficult to understand is that all the earliest, pre-gospel Christian epistles display the same silences as Paul. It is only in the second century AD that Jesus begins to be linked with the time of Herod and Pontius Pilate and that, further biographical details emerge. In *Antiquities*, Josephus tells us that Pilate was appointed Procurator of Judea in 27 AD and his provocative attack on the Samaritans in 36-7 AD resulted in his being recalled to Rome. According to Eusebius, Pilate chose to commit suicide rather than see himself publicly disgraced.

So with even the timeline of his birth uncertain, how can we be sure that we learned about the correct historical Jesus? The Gospel Jesus, with whom we became familiar in Sunday School, appears to be something of a patchwork character, partly Sun-God, partly mythical, partly pagan, and partly based on a variety of historical characters, found in various writings including the Talmud and Toldoth Jeshu. The pagan philosopher and atheist **Celsus,** in 178 AD, wrote what is probably the very first attack on the Christian cult. In this work entitled *Alethes Logos* (True Word), he states that Miriam-Mary's betrothed husband (a carpenter) turned her out when, due to an adulterous affair, she became pregnant to a Roman soldier stationed in Bethlehem. (ben Panthera again.) He intimates that Jesus himself was a sorcerer having studied magic in Egypt where he was taught certain mysteries and gained certain miraculous powers, which he later used to proclaim himself a God. Celsus reinforced his story with quotes from the earlier *Sepher Toldoth Jeshu*. The Jews of course reject that Jesus was the Messiah so it possibly does not concern them that the ancient Jewish Talmud as well as the later Toldoth Jeshu both contain some interesting and somewhat uncomplimentary stories about Jesus and the early Christian origins. They mostly classify Miriam–Mary as an adulteress or prostitute and record Jesus as a bastard son.

In their work *He Walked Among Us*, Josh McDowell and Bill Wilson state, on the authority of Joseph Klausner, that the phrase *'such-an-one'* is often used for Jesus in the Ammoraic period (the fifth century). [21] This term is also used in the Talmud and what makes it of interest is that Rabbi Shimeaon ben `Azzai said;

> *"I found a genealogical roll in Jerusalem wherein was recorded, that 'Such-an-one' (Jesus) is the bastard son of an adulteress."*

Now this Rabbi ben 'Azzai was no lightweight. He was an extremely learned and pious man who would have dismissed an errant scroll in an instant, and accordingly is considered a most credible source. As an ascetic celibate, ben 'Azzai was one of just four Rabbi's who according to Talmudic tradition, were fit to 'enter paradise'. [22]

According to the Jewish *'Tractate of Talmud'*, the *Chagigah,* a certain person had a dream in which he saw the punishment of the damned. In this dream, *"He saw Mary the daughter of Heli amongst the shades..."* [23] The Bible teaches Christians to have faith in dreams. For example Daniel placed a lot of stock in dreams, as was the custom in those times. Whether or not we give this dream any credibility it still reveals the thoughts of the writer in that contemporary period and indicates that:

(i)   The adulteress story would have to be considered true for Miriam–Mary to be amongst the dammed.

(ii)   It must have been considered that Jesus was indeed the bastard son of an adulteress

(iii)   It would make more sense if Mary was historically the daughter of Heli. In the Bible, Joseph is recorded as the son of Heli but also as the son of Jacob. The fathers of Jacob and Heli themselves are shown respectively as Matthan and Matthat; the similarity indicating the same person, so it is unlikely that either was the father of Mary, though Heli would likely be her father in law. We cannot be sure of the pedigree of Miriam-

Mary, but authentication of the above passage would make her Joseph's sister.

Matthew 1 : 15-16 Joseph's father was **Jacob** son of Matthan.

Luke 3 : 23 Joseph's father was **Heli** son of Matthat.

All this evidence certainly cannot be made to accommodate the Immaculate Conception and strangely, the virgin birth wasn't orchestrated until 325 AD and wasn't promoted by the church until **some 700 years** after the conventional birth date of Jesus. The 'virgin birth' is unquestionably fraudulently added church doctrine. The reality is we all really do know that virgins don't have babies and even if Almighty God was involved it would make no sense for him to do it this way when any number of pagan Gods were supposedly born of virgins, long before Jesus. Surely a true God could be more imaginative and original. We will devote more time to this subject later.

The early Christian Church father, **Adamantius Origen** 185 – 251 AD was so taken with the words of **Matthew 19 : 12** about *"men who made themselves eunuchs for the sake of the kingdom of Heaven"* that he applied the passage literally and castrated himself. Origen strongly defended his faith against the previously mentioned, *'Alethes Logos'* of Celsus (c. 170 CE). He referred to Jesus as an Angel and he inadvertently left us the only quotes we now have from the otherwise deliberately destroyed work of Celsus. For example in the following quote, Origen repeats the Jesus ben Panthera story that Celsus claimed he heard from a Jew;

> *But let us now return to where the Jew is introduced, speaking of the mother of Jesus, and saying that "when she was pregnant she was turned out of doors by the carpenter to whom she had been betrothed, as having been guilty of adultery, and that she bore a child to a certain soldier named Panthera;" and let us see whether those who have blindly concocted these fables about the adultery of the Virgin with Panthera, and her rejection by the carpenter, did not invent these stories to overturn His miraculous conception by the Holy Ghost: for they could have falsified the history in a different manner, on account of its extremely miraculous character, and not have admitted, as it were against their will, that Jesus was born of no ordinary human marriage.* [24]

We have an interesting comment by Sam Shamoun in a piece called, *'Jesus in the Rabbinic Traditions.'* He suggests how the Panthera story can agree with the Biblical genealogy;

> *"It is noteworthy that Origin himself is credited with the tradition that Panthera was the appellation of James (Jacob), the father of Joseph, the father of Jesus..."* Shamoun goes on stating that the widespread belief that Panthera was indeed the father of Jesus was documented by many writers; *"So too, Andrew of Crete, John of Damascus, Epiphanius the Monk, and the author of Andronicus of Constantinople's 'Dialogue Against the Jews', all name Panther as an ancestor of Jesus..."* [25]

Apparently, as shown above, Origen once wrongly thought that Panthera was really a nickname of Jacob, the father of Joseph. This would make Jesus his grandson, and now it is clearly recognised as an error and fortunately we are not asked to believe that Mary had an affair with her betrothed's father. Judging from the documented treatment of young women by soldiers in the Holy Land at that time, I think Jesus being the result of an affair with a soldier or resulting from rape is really quite plausible. There is simply far too much contemporary documentation of the Panthera story to disregard it. In a court of law there would surely be sufficient evidence from a myriad of sources to have it accepted as fact. We may not like what we hear but these ancient scribes had no obvious hidden agenda and accordingly, have a right to be heard. Just because we weren't taught this does not make it wrong; it holds far more supporting evidence than the lone Bible story does. The early church and its parishioners also must have had grave concerns about the documentation citing Panthera's parenting of Jesus. Zealous Christians in the time of St. Augustine sought out and destroyed every copy of Celsus' — *Alethes Logos* and today we only know of it from Origen's rebuttal. It seems the Roman Catholic Church also censored even the Origen documents sometime in the seventeenth century, in an attempt to totally erase the mention of Jesus ben Panthera. [26] This indicates grave concerns by the Church about this material that could totally scuttle the virgin birth myth. What makes this scenario of Panthera so intriguing is that a tomb has now been discovered near Bingerbruck (Bingerbnick), Germany, documented as the resting place of a Roman soldier, Julius Panthera. The inscription reads;

> *"Tiberius Julius Abdes Panthera of Sidon, Phoenicia, aged 62, a soldier of 40 years service, of the first cohort of archers, lies here...."* [27]

The Tomb of Panthera, believed to have been the father of Jesus, found in Bingerbnick, Germany.

The inscriptions (and possibly the tomb) do not appear to date from the time of Christ unless they have been rejuvenated and as a result of this many Bible scholars don't even consider that they may be genuine. Research indicates however that this tomb may have been erected, maintained and even renovated by a group like the Knights Templar to cast light on the secret of Panthera to which they seem to have been privy. Tony Bushby says that the priest Saniere of Rennes la Chateau erected it and this is quite plausible too, although it does appear to be considerably older than the time of Saniere. [28] The tomb has since been moved to the museum at Bad Kreuznach. This and the fact that a Roman officer of this name actually did serve with the first cohort and was transferred to service in Germany (Rhineland) around 9AD, gives this scenario increased credibility. Professor Morton Smith of Columbia University certainly thought so when he stated that this tomb might perhaps be, *"our only genuine relic of the holy family"*.

We have now researched several early sources that state that Jesus was the son of Panthera. This tenacious story must hold some considerable credence because its documentation was so incredibly widespread and because **Tiberius Julius Abdes Panthera** was a known Roman army officer. There is however more to it than that, and this is a crucial point, because Panthera was in fact the son of **Augustus Caesar**. Now Caesar had been deified, after his death; is it such a leap of faith to see Caesar's grandson (Jesus) recorded as "the son of God." If true, this link from Jesus right to the Emperor Augustus Caesar would certainly go a long way towards explaining Pilate's deliberation at Jesus' trial, now wouldn't it?

In addition Jesus' mother Mary-Miriam was said to be the sister of Queen Helene (Salome) making Jesus her nephew and giving him a right royal pedigree on the sides of both parents. We need to study Panthera further. From ancient mythology we can note that the first creature killed by Hercules was a Nemean Panther, and from its skin he made a cloak which supposedly rendered him invincible. Ancient Egyptian records tell of a mystery school based on the rites of Osiris, whose members called themselves 'Panthers' and wore cloaks similar to that of Hercules. Later Egyptian priests wore an assortment of feline skins in their rituals; the particular fur indicating the level of initiation and at times the feline pelts were covered in decorations of stars. Wild beast fur became the insignia of authority and showed a degree of initiation into the 'Panther' mysteries. [29] Of interest to us is that Emperor Augustus Caesar was one, known to be initiated into the highest Panther mysteries of Egypt. [30] This would certainly make it easy to believe that Augustus Caesar might pass this knowledge on to his son and if it was a strong motivation in his life, immortalize it as his son's given name or title. Bushby tells us;

> *"In later times, those who achieved initiation into the highest Panther Mysteries were awarded the appellation 'Panther', and that title was included into their family and given names."* [31]

The fact that Jesus went to Egypt and there learned mysteries and miracles simply confirms the likelihood that he too became an initiate and also adds credence to the hypothesis that Panthera was really his father. Another consideration is whether Jesus was actually dark skinned. Several of the Pagan Gods we will encounter later in this book were depicted as being black skinned. The name 'Panthera' (Panther in English) is thought by some to be a nickname indicating that the possible father of Jesus was in fact black like a panther. Kersey Graves tells us;

> *"In the pictures and portraits of Christ by the early Christians, he is uniformly represented as being black. And to make this the more certain, the red tinge is given to his lips..."* [32]

If we look to the Bible; **Solomon 1 : 5-6** *"I am black but comely, o ye daughters of Jerusalem, as the tents of Kedar, as the curtains of Solomon. Look not upon me because I am black, because the sun hath looked upon me ..."*

Now it has long been considered that this passage refers to Jesus Christ, and Graves supports this point as well. Throughout Europe but particularly in France, Portugal and Spain there are many depictions of 'Black Madonnas' and 'Black Christs' so we cannot discount the possibility that Jesus was black, or that the black depictions were a signpost to his initiation in the panther mysteries of Egypt.

It appears that Jesus had a royal pedigree that made Pilate sit up and take notice and may have even been accepted as the potential King of the Jews by Rome. His lack of descent from David, and the timing of his birth, are the things that hampered his acceptance by the Jewish Church leaders, who sought to have him crucified. No other scenario makes any sense. The Magi, the wise men, who brought presents for the newborn King did not get it wrong. They came looking for a genuine, dynastic King, not a carpenter. In addition the whole "virgin birth" lie was to elevate and align Jesus with the pagan Gods supposedly resulting from virgin birth and to cover up his shortcomings as the true King and Messiah.

Some Biblical difficulties

The entire Jesus pedigree within the Books of the Bible is problematic;

Matthew 1 : 17 There were **twenty-eight** generations from David to Jesus.

Luke 3 : 23 –31 There were **forty-two** generations

Matthew 1 : 6-16 The lineage of Jesus is traced through David's son, **Solomon.**

Luke 3 : 23 The linage is traced through David's son, **Nathan**.

Luke and Matthew both definitely state that **the Holy Ghost** was Jesus' father.

Luke and Matthew both definitely state that **Joseph** was Jesus' father.

Matthew 1 : 20 The angel spoke to **Joseph**.

Luke 1 : 28 The angel spoke to **Mary**.

Matthew 1 : 18-21 The Annunciation occurred **after** Mary had conceived Jesus.

Luke 1 : 27-32 It occurred **before** conception.

Matthew 1 : 20-23 An angel announces to **Joseph** that the child Jesus will be "great," the "son of the Most High"

Luke 1 : 28-37 The same things are told to **Mary**

Matthew 3 : 3 John the Baptist prophesied the ministry of Jesus. (Jesus was his cousin living in the same locality and only 6 months younger than John so this would not have been difficult.)

Matthew 3 : 16-17 states that John the Baptist was preparing the way for Jesus. At his baptism there were miracles including the voice of God from Heaven.

Mark 1 : 9-11 confirms that the baptism of Jesus brings forth the voice of God.

Mark 3 : 21-23 Despite this, Jesus' own relatives and neighbours **didn't realize he was the Messiah** and attempted to constrain him, thinking that he might be out of his mind.

Matthew 3 : 11-17 Somehow John the Baptist only realized the true identity of Jesus as the Messiah at the time of Jesus baptism, yet the very purpose of John's baptism was to reveal Jesus to Israel.

John 1 : 29-34 shows the same as above, finishing with, "I saw, and bare record that this is the Son of God." Two of John's disciples actually abandon John and follow Jesus.

Matthew 11 : 2-4 to make a mockery of the Biblical record, some time well after the Baptism, John the Baptist in prison sends his disciples to ask **if Jesus is the Messiah**. Hello!

John the Baptist was originally thought to be the awaited Messiah and in that time had a huge following. He is recorded as a cousin of Jesus and is thought by serious scholars to have been from a wealthy family of a royal linage. Origen stated, *"There are some who said of John (the Baptist) that he was the anointed"*. This is confirmed by Dr. Franz Hartmann who recorded that John *"was of a noble family and had many influential friends"* [(33)]

Worth noting too is the thoughts of Jesus documented in the Gospel of Thomas. When the Disciples enquire who will be the leader when Jesus departs, he makes this surprising admission;

"Wherever you are, you are to go to James the Righteous, for whose sake Heaven and Earth came into being."

This statement would likely promote Jesus' brother James as the Messiah and would suggest that Jesus viewed the strict upholding of Jewish law, the stance of James, as the future direction for the Christian Church.

Twin Messiahs

There is a school of thought that simply will not go away, that there were actually twin Messiahs. There is evidence that the Jews were expecting two Messiahs, a High Priest descended from Aaron and a King descended from David. It appears that this would be a necessity because of the separation of powers of Church and State required by the laws of Moses. If this could be achieved by twin brothers with joint linage from both Aaron and David, it would have been a remarkable achievement, certainly taken as a sign and omen from Almighty God.

This painting is believed to contain 'secrets' exposed to Da Vinci & Michaelangelo by Pope Leo X.

Leonardo da Vinci was just one of the intelligentsia who believed in the secret of the twin Messiahs and actually showed the disciple Judas Thomas as looking identical to Jesus in his painting of '*The Last Supper*'. **Pythagoras** was another who believed this to be true and the artist **Raphael** (Sanzo Raphello, 1483-1520) painted twin Messiahs in his work '*La Belle Jardiniere*' which shows Miriam–Mary with twin boys. The Church however later promoted that one was Jesus and the other John the Baptist, six months his senior. **Michelangelo's** (Michelangelo Buonarroti 1475-1564 AD) painting of the 'Sibyl of Tarquin' on the ceiling of the Sistine Chapel, shows two identical assisting genii looking over the Sibyl's shoulder. Many of his other paintings and sculptures also carried this theme. This was his pictorial cryptogram to show he believed the twin Messiah motif as well. Persistent rumours alleged that a secret was confided to both da Vinci and Michelangelo by the Borgia Pope. Pope Leo X (Giovanni de Medici, 1513-1521 AD) was a self confessed 'pleasure loving' homosexual and one of his partners was Michelangelo. If the birth of twin Messiahs was actually true then it is a secret that was kept from the Bible by ensuring any mention was removed and by particularly excluding those books that carried this story. The works of da Vinci and Michelangelo certainly give us a hint so we should now look further at the disciple, known as "doubting Thomas" in the Bible;

John 11 : 16 *Then said Thomas, which is called Didymus, unto his fellow disciples,*

Now this is a pleonasm since *Thomas* is a sobriquet that in Hebrew means 'twin'. The problem is that *Didymus* in Greek also means 'twin' and accordingly Thomas must be named **'Twin called the twin'**. This makes it apparent that Thomas was somebody's twin, so who's? Dr Barbara Theiring states that it is possible that the entire story of the twin comes from the fact that Thomas was actually a member of the Herod family who lost his birthright when his parents divorced in 5 BCE. Thus he was considered a 'twin' with the Biblical Esau who similarly lost his birthright. [34] Earlier we debunked the herodian descendency of Jesus. I also believe that the story is a bit too tenacious to be based on this kind of joke or word pun. There certainly seems to be more substance to it than that.

It is somewhat ironical that despite widespread usage, the very early, apocryphal, **Gospel of Thomas** was not selected for inclusion in the Bible and accordingly suffered some considerable suppression. If this book was actually written by Thomas Didymus one would reasonably expect its inclusion in the Bible. As a follower and disciple of Jesus and an eyewitness to his preaching, to his overall message and ultimately to his resurrection, Thomas had a legitimate message to contribute. In this gospel Thomas describes himself as **Judas Thomas**, (Judas the twin). We have two versions of The Gospel of Thomas today. The first was discovered in the late 1800's among the *Oxyrhynchus Papyri*, and consists of fragments of a Greek version, which has been dated to c. 200 AD. The second is a complete version, in Coptic, from Codex II of the Nag Hammadi corpus. This well and truly predates the accepted canonical gospels, and as such should have some considerable validity.

It is recorded in the Bible that Jesus had a brother Judas, Juda or Jude;

Matthew 13 : 55 *Is not this the carpenter's son? Is not his mother called Mary? And his brethren, James and Joses, and Simon, and Judas?*

Mark 6 : 3 *Is not this the carpenter, the son of Mary, the brother of James, and Joses, and of Juda, and Simon? And are not his sisters here with us?*

Jude 1 : 1 *Jude, the servant of Jesus Christ, and brother of James, to them that are sanctified by God the Father, and preserved in Jesus Christ:*

The plot thickens because in **The Acts of Thomas**, another early manuscript not included in the Bible, it states that when Jesus appears to a young man, *"...he saw the Lord Jesus in the likeness of the apostle Judas Thomas... the Lord said to him, "I am not Judas who is also Thomas, I am his brother"*. That's pretty definite. Does the reader fully comprehend the enormity of what is recorded here! Jesus brother Judas is in fact his twin brother Judas Thomas and is the same Thomas Didymus as listed in the Bible as a disciple. Elaine H. Pagels, the noted religious historian; the Harrington Spear Paine Foundation, Professor of Religion, Princeton University, states on The Gospel of Thomas;

This book opens with the lines, "These are the secret words which the living Jesus spoke, and the twin, Didymos Judas Thomas wrote them down." Then there follows a list of the sayings of Jesus. Now this raises all kinds of questions. Did Jesus have a twin brother? Actually the name Thomas Didymos — well, Thomas is Hebrew for twin. Didymos is Greek for twin.... The implication here is that he is Jesus' twin. But this character, of course, also appears in the Gospel of John, he's one of the disciples, the twin. Here he appears as if he's Jesus' twin, and he is one who knows secret teaching, which Jesus hasn't given to all other people. [35]

The Gospel of Thomas also states that persons *'who find the interpretation of these secret words will not taste death.'*

The twin motif occurs throughout the *Acts of Judas Thomas*. Now if you are ready to handle another talking donkey, an ass's colt in the Fourth Act of this book, addresses him as '*twin of Christ*' leaving no doubt that they are considered twin Messiahs at that time; well at least by donkeys anyway. A devil-incubus asks Thomas in the Fifth Act, "*Wherefore are you made like unto the Son of God who has done us wrong? For you resemble him altogether as if you were born of him.*" Others note the strong resemblance, including a murdered girl restored to life after her sojourn to hell in the Sixth Act. Fairly bizarre stuff, but despite the suppression of most of the documents taking this stance, those remaining strongly indicate that Judas Thomas was considered the twin of Christ.

We stated earlier that today's King James Version of the Bible differs in a number of details from the KJV of 1611. The 1611 editions have "*Then cometh Judas*" instead of "*Then cometh Jesus*" in **Matthew 26 : 36.** Whether this is a printing error or there was confusion with the twin brothers can only be guessed at. The ancient, Hymn in Praise of the Manicheans' God, Mani reads;

> "*Hail to your twin and to your Glory; that have come forth with you! You have come with salvation, oh Twin of the Gods! You have come with salvation, oh dearest and most Beloved One! Hail to the bright Gods of whom you are born!*"

There is a tradition that Jesus escaped the crucifixion and disbanded the disciples, sending them to far off lands to spread the gospel. We read in the **Acts of Thomas**:

> *According to the lot, therefore, India fell unto Judas Thomas, which is also the twin: but he would not go, saying that by reason of the weakness of the flesh he could not travel, and 'I am an Hebrew man; how can I go amongst the Indians and preach the truth?' And as he thus reasoned and spake, the Saviour appeared unto him by night and saith to him: "Fear not, Thomas, go thou unto India and preach the word there, for my grace is with thee." But he would not obey, saying: 'Whither thou wouldest send me, send me, but elsewhere, for unto the Indians I will not go'.*

> *And while he thus spake and thought, it chanced that there was there a certain merchant come from India whose name was Abbanes, sent from the King Gundaphorus, and having commandment from him to buy a carpenter and bring him unto him.*

(Gundaphorus is a historical personage who reigned over the Northern part of India in the first century after Christ. Contemporary coins bear his image and the king's name in Greek as Hyndopheres)

Now the Lord seeing him walking in the market place at noon said unto him: Wouldest thou buy a carpenter? And he said to him: Yea. And the Lord said to him: I have a slave that is a carpenter and I desire to sell him. And so saying he showed him Thomas afar off, and agreed with him for three litrae of silver unstamped, and wrote a deed of sale, saying: I, Jesus, the son of Joseph the carpenter, acknowledge that I have sold my slave, Judas by name, unto thee Abbanes, a merchant of Gundaphorus, king of the Indians. And when the deed was finished, the Saviour took Judas Thomas and led him away to Abbanes the merchant, and when Abbanes saw him he said unto him: Is this thy master? And the apostle said: Yea, he is my Lord. And he said: I have bought thee of him. And thy apostle held his peace.

And on the day following the apostle arose early, and having prayed and besought the Lord he said: I will go whither thou wilt, Lord Jesus: thy will be done. And he departed unto Abbanes the merchant, taking with him nothing at all save only his price, for the Lord had given it unto him, saying: Let thy price also be with thee, together with my grace, wheresoever thou goest. [36]

Tradition says that Thomas journeyed as a missionary to both Parthia and India. This is supported by Eusebius of Caesarea who records that Thomas became a missionary in Parthia. The Acts of Thomas state that he was later martyred in India. The Syriac-rite Christians of Malabar, India, to this day claim St. Thomas as their founder. Saint Thomas' Mount in Madras, India is the traditional site of his martyrdom. In Kashmir India, a tomb still exists, surprisingly, aligned East-West as Jewish tombs are and not North-South like Asian tombs. Local customs say it is the tomb of Judas Thomas and some even say of Jesus. As we briefly mentioned, a king by the name of, **Guduphara (Gundaphorus)** actually reigned in the Punjab area south of the Himalayas about the year A.D. 46. [37] This is a quite astonishing correlation and certainly makes the story from the 'Acts of Thomas' worth investigating.

We must exercise caution however, because this could still be allegory, since the twin Messiah theme was something held in awe in those times and is not uncommon amongst the pagan Gods. It is seen in Zoroastrianism, and so too with many Gods from The Buddha to Quetzalcoatl, each being recorded as a twin. The God of Ancient Mexico, Quetzalcoatl was a **twin**; the Buddha's soul-**twin** was Vajrapani. The roles of the 'favrashi' in Zoroastrianism and Vajrapani in Buddhism are not entirely unlike the twin motif of Judas Thomas and Jesus. [38]

The Gospel of Thomas tells us that when Thomas arrived in India, either for missionary work or in service of the King, he gained Indian followers by performing exorcisms and resurrections, but was eventually sentenced to death after converting the wives of King Misdaeus and his kinsman Charisius. This is supported below;

"The extravagance of the legend may be judged from the fact that in more than one place (cap. 31, p. 148) it represents Thomas (Judas Thomas, as he is called here and elsewhere in Syriac tradition) as the twin brother of Jesus. The Thomas in Syriac is equivalent to Didymos in Greek, and means twin. The story itself runs briefly as follows: At the division of the Apostles, India fell to the lot of Thomas, but he declared his inability to go, whereupon his Master Jesus appeared in a supernatural way to Abban, the envoy of Gundafor, an Indian king, and sold Thomas to him to be his slave and serve Gundafor as a carpenter. Then Abban and Thomas sailed away until they came to Andrapolis, where they landed and attended the marriage feast of the ruler's daughter. Coming to India, Thomas undertook to build a palace for Gundafor, but spent the money entrusted to him, on the poor. Gundafor imprisoned him; but the Apostle escaped miraculously and Gundafor was converted. Going about the country to preach, Thomas met with strange adventures from dragons and wild asses. Then he came to the city of King Misdai (Syriac Mazdai), where he converted Tertia the wife of Misdai and Vazan his son. After this he was condemned to death, led out of the city to a hill, and pierced through with spears by four soldiers. He was buried in the tomb of the ancient kings but his remains were afterwards removed to the West. [39]

At the wedding of the ruler's daughter, mentioned above from the Acts of Thomas we see an unsettling incident: Thomas prayed to the Lord Jesus, invoking him as, among other things, *"he that reveals hidden mysteries and makes manifest words that are secret."* At the end of his prayer he blessed the young couple, and then he appeared to leave the room. When the newlyweds thought they were alone, they found to their astonishment that *"Thomas was still standing before them. Rather, he seemed to be Thomas; however, the intruder identified himself as Jesus, having the appearance of Judas Thomas, his twin."* (40)

This document indicates that the twins were close to identical and really leaves some Bible stories open to conjecture. Remember the Bible version that quotes 'Judas' instead of 'Jesus' in **Matthew 26 : 36.** Tony Bushby tells us it was Judas Thomas and not Jesus who was meant to be crucified, and that a switch was arranged. It seems that this selling into slavery was required after Thomas escaped crucifixion by offering a substitute to be killed, thus causing his birthright to be forfeited. Bushby correctly states that this was an old tradition dating back to ancient Sumer and we will cover this later. (41)

Could this explain the strange silence for at least 150 years about the crucifixion of Jesus? Could it be that his twin brother was the one tried by Pilate and could it be that Simon of Cyrene was the substitute (or whipping boy)? This would mean that Jesus was doing Thomas a favour by selling him into service, ensuring his employment with a civilized King who would recognize his past royalty and treat him well. Of course this is further suggested when Jesus gave Thomas the price he got for him. The Acts of Thomas place both Jesus and Thomas in Taxila (now in Pakistan) at the court of King Gundafor in the twenty-sixth year of his rule (47 A.D.). Jesus and Thomas would have been 54 years old, at that time. According to this source, Jesus then travelled on to Kashmir, from where he made periodic journeys to other parts of India. Since the Essene doctrine appears to have been a form of Buddhism similar to that taught at the Alexandria school of Pythagoras, this would then offer no surprises if Jesus sojourned in Asia for some time.

We saw Jesus referred to as Ben Stada in the Talmud and it is interesting to find this story parallelled in an ancient work called the **Safed** or **Mehgheehlla Scroll.** This document was discovered near Lake Tiberius in 1882 by a Jewish, Russian physician Dayve Boris de Waltoff (b. 1865). Tony Bushby reports on this document;

"In this old text, there were two brothers called Yeshai and Judas ben Halachmee who

were the illegitimate twin sons born of a fifteen-year-old girl called Stadea. The closeness of the name Stada in the Talmud to the Stadea in the Safed Scroll is extraordinary, and the slight difference in spelling can be explained by variations in translations. The interesting point here is that the name ben Halachmee was the name of Stadea's later husband, not the biological father of her sons. Unfortunately, no mention is made of the real father's name, but ben Halachmee was the name given to Stadea's illegitimate twin boys." [42] We find further documentation that Jesus was **Yeshai ben Halachmee**, and that the account of his birth in the Bible is an allegorized version of the Hindu account of the birth of Krishna. [43]

In the **Safed Scroll**, the brothers Yeshai and Judas were raised by the Essenes, most likely at Qumran, but in time the heretical religious views of Yeshai angered the Jewish priests to a point where they turned on him. He was handed over to the Romans charged with inciting the people to rebel against the Roman Government. Jesus (Yeshai) obviously considered himself to be the Messiah and he believed a requirement to rid the Holy Land of the Romans was a primary objective of the Jewish Messiah. He was found guilty and sentenced to death, but escaped the Holy Land, and travelled to India. [44]

Was Jesus born on 25 December?

There is something wrong if the only Son of God came to Earth and taught us a better way of life, did earth-shattering miracles and even died for our salvation and nobody can even remember the date. The Eastern Churches claimed it was 6 January, now called the 'Epiphany'. This date corresponded to the 'birth' of Mithras but was also a baptismal date and even in ancient Egypt, the "Festival of the Immersion" was held on this day. The Basilidians celebrated Christ's birthday on the 25 April and according to Clement of Alexandria various other sects celebrated it on the 25 May. In fact we don't even know the year of Jesus' birth. The Bible tells us that Jesus was born while Herod the Great was still alive. Herod died in 4 BCE so if we believe the Bible's accuracy, we can easily dismiss any dates after this time. Some confusion comes from the tax census at the time when Joseph and Mary were required to travel to Bethlehem. This census is actually documented in history. The Syrian governor Quirinius (Cyrenius) was appointed by Rome to oversee the Holy Land and immediately ordered this census in 6 AD. This was however not the year of Christ's birth. Jesus at this time was ready for the Jewish "Born Again" ceremony, the forerunner of the Bar Mitzvah, which occurred at age 12, so it was in fact the "second birth" and not the actual birth that was celebrated at this time. Thus 12 years prior would put his actual birth at 7 BCE (while Herod was still alive). This meets all criteria and it appears from various sources that Jesus was actually born Sunday, 1st. March 7 BCE. Once we realize the Bethlehem episode was the 'second birth' or 'born again' ceremony the Bible record makes more sense;

> **Luke 2 : 1-5** *"And it came to pass in those days, that there went out a decree from Caesar Augustus that all the world should be taxed. (And this taxing was first made when Cyrenius was governor of Syria.) And all went to be taxed, every one into his own city. And Joseph also went up from Galilee, out of the city of Nazareth, into Judaea, unto the city of David, which is called Bethlehem; (because he was of the house and lineage of David) to be taxed with Mary his espoused wife, being great with child.*

There is however considerable error in the above passage, showing many signs of later tampering. Firstly we know the family did not leave from Nazareth because we have seen that it didn't exist at that time and if it had, the early contemporary name of Natzrat would have been recorded. Next Joseph was not a lowly carpenter sent to his birthplace to be taxed. His belonging to the tribe of Judah and the Kingly linage of David makes it highly unlikely that he would be required to make this journey to be taxed. If he made this journey at all it was for the "born again" ceremony of Jesus, who was in line to be King. It is of course possible that Mary was actually "great with child" but this unborn child would have been one of the brothers or sisters and not Jesus. Because of the inferred illegitimacy of Jesus there were factions who switched allegiance between Jesus and his brother James. Even their father Joseph was undecided. James was however born in 1 AD. Jewish custom called for a 6 year wait for the second Royal son and in this case a little longer for the child James to be 'correctly' born in the royal month of September. [45] This further supports the 7 BCE timeframe for the birth of Jesus.

We should note too that a mountain of literature was available at the time of Christ, supporting John the Baptist as the Messiah. It is claimed too that John was born in Bethlehem and it could be that the scribes found it necessary to carry this location over to Jesus as well. The apocryphal **Book of James** (the protoevangelium) describes the slaughter of the innocents much the same as the Gospels, however in this Book the messianic infant sought by Herod was actually John, and not Jesus.

Before the event of Christianity an Asiatic religion swept into Rome and made its home on the Vatican hill before that location was commandeered for Christianity. Mithras was an Aryan Sun-God, called by the Romans, **Sol Invictus** "The Invincible Sun". The date, **25 December** was the date of the European winter solstice of the sun. Accordingly, it was a major celebration day for several pagan cults but particularly for the Mithras, Sol Invictus worshippers. In 274 AD, Aurelian adopted the 25 December as the day to celebrate the renewal of 'The Invincible Sun'. His successor, the Byzantine Emperor Constantine was a Sol Invictus worshiper and was called the 'Sun Emperor'. When for political reasons, he later changed the official religion of the Roman Empire to Christianity it was a further concession he granted to the sun worshipers that the circle of the Sun emblem could be incorporated with the cross and in time became the Christian halo. In addition their cult's main celebration day would remain in the Christian calendar by stating that it was Jesus' birthday. This was nonsense but it fooled the world. This point is further supported by **Luke 2 : 8** *Now there were in the same country shepherds living out in the fields, keeping watch over their flock by night.* The 25th December is approaching mid winter in the Holy Land being well north of the Tropic of Cancer and the animals would have been kept in stables at this time. The shepherds stayed in the fields in nice weather and of course March (if Jesus was born 1 March) would have been their springtime.

The Jewish Rabbi

There is now a myriad of erroneous documentation that the Jewish Rabbi, Jesus, spoke Aramaic and all this without a shred of supporting evidence. I have read so many times that Jesus spoke Aramaic that I seriously wonder about where the authors get their information. To a Jew, this is the ultimate blasphemy and is so often repeated by otherwise intelligent scholars, that it just dumbfounds me. Jesus' mother was the Jewess Miriam (Mary) the daughter of the High Priest and of the priestly tribe of Levi. Jesus was a Jew and being Jewish, he obviously spoke Hebrew. Why would he speak the language of another culture? This is just nonsense although a high percentage of scholars now believe it from hearing it and reading it so often. Aramaic was a language widely used in diplomacy of the ancient Near-East and was used extensively for international communication. Some technical words in Hebrew used the Aramaic loan words but otherwise it was an entirely separate language. It is of course possible that Jesus as a learned man had some knowledge of Aramaic however as a Jew his primary language was most certainly Hebrew. Professor Martin Buber stated;

> *"Jesus undoubtedly, when addressing his people, spoke in the Hebrew tongue."* [46]

Dr David Flusser of Hebrew University said;

> *"We can only be as certain that Jesus and his disciples spoke Hebrew as we can be certain that he was a Jew and lived in Eretz Yisrael. If Jesus was a Jew who lived in this place during that purported time, the question then is, 'did he speak his mother tongue'?"* [47]

To any thinking person this is a fairly simple rhetorical question and the answer is that if Jesus was a real Jewish person of course he spoke the language of that time and place and that was of course, Hebrew!

The argument that much of the Old Testament was written in Aramaic (which I have read again and again) also doesn't stack up. The truth is that many books of the Bible contained a little Aramaic, usually in the form of Aramaic loan words, however that doesn't convey the reality of the matter. The Old Testament books were originally written in Hebrew but for example, proclamations by foreign monarchs would be shown in the more suitable Aramaic. The exceptions were Daniel and Ezra which had sections of Aramaic but were certainly written in the Hebrew script. We can see this in **Ezra 4 : 11–16** showing a letter from Samaritan officials to the King Artaxerxes and **17–22** showing his reply. Much of the New Testament was written in Greek with a few words drawn from Aramaic. Not just ordinary Greek however, the special first century Greek vernacular is known as 'Koine' and this is what was used in the Hellenistic period in the Holy Land. It is argued however that even the New Testament was drawn from Hebrew and checking the Greek format shows up an original Hebrew structure. For example, the ease of translating the Gospels from Greek back to Hebrew indicates that an original Hebrew was used.

We saw earlier how the Church of Rome hi-jacked the Jewish religion, adopted its history and claimed its patriarchs for the new religion of Christianity. In addition it turned the original Jewish scripture into the Christian Latin Bible in the time of Constantine. This was the commencement of the movement that translated the various names of God to the insipid and meaningless '**Lord**', changed Rabbi to '**Master**' and also suggested that Jesus did not speak **Hebrew.** This is all just part of the conspiracy to mask the Jewish-ness of Jesus. Jesus was a Rabbi, which meant he had attained and received the *smechah* or full ordination. In the Greek texts of the Bible alone, Jesus is addressed 14 times as "Rabbi; despite this today's English Bible's have his disciples call him, 'Master'. Now Rabbi doesn't mean Master at all; it means Rabbi. Jesus was known to study the scriptures and gave the lesson in the Tabernacle, and this quite obviously in Hebrew. Our stance is confirmed by the Jewish writer and archaeologist Vendyl Jones;

> "...the Jews gave the world the Bible. The Jewish Scripture is the premise for both, Christianity and the Islam as well as Judaism. Many other religions use it to some degree. The language of Jesus and the original Gospels was Hebrew. Except for Paul's writings to the Gentiles, the Greek testaments are full of Hebrew words and structure. Why is this so? What other nation on earth could say, "We gave you the word of God." [48]

The Romans made Jesus as Roman as possible. The great artists painted images to fit the thoughts of their vernacular. Never depicted were the hooked nose and Semitic features. For a white Caucasian audience the images show a white Caucasian Jesus. In Fiji recently I went with my family to the Catholic Church of Naiserlagi, 25km east of Raki-raki, where we viewed a fresco of a crucified Christ. There he is depicted as Polynesian, looking quite Fijian, black skin and resplendent in a masi patterned sulu, with a tanoa bowl of Yaqona (kava) complete with cowry shell at the foot of the cross. Off to the side his mother Mary is weaving a pandanus floor mat.

Jean Charlot's depiction of a "Black Jesus" in a Fijian Church.

Jean Charlot's mural.
Was Jesus a carpenter?

The Church of Saint Francis Xavier
at Naiserelagi, Fiji

This mural was commissioned in 1962 by the then chaplain, Monsignor Franz Wagner (former chaplain and singing tutor to the Von Trapp children in the *Sound of Music*) who had been sent to Fiji as a disciplinary posting by the Catholic Church. His friend the French muralist Jean Charlotte and his son Martin came to Fiji seeking him out and were on hand to add their artistic touches to the Naiserlagi Catholic Mission church as it was plastered. Depicting Gods in a local, contemporary vernacular is not a new phenomenon;

"Nowhere in the world were there gods who did not speak the language, follow the customs, enjoy the food and dress in the fashion of their constituency – over and above their clear disposition to favour their own kind in any controversy. Clearly, people around the world created gods in accordance with their own needs, and consistent with their own cultural settings." [(49)]

Disciples & Desposyni

Although Jesus had many followers loosely called Christians, the Bible tells us he had twelve intimate personal followers called disciples. There were twelve tribes of Israel, so it seems someone, somewhere, decided that there should be twelve disciples. The earlier Talmud however states;

"Our rabbis taught: Yeshu had five disciples - Mattai, Nakkai, Netzer, Buni, and Todah." [(50)]

Of the five disciples only Mattai (Matthew) and Todah (Thaddaeus) correspond to the twelve listed in the Bible. The case for Jesus having just five disciples is supported by the fact that other Jewish Rabbis in the Talmud such as Yohanan ben Zakkai and Akiba each had five disciples. [(51)] In addition many other spiritual leaders from antiquity like Confucius had five disciples. The Bible intimates that Jesus' cousin John the Baptist also had 5 disciples, two of whom later abandoned him and joined Jesus. The first part of the Christian Bible is derived from the Jewish writings so it is not plausible for us to think that the original source is the one in error. What is more of a revelation however, is that the disciples of the Bible appear to be part of a dynasty, several being close relations of Jesus, and many being zealots. These zealots (zealous before the Law) were a militant group who wanted to free the Holy Land from the Romans. Jesus himself is often depicted as quite militant and possibly his whole band were zealots.

Luke 22 : 36 *Then said he (Jesus) unto them, But now, he that hath a purse, let him take it, and likewise his scrip: and he that hath no sword, let him sell his garment, and buy one.*

This may not fit our mind picture of gentle peaceful disciples extolling peace and love in any way shape or form, however there is much evidence to support it.

In the work '*Ecclesiastical History*', **Eusebius Pamphilius**, Bishop of Caesarea (260 – 339 AD) confirmed that the ancient Greek word '*Desposyni*' meaning 'heirs' was reserved in the writings of **Julius Africanus** to mean those of the same family descent as Jesus. The term was specifically confined to the immediate heirs and relatives of Jesus as one might today determine the hub of a royal family or dynasty. [52] We find that the disciples of Jesus were included in the Desposyni and accordingly we must accept that they were relations and heirs. Since we can show that several actually were relations, I propose that with the Desposyni and with the Disciples we are looking at a Messianic family dynasty, trying to regain the throne of Antigonus from the Romans. Since there were known zealots amongst them we can further conclude that their primary purpose was to overthrow the rule of Rome by force, and locate Jesus on the throne of the Holy Land. When thoroughly outgunned and all became hopeless, they then claimed that their kingdom is not of this world, and so was born the Kingdom of God.

The Roman Church was terrified that the family of Jesus may put up a leader to take back the Jewish religion and blow the whistle on their fraudulent hijacking. Particularly after the trouble and rebellion in the Holy Land, the Roman Emperors from Vespasian (69-79 AD) through to Hadrian (117-138 AD) tried to capture those considered to be Desposyni or relatives of Jesus and descendants of King David. The second century historian Hegesippus, reported in *Hypomnenata* (memoirs) that Vespasian ordered that no member of the Messianic dynasty should be allowed to live, and all descendants of King David should be found and destroyed. Domitian (81-96 AD) specifically instigated an inquisition of the remaining family members of Jesus' brother, Jude (Thaddaeus). This event is recorded by Eusebius who states that when these family members were questioned about "Christ and his Kingdom" they replied that "*the kingdom was not of the earth, but of the sky, and at the end of the world, Jesus would appear to give to everyone according to his works.*" Domitian considered that they were quite mad and backed right off, but his successor, Trajan (98-117 AD), still saw them as a threat and had them all killed. [53] The persecution of early Christians by authorities certainly led to subterfuge of identity apparent in the many name changes and strange identities adopted by these believers; and this is what makes identification so very difficult today.

Fr. Malachi Martin, a Jesuit professor who served with Pope John XXIII relates that in 318 AD a delegation of Desposyni journeyed to Rome where they were given an audience with Bishop Silvester in the Lateran Palace. Their spokesman called Joses argued that the Church should be rightfully centered in Jerusalem not in Rome and that a member of their Desposyni and genuine descendant of the Saviour should be the rightful Bishop of Jerusalem. They also suggested that the Bishops of other centers like Alexandria, Antioch and Ephesus should also be selected from those related to Christ, and descendants of King David. [54] Bishop Silvester was in no position to override the demands of Emperor Constantine no matter how reasonable their requests; needless to say these requirements were not met.

They were actually told that the teachings of Christ had now been superceded by a doctrine that was more amenable to the requirements of Imperial Rome and that the power of salvation no longer rested in Jesus Christ but in fact with the Emperor (Constantine).

Now this is documented fact; it actually happened! How do you think this hi-jacking of the teachings of Jesus into a Roman powerbase would sit with Christians today? It seems to sit just fine because the believers are still being fed this garbage by the Roman Church today, and just look how many turn up for yet another helping each week. We said earlier that power overrules orthodoxy and here is your proof!

"God saw that a man, son of a woman, was to come forward in the future, who would attempt to make himself God and lead the whole world astray, and if he says he is God he is a liar. And he will lead men astray, and say that he will depart and will return at the end of days."

The learned Rabbi Eliezar, writing about AD 160 (Quoted by Christian Author Michael Green, *'Who is This Jesus?'* Nashville: Thomas Nelson Publishers, 1992, p. 60)

CHAPTER FIVE

THE CRUCIFIXION

"And if Christ be not risen, then is our preaching vain and your faith is also vain".

1 Corinthians 15 : 14

Jesus Unknown to First Century Historians

The whole tenet of the Christian's belief in redemption is that Jesus (the son of God) came in the flesh and became a blood sacrifice for the remission of sin. This we were taught is the thing that drives the Devil wild; the power in the shed blood of Christ.

> **1 John 4 : 2** *Every spirit that confesseth that Jesus Christ is come in the flesh is of God and every spirit that confesseth not that Jesus Christ is come in the flesh is not of God.*

Despite this, in the Bible we find silly anomalies like the demons that were present in the possessed man Legion, crying out before they were cast into the herd of swine;

> **Matthew 8 : 29** *"And behold they cried out saying, 'What have we to do with thee Jesus thou Son of God? Art thou come hither to torment us before the time?"*

This passage has demons acknowledging that Jesus is the Son of God which by the John passage above indicates that the Demons must be of God!

Reading from **Luke 24 : 36** we find Christ, after the crucifixion, in the flesh eating honeycomb and fish before being parted from the disciples and then being carried away to his position in heaven. He even quotes, *"for a spirit hath not flesh and bones, as ye see me have"*. Why then does Paul tell us;

1 Corinthians 15 : 50 *Flesh and blood cannot inherit the kingdom of heaven.*

Well it sure looks like someone got it wrong! In addition Jesus supposedly didn't rise to be with his father until some weeks after his death.

After telling the 'thief' on the cross that, that day he would be with him in paradise, he stayed on for many days. Now this is a crucial point; if Jesus survived the crucifixion, this is a major problem for the church!

It is imperative to the Christian religion that Jesus died for the remission of sins as the ultimate blood sacrifice. On the third day he rose again, conquering death, and therein is a Christian's salvation. He was supposedly the first to overcome death and rise to Heaven making this a one time, unique and momentous occasion. Are you ready for a shock! It wasn't always this way in Church doctrine with early Bibles claiming the death of Jesus was a ransom paid to the Devil, and nothing whatever to do with salvation. This means that all the remission of sin is a fraudulent later addition, and that is another real problem for the Christian Church. If the Bible records of the crucifixion are actually fraudulent as they certainly appear to be, then we must be concerned that the entire resurrection package in the Christian religion is fraudulent and the concern is that accordingly any Christ endorsed salvation is totally worthless.

Let's look at some facts:

Firstly the crucifixion of Jesus was unknown to first century historians and church fathers. The contemporary writers, from the time that Jesus is thought to have lived, left a veritable library of literature, in which not one mention of Jesus or of his apostles or his disciples appears. These writers and historians include: **Arrian, Apollonius, Hermogones, Damis, Aulus Gellius, Appion of Alexandria, Philo Judaeus, Juvenal, Quintilian, Silius Italicus, Phlegon, Pausanias, Dio Chrysostom, Favorinus, Seneca, Dion Pruseus, Martial, Lucanus, Statius, Phaedrus, Florus Lucius, Columella, Lysias, Theon of Myrna (Smyran), Pliny the Elder, Paterculus, Persius, Justus of Tiberius, Ptolemy, Valerius Maximus, Quintius Curtius Rufus, Valerius Flaccus, Pomponius Mela** and even the Roman Consul, **Publis Petronius**. [1]

Furthermore the crucifixion was not mentioned by the usual learned historians, the likes of **Tacitus, Suetonius, Epictectus, Cluvius and Plutarch**. [2] We could add to the list **Phaedrus, Pliny the Younger** and **Lucian**. None of them even mentioned Jesus, his remarkable works or his crucifixion. Now we must make the effort to grasp what is being said here and comprehend its implications. We were taught that Jesus was the 'King of the Jews' yet he is also absent from any list of Jewish Kings. So the question now is, if Jesus Christ really existed and did the miraculous things attributed to him, and was even anointed as the King of the Jews, why did the great historians who were his contemporaries' not even hint at his existence or in any way mention the miracles or the works he is alleged to have done? All these writers and historians were at the right place in roughly the right timeframe and could hardly have failed to know something of Jesus and the amazing events said by the Bible writers to have taken place in the city of Jerusalem. In the case of **Justus of Tiberius** mentioned above, he was a native of the Holy Land in Jesus' time, and wrote a comprehensive history of that period. He actually lived at the time in Galilee, the supposed home of Jesus. Though his work perished, **Photius of Constantinople**, (his name means 'enlightened') a Christian scholar and critic of the ninth century, who scrutinized Justus' work, declared;

> *"He (Justus) makes not the least mention of the appearance of Christ, of what things happened to him, or of his wonderful works that he did."* [3]

With a little research we find too that contrary to popular belief amongst Christians, the crucifixion received no mention whatever from **Flavius Josephus** who covered that location and period of history impeccably. It is sometimes mis-quoted that Josephus recorded;

> *"Now there was about this time Jesus, a wise man, if it be lawful to call him a man.... He was the Christ, and when Pilate condemned him to the cross...he appeared to them alive again the third day."*

Christians, please don't be fooled, <u>this is a forgery</u> that was added to the Josephus text many years later. It sounds just a bit too pat, and rightly so because Josephus never wrote it. Christian defenders, as early as **Clement of Alexandria** (150-215 AD) never cited it and certainly would have if they had that record. **Origen** (185-254 AD), who dealt extensively with the works of Josephus, documented categorically that Josephus (who of course was a Jew) did not believe Jesus to be the Messiah nor proclaim him as such. **Bishop Eusebius**, in 324 AD, first mentions this passage attributed to Josephus (twice), and is likely the forger of it. [4] The authenticity of this fraudulent passage attributed to Josephus is completely discounted by even Christian scholars today.

The Bible is left standing pretty much alone on the life and death of Jesus, and on top of the other errors and irregularities we have already encountered, is not looking solid at all. Scholars have always questioned whether the Bible can be actually proved right or wrong or even if some parts can be confirmed or denied by history. The Dominican father, Roland de Vaux, who worked on the Dead Sea Scrolls, one of the most prominent figures in the history of Biblical antiquity, stated that the capacity of the Jewish and Christian faiths to actually survive was dependent upon the agreement between 'religious' and 'objective' history. He stated;

". . . if Israel's historical faith does not have its roots in history, then it is wrong and the same is true of our faith." [5]

As we uncover a Bible full of problematical documentation we experience the errors, contradictions and inconsistencies, and as we research the Bible's departure from history, we are forced to concede that the answer to the above is almost certainly in the negative. What now makes this situation more astonishing is that another important crucifixion <u>was</u> mentioned by many of the writers named above. As previously stated, **Antigonus** the heroic Maccabee, with the support of Julius Cesar, regained control of the Holy Land in 40 BCE just 33 years before the likely birth of Jesus. The title Maccabee meant *'Hammer of God'*, certainly indicating strength and steadfastness. Antigonus ousted Herod from the Holy Land, claiming himself to be the rightful **'King of the Jews'** and re-claimed his crown in Jerusalem. With the demise of Caesar soon after, however, he met with strong opposition from Herod and his ally Marc Antony. No matter what he did, Antigonus was totally 'outgunned' by the power of Rome and finally after 6 years the inevitable happened. In the words of Dio Cassius;

"Antony now gave the kingdom to a certain Herod, and having stretched Antigonus on a cross he scourged him, a thing never done before to any other King by the Romans, and he then put him to death". [6]

So here we have a clearly documented 'scourging and crucifixion' by the Romans, in the Holy Land, of a Jewish leader who called himself the 'King of the Jews'. As well as the above documentation by Dio Cassius, this event was covered by Plutarch, Strabo and others. In fact, for years to come, a deep sympathy was felt throughout the Holy Land for 'the crucified King of the Jews', but this certainly referred to Antigonus and not Jesus. We can't help but wonder if this story was hi-jacked into the Bible. It would seem fairly apparent that it was, but we have a lot more to cover.

We discovered earlier that parts of the *'Sepher Toldoth Jeshu'* as recorded in the Jewish Talmud and quoted by Celsus, places Jesus as a contemporary of Janneus the Sadducee, the King of Judea who reigned from 106 to 79 BCE and of Simeon ben Shetach who lived in 90 BCE. Ironically King Janneus and his wife Queen Alexandra Salome had a son Aristobulus II who was in fact the father of Antigonus. Yes! This means that King Janneus was actually the grandfather of Antigonus and Jesus was said to be a contemporary. If history had repeated, and the crucifixion of Antigonus had actually been followed by the crucifixion of Jesus; a second 'King of the Jews' scourged and crucified, this would have been even more newsworthy. Why then is there not one mention of this outside the Bible? The Antigonus scourging and crucifixion at the hands of Marc Antony is absolutely documented empirical fact; it is historical fact. The crucifixion of Jesus is recorded in the Gospels of the Bible only. How can we account for total silence for 150 years after the supposed event by every known writer of the time? This is more particularly implausible, when a duplication of the manner of death of Antigonus, by Jesus, would have made it doubly newsworthy?

So were Antigonus and Jesus the same person? I don't really think so; Antigonus was certainly a Messiah and certainly 'The King of the Jews' however he was not a Rabbi. Although he carried the title "Hammer of God" he was never called the Son of God. Actually neither was Jesus until 325 AD when deified by Rome. It is certainly crazy too, that Jesus was supposedly crucified for saying he was the Son of God when this deification did not take place until almost three centuries later in 325 AD. It seems likely that Jesus' decent from Augustus Caesar, through Panthera is not only correct, it is what made Pilate sit up and take notice. He certainly did not wish to be responsible for the capital punishment of the grandson of the deified God, Caesar. This is what could have labelled Jesus the Son of God and it is possibly this that founded the major religions of the world. It now seems even more likely that the entire story of scourging and crucifixion is veiled allegory, plagiarized from the Antigonus record.

Among the works saved from the fire in the Alexandrian Library was a work entitled 'The Life of Apollonius of Tyana', written by the Athenian author Flavius Philostratus (c.170-245AD). The amazing thing about this book written at the beginning of the Third Century AD, a hundred years prior to the Council of Nicea, is that it too made no mention whatsoever of the existence of Jesus, or of Christianity. Dr Raymond W Bernard, B.A., M.A., Ph D. tells us that instead, it presented **Apollonius of Tyana** as the universally acclaimed, charismatic leader and world teacher of the First Century, revered from one end of the Roman Empire to the other by everyone, from the lowest slave to the Emperor himself. [7] Dr. Bernard goes on to state;

"For Philostratus in his book described a character born in the very year of the birth of Christ who, in every respect, was the equal, if not the superior, of the Christian messiah."

The Bible's life and deeds of Jesus precisely mirror those recorded elsewhere for Apollonius of Tyana.

Apollonius, was born in Tyana, Cappadocia, in the south of present day Turkey and was considered a demi-God in his own lifetime. His birth was supposedly announced by an angel and informed scholars today believe that New Testament teachings stem not from Jesus, but rather from Apollonius of Tyana. He went on to preach the word of God but also prayed to the Sun, as did the Manicheans.

Apollonius performed miracles and healings and was a supporter of Essene doctrine, based on the Buddhist school of Pythagoras. He set up a school himself at Ephesus. Almost all available records about Apollonius of Tyana were destroyed by Constantine soon after the Council of Nicea, as it specifically threatened the Christian message. [8]

Some details of the infancy of Apollonius of Tyana are included in a work by Maximus of Agae and additional information about his life, death and resurrection is included in the memoirs of his disciple Damis of Nineveh. Many serious scholars believe that the records we have of the life of Apollonius and that of Jesus in the New Testament are equivalent writings. Several suggest that they could have been one and the same person. Thus our research indicates that the personage of Jesus was allegorically based on the 'Teacher of Righteousness' and on Apollonius of Tyana, with the crucifixion of Antigonus thrown in and then the characters Yeshai ben Halachmee and Jehoshua ben Panthera added. As a result we still have no assurance of the timeframe for the life and death of Jesus; likely because it is pure allegory;

> "Using the Bible references, Jesus was born in 7 BCE ... however there are sufficient sources making him a contemporary of King Janneus, to question the Biblical record. H. P. Blavatsky states that Jesus was born around 107 BCE, and quotes an obscure passage from a 'secret work', which could be interpreted to mean that he died in his 33rd year (i.e. in 75-74 BCE)" [9]

With some diligence in our studies we can actually identify the secret work referred to in the above quote? The secret information was that;

> "Shankaracharya, the great Vedantic teacher of India, who was born in 510 BCE, chose to die in his 33rd year. A commentary explains: 'At whatever age one puts off his outward body by free will, at that age will he be made to die in his next incarnation against his will'" [10]

In the Talmud we find a most unusual character called Balaam. This person appears to bear little resemblance to the pagan priest Balaam in the Bible, whom we saw with the talking donkey in the introduction of this book. In the Talmud, Balaam seems to denote Jeshu – and is said to have died when he was 33 years old. The Bible does not indicate how old Jesus was when he died, though it is accepted that he began his ministry at the age of 30 as is common for Rabbi's. The accepted opinion among Christians today is that his mission lasted 3 years, and that he was crucified in his 33rd year although there is no real evidence for this. **Bishop Irenaeus** specifically stated that Jesus' ministry lasted 20 years, or until he was 50 years of age. Irenaeus claimed he heard it from the martyr **Polycarp** who had received the information directly from **St. John**. This is fairly unlikely and the truth is we don't really know for certain when Jesus was born, or when he died, or even if he was actually crucified.

The Sacrificial Lamb of Passover

From the time of the original Passover in Egypt, around the fourteenth century BCE, the Jews celebrated the sacrifice of a Passover lamb;

Exodus 12 : 21 *Then Moses called for all the elders of Israel, and said unto them, Draw out and take you a lamb according to your families, and kill the passover.*

2 Chronicles 35 : 7 *And Josiah gave to the people, of the flock, lambs and kids, all for the passover offerings,*

We should now consider that the crucifixion of Christ is not only inspired by the crucifixion of Antigonus the 'King of the Jews', but even more so is an allegoric device based on the sacrifice of the Passover lamb. This is what St. Paul said in his letters;

1 Corinthians 5 : 7 *For even Christ our passover (lamb) is sacrificed for us:*

Ask yourself this, "When did the crucifixion of Christ supposedly take place?"

John 19 : 14 *And it was the preparation of the passover, and about the sixth hour: and he (Pontius Pilate) saith unto the Jews, Behold your King!*

Of course it was right at the time of Passover; this being the perfect vehicle to magnify the impact of the atonement sacrifice supposedly made by the crucified King of the Jews. Accordingly the divine drama was enacted precisely on 13 Nissan the time of the Passover. Would you rather believe that the Romans just happened to randomly choose this date or that they worked to fulfill the Jewish doctrine? How accommodating! The lamb was of course symbolic of the 'innocent' being slaughtered to redeem the guilty'.

The Bible Record

At the time of Christ, the Jewish Sanhedrin had the power to order death by "stoning" and there are many cases of this capital punishment in the Bible. The Romans say the Jews killed Jesus and this is meant to explain away their anti Semitic feeling to this day. This is not true as the Roman method of capital punishment for crimes against the Empire was "crucifixion". Full stop. In reality the Romans crucified Antigonus and in the Bible the Romans crucified Jesus. The story of Pilate washing his hands does not alter a thing. If the crucifixion is in any way true then Jesus was crucified for seditious crimes against the Roman Empire. In like manner to Antigonus, the greatest of Jesus' crimes against Rome was possibly his linage as the King of the Jews. In truth; it said so, on the sign the Bible claims they placed over his head. Today clergy promote that this sign was meant to mock and deride Jesus. I believe that there is no hint of that. It simply outlines his crime as a deterrent to others as was the Roman practice. See what you think;

> **John 19 : 19 – 22** *And Pilate wrote a title, and put it on the cross. And the writing was 'JESUS OF NAZARETH - THE KING OF THE JEWS'. This title was then read by many of the Jews: for the place where Jesus was crucified was nigh to the city: and it was written in Hebrew, and Greek, and Latin. Then said the chief priests of the Jews to Pilate, 'Write not, The King of the Jews; but that he said, I am King of the Jews.' Pilate answered, 'what I have written I have written.'*

Pilate's observation indicates that there was argument not by the Romans but by the Jews over his legitimacy as King. Also we would hope and expect, that Pilate would have written 'Jesus the Nazarene', not the ridiculous, 'Jesus of Nazareth'.

Whatever Pilate wrote, the Gospels don't even agree on the inscription above the cross:

> **Matthew 27 : 37** *"This is Jesus the King of the Jews."*
>
> **Mark 15 : 26** *"The King of the Jews."*
>
> **Luke 23 : 38** *"This is the King of the Jews."*
>
> **John 19 : 19** *"Jesus of Nazareth, the King of the Jews."*

A sign stating 'King of the Jews' over the head of Antigonus would certainly have been truthful and this reinforces that this was the source of the crucifixion myth. The record of Jesus' final words at the crucifixion differs too;

> **Matthew 27 : 46-50** *"My God, my God, (Eli! Eli!) Why hast thou forsaken me?"*
>
> **Mark 15 : 34-37** *"My God, my God, (Eloi! Eloi!) Why hast thou forsaken me?"*
>
> **Luke 23 : 46** *"Father, into thy hands I commit my spirit."*
>
> **John 19 : 30** *"It is finished."*

The Matthew record is unlikely since it was originally recorded *"Eli, Eli, lama sa-bach-tha-ni?"* "Eli! Eli! lama" is Hebrew then "sabachthani" is Aramaic the language of the Arameans who were established in Mesopotamia in the 13th Century BCE and later spread into Syria, Palestine and much later into Persia. Marks account is no better because in this record the "Eloi, Eloi" is Aramaic; "lama" is Hebrew, and "sabachthani" is again Aramaic. The Hebrew Holy books render this phrase as Jesus may have said it in Hebrew, *"Eli! Eli! lama 'ahzavtini"*. The problem is that in the second and third centuries there was considerable translating from Hebrew to Aramaic before translating into Greek from which our English versions came in turn. There are vast differences between the Aramaic versions and the Greek and English versions, even to the extent that the book of **'3 Corinthians'** in Aramaic does not exist in the other languages. [11] Now the versions of Jesus' words from Matthew and Mark are of further interest because believe it or not they are not original. In the Book of Psalms, these were the very words (in Hebrew) of King David;

Psalms 22 : 1 *"Eli! Eli! lama 'ahzavtini". My God, my God, why hast thou forsaken me? Why art thou so far from helping me, and from the words of my roaring?*

What is the likelihood of Jesus wreaked with pain and frustration on the cross, at the point of death, repeating the very words of King David for some prophetic reason? There is further thought that the actual words spoken by Jesus were *Eli Eli lamah azabutha-ni?* Almost the same phonetically. Surprisingly this in English means *My God, my God, how thou dost glorify me!* This is relevant because it is the final part of the 'mystery school' initiation ceremony outlined in the ancient Egyptian Book of the Dead. It was cried out in a crucifixion ritual whilst tied to an Ankh; an Egyptian cross. [12] This is a bit too close for comfort and as our study continues it becomes more and more likely that the death of Jesus on the cross, did not happen in reality. It follows precisely the ritual of an Egyptian mystery school.

The Talmud spells out that in accordance with Jewish law; Jesus was *"stoned and then hanged on a tree"*. In hymns, we sang the composers words about Christ's crucifixion, metaphorically stating how they 'nailed him to a tree.' Now we must wonder just how metaphoric this was. Both Paul and Peter, whose original letters and writings were used when the gospels were eventually compiled, stated that Jesus was 'hanged on a tree'.

Acts 5 : 30; *The God of our fathers raised up Jesus whom ye slew and hanged on a tree,*

Acts 10 : 39; *....whom they slew and hanged on a tree.*

Is there something we are not being told? Somewhat surprisingly the Bible states that this is God's way of dealing with a rebellious son;

Deuteronomy 21 : 22; *a rebellious son should be killed by stoning and hanging in a tree.*

Galatians 3 : 13; *Christ hath redeemed us from the curse of the law, being made a curse for us; for it is written, Cursed is every one that hangeth on a tree.*

King David's son Absalom was slain when he rebelled against his father.

Samuel 18 : 10; *And a certain man saw it, and told Joab, and said, Behold, I saw Absalom hanged in an oak tree.*

Incidentally, Absalom was then thrown in a pit and stoned.

What They Didn't Tell Us

There is a thought that the crime that led to the capital punishment of Jesus was perhaps not against Rome but against Jewish law when Jesus took a handwritten scroll from the Temple of Jerusalem. This was indicated by an ancient writing titled *"The Narrative of Joseph of Arimathea"*;

"At the fourth and fifth hours they went out and found Jesus walking in the street. Towards evening they obtained a guard of soldiers. They came to Jesus and saying, "Hail Rabbi" they took Jesus to the High Priest who examined him. Jesus was held captive upon Sarra's word...On the next day, being Wednesday at the ninth hour, they brought him to the Priests hall and asked; "Why did you take away the Torah scroll?" He was silent." [13]

In the first chapter of *"The Narrative of Joseph of Arimathea"* it actually records that Judas Iscariot was the accuser and mentions Sarah the prophetess as the daughter of Caiaphas, who stirs up the crowd against Jesus;

And on the third day, before Jesus was laid hold of, Judas says to the Jews: Come, let us hold a council; for perhaps it was not the robber that stole the law, but Jesus himself, and I accuse him. And when these words had been spoken, Nicodemus, who kept the keys of the sanctuary, came in to us, and said to all: Do not do such a deed. For Nicodemus was true, more than all the multitude of the Jews. And the daughter of Caiaphas, Sarah by name, cried out, and said: He himself said before all against this holy place, I am able to destroy this temple, and in three days to raise it. The Jews say to her: Thou hast credit with all of us. For they regarded her as a prophetess. And assuredly, after the council had been held, Jesus was laid hold of. (14)

The second chapter continues;

And on the following day, the fourth day of the week, they brought Him at the ninth hour into the hall of Caiaphas. And Annas and Caiaphas say to Him: Tell us, why hast thou stolen our law, and renounced the ordinances of Moses and the prophets? And Jesus answered nothing. (15)

All sorts of confusion break loose and Sarra (Sarah) is threatened;

And the evening of the fourth day being ended, all the multitude sought to burn the daughter of Caiaphas, on account of the loss of the law; for they did not know how they were to keep the Passover. And she said to them: Wait, my children, and let us destroy this Jesus, and the law will be found, and the holy feast will be fully accomplished. And secretly Annas and Caiaphas gave considerable money to Judas Iscariot, saying: Say as thou saidst to us before, I know that the law has been stolen by Jesus, that the accusation may be turned against him, and not against this maiden, who is free from blame. And Judas having received this command, said to them: Let not all the multitude know that I have been instructed by you to do this against Jesus; but release Jesus, and I persuade the multitude that it is so. And craftily they released Jesus. (16)

Now this scenario is actually more believable than the Bible's rendition where Jesus has been accused of being a King and amazingly the Jews say 'we have no king but Caesar'. This is something they would never have said and makes that report highly implausible. In addition it explains those either side of him being termed robbers and there is a plausible reason why Jesus would steal a handwritten scroll. Let's look further at this document;

"And going out at the fourth hour, and at the fifth, he finds Jesus walking in the street. And as evening was coming on, Judas says to the Jews: Give me the aid of soldiers with swords and staves, and I will give him up to you. They therefore gave him officers for the purpose of seizing Him. And as they were going along, Judas says to them: Lay hold of the man whom I shall kiss, for he has stolen the law and the prophets. Going

up to Jesus, therefore, he kissed Him, saying: Hail, Rabbi! It being the evening of the fifth day. And having laid hold of Him, they gave Him up to Caiaphas and the chief priests, Judas saying: This is he who stole the law and the prophets. And the Jews gave Jesus an unjust trial, saying: Why hast thou done these things? And he answered nothing. [17]

So now we must ask, "Why did Jesus need an original Hebrew scroll of the Torah?" We are told that Jesus spent his early life in Egypt and it seems likely that there he gained initiation in the Egyptian mystery schools. Recall that he supposedly removed sacred teachings by scratching the information on his skin. In the Jewish, Palestinian Gemera it states;

"He who scratches on the skin in the fashion of writing is guilty, but he who makes marks on the skin in the fashion of writing, is exempt from punishment. Rabbi Eliezer said to them: But has not Ben Stada (Jesus) brought (magic) spells out of Egypt just in this way?" [18]

These marks on the skin were presumably not writing as in letters or words, since they are referred to as 'marks in the fashion of writing' which seems to indicate diagrams, drawings, sigils, or perhaps even hieroglyphics. It is also said that he copied the characters from the cubic stone in the Holy of Holies onto a piece of parchment and attached it to his thigh, however that would likely be in Jerusalem and not the main charge of smuggling secrets out of Egypt by marking it on his body. It could even be that a mystery code was documented without involving writing proper. This is confirmed;

Mishnah.[104b] *"But did not Ben Stada bring forth witchcraft from Egypt by means of scratches [in the form of charms] upon his flesh?"*

The **Tosephta** adds yet another variant of this tradition;

"He who upon the Sabbath cuts letters upon his body is, according to the view of Rabbi Eliezer guilty, according to the view of the wise not guilty. Rabbi Eliezer said to the wise: Ben Stada surely learned sorcery by such writing." [19]

The same story is also handed on in the **Babylonian Gemara**, but with a very striking variant;

"There is a tradition: Rabbi Eliezer said to the wise men, has not Ben Stada brought magic spells from Egypt in an incision in his body?" [20]

The Talmud refers to Jeshu ben Pandera, who we certainly identified as Jesus, who is said to have been the disciple of Joshua ben Perachiah, who we identified in the last chapter as Jesus' Uncle, who in the Talmud report, fled with Jeshu to Alexandria in Egypt, where Jeshu is said to have learned Egyptian magic. Blavatsky states that Y'shua studied and was initiated into the Mystery Schools in Alexandria and was consecrated as a High Pontiff of the Universal Secret Doctrine by the Egyptian Priests. Described as a learned man, Jeshu was expelled for heretical tendencies from the school over which Joshua presided and was cursed and driven out for heretical leanings. [21] According to the Talmud, Jeshu became a religious teacher, had several disciples, and preached to ordinary people. He was accused of practising sorcery, deceiving Israel and estranging people from God. After being tried and convicted, the Talmud records, he was stoned to death and his body was then hung up as a warning to others.

It seems well established that Jesus brought secrets out of Egypt by marking the information on his skin. So why did he need a handwritten Temple scroll of the Torah? The reason is that Jesus had learned that there was hidden material in the Torah and wished to identify and share the information with the laity. He learned the secret information whilst in Egypt but now he needed a handwritten Jewish Torah written in the twenty-two letters of the Hebrew alphabet to decode the data he had and make this information known to all men. The Priests and High Priests understood only the literal sense of the Torah and wished to protect their own office and prestige, so accordingly sought to have Jesus killed. The original Jewish writings create a more believable scenario than the Bible gives us.

G. de Purucker says that Jesus;

"came at a time of a downwards-running cycle in order to sow some seeds at least of spiritual light, preceding a time which was going to be spiritually dark". His mission quickly proved to be a failure, because although the cyclic time for an avatar (God who came down) had come, everything was working against the spiritual forces for which he opened the way, and within less than a hundred years the teachings that he had left behind had degenerated. For instance, the doctrines of reincarnation and karma were replaced by the irrational and unjust dogma that belief in Jesus is sufficient to absolve us of all our sins and secure us an eternity of heavenly bliss, while unbelievers

will suffer eternal torment in hell. [22]

Several sources confirm that Reincarnation and Karma were included in original Christian dogma along with Astrology and Astronomy which were removed around the time of Constantine. This would further support that Buddhist doctrine from the Pythagoras school at Alexandria and embraced by the Essenes, was taught by Jesus. Josephus documented in the 'Wars of the Jews' that the Essenes were practiced in the art of healing and sourced their knowledge from the ancients. This would seem likely because the word Essene; '*essenoi*' in Greek and '*asayya*' in Aramaic, actually meant physician or healer.

A Substitute Crucified

By the second century AD, suggestions were being circulated in the Christian world that someone other than Jesus had been crucified on Golgotha. In 325 AD Constantine's pseudo-orthodoxy, finally arrogantly declared that Jesus did die on the cross and thinking other than this amounted to heresy. It was only with this power play that these suggestions were finally silenced. We might guess that if there was such doubt right from the time of Christ until the Council of Nicea, and with other evidence we have uncovered, we certainly have reason to question the validity of the crucifixion today.

Constantine's declaration had some problems. The Gnostics viewed Jesus as divine, and supposedly composed wholly of spirit, without flesh. Because of this they couldn't visualize a spirit nailed to a cross. They searched the scriptures and sought out ways to explain how the crucifixion of Jesus could have taken place. This is what three of the informed Gnostics of that time had to say;

Marcion (100-160 AD) This famous Gnostic denied the salvation of the body; believing that only the <u>souls</u> of men would be saved. Marcion believed the flesh of Christ to be imaginary, and his birth to be a phantom and a magical trick. He taught that there were actually two Gods; the angry God of the Old Testament who punishes, and the kind God of the New Testament who pities man.

Basilides (120-160 AD), believed that it was certainly not Christ who died on the cross, but rather the substitute Simon of Cyrene, who was constrained to carry the cross in his stead. Simon and Jesus then switched likenesses he claimed, allowing Jesus to stand off laughing at his tormentors. The writings of Basilides were systematically destroyed by the Catholic Church.

Cerinthus (c.150 AD) taught that Jesus was a physical man until the time of his baptism when the voice from Heaven declared that he had at that instant become the Son of God. Accordingly, Cerinthus claimed that Jesus left his body before his crucifixion and thus never suffered. He did not accept that Jesus had yet been resurrected although he possibly had been crucified. [23]

No less an authority than **Irenaeus** confirmed the writings of the Gnostic **Basilides** and recorded that Jesus did not suffer crucifixion at all. He further documented, '*Rather a certain Simon of Cyrene was compelled to bear his cross for him…and through ignorance and error it was he who was crucified.*'

This consistent choice of Simon of Cyrene is enlightening since the Bible seems to be trying to tell us something with its various mentions of this character. Firstly, the location of Cyrene is actually in Libya and the fact that Simon was a distant stranger in the land, could have made a hoax more possible. Next the following texts give a different story than the one we were fed in Sunday School;

> **Matthew 27 : 32** *And as they came out, they found a man of Cyrene, Simon by name: him they <u>compelled to bear his cross.</u>*

> **Mark 15 : 21** *And they <u>compel</u> one Simon a Cyrenian, who passed by, coming out of the country, the father of Alexander and Rufus, to bear his cross.*

> **Luke 23 : 26** *And as they led him away, they <u>laid hold upon</u> one Simon, a Cyrenian, coming out of the country, and on him they laid the cross, that he might bear it after Jesus.*

The non-canonical **Acts of Thomas**, supposedly written before the other Gospels by the brother and disciple of Jesus state;

> "*I did not succumb to them as they had planned, and I did not die in reality, but only in appearance; I was laughing at their ignorance.*"

In the Gnostic **Acts of John;** Jesus states;

"I have suffered none of the things which they will say of me; even the suffering that I showed to you, and to the rest of my dance, I will that it be called a mystery."

These stories from various sources are amazingly consistent. The Holy Bible could be seen to clandestinely support their stance that the crucifixion was a hoax, with the reports of Simon of Cyrene being compelled to carry the cross. We should check another non-canonical work;

Acts of Pilate Chapter 10 : 99-100, *But as He, from the many blows and the weight of the cross, was unable to walk, the Jews, out of the eager desire they had to crucify Him as quickly as possible, took the cross from Him, and gave it to a man that met them, Simon by name, who had also two sons, Alexander and Rufus. And he was from the city of Cyrene. They gave the cross, then, to him, not because they pitied Jesus, and wished to lighten Him of the weight, but because they eagerly desired, as has been said, to put Him to death more speedily.*

The Koran is a considerably later record than the Bible and is adamant that a substitute was crucified instead of Christ. In fact the Koran states;

Sura 4 : 157 *"And for claiming that they killed the Messiah, Jesus, son of Mary, the messenger of God. In fact, they never killed him, they never crucified him - they were made to think that they did. All factions who are disputing in this matter are full of doubt concerning this issue. They possess no knowledge; they only conjecture. For certain, they never killed him."* [24]

The Muslim world generally believes that God performed a miracle to cause someone else to suddenly look exactly like Jesus and to be crucified in his place. Some Gnostics also follow this line of thought. Speculation as to who this person was, includes; Judas Iscariot, Simon of Cyrene, another of the disciples or even one of the Roman soldiers.

Muslim writer, **Yusuf Ali** records;

'The Qur'anic teaching is that Christ was not crucified nor killed by the Jews, notwithstanding certain apparent circumstances which produced that illusion in the minds of some of his enemies.' [25]

Abdul-Haqq comments;

'The teaching of the Koran that Jesus Christ did not die upon the cross implies that

the entire Christian movement is based on a unique deception in history.' [26]

With all this evidence we must consider that they just may be correct. We were taught in Sunday School that Simon volunteered to assist Jesus in carrying the cross and in the movies he gave him a drink of water. That is not what is recorded here. Words like 'laid hold of' and 'compelled' tell a different story. I think we were 'sold a pup!'

We mentioned earlier a practice existing from Sumerian times where a King or ruler could insert a substitute (the whipping boy) for punishment, but in so doing would effectively forfeit his kingship and birthright. There is in fact an unusual story told by the Sumerians in a piece called, '*Inanna's Descent to the Underworld'*. In this tablet Inanna abandoned the "Great Heaven" and descended to Earth to the Underworld; likely meaning the 'down under' continent of Africa. To later ascend from the underworld was apparently a serious misdemeanour. Here the Anunnaki fastened the "eyes of death" on Inanna in what could be the origin of the 'evil eye'. In this case it was highly effective because the text goes on to state; it killed her and they hung her corpse on a stake. Three days later EN.KI arranged for the 'water of life' and the 'food of life' to be administered, and effected her resurrection. Is this sounding familiar, 'hung on a stake', 'resurrection after three days', 'descended to the underworld'. This substitute, (whipping boy) practice was apparently allegorically applied to Jesus. Following that, '*Inanna's Descent to the Underworld'* then tells us;

> *"The Anunnaki Gods seized her (saying), 'who of those who ascended from the underworld ever did get up scot-free? If Inanna is ascending from the underworld, let her give a substitute as a replacement for her'."* [27]

The text continues with **Dumuzi** being dragged away as her divine substitute. There are other lesser examples available, one from *The Epic of Gilgamesh*, sufficient to indicate that this 'substitution' seems to have been an accepted practice of the Sky-Gods. Another case is shown when the Anunnaki found the mining too hard and staged a mutiny. A God named **Geshtui** was *"called and cast for destruction"* [28] This was certainly a substitute death to redeem the rebellious ones. In ancient Europe the King was sacrificed at the seventh full moon after the shortest day of the year. When resistance mounted to this practice, it was approved that a Priestess could substitute a surrogate boy-king called an *'interex'* who died in place of the king. [29] The Biblical practice of releasing a criminal on special occasions, as was offered with the 'robber' Barabbas, appears to have no factual basis in history. The ring-in of a substitute, however, certainly holds allegoric relevance in the light of the Sumerian practice shown in Sumerian epic literature.

The Insurrection

Dr. Barbara Thiering states;

> *"Jesus was no solitary preacher appearing suddenly on the shores of Galilee. He was a central figure in a major political movement which was working at overthrowing the pagan Roman Empire."* [30]

If Jesus was actually crucified by the Romans, it was for sedition against Rome. The job of the Messiah was to attempt to overthrow the Roman occupation. If he didn't do this he was falling down on the job. If the Bible story is correct, ask yourself this, "How many soldiers were dispatched to arrest Jesus?" Take a pen now and write down how many you understand were involved. From Sunday School, if we thought about it at all, we received the impression of maybe 10 to 20 soldiers, say 50 tops. Where did we get that impression?

> **Matthew 26 : 47 & Mark 14 : 43** *And while He was still speaking, behold, Judas, one of the twelve, with a great multitude with swords and clubs, came from the chief priests and elders of the people.*

Now we can actually be much more precise than that because the original word translated as *"a great multitude"* was actually a Roman **"cohort"**. This has been widely researched by Bagient, Leigh & Lincoln in their classic book, "The Messianic Legacy";

> *"A cohort was one tenth of a legion — six hundred soldiers. If, that is they were regular Roman soldiers. A cohort composed of auxiliaries, as those in the Holy land were, would number at least five hundred troops, and sometimes as many as two thousand; — seven hundred and sixty infantry and one thousand two hundred and forty cavalry."* [31]

The above writers go on to draw the obvious conclusion by asking the question, would Pilate or any other Roman Governor, mobilize between six hundred to two thousand troops to arrest just one man, particularly a man extolling peace and love. This would be obvious overkill. Our "mind picture" from Sunday School is obviously quite wrong and the Roman authorities were faced here with a very major political revolution. Imagine between 600 and 2000 police or troops being mobilized at a football match or insurrection today; it would be a very major event and reported in all media. There is no doubt then; that Jesus was involved in a very major political insurrection against Rome, no matter how unsuccessful.

If we can appreciate that Jesus failed as the Messiah, we might ask then, if the Jews in fact consider a much later "King David" to be the successful Messiah. Self-government for Israel was not achieved right from 63 BCE until 1948, when it became a new nation with **David ben Gurion** as its Prime Minister. Now it seems this great leader was in fact a descendant of King David and his son Solomon and was the first to successfully remove all unwanted "Kittim" and achieve self-rule in Israel. Was David ben Gurion then in fact the long awaited Jewish Messiah?

Those Crucified With Jesus

The Bible's account of the offer to release Jesus in lieu of the 'robber', called **Barabbas** is extremely difficult to accept. This causes considerable heartburn for the following reasons:

- Firstly no record can be found of any Jewish or Roman custom of releasing a prisoner on a special occasion.
- We don't know who he was however early Bibles named Barabbas as **Jacob Barabbas** [32]
- One of two disciples chosen to replace Judas Iscariot, was named **Joseph** (the same as Jacob) **called Barsabas,** surnamed Justus. [33]
- Crucifixion was a punishment for sedition against Rome not for robbery. Those crucified with Jesus are separately called, 'robbers', 'thieves' and 'malefactors'.
- Possibly Barabbas was a zealot involved in the insurrection with Jesus.
- Abba means 'father' and accordingly **Bar Abbas** means "son of the father" sounding like Barabbas could be Jesus' own son.

• Despite this sounding quite plausible, the two men crucified with Jesus are elsewhere called **Dysmas** and **Gestas**. [34]

In addition:

Matthew 27 : 44 Both of those who are crucified with Jesus taunt him.

Luke 23 : 39–42 Only one taunts Jesus, and he is rebuked by the other for doing so.

Luke 23 : 43 *And Jesus said unto him, Verily I say unto thee, today shalt thou be with me in paradise.*

So why would Jesus make this crazy, unachievable promise? How could he possibly be with him that day in paradise when: **John 20 : 17** and **Acts 1 : 3** make it clear that Jesus was not raised until the third day and then did not ascend until at least forty days later. Why would he lie under pain of death to the 'robber'?

Was Jesus Really Crucified and Resurrected?

The second century Church Father, Irenaeus, was crucially important to the formation of the Catholic Church's early doctrine, yet in all his extensive writings he never once mentioned the crucifixion, or the resurrection of Jesus Christ. [35] In fact it gets worse for Christian believers, Bishop Irenaeus emphatically states that Jesus declined towards old age and specifically states that his ministry in the Holy Land lasted for 20 years until he was 50. In his work *Against Heresies*, Irenaeus claimed Jesus then remained in "Asia" with his disciple John and others, up to the times of the Emperor Trajan, before finally dying in very advanced years. [36]

The uncanonical Gospel of Philip states that the entire crucifixion passion was allegoric and ridicules the ignorant Christians who believe that the story of the resurrection was to be taken literally;

"Those who say they will die first and then rise again, are in error. They must receive the resurrection while they still live." [37]

Now what Philip is referring to is a mystery school initiation ceremony that includes a symbolic 'death' and subsequent resurrection and was practised, naturally, whilst one is still alive. The archaeologist and writer Dr Barbara

Thiering said this;

> *"Jesus did not die on the cross. This central fact, and the account of what did happen, is given in the pesher of the Gospels and Acts. The Book of Revelation is another of the sources, and when treated by the same technique, not only confirms the fact but gives a detailed account of the movements of Jesus after the crucifixion that fits in exactly with the account in the Book of Acts."* [38]

Thiering states further that *"Jesus was pardoned, by Pilate, through the influence of the Herods…"* proving he was still alive, *"on Wednesday 16 Dec 33 AD"* at about age 40. [39] What possible reason could the scribes of Dr Thiering's source have for recording his pardon if it were not true? More particularly if it was common knowledge that Jesus had died on the cross, it would be ludicrous to document such a piece. They would certainly not wish to risk the wrath of Pilate and Herod for false reporting.

The <u>Gnostics</u> recorded that belief in a literal resurrection was; *"…the faith of fools"*.

The <u>Manicheans</u> felt that Jesus was a God and never walked the Earth as flesh and Blood and accordingly dispute that any crucifixion ever took place.

The <u>Unitarians</u> thought Jesus had been a prophet not a God and if any crucifixion actually took place then it was not for the redemption of mankind.

We can today read documents believed by some to have been written by the Biblical Barnabas, the colleague of St Paul. In the non-canonical *Gospel of Barnabas* it is stated quite categorically that Jesus Christ was <u>not</u> crucified but was carried towards heaven by four angels. In complete contradiction, Saint Paul emphatically tells us he knows *'nothing except Christ Jesus and him crucified'*. It seems the dispute between Barnabas and Paul mentioned in Acts was about this very subject. Despite his stand, St Paul himself knew that parts of Jesus resurrection defied belief and wrote;

Acts 23 : 8 *For the Sadducees say that there is no resurrection.*

This was because sections of the Sadducees as well as many other early Christians and contemporary Jews disputed the crucifixion and in line with this, naturally had problems with the resurrection. This is not a lone quote with the gospels maintaining this theme;

Matthew 22 : 23 & **Mark 12 : 18** *The same day came to him the Sadducees, which say that there is no resurrection.*

We need also to explain the following;

2 Kings 4 : 32-37 A dead child is raised (well before the time of Jesus).

Matthew 9 : 18-25, John 11 : 38-44 Two dead persons are raised (by Jesus himself).

Acts 26 : 23 Jesus was the first to conquer death.

Regarding the 'gift' of the Holy Spirit after the Resurrection;

Mark 1 : 14 Jesus began his ministry after the arrest of John the Baptist.

John 3 : 22-24 Before the arrest of John the Baptist.

Luke 1 : 15 John the Baptist had the Holy Spirit from before his birth; six months before the birth of Jesus.

Luke 1 : 41 John's mother Elizabeth was baptized in the Spirit before Jesus was born.

Luke 1 : 67 So was his father Zachariah.

Luke 2 : 25 So was Simeon.

Luke 11 : 13 The Holy Spirit is obtained by prayer presumably at any time.

John 7 : 39 The Holy Spirit cannot come into the world until after Jesus has departed.

John 16 : 7 The Holy Spirit cannot come into the world until after Jesus has departed.

Acts 1 : 3-5 The Holy Spirit cannot come into the world until after Jesus has departed.

John 20 : 22 In his first resurrection appearance before the assembled disciples, Jesus gives them the Holy Spirit.

Acts 1 : 3-5 The Holy Spirit was received much later at Pentecost.

This hotch-potch mess certainly does not aid the Bible cause. Independent records have Jesus alive well after the supposed crucifixion. It is fairly well recorded that in middle age, Jesus visited Persia, where he was known as '**Yuz Asaf**,' meaning '*leader of the healed*.' Tradition says he preached throughout Persia. Accounts such as Agha Mustafai's *Jami-uf-Tawarik* (Vol II) confirm that, **Yuz Asaf** and **Jesus** were one and the same man. The court poet of Emperor Akbar of India supported this when he recorded Jesus as '*Ai Ki Nam-i to:Yus o Kristo*', or '*Thou whose name is Yuz or Christ.*' [40]

Mark Mason goes on:

"There is a grave in the middle of Srinagar's old town, which is supposedly the grave of Judas Thomas, yet many people believe it to be the grave of Jesus himself. The building later erected around the gravestone is called Rozabal, meaning 'tomb of a prophet.' Above the passage to the actual burial chamber is an inscription explaining that Yuz Asaf entered the valley of Kashmir many centuries before, and that his life was dedicated to the search for the truth". [41]

In March 2002 a World News item claimed that this Indian tomb was to be excavated and DNA samples taken from any remains in an attempt to finally lay these persistent rumours to rest. Now how will they be sure? I guess that comparisons will be done against known descendants of Jesus, or will this upset the Vatican and other groups? There has been deafening silence about it ever since!

What Was Recorded

The Roman chronicler, Publius Cornelius **Tacitus** (c. 56-109) gives us the only early record outside the Bible; of the insurrection that led to the crucifixion of Jesus (and this record is hearsay) documented well after the event. He recorded that he heard that the Romans crucified Jesus as a political revolutionary. [42] The fact that this capital punishment was by crucifixion substantiates that his misdemeanour would be some form of sedition against Rome. The writings of Tacitus cover Roman history from around 14 – 46 AD and the *Annals - (After the Death of the Deified Augustus)* are generally regarded above his other works, as authentic and historically accurate. In Annals, Tacitus makes mention of '**Christus**' [43] At this time it was possibly Judas Thomas documented since he went by the name of Judas Chrestus. We have no way of knowing if Jesus the Christ or Judas Chrestus is referred to here. In fact *Chrestus* meant '*Good and Holy*', while *Christus* meant '*anointed*', so some believe Jesus evolved from Chrestus to Christus. I think it is more likely that Chrestus (Good and Holy) was Judas Thomas and at the next level was Christus (anointed) meaning Jesus. As Madame Helena Blavatsky explains:

> *Western Theosophists accept the Christos as did the Gnostics of the centuries which preceded Christianity, as do the Vedantins their Krishna: they distinguish the corporeal man from the divine Principle which, in the case of the Avatara, animates him.* [44]

Part of the Tacitus report in the *Annals*, talking about the time after the great fire of Rome in 64 AD, reads:

> *"Nero fastened the guilt and inflicted the most exquisite tortures on a class hated for their abominations, called 'Chrestiani' by the populace. <u>Chrestus</u>, from whom the name had its origin, suffered the extreme penalty during the reign of Tiberius at the hands of one of our procurators, Pontius Pilatus, and a most mischievous superstition, thus checked for the moment, again broke out not only in Judaea, the first source of the evil, but even in Rome, where all things hideous and shameful from every part of the world find their centre and become popular".* [45]

The quotations, *'hated for their abominations'*, *'first source of the evil'* and *'things hideous and shameful'* refer to a widely held belief at the time that the Christian Eucharist was a cannibalistic feast that actually involved eating the flesh and drinking the blood of a sacrificed human, usually an infant. Tony Bushby supplies considerable evidence that this is truly what was practiced. [46]

St. Justin Martyr was appalled by the early followers of Chrestus. He reported;

> *"... All who take their opinions from these men are, as we before said, called <u>Chrestians</u>...and whether they perpetrate those fabulous and shameful deeds - the upsetting of the lamp, and promiscuous intercourse, and eating human flesh."* [47]

Justin Martyr also accused them of breeding children, specifically to hire out for their religious orgies;

> *"And any one who uses such persons, besides the Godless and infamous and impure intercourse, may possibly be having intercourse with his own child, or relative, or brother. And there are some, who prostitute even their own children and wives, and some are openly mutilated for the purpose of sodomy; and they refer these mysteries to the mother of the Gods, and along with each of those whom you esteem Gods there is painted a serpent, a great symbol and mystery.* [48]

The Governor of Bithynia wrote to the Emperor Trajan in 110 AD for advice on how to deal with this Chrestiani sect whose superstitions were not confined to the Cities he claimed, but were spreading through the villages and countryside as well.

The later Roman historian **Suetonius** (Gaius Suetonius Tranquillus - AD 117-138) documented the name 'Chrestus' in his work 'Lives of the Caesars', (Divas Claudius) Life of Claudius. Here we read;

> "Because the Jews at Rome caused constant disturbances at the instigation of <u>Chrestus</u>, he [Claudius] expelled them from the city [Rome]." ... "Nero inflicted punishment on the Christians, a sect given to a new and mischievous religious belief." 25:4 He banished from Rome all the Jews, who were continually making disturbances at the instigation of one <u>Chrestus</u>." (49)

As well as being an accomplished historian, Suetonius was also the Roman Secretary of State so we would expect his record to be somewhat credible and accurate; he would be in serious trouble with the Emperor if it was not. By this record, if Chrestus (referring to Jesus) was causing disturbances in Rome after 41 AD as reported by the Secretary of State, well he certainly wasn't dead and the Church has some explaining to do! The next writing we examine seems quite juvenile in its content and is from the very suspect book called: **The Acts of Pilate;**

> "Then Pilate ordered the curtain of the tribunal where he was sitting to be drawn, and says to Jesus: Thy nation has charged thee with being a king. On this account I sentence thee, first to be scourged, according to the enactment of venerable kings, and then to be fastened on the cross in the garden where thou wast seized. And let Dysmas and Gestas, the two malefactors, be crucified with thee." (50)

The prior documentation of the scourging and crucifixion of Antigonus makes it clear that nothing like this had been done before by Rome, to a Jewish King. The above piece claims, 'according to the enactment of venerable kings' which indicates that not many years later, it was now standard practice. The line, "Thy nation has charged thee with being a king" seems a peculiar way to describe Christ's seditious crime against Rome. Note too that here we see 'malefactors' and not 'robbers' indicating that they could have possibly been involved in an insurrection with Jesus. The way they are introduced to

Jesus in the above passage makes it seem quite apparent that he would know whom Dysmas and Gestas are. This gives the impression that they were associates, involved in the same insurrection.

At the crucifixion of Jesus we are told;

Matthew 27 : 51-54 *" And, behold, the veil of the temple was rent in twain from the top to the bottom; and the earth did quake, and the rocks rent; And the graves were opened; and many bodies of the saints which slept arose, And came out of the graves after his resurrection, and went into the holy city, and appeared unto many."*

The rending of the temple curtain is easy to explain; that comes directly from the Egyptian 'Book of the Dead' and takes place at the end of the 'mystery school' initiation where in front of the new initiate who has been tied to an ankh cross, the black curtain is rent to both symbolically and actually let in the light. The second part however is plainly something else. Now this is a pretty amazing occurrence described here; certainly one of the most amazing sequences to be found in the Bible and if it were true, quite possibly the single most amazing occurrence the world has ever seen. Why then is it not documented by even one of the philosophers, historians and scribes outside of the Bible? Why isn't Jerusalem famous for this outstanding event? Seneca and Pliny the Elder minutely document the events of this area at this precise time, yet fail to even mention in passing, this earth-shattering event. This must be considered somewhat strange. A few other problems spring to mind. For example, when the saints came out of their graves; who were they, since by the time of Christ's supposed crucifixion there were but few Christians, and probably no saints. Next when their bodies were somehow rejuvenated was their rotted clothing rejuvenated as well, or were they moving around naked. Were they in dire need of food and drink and did they find time for a quick bath, manicure and haircut. For what purpose were they re-animated; what tasks did they undertake and for how long did they live the second time? If Jesus was the first one to ever "overcome death" how is it that these saints did it first? I feel Matthew should have at least satisfied our curiosity with a more complete description. Why did they venture into the Holy City? What was achieved; did these saints then die again? Did they still have the diseases and maladies that they previously died of? Were they all still contagious and did they actually cause an epidemic in that city?

No, sorry this is palpable nonsense. I cannot even start to give credibility to this twisted rubbish. The writers were trying for a dramatic spectacle at the death of their God, believing they held captive an extremely gullible audience who got off on this sort of religious fervour. I think even the Christian readers would understand that this is simply nonsense, unsuitable for any Holy Book and unworthy of any credence!

In Chapter V of 'The Epistle of Ignatius to Mary at Neapolis, near Zarbus' we find Ignatius protecting the stance that Christ died and was resurrected, however he openly admits that of the local populous, there are many who don't believe this;

> *"Avoid those that deny the passion of Christ, and His birth according to the flesh: and there are many at present who suffer under this disease."*

It appears that the 'disease' of unbelief was rife soon after the supposed event. Nothing has really changed today. Many of us still have this disease; in fact as more people become knowledgeable in the subject, this malady reaches epidemic proportions! We must not lose sight of the fact that Jesus was a Jew (some say the King of the Jews) and yet the Jewish religion denies his resurrection, denies that he was the Son of God and denies that he is capable of saving anybody. Let's not forget that it was these Jewish folk who wrote the first versions of the Bible that were hijacked by the Christians.

Miracles & Magic

The word 'magic' originally had no connotation of trickery at all but rather of secret knowledge. It was derived from the Sumerian word for 'secret', 'hidden' or 'profound'. For some reason the Church still teaches that miracles are good and of God, while magic is bad and of the devil. This is not the original context. To all intents and purposes they are one and the same. Jesus supposedly learned magic in Egypt, which he possibly used to perform his miracles. The word, *Magi* became a standard term for the Zoro-astrian priesthood in Persia and a magician or a person endowed with 'secret knowledge' in that area was known as a *Magus*. Egyptian priests were called '*magicians*' and this title along with 'Magi' and 'Magus' indicated that they held secret knowledge or were initiated into the mysteries of the Gods. We should recall the **Magi** (wise men) who visited after the birth of Christ and also the contemporary of Jesus named **Simon Magus**.

The **Didache** is an ancient Christian text that pre-dates the Bible's New Testament, written around 140 A.D., and supposedly compiled from the teachings of the twelve apostles. Parts of the Didache have been found included in various other religious texts and it seems to have been warnings and instructions for the early Church. Sections of this document specifically condemn the use of magic.

> "Although Simon Magus and Elymas, (bar Jesus) that child of the devil (Acts, xiii, 6 sqq .) served as deterrent examples for all Christians, it took centuries to eradicate the propensity to magic. St. Gregory the Great, St. Augustine, St. Chrysostom, and St. Ephraem inveighed against it." [51]

The condemnation from a Church perspective arose from the fact that the practitioners of magic had to seek assistance from other entities, not being able to produce it themselves. They then 'turned away' Christians who seemed to have a strong desire for these esoteric spectacles and flashy miracles. The book *"The Keys of Solomon"* is a reference still utilized today in conjuration and in the seeking of such assistance.

Simon Magus the Holy God

Simon Magus was a Samaritan from the town of Gitto who was at least a partial supporter of Jesus. He is mentioned in the Bible; trying to buy from the disciples the power of healing the sick and casting out devils to add these tricks to his repertoire.

> **Acts 8 : 9** *But there was a certain man, called Simon, which beforetime in the same city used sorcery, and bewitched the people of Samaria, giving out that himself was some great one.*

> **Acts 8 : 18-19** *And when Simon saw that through laying on of the apostles' hands the Holy Ghost was given, he offered them money, saying, 'Give me also this power, that on whomsoever I lay hands, he may receive the Holy Ghost.'*

Later, Justin Martyr complained to Rome about Simon Magus in this following piece;

> *"And because after Christ's ascension into heaven the devils put forward certain men who said that they themselves were gods; and they were not only not persecuted by you, but even deemed worthy of honours. There was a Samaritan, Simon, a native of the village called Gitto, who in the reign of Claudius Caesar, and in your royal city of Rome, did mighty acts of magic, by virtue of the art of the devils operating in him. He was considered a god, and as a god was honoured by you with a statue, which statue was erected on the river Tiber, between the two bridges, and bore this inscription, in the language of Rome: "Simoni Deo Sancto" (Simon the Holy God.)* (52)

It seems remarkable that we were taught about the peaceful Jesus whose only wish was to improve the lot of mankind, and he was crucified by the Romans for doing miracles and saying he was the Son of God, when a contemporary Magician claiming that he was God himself, had his statue erected in Rome. It seems that Simon Magus impressed the next Roman Emperor Nero sufficiently to gain his support in Rome and it seems it was probably Nero, and not Claudius, who erected the statue to him in Rome between the bridges on an island in the River Tiber. Simon became fairly cocky with his newfound fame and then claimed he was a God of virgin birth. What a turn of events. Surprise! Surprise!

Nesta Webster in the book *'Secret Societies and Subversive Movements'* states;

> *Indeed, the man generally recognized as the founder of Gnosticism, a Jew commonly known as Simon Magus, was not only a Cabalist mystic but avowedly a magician, who with a band of Jews, including his master Dositheus and his disciples Menander and Cerinthus, instituted a priesthood of the Mysteries and practised occult arts and exorcisms… Simon, indeed, crazed by his incantations and ecstasies, developed megalomania in an acute form, arrogating to himself divine honours and aspiring to the adoration of the whole world. According to a contemporary legend, he eventually became sorcerer to Nero and ended his life in Rome.* (53)

Study of this subject tells us that the 'contemporary legend' mentioned above is in fact the third century writings of **Hippolytus**, who lucidly states that Simon Magus came into conflict with St Peter in Rome, and died there in a magic competition. Writings of the educated **Bishop Clement** confirm the story of a magic competition between the disciple Simon Peter and the magician Simon Magus in front of Emperor Nero. Simon Magus supposedly tried to fly from a tower to prove he was God, and was apparently making a fair job of it until Peter challenged the devil that gave Simon his power. As a result Simon crashed to the ground and was smashed into four pieces, I guess, effectively proving once and for all that he really wasn't. This is crazy stuff; this is Harry Potter without a broom. The loss of his champion Simon Magus, enraged Nero and somehow this led to the upside down crucifixion of Peter and the beheading of St. Paul on Nero's instructions. Most students of classical ancient history recognise that regardless of this silly story, the Emperor Nero himself was more than a little crazy, so accordingly it is certainly not easy to ascertain what may have really happened. *Eusebius of Caesarea* mentions Simon Magus in *Church History:* and this sounds very similar to the record of Justin Martyr:

"After Christ's ascension into heaven the devils put forward certain men who said that they themselves were Gods; and they were not only not persecuted by you, but even deemed worthy of honours. There was a Samaritan, Simon, a native of the village called Gitto, who in the reign of Claudius Caesar, in your imperial city did some mighty acts of magic by the art of demons operating in him, and was considered a God, and as a God was honoured by you with a statue, which was erected in the river Tiber, between the two bridges, and bore this inscription in the Latin tongue, Simoni Deo Sancto, that is, To Simon the Holy God. And nearly all the Samaritans and a few even of other nations confess and worship him as the first God. [54]

This certainly seems to be the source of Justin Martyr's story; being almost identical. The purpose of this section is to show how the populus of the Holy Land and indeed Rome would so easily adopt and take in a magician of the calibre of Simon Magus. This was prime entertainment. It goes further however in showing that in that day and age the populous loved any outdoor spectacle; however it also indicates that in total contrast, Jesus must have finally caused a pretty major insurrection for it to lead to his crucifixion.

Dr. Barbara Thiering believes Simon Magus, the Disciple Simon and Lazarus who was 'raised from the dead' were one and the same person and this would be worth consideration. (55)

More Confusion

We mentioned there is 150 years silence following the Bible's report of the crucifixion and a likely reason is that this record contained the life and miracles, not of Jesus, but of Apollonius of Tyana. As a result the entire record was eradicated by Constantine because it interfered with the direction he planned for the Roman Church. We must therefore of necessity look to the material from before and after the event that we have just covered. To gain some small inkling of the research problems associated with the Crucifixion, we must now use the Bible as a primary source for that missing period. This tack is fraught with danger, as the following will show;

> **Luke 24 : 33–36**; *And they rose up the same hour, and returned to <u>Jerusalem</u>, and found the eleven gathered together, and them that were with them, saying, The Lord is risen indeed, and hath appeared to Simon… And as they thus spake, Jesus himself stood in the midst of them, and saith unto them, Peace be unto you.* We see Christ, after the crucifixion, in the flesh eating honeycomb and fish before being parted from the disciples.

> **Matthew 28 : 16–17**; *Then the eleven disciples went away into <u>Galilee</u>, into a mountain where Jesus had appointed them. And when they saw him, they worshipped him: <u>but some doubted</u>.*

Jesus had arranged to meet the disciples, after the resurrection, in **Galilee.** No wonder some doubted because the Bible also states that it was in **Jerusalem** – some 100 miles away! If the disciples of Jesus doubted at that time, what hope is there for us today. Despite what Matthew records above about Jesus' appearance in Galilee, we find **Matthew 28 : 8–9** states that Jesus had already appeared <u>near the tomb</u>.

Luke 24 : 13–15 puts it in the vicinity of <u>Emmaus</u> (seven miles from Jerusalem).

John 20 : 13–14 says it was right <u>at the tomb</u>.

The same evening of the resurrection is the time of his ascension for **Luke 24 : 1–59**, with verse **51** un-ambiguously stating;

> "*And it came to pass, while he blessed them, he was parted from them, and carried up*

into heaven." This certainly describes the ascension of Jesus and yet we are told in Acts that it occurred 40 days later;

Acts 1 : 3; *To whom also he shewed himself alive after his passion by many infallible proofs, being seen of them forty days, and speaking of the things pertaining to the kingdom of God.*

We should note that 40 days was a standard Biblical measurement similar to the archetypal twenty pieces of silver. In fact it originated in early astronomy where it required 40 days for a star (or the planet Venus) to move in the heavens to the next datum point. Surprisingly however, John tells us that after the resurrection Jesus appeared to Mary Magdalene, and then joined the disciples at the Sea of Tiberias;

John 21 : 1 *After these things Jesus shewed himself again to the disciples at the Sea of Tiberias; and on this wise shewed he himself.*

If we read Mark however we discover;

Mark 16 : 14 *Afterward he appeared unto the eleven as they sat at meat, and upbraided them with their unbelief and hardness of heart, because they believed not them who had seen him after he was risen.*

This took place in Jerusalem then in **verse 19** Jesus is received up in Heaven. Perhaps part of the Jesus repertoire of miracles was the power to bi-locate, unless the Gospel scribes were complete morons, it certainly seems here that this is so. Many other details of the crucifixion, resurrection and ascension are disparate. This, of course, is human nature when different witnesses describe an event; however this is supposed to be the infallible word of God. To clearly evaluate the above;

Matthew: Jesus was to meet the disciples in **Galilee** after the resurrection. Although they were close colleagues who knew him well, strangely some doubted it was really him. No ascension occurs.

Mark: The ascension took place while the disciples were gathered together in **Jerusalem**.

Luke: Christ, in the flesh after the crucifixion, eats honeycomb and fish before being parted from the disciples. The ascension took place after supper, at **Bethany**.

John: Jesus meets the disciples by the **Sea of Tiberias** and eats fish and bread with them. No ascension is recorded - it simply states that Jesus was later received in Heaven.

Acts: Makes it clear the ascension was 40 days after the resurrection and occurred at **Mt. Olivet**.

When Jesus was questioned by the High Priest and then Pilate, we were taught that 'Like a lamb, he opened not his mouth.' Read it for yourself;
Matthew 27 : 12–14 *Jesus speaks not a single word and answers not a single charge at his hearing before Pilate.*

In total contradiction, considerable dialogue is outlined in the scriptures. We won't go into the full dialogue but give the specific answer from each case:

Matthew 26 : 63-4 *And the high priest answered and said unto him, I adjure thee by the living God, that thou tell us whether thou be the Christ, the Son of God. Jesus saith unto him, Thou hast said: nevertheless I say unto you, hereafter shall ye see the Son of man sitting on the right hand of power, and coming in the clouds of heaven.*

Mark 14 : 61-2 *Again the high priest asked him, and said unto him, Art thou the Christ, the Son of the Blessed?*
And Jesus said, I am: and ye shall see the Son of man sitting on the right hand of power, and coming in the clouds of heaven.

Mark 15 : 2 *And Pilate asked him, Art thou the King of the Jews? And he answering said unto them, Thou sayest it.*

Luke 23 : 3 *And Pilate asked him, saying, Art thou the King of the Jews? And he answered him and said, Thou sayest it.*

Luke 22 : 66-7 *And as soon as it was day, the elders of the people and the chief priests and the scribes came together, and led him into their council, saying, Art thou the Christ? Tell us. And he said unto them, If I tell you, ye will not believe. And he said unto them, Ye say that I am.*

In each of the above Jesus gives answers some with considerable dialogue. Again we find in **John 18 : 34 – 37** that he answers all Pilate's questions:
"Sayest thou this thing of thyself, or did others tell it thou of me? My kingdom is not of this world: if my kingdom were of this world, then would my servants

fight, that I should not be delivered to the Jews: but now is my kingdom not from hence. Thou sayest that I am a king. To this end was I born, and for this cause, came I into the world, that I should bear witness unto the truth. Everyone that is of the truth heareth my voice".

Further conflict to the stories of the trial, crucifixion and ascension are caused by more contradiction. After the trial, we see conflict in a very important area regarding the dress of Jesus;

Matthew 27 : 28 A **scarlet** robe (a sign of Priesthood).

Mark 15 : 17 A **purple** robe (a sign of Royalty)

What was he given to drink on the cross?

Matthew 27 : 48 He was given vinegar to drink.

Mark 15 : 23 He was offered wine with Myrrh in it and he didn't drink it.

Luke 23 : 36 The soldiers mocked him by offering vinegar.

John 19 : 29-30 Jesus asked for it and they filled a sponge with vinegar and put it upon hyssop and Jesus drank it.

So how close were the women to the crucified Christ?

Matthew 27 : 55 Many women from Galilee including Mary Magdalene and the other Mary afar off.

Mark 15 : 40 the same women, afar off.

Luke 23 : 49 The same women from Galilee with no mention of the two Mary's looked on from afar.

John 19 : 25-26 There were Mary his mother, Mary the wife of Cleophas and Mary Magdalene plus the disciple Jesus loved and they were at the foot of the cross so Jesus could speak to them.

Matthew 28 : 1 The first visitors to the sepulchre were Mary Magdalene and the other Mary (**two**) and it was toward dawn when they arrived and an angel rolled away the stone.

Mark 16 : 1-2 Both of the above plus Salome (**three**) and it was after sunrise and they wondered how to remove the stone.

Luke 23 : 55, Luke 24 : 1 & 10 Mary Magdalene, Joanna, Mary the mother of James, and other women plus women from Galilee following Joseph (probably a large crowd but **at least ten**) It was at early morning and they saw into the tomb so the stone was not in place.

John 20 : 1 Mary Magdalene only **(one)** and it was still dark and the stone had been rolled away.

Matthew 28 : 1-2 The stone was still in place when they arrived. It was rolled away later.

Mark 16 : 4, Luke 24 : 2 and **John 20 : 1** The stone had already been rolled away.

Matthew 28 : 2 One angel arrived during an earthquake, rolled back the stone, then sat on it outside the tomb.

Mark 16 : 5 No earthquake is mentioned, only one young man sitting inside the tomb.

Luke 24 : 2-4 No earthquake, two men suddenly appear standing inside the tomb.

John 20 : 12 No earthquake, two angels are sitting inside the tomb.

Matthew 27 : 62-66 A guard was placed at the tomb the day following the burial for the express purpose of preventing the disciples from removing the body.

Mark 15 : 45-46, Luke 23 : 52-56, John 19 : 38-42, John 20 : 1-6 No guard is mentioned. This is important since we saw earlier this chapter, documents suggesting that Jesus' body was stolen and his Resurrection faked by the disciples.

Mark 16 : 1-5, Luke 24 : 1-4 Mary Magdalene and other women enter the tomb with spices to anoint the body. They were aware that the stone had been rolled away but were not aware of any guard.

John 20 : 1-2 Mary Magdalene alone approached the tomb, saw the stone rolled away and ran to get Peter.

Luke 23 : 55-56 The women followed Joseph to the tomb, saw how the body had been laid, then went to prepare spices with which to anoint the body.

John 19 : 39-40 Nicodemus brought 100 lbs. of myrrh and aloes with him and anointed the body as the women should have noticed.

John 20 : 1-2 Mary ran to tell Peter and the other disciple that the body had been stolen. She would have been horrified that the body had been stolen. She would not be feeling "great joy" as stated by Matthew.

Matthew 28 : 6-8 The women ran from the tomb "with great joy".
The persons interacting with the risen Lord is also way out of wack;
the order of Resurrection appearances was;

Matthew 28 : 1-18: Mary Magdalene and the other Mary, then the eleven.

Mark 16 : 9-14 It was Mary Magdalene, then two others, then the eleven.

Luke 24 : 15-36 It was two others, then Simon (Peter?), then the eleven.

John 20 : 14 & **John 21 : 1** It was Mary Magdalene, then the disciples without Thomas, then the disciples with Thomas, then the eleven disciples again.

1 Corinthians 15 : 5-8 It was Cephas (Peter), then the 'twelve' then 500+ brethren.

Acts 1 : 15 says there were only about 120, then James, then all the Apostles, then Paul?

John 20 : 17 On his first appearance to Mary, Jesus forbids her to touch him since he has not yet ascended to the Father.

Matthew 28 : 9 On his first appearance to them, Jesus lets Mary Magdalene and the other Mary hold him by his feet.

John 20 : 27 A week later, although he has not yet ascended to the Father, Jesus tells Thomas to feel his wounds.

If any of this convoluted mess is true then the whole bunch needed a course on organizational skills. They were running around 'willy nilly' not seeing what had been done and what needed to be done. The scribes were hopeless too; they couldn't get their story straight on even one item. Think too of the later Bible compilers who edited this conflicting hotch potch. The reporting of events is a contradictory mess, and it is hard to glean a word of truth from it. When we examine the timeframe it gets even worse.

Mark 15 : 25 *And it was the third hour, and they crucified him.*

Luke 23 : 44 *And it was about the sixth hour, and there was darkness over all the earth until the ninth hour.* So if it was dark how did they observe from afar?

John 19 : 14-15 *And it was the preparation of the Passover, and about the sixth* *hour: and he saith unto the Jews, Behold your King! But they cried out, Away with him, away with him, crucify him.*

We can prove the crucifixion had to be after the sixth hour since Jesus was still before Pilate and had not yet been sentenced at that time. Scriptures quoted early this chapter indicate Jesus was crucified on the Day of Preparation, the day before Passover however there is difficulty gleaning that information from other Bible records.

Matthew 26 : 18-20 & 57, Matthew 27 : 1-2, Mark 14 : 16-18, Mark 14 : 53-72, Mark 15 : 1 Jesus' initial hearing was on the night of the Passover in front of Caiaphas the High Priest and the scribes and elders of the Sanhedrin. In the morning after Passover he was taken to Pilate.

Luke 22 : 11-16, Luke 22 : 54, Luke 22 : 66-67 The initial hearing took place in the morning on the day of Passover in front of the High Priest Caiaphas. Then there was an inquiry held by the Sanhedrin.

John 18 : 12-28, John 19 : 14 It took place the day before Passover, on the Day of Preparation. There was no appearance before the Sanhedrin, only the private hearings before Annas who was father-in-law to Caiaphas the High Priest.

Herod and his Sadducee High Priest were ruthless in guarding their positions and were particularly down on the dynasty of Zadok priests (Essenes) who with a following just may start a movement to usurp their titles. The position of High Priest was jealously sought after as it included the presidency of the Great Sanhedrin and carried responsibility for the suppression of any revolutionary or heretical doctrine. Any potential claimants for the position of High Priest were marked for particular vengeance as in the supposed case with Annas, father in law of the High Priest Caiaphas leading the Great Sanhedrin to condemn Jesus for blasphemy. This is well summarized (perhaps allegorically) by the following;

"His crime was revolutionary insurgency and a valid Zadoki claim to both the throne of Israel and position of High Priest. The same set of circumstances had already led to the death of Hezekiah and his son Judas the Galilean. It was also the reason that John the Baptist was beheaded. In 62 CE the High Priest Ananus had the next

THE CRUCIFIXION

leader, James the Righteous, stoned for the same reason. Josephus wrote that their persecution was not so much because they claimed the throne, but because they were entitled to it." (56)

While trying to unravel the Bible contradictions we should spare a thought for Judas who doesn't know if he is coming or going;

Luke 22 : 3–23 Satan entered Judas before the supper.

John 13 : 27 It was during the supper.

Matthew 26 : 14-25, Mark 14 : 10 –11, Luke 22 : 3–23 Judas had already made his bargain with the chief priests before the meal.

John 13 : 21-30 After the meal.

Matthew 26 : 20-29, Mark 14 : 17-28, John 13 : 21-30 Jesus forecasts his betrayal prior to the communion portion of the supper.

Luke 22 : 14-23 After the communion portion.

Matthew 26 : 26-29, Mark 14 : 22-25 The order of the communion was: bread, then wine.

Luke 22 : 17-20 It was: wine, then bread.

Matthew 26 : 49-50, Mark 14 : 44-46 Jesus is betrayed by Judas with a kiss, then he is seized.

Luke 22 : 47-48 Jesus anticipates Judas' kiss however no actual kiss is mentioned.

John 18 : 2-9 Jesus voluntarily steps forward to identify himself negating any need for Judas to identify him. No kiss is mentioned.

Matthew 27 : 3-7 The chief priests bought the potters field in which to bury Judas who had hanged himself.

Acts 1 : 16-19 Judas bought the field with his reward (not as a burial plot) but then after falling his body burst open and his bowels gushed out.

So what are we to believe and what are we to reject. We have seen nothing but contradiction. From our studies, it seems that Jesus was never crucified or certainly did not die on the cross and this would also rule out the resurrection, branding the Bible stories as fraudulent. The late British scholar John Allegro, the first to publish translations of his section of the Dead Sea Scrolls, went on to draw conclusions that he doubted the validity of Jesus as an historical figure; in part because he could not explain the absence of Jesus from the Scrolls record. Allegro was well known in the mid Eighties for his criticism of the Catholic scholars involved in translating the Dead Sea Scrolls for their tardiness in publishing their parts of the scrolls; that finally led to accusations of straight out suppression of material that would compromise the Catholic Church and its Christian message. This very thing also happened in the time of Constantine so very little has changed to this day.

John Allegro went on to publish a work that correctly confirmed that drugs were used to varying extents among religious cults and in the mystery schools of the ancient Middle East. Allegro claimed that most religious experiences both pagan and Christian could be attributed to use of these drugs plus the hallucinogenic drug, psilocybin (present in magic mushrooms). [57]

The Bible is made up of a collection of works of various unknown writers who have left us with confusion and contradiction on almost every facet of the crucifixion and resurrection. A succession of scribes has documented their own version of events to arrive at this contradictory mess that is either fraudulent, incompetent or both. We can be certain that Almighty God has taken no part in producing this work.

"I deny the existence of any divinity that requires to be worshipped with blood, with the death stroke and with sacrificial rites."
Pharaoh Akhenaten.

CHAPTER SIX

ALL THE OTHER SAVIOURS

"For as I passed by, and beheld your devotions, I found an altar with this inscription, 'to the unknown God,' whom therefore ye ignorantly worship, Him declare I unto you."

Acts 17 : 23 (KJV)

The Uniqueness of Christ's Sacrifice

As we concluded in the previous chapter, it seems to be virtually impossible to find collaborating evidence in support of the Biblical story of the crucifixion of Christ. The name Jesus is also not mentioned in the Dead Sea Scrolls. Dr. Yigel Yadin, Professor of Archaeology at Hebrew University went on record as stating that the absence of the name Jesus or any mention of the Early Church was "strange". Every indication is that these scrolls date from the first century of the Christian era; and this would make the exclusion of any mention of Jesus, 'strange' to the extreme, and this is quite an under-statement. John Allegro who worked so hard on the translations of the Dead Sea Scrolls often faced criticism from the Catholic scholars working on the project who he accused of delaying and even suppressing information that did not support the Church's stance on Jesus. This criticism was fanned into open hostility when the Catholics attempted to discredit him in the London Times. In answer to a critique of his work by Father Roland de Vaux; John Allegro responded in September of 1956, drawing attention to the omission of Jesus as the 'Son of God' from the scrolls;

"You go on to talk blithely about what the first Jewish-Christians thought in Jerusalem, and no one would guess that your only real evidence - if you can call it such - is the New Testament, that body of much worked-over traditions who's 'evidence' would not

*stand for two minutes in a court of law... As for Jesus as a 'son of God' and 'Messiah'-
I don't dispute it for a moment; we now know from Qumran that their own Davidic
Messiah was reckoned a 'son of God', 'begotten' of God – but that doesn't prove the
Church's fantastic claim for Jesus that he was God himself. There's no 'contrast' in their
terminology at all – the contrast is in its interpretation."* [1]

Against this total lack of evidence of a crucifixion, we did find several
reports of Jesus still being alive long after the supposed crucifixion. This
coupled to Barbara Thiering's evidence that Jesus Christ was pardoned in 33
AD, by Pilate and the Herods, again brings into question the events of his
birth, life, deification and particularly his crucifixion. No scribe would risk
severe punishment by suggesting Jesus was pardoned if it was not so, at the
least he would be a laughing stock. It would be pretty stupid to state that he
had been pardoned if everyone knew he had been crucified. It would seem
fairly apparent that Jesus would need to have escaped death on the cross, to
be in a position to receive a pardon, wouldn't it?

So after careful and exhaustive study the conclusion looms that there
must be considerable doubt that Christ really died on the cross at Calgary
and it is far more likely that the story of Antigonus was adopted into the
Christian religion. If we accept this conclusion then it becomes likely that
Jesus was an allegoric, mythical being made up of a composite of other
personalities like the Teacher of Righteousness, Apollonius of Tyana and
Antigonus. We are now struggling with a creedal skepticism but our doubts
are certainly warranted. In a court of law there would be sufficient evidence
with eyewitness accounts and documentation, to determine that Jesus did
not die on the cross. The Bible is the <u>only</u> document with a first hand record
that he did, and it cannot be relied on for two reasons. Firstly there are many
cases of obvious tampering by factions with their own agendas and secondly
it has proved to fall down again and again with a myriad of errors through
translation, misunderstandings and fraudulent manipulation to enhance the
story. If you wish to contradict this conclusion, then you find the supporting evidence that refers to the life and sacrifice of Jesus and find evidence
that refutes that which states he survived. I don't believe it exists.

There is also a third consideration and that is that the prime elements of the birth, life, death and deification of Christ follow precisely the ritual traditions of ancient pagan religious practice. Even if for a moment, we were to assume that despite the Bible being a lone source of the crucifixion story, it is totally correct; then the uniqueness of Christ's conquering of death and eventual resurrection to Heaven is somewhat diluted anyway, by much older, identical stories contained in many and various oriental and pagan religions from around the world. We were never taught this stuff and this is what we will look at now. Most people I talk to have never heard of these things because the church has held them back for many years. In fact we will now see that the 'sacrifice for redemption' theme is far from uncommon as a motif in many, many, global religions. It appears to have originated with the ancient 'Kill the King' ritual where the King (as the most prestigious member of the tribe) was sacrificed to the Gods as the ultimate sacrifice, for appeasement, in times of trouble. Deification of the Regent was also commonplace. The German scholar Erich Zehren had this to say;

> *"...The Sumerian and Semitic kings assumed the role of the suffering, dying and resurrected god. For whatever happened in heaven must also happen on Earth and be represented in the sacred cult."* [2]

Erich Zehren went on to document that the archaeologist Wooley found evidence during the excavation of Ur that showed it was common practice in ancient Sumer for the king's body to be removed from his tomb to simulate resurrection. [3] We saw earlier that this is precisely what the Pharisees and Sanhedrin feared the disciples might attempt to do in the case of Jesus. Now these myths and stories require careful consideration because they predate the Bible by some considerable time, a couple of thousand years in some cases. This is hard evidence to refute because we saw earlier that pagan influences had certainly been adopted into the Nativity scene and other areas of the Christian religion. From my university studies I knew of parallels to Christ's birth and death amongst pagan religions. I even had clergy explain that the 'devil' had gone back in time to seed the earlier religions and generally plant evidence, so a counterfeit existed by the time Christ arrived. This is a pretty flimsy argument but it is in no way original. In ancient times, Saint Justin stated that the sacred things of the Christian religion including the Eucharist had been counterfeited by the devil;

"... *this very solemnity, the evil spirit introduced into the mysteries of Mithra.*" [4]

The dogma of the Christian religion has proved to be based on fear and intimidation through a process of indoctrination and this process works to deprive its followers of any form of knowledge that might be adverse to its own creed, so the laity will believe something as ludicrous as this time-travelling devil before they will make any attempt to gain even a fleeting knowledge of the subject from alternate sources. I didn't ever subscribe to this 'time traveller' theory and I don't believe even the most credulous Christian would, except in an act of outstanding faith or as an act of total desperation. To add to the likely deception, we will now establish that Jesus offered virtually nothing that was in any way innovative or new. It is not reasonable to believe that a God walked the Earth two thousand years ago, offered nothing that was new to mankind and then vanished without a trace. We will find also that the most part of the Christian message, that was not hi-jacked from the Jewish religion, was in fact borrowed from ancient pagan sources, effectively negating any reasonable chance for the involvement of the hand of Almighty God. I would think the Christian Bible itself sets the stage to refute the uniqueness of the Jesus office as the Son of God in the following passage:

John 3 : 13 *Only the Son of Man (Jesus) has ever ascended to heaven.*

Are we meant to believe this passage in John is the word of God? That is not what the Bible states elsewhere. What about Enoch, Elijah and the 'robber' on the cross? What about Abraham and Lazarus? Read for yourself:

Hebrews 11 : 5 *Enoch was translated to heaven.*

2 Kings 2 : 11 *Elijah went up to heaven.*

Luke 23 : 43 *And Jesus said unto him, Verily I say unto thee, today shalt thou be with me in paradise.*

2 Corinthians 12 : 2-4 *An unnamed man, known to Paul, went up to heaven and came back.*

Luke 16 : 20-24 *And it came to pass, that the beggar died, and was carried by the angels into Abraham's bosom: the rich man also died, and was buried; And in hell he* *lift up his eyes, being in torments, and seeth Abraham afar off, and Lazarus in his bosom. And he cried and said, Father Abraham, have mercy on me, and send Lazarus that he may dip the tip of his finger in water, and cool my tongue; for I am tormented in this flame.*

We find the Bible contradicting itself, stating that only Jesus ever ascended to Heaven, then it describes several others who did just that; and it doesn't stop there either. Let's continue with one of the best-known quotes from the Bible:

John 3 : 16 *For God so loved the world, that he gave his only begotten Son,*

The Bible is adamant and in fact its doctrine revolves around the fact that Jesus was (or is) the only begotten Son of God. This is part of the Apostles Creed that we recited with such fervour. To show it is not a lone quote;

John 1 : 18 *No man hath seen God at any time, the only begotten Son, which is in the bosom of the Father, he hath declared him.*

Are we to believe these two verses above from John? We can easily see that these statements *"no man hath seen God at any time"* and that Jesus was his *"only begotten son"* are not consistent with the Bibles other books and verses. In **Exodus 24:9-12** and **Genesis 17:1**, the Bible tells us both Moses and Abraham not only met with God and saw him face-to-face but in fact sat down to eat with him. Abraham entertained God and his entourage. The Bible contradicts the "only begotten Son of God" in a number of ways also effectively disputing the uniqueness of Christ's mission and the fact that he alone was supposedly the only Son of God;

Luke 3 : 38 *Which was the son of Enos, which was the son of Seth, which was the son of Adam, which was the son of God.* So Adam too was called the Son of God.

Daniel 3 : 25 *He answered and said, Lo, I see four men loose, walking in the midst of the fire, and they have no hurt; and the form of the fourth is like the Son of God.*

To whom was the writer of Daniel referring? Jesus was not born for many years to come and was certainly not on the scene as a person in Old Testament times and was totally unknown in the Old Testaments pages, so how would Daniel know what he looked like. Which Son of God did

Daniel mean here?

> **Hebrews 7 : 1 – 3** *For this Melchizedek…. Without father, without mother, without descent (or descendants), having neither beginning of days, nor end of life; but made <u>like unto the Son of God</u>; abideth a priest continually.*

So before Jesus was born, Melchizedek was like the Son of God.

> **Jeremiah 31 : 9** *They shall come with weeping, and with supplications will I lead them: I will cause them to walk by the rivers of waters in a straight way, wherein they shall not stumble: for I am a father to Israel, and <u>Ephraim is my firstborn</u>.*

So actually Ephraim (the son of Jacob/Israel) was really the firstborn son of God.

> **1 Chronicles 17 : 12-13** *He (Solomon) shall build a house for me, and I will establish his throne for ever. I will be his Father, and <u>he shall be my Son</u>; I will not take my steadfast love from him, as I took it from him who was before you.*

The Bible passages above confirm that Adam, Melchizedek, Ephraim and also Solomon were sons of God and yet Jesus was supposedly his <u>only begotten son</u>. The Bible goes further to use the lofty title 'Son of God' for lowly mankind striking another blow to the uniqueness of this term;

> **Hosea 1 : 10** *Yet the number of the children of Israel shall be as the sand of the sea, which cannot be measured nor numbered; and it shall come to pass, that in the place where it was said unto them, Ye are not my people, there it shall be said unto them, <u>Ye are the sons of the living God</u>.*

> **Romans 8 : 14** *For as many as are led by the Spirit of God, <u>they are the sons of God</u>.*

This of course doesn't make any sense but there's more. Satan (Lucifer) was supposedly created as a Son of God, in fact his most beautiful creation (perhaps more beautiful than his 'brother' Jesus);

> **Job 1 : 16** *Now there was a day when the <u>sons of God</u> came to present themselves before the Lord, and Satan came also among them.*

This may not sound correct yet it is repeated to be sure the reader understands;

> **Job 2 : 1** *Again there was a day when the <u>sons of God</u> came to present themselves before the Lord, and Satan came also among them to present himself before the Lord.*

So we find that there were plural Sons of God and Satan (Lucifer) was certainly classed as a Son of God. Now the name Lucifer means quite literally "day star" or "morning star" so what is it that Job is trying to tell us in this next passage?

Job 38 : 7 *When the morning stars sang together, and all the <u>sons of God</u> shouted for joy?*

This confirms that the sons of god were many and this cannot be coincidental since there is obviously some hidden meaning here. It seems all the Sons of God were 'morning stars' (or Lucifers) but for now suffice to say the Bible contradicts the uniqueness angle and these are pretty important issues to get wrong. This is not what we were taught! In addition Job makes it clear that the "Sons of God" existed before the creation of man, so men like Adam and Solomon are certainly not meant here.

If we keep an open mind we will discover that there is a rational explanation contained in the evidence that follows and this will be the subject of a following book. To understand the next chapters and to fully appreciate just who the plural, 'Sons of God' were, it is imperative that we firstly recognise that Jesus was <u>NOT</u> the singular, only begotten Son of God. That was a nonsense passage added to the New Testament in conflict with other passages as we have just seen. In following chapters we will ascertain precisely who the sons of God were;

Genesis 6 : 2 *That the <u>sons of God</u> saw the daughters of men that they were fair; and they took them wives of all which they chose.*

Genesis 6 : 4 *There were giants in the earth in those days; and also after that, when the <u>sons of God</u> came in unto the daughters of men, and they bare children to them, the same became mighty men which were of old, men of the shem.*

It may be somewhat confusing when contradictions are pointed out, not from alternate sources but from the same Bible. This in turn leaves the Christian doctrine in tatters and its Bible exposed as a work that is plainly in error.

The 'Holy' Ghost

We all heard about the Holy Ghost (or Holy Spirit) found within the Godhead and a third part of the Christian Trinity, although many Christians remain somewhat confused and uncomfortable with the worship of this Deity. It would likely alarm most Christians to learn that this Ghost is of very ancient pagan design and did not even enter the Christian record until the Council of Nicaea in 325 AD. This is despite a fraudulent record, added to the New Testament, claiming that the disciples of Jesus came in contact with this Holy Ghost in the first century, on the day of Pentecost. Some writers insist that "The Ghost" was an archetype of early paganism whilst others claim that the Indian God, Lord Krishna actually developed from the early record of this Ghost. From the time of Christ, a disciple of Apollonius called Damis the Assyrian (also recorded as Damis of Nineveh) documented in his work *'Memoirs'*, that his master actually raised the ghost of **Achilles**. Alexander the Great and many other world leaders were fascinated with the story of Achilles and it seems this could be the original entity that became the 'Holy' Ghost. In the early third century, Flavius Philostratus wrote a work called; *'Life of a Ghost'*. Bishop Eusebius saw that attributes of the Ghost in these writings had been applied to the personage of Jesus and worked hard to suppress all documentation about the Ghost. Nevertheless in time this 'Holy' Ghost was added to the Bible.

The nineteenth ecumenical council opened under Pope Paul III, at Trent on 13 December, 1545, and closed there on 4 December, 1563. It was proclaimed at this council that it was the authority of this Ghost that kept the Church on track and aided its infallibility and venerated it's inclusion in the Godhead. The following passage of questioned authenticity shows that a section of Christianity just after the time of Christ, had never heard of this Ghost;

> **Acts 19 : 2** *"Have ye received the Holy Ghost since ye believed?" And they said unto him, "We have not so much as heard whether there be any Holy Ghost."*

The Sadducees had apparently never heard of the Holy Spirit as well;

> **Acts 23 : 8** *For the Sadducees say there is no resurrection, neither angels, nor <u>spirit</u>; but the Pharisees confess both.*

The Ghost certainly precedes Christianity and likely pertains to both Achilles and possibly Krishna. After considering it's early pedigree, to give allegiance to this ghostly entity within the Christian Trinity in this day and age, would be naive to the extreme.

Requirements to be a God

The actual state of Godship carried an inherent expectation of meeting certain criteria that was, despite its global nature, amazingly similar. In ancient texts we find a generic sameness in the attributes that led to the deification of the various pagan Saviour Gods. The Christian may not realise that outside the Bible this evidence is readily accessible and plentiful. Being born in a stable or grotto with animals and shepherds attending plus the visitation of wise men was also a regular theme. Virgin birth was not only common; it was an ancient obsession and a virgin 'Queen of Heaven' was worshipped from distant antiquity. In fact German archaeologists excavating the ancient city of Uruk, (one of the oldest cities on Earth) found evidence of a virgin 'Queen of Heaven' who had been worshipped there from the most ancient times. The timing of religious re-birth to a specific time of year like the winter solstice was also congruent. We need to investigate this subject to clearly demonstrate that the Bible in reality fits harmoniously in with a plethora of pagan religions and does not in any way offer the unique message we were sold. We can start with the numerous documented references to universal 'Sun Gods' all of whom are born in a time of spiritual awakening at the European winter solstice of 23-25 December and eventually die only to be resurrected at the season of Easter. Sound familiar?

Kuhn explains that the *Logos* and the *Christos* were 'cosmic forces' in ancient philosophy and the Christians took these solar entities and confused them into the character of Jesus. For this reason the true facts surrounding the historical Jesus had to be abandoned in favour of the universal doctrine.

Kuhn put it this way:

To indicate the universality of the Sun-god myth it is only necessary to enumerate some thirty of the chief figures known as Sun-Gods amongst the nations about the Eastern Mediterranean, before the advent of Jesus. There were in <u>Egypt</u>, Osiris, Horus,

Serapis, Hermes or Taht (Thoth), Khunsu, Atum (Aten, Adon, the Adonis or Phrygia), Iusa, Iu-sa, Iu-em-hetep; in <u>Syria</u>, Atis, Sabazius, Zagreus, Kybele (feminine); in <u>Assyria</u> Tammuz; in <u>Babylonia</u>, Marduk and Sargon; in <u>Persia</u>, Mithra, Ahura-Mazda and the Zoroasters; in <u>Greece</u>, Orpheus, Bacchus (Dionysus), Achilles, Hercules, Theseus, Perseus, Jason, Prometheus; in <u>India,</u> Vyasa, Krishna, Buddha; in <u>Tibet</u> the Boddhisattvas; besides many others elsewhere." [5]

David Pratt, in his book; *"Who Was the Real Jesus?"* made these comments that support what Kuhn had to say about the similarity of Jesus to the Sun-Gods;

"The gospel figure of Jesus is a Jewish adaptation of the mythical 'God-man' found under many different names in ancient pagan mystery religions: in <u>Egypt</u> he was Osiris, in <u>Greece</u> Dionysus, in <u>Asia Minor</u> Attis, in <u>Syria</u> Adonis, in <u>Italy</u> Bacchus, in <u>Persia</u> Mithras. All the major elements of the Jesus story, from the virgin birth to the crucifixion and resurrection, can be found in earlier stories of pagan 'God-men'." [6]

Like Plato, St Epiphanius of Salamis also recognised the God within the individual heart and stated that 'Krist' was the identity of this inner spirit. The obvious similarity to the name of Jesus Christ, the name that the Bible records as 'above every other name' is accordingly worthy of study. The title 'Christ' corresponds with a string of 'Krist' Gods possibly commencing in Egypt a thousand years before Jesus, where this name was engraved on the basalt Palermo stone. It seems that separately, Krist was a name given to the Egyptian God Horus born of the virgin Isis and appears to be a concept or title passed down to various deified figures from many different regions around the world. In addition to 'Krist', the Gods, 'Chris of Chaldea' and the early Indian God 'Krishna' who all date from well before the Biblical times are examples of 'Krist' titles.

We saw that Jesus' name was altered to Yehoshua and then shortened to Yesu. The Greek word 'Jesus' is said to duplicate the Hebrew name Yesu, the supposed name used by the man from Galilee. St Epiphanius recorded "Men of Yesu" as a heretical sect of healers existing in the Roman territory and specifically associates them with 'Jesus the physician'. The worship of a God called Yesu however is much older than that, being a member of the Druidic trinity; **'Yesu'** along with **'Beli'** and **'Taran'** were worshipped from a time of great antiquity.

We must be cautious because in antiquity Gods took the names of other Gods they conquered. Thus an 'all-conquering' God would have a multi facetted personality to go with his multiple names. As Stuart Nettlefold comically put it;

> *"Conquering Gods their titles take*
> *From the foes they captive make."* [7]

Similar Saviours

The religion of Mithraism catered only for men and its mysteries were dispensed in grades of initiation. These were **Corax** (raven); **Nymphus** (bridegroom); **Miles** (soldier); **Leo** (lion); **Perses** (Persian); **Heliodromus** (sun's courier) and finally **Pater** (father) each having secret initiation rituals, secret meals and each dedicated to a planet. Their temples were built in natural caves or in the basements of houses made to look like the cave in which Mithras had killed the divine bull (tauroctony); the symbol of life through death. The early Christian Church denounced this religion as a blasphemous mockery of Christian rituals, and this despite Mithraism being at least a millennium older than Christianity. The Roman Church had a lot of problems with Mithraism along with the cult of Zoroaster. It is recorded in some ancient texts that as a real person, the prophet Zoroaster was a pupil of no less than Abraham, and most particularly in the study of astronomy, astrology and time-keeping. Abraham is also quoted by Josephus as teaching these same things to the Egyptians. **Zarathustra** is the original Persian form of Zoroaster and the time frame for this prophet is fairly uncertain, although somewhere within the wide range of 2000 BCE to 5000 BCE is usually quoted. It is unlikely that Abraham (c. 2000 BCE) was actually his tutor although Zoroaster supposedly spread his philosophy by converting kings and princes who would then convert the people of their lands.

Mithraism was an ancient pagan 'mystery religion' mainly located in Persia that finally spread to Rome in the 1st century BCE. It was an offshoot of **Zoroastrianism**, which recognized Ahura Mazda as God. There are unequivocal, obvious parallels between this religion and the Christian religion and it is easily proved with certainty that the worship of Mithra predated the birth of Christ since Mithras first appears as an Aryan sun-god in Sanskrit and Persian literature from around 1400 BCE. To gain insight into the similarities, this religion, Mithraism;

(i)   *Postulated the Apocalypse and the Day of Judgment.*

(ii)   *Prophesied the resurrection of Mithras and proclaimed a second coming.*

(iii)   *Included a bread and wine ceremony identical to the Christian Eucharist.*

(iv)   *Involved a sealing of the forehead in a baptism ceremony.*

(v)   *Taught the concept of both Heaven and Hell.*

In addition Mithras was:

(i)   *Born of a virgin in a grotto that also housed animals.*

(ii)   *Attended by shepherds and regaled with gifts brought from afar.*

(iii)   *Born at the time of the winter solstice, 25 December. (The Roman Emperor Aurelian decreed that this should be the official birthday of Mithra.)*

(iv)   *The sole creator of the Universe.*

(v)   *Depicted with a halo (nimbus) around his head.*

(vi)   *Believed to have partaken of a last supper with his followers before he ascended to heaven.*

(vii)   *His followers believed he would come again to raise the dead for a final judgement, after the world had been destroyed by fire.*

(viii) *A Mithra styled baptism would obtain immortal life for his followers and believers could gain atonement from the resurrection of their saviour since he had conquered death.*

(ix)   *The later Roman section of this cult chose a leader they called 'Papa' (the same title as Pope).*

(x)   *Believers celebrated a sacred meal of bread and wine identical to the Catholic Eucharist which they called the <u>Myazda</u> in remembrance of Mithra (and apparently Ahura Mazda).*

(xi)   *Their service employed bells, candles, incense, holy water and involved chanting mantras.*

Taken by the similarities of Mithraism to Christianity, Knight and Lomas state;

"This is not a case of similarities; we're talking about total interchangeability." They

go on, *"The cult of Mithra is particularly awkward for Christians who do not subscribe to the satanic time-traveler theory. Mithraism is a Syrian offshoot of the more ancient Persian cult of Zoroaster, which was introduced into the Roman Empire about 67 BCE. Its doctrines included baptism, a sacrament meal, belief in immortality, a saviour God who died and rose again to act as a mediator between man and God, a resurrection, a last judgment and heaven and hell."* [8]

A fundamental difficulty for the Christian Church is the fact that the central myth involved in Christianity actually predates Christ and the Bible by many hundreds, if not thousands of years. If we specifically look at the Bible's cataclysmic stories we will find too that these are in no way original or unique. Dr. Immanuel Velekovski describes a global scenario of doom and cataclysm separating the world's eons. This takes away the uniqueness of other Bible stories, in placing a global theme on the Biblical flood, the plagues of Egypt and the predicted 'end of the World' cataclysm. The global pagan records usually have the world destroyed in turn by (i) **Flood** and inundation, (ii) **Fire** sometimes with accompanying brimstone then (iii) **Wind** and tempest. [9]

We should consider too that the crucifixion of Christ shares a motif of regent sacrifice that was at the time, both pagan and global. The Christian communion or Eucharist with it's "this is my body…. take eat" and "this is my blood that is shed for many" is itself a parody of the cannibalistic feast ritual that followed the sacrifice of the King. As we continue looking at ancient cults from around the world, it becomes quite apparent that the much later Christianity borrowed and adopted these rituals. As we saw, Paul himself states that it was not at all necessary to be truthful in this endeavour, believing that it was no sin to lie for the glory of God.

Romans 3 : 7 *For if the truth of God hath more abounded through my lie unto his glory; why yet am I also judged as a sinner?*

It becomes likely that Paul with little regard for the truth, "matched miracles" when he encountered the followers of pagan Gods, to convert these heathens to Christianity. Accordingly he attributed stories of virgin birth and overcoming death to Jesus to spread the all-important message. Remember Paul had no Bible and had supposedly never met Jesus; he spent almost no time with the disciples of Jesus and his entire doctrine was what he made up and we can see now just how much was based on prevailing pagan religion from the Holy Land. In addition we should recognise the ancient practice of embedding sufficient actual history into the very tissue of cultural and religious doctrine, to make it credible.

Crucified Contemporaries of Christ

Helena Blavatsky stated that the story of Jesus was invented in totality some time after the 1st century AD. Apart from the letters of Paul, this is pretty much what our research is showing as well. Jesus, she says, is a deified personification of the glorified type of the great Hierophants of the Temples, and his story, as told in the New Testament, is allegory, assuredly containing profound esoteric truths, but still an allegoric record.

> *"Every act of the Jesus of the New Testament, every word attributed to him, every event related of him during the three years of the mission he is said to have accomplished, rests on the programme of the Cycle of Initiation, a cycle founded on the Precession of the Equinoxes and the Signs of the Zodiac."* [10]

It is true that back in the age of **Taurus,** mankind engaged in Bull worship, moving to the Fish symbol heralding the 'fishers of men' in the age of **Pisces** and now embraces the resurgence of Buddhist philosophy of peace and understanding as we herald in the 'age of **Aquarius**'. G. de Purucker supports this stance and recorded in a similar vein:

> *"...the 'Gospel' story is merely an idealized fiction, written by Christian mystics in imitation of esoteric mysteries of the 'Pagans', showing the initiation trials and tests of the candidate for initiation; and it is not very well done, there being much error and many mistakes in the 'Gospels'."* [11]

It seems that after dispatching Antigonus, the 'King of the Jews' in 34 BCE, Rome adopted a policy of zero tolerance on Jewish messiahs. No clergyman ever told me of the crucifixion of additional Jewish Messiahs in the Holy Land, from around the time of Jesus. The historian Josephus, who is known as a fairly reliable source, however documents three Jewish 'Messiahs' from the first century, who were crucified by the Romans: **Yehuda of Galilee** (6 AD), **Theudas** (44 AD), and **Benjamin the Egyptian** (60 AD).

From **Acts 5 : 34–35** we can see that the disciple Judas Thaddaeus - is called 'Theudas'.

It seems that Joses, the brother of Jesus, was likely this disciple, and it is possibly his crucifixion in 44 AD that is referred to above. A probable reference to Benjamin the Egyptian exists in the Bible;

> **Acts 21 : 37–38** *And as Paul was to be led into the castle, he said unto the chief captain, May I speak unto thee? Who said, Canst thou speak Greek? Art not thou that Egyptian, which before these days madest an uproar, and leddest out into the wilderness four thousand men that were (sinners) murderers?*

Josephus is easily sourced reference, so the Church simply must be aware of these facts. Despite this we certainly see a reluctance to disclose information to the laity. We must also consider why is it, that all this documentation exists for other crucifixions, but there is no supporting evidence whatsoever for the Bible's story of Jesus Christ?

The Purpose of The Crucifixion

I always had trouble with the whole purpose of the crucifixion of Jesus. The concept of the innocent redeeming the guilty defies logic. I appreciate that Jesus was to become the 'Lamb of God' to take on the sins of the world and present to God the Father, the ultimate blood sacrifice. He was to die for mankind, for you and me. Answer me this then; how did Jesus being crucified for seditious crimes against Rome achieve that for us? Does this mean that the capital punishment of someone on America's 'death row' can also help? But Jesus was innocent, you say! What if the 'death row' inmate is also innocent? In addition why did God require the sacrifice of his only son, to appease himself, when he makes the rules? To believe that the death of Jesus was necessary for the appeasement of a petulant deity, one must believe firstly in the redemption inherent in blood sacrifice, and ultimately in human sacrifice, and I for one, certainly have trouble with that. If we think about it the entire concept is barbaric!

When the Biblical 'King of the Jews' attempted to overthrow the Romans, resulting in his capital punishment as a subversive against Rome, wasn't this a totally, totally unrelated event to our salvation. What did it have to do with dying for the sins of man? Viewing it within the context of the long-established ancient practice of regent sacrifice is the only motif that makes any sense. The Eucharist theme is also entirely consistent with this pagan practice. Fitting it to the Passover Lamb sacrifice is a nice twist as well. Remember, crucifixion was a Roman punishment for sedition against the Empire. The Bible stresses that Jesus died for your sins. How is it that if you can accept this within your belief mechanism – then you are saved; yet if through a questioning mind, education, lack of indoctrination or whatever, you simply can't swallow this highly implausible story, you can look forward to eternal torment? Can we at least ask why? Just like the required punishment of an <u>innocent</u>, to 'save' the <u>guilty</u>, it just makes no sense whatever.

Twenty-three Crucified Saviours

Further research began to show that there were many of the world's supposed 'saviours' additional to both Jesus and Mithras who were said to have been sacrificed for the redemption of their followers, and these all seemed to fall within the regent sacrifice context. I decided to research this subject much further and about this time a book called 'The Worlds Sixteen Crucified Saviours' written by Kersey Graves came into my possession. This is an amazing book in its own right but more particularly because it was written a hundred and thirty years ago in 1875. Graves had information not readily available today, but of course had no access to more modern finds like the Dead Sea scrolls or Nag Hammadi corpus. Graves focuses on a total of sixteen saviours however we will uncover information on several others that would convince even the most determined sceptic that this motif of a crucified King is neither unique nor original as it pertains to Jesus. Graves is totally adamant that the information he has uncovered dispels the slightest chance that the Bible story of Jesus being the saviour of the world is in any way unique, original or true. He passionately addresses the clergy:

> "Friends and brethren – teachers of the Christian faith: Will you believe us when we tell you the divine claims of your religion are gone – all swept away by the "logic of history," and nullified by the demonstrations of science? The recently opened fountains of historic law, many of whose potent facts will be found interspersed through the pages of this work, sweep away the last inch of ground on which can be predicated the least

show for either the divine origin of the Christian religion, or the divinity of Jesus Christ. For these facts demonstrate beyond all cavil and criticism, and with a logic force which can leave not the vestige of doubt upon any unbiased mind, that all its doctrines are an outgrowth from older heathen systems. Several systems of religion essentially the same in character and spirit as that religion now known as Christianity, and setting forth the same doctrines, principles and precepts, and several personages filling a chapter in history almost identical with that of Jesus Christ, it is now known to those who are up with the discoveries and intelligence of the age, were venerated in the East, centuries before a religion called Christianity, or a personage called Jesus Christ were known to history. [12]

Graves looks at saviours who suffered crucifixion but also offers information on other 'Gods' who displayed supposedly unique Christian precepts, in many cases hundreds of years before the time of Christ. His research into pagan, heathen Gods, finds (as we did) that there are set criteria, such as virgin birth and associated miracles, that over the centuries have become the expected attributes of a God. In like manner it is my intention to as fairly as possible, consider the attributes of the ancient pagan Gods and compare them to the Biblical Jesus in line with similar criteria of twelve such attributes. Let's now look at these specific criteria that the Christian Church would readily teach as peculiar to Christ, unique to his status and necessary to his deification;

1. **Prophecies of the Coming Messiah.**
2. **Immaculate Conception and Parthenogenesis** (literally, virgin birth).
3. **Stars Predict and Illuminate the Birth.**
4. **Shepherds, Angels and Wise Men with Gifts Attend the Birth.**
5. **Birth Date of 25 December.**
6. **Of Royal Descent but Humble Birth.**
7. **Threat to the Infant by the Incumbent Ruler.**
8. **Healing, Miracles and Remission of Sin.**
9. **Dualistic Involvement of a Serpent or Satan.**
10. **Sacrifice by Crucifixion as Atonement for Unworthy Man.**

11. Descent into Hell and Miraculous Resurrection
12. The Eucharist of the body and blood.

Prepare for some surprises as we take them one at a time:

1. Prophecies of the Coming Messiah

The clergy would have us believe that there are several prophecies predicting the event of the birth and death of Christ. I personally believe that not one of these prophecies will withstand any amount of scrutiny. The Jewish church does not accept that Jesus was the Messiah and does not recognise any predictions in their Talmud texts. Since the Bible's Old Testament is borrowed from those texts it is difficult to see how Christians can now find these prophecies recorded there. For example the prophesy of Isaiah, *"Unto us a child is born."* This context shows that it is the writer's own child being spoken of and the semantics clearly indicate that the child is already born, effectively negating any divine or inspired prophetic involvement. In addition, predictions of the birth of 'Messiahs' were both common and global, for example Graves states;

> *"Most religious countries and more than a score of religious systems had a standing prophesy that a divine deliverer would descend from heaven and relieve them from their depressed state, and ameliorate their condition."* [13]

Bala an ancient prophet of India long predicted that at the end of their *'Cali Yug'* period, a divine child would be born who would miraculously understand all things including the Holy Scriptures and that he would bring justice and truth and remove all sin. The birth of **Krishna** was believed to have fulfilled what had been recorded in all their sacred books. [14]

We were taught that the Bible's book of Micah contains a prophesy of the birth of Christ;

> **Micah 5 : 2** *But thou, <u>Bethlehem Ephratah</u>, though thou be little among the thousands of Judah, yet out of thee shall he come forth unto me that is to be <u>ruler in Israel</u>; whose goings forth have been from of old, from everlasting.*

To make this prophesy work, we would have to disregard a few basic facts. Firstly Jesus never ruled in Israel. Secondly it is highly unlikely that Jesus was born in Bethlehem. Furthermore, Bethlehem was acknowledged as an ancient centre of the Tammuz cult, so if a ruler coming out of Bethlehem is being spoken about, the Biblical scribe in Micah is most likely talking about Tammuz and not Jesus.

2. Immaculate Conception and Parthenogenesis (literally, virgin birth). **Mithra** was born of a virgin in a stable on 25 December around 600 BCE (based on an even older Sanskrit record from 1400 BCE). The resurrection of Mithra was celebrated at Easter. The quoted birth of the Egyptian God **Horus** was to the virgin **Isis** and it is recorded that the mother of **Hercules** was a virgin who "knew only **Jove**" (meaning the Roman God Jupiter equivalent to the Greek Zeus). The Holy virgin **Devaki** (Yasoda) gave birth to the Indian god **Krishna**. The virgin **Pythais** mother of **Pythagoras**, conceived by a (holy) ghost. **Aleides** was born in 1280 BCE of the virgin **Alemene**. The Persian God, **Zoroaster** was born of an immaculate conception. **Juno** of Greece was a virgin when she bore the god **Mars**. This same mother had **Vulcan** by a 'holy wind ghost'. **Plato** was said to be born of his mother **Paretonia** by the god **Apollo** and not her husband **Ariston**. The Mexican saviour God **Quexalcotal** was born of the Queen of Heaven called **Suchiquecal**, without the aid of a man. The virgin **Maia** conceived the Chinese god **Xaca** with the aid of a white elephant. The first Chinese monarch and Saviour, **Emperor Yu** was conceived when his mother was struck by a star. She was the virgin **Shing–Mon** and actually conceived this deity from a water lily. **Tamerlane** of Bermuda was conceived by his mother with the aid of the 'God of Day', whilst **Genghis Khan** of Tartary, without earthly father was the son of the Sun. Egyptian God **Julis** (or Zulis) was born of the beautiful virgin **Cronis Celestine** by way of divine, immaculate conception and **Osiris** too was the result of virgin birth, from **Ceres** his mother. The virgin mother of the Druid God **Hesus** was **Mayence**; of the Egyptian **Bacchus** was **Semele**; while of the Grecian **Bacchus** was **Minerva**. A God was responsible for immaculately conceiving **Buddha** with his mother **Maya** still a virgin, while saviours **Tein** and **Chang-Ti** according to Chinese history were both born of virgins. Oddly enough the (step) fathers of both Buddha and Krishna as well as Jesus are recorded as being carpenters. In addition, the *Asiatic Researches* documents the *"only begotten son of*

God," one **Salvahana** of Cape Mountain, as the son of a virgin mother and a carpenter by the name of **Taishnea**. Almost all of these Saviours are noted as the "first born" or "only begotten" <u>son of God</u>. The god, **Arion** too was the result of immaculate conception by the gods in the citadel, which resulted in a ten-month pregnancy. It is interesting to note also that records exist stating the gestation of **Hercules, Sakia, Confucius, Guatama the Buddha, Scipo, Solomon** and even **Jesus Christ** supposedly took ten months.

The obsession for Gods to be born of a virgin probably says more about the upper echelon of the Church, that they would require this amazing and quite impossible biological feat. The laity have only themselves to blame if they actually believe this rubbish and it makes them prime targets for the rest of the nonsense the Church would have them accept. Sargon the Akkadian ruler who was deified in the third century BCE was also credited with parthenogenesis. King Sargon was likely the prototype Moses, supposedly found as a baby in a floating basket many years before the time of Moses. A record supposedly from Sargon himself, exercising a remarkable memory goes thus;

> *"My mother was a 'priestess' (bride of God). I had no father. My mother conceived me and gave birth to me in secret. She laid me in a basket of reeds and closed the door with bitumen. She set me afloat upon the River Euphrates but it did not drown me. It bore me away."*

So without the aid of a father, Sargon's mother, a (virgin) priestess was able to conceive him. He overcame a difficult and deprived childhood to become a great king and was in due course deified, because he held all the traits and qualifications required of a God.

3. Stars Predict and Illuminate the Birth

The ancients were really fascinated by astrology and astronomy and vehemently sought astral signs and harbingers. Comets were thought to precipitate catastrophes or announce in the new ages. **Abraham, Julius Caesar, Pythagoras, Yu, Confucius** and **Krishna,** like **Jesus Christ** all had a star heralding their arrival. **Virgil** declared in 60 BCE that a star guided

Aeneas in his journey westward from Troy and **Pliny** reported in *Natural History Book II* that the citizens of Rome thought they had seen a God in the form of a man in a comet or star. [15] In the case of Jesus however, we must look again at what the Bible records.

Matthew 2 : 2 *we have seen his star in the east.* Note it does not say **a** star; it clearly references astrology with **his** star. The wise men came from the east and this passage must be communicating that at home, in the east, they saw his astrological star, not that as they headed west to arrive at his birth place, they continually looked over their shoulder at the star in the east from whence they had come.

> *"In the history of the Hindu saviour Krishna, we are told that, "As soon as Nared, who having heard of his fame, had examined the stars, he declared him to be from God; i.e. the Son of God."* [16]

A star predicted the birth of Julius Caesar:

> *"The Roman Calcidius speaks of "a wonderful star, presaging the descent of a God amongst men."* [17]

4. Shepherds, Angels and Wise Men with Gifts Attend the Birth

Magi or wise men visited several of the world's saviours and in many cases the new born were also adored by shepherds. Well before the birth of Christ we find recorded that angels attended the birth of **Confucius** of China in 598 BCE. Graves states that there were five wise men who came to visit Confucius whilst celestial music played and angels attended the scene. On the occasion of his birth in 1200 BCE, **Krishna** was visited by *devatas* (angels), shepherds and wise men all impressed by his potential for future greatness. [18] These learned men even presented him with gifts of (wait for it) gold, frankincense and myrrh. The sacred Indian *Ramayana* holds a passage where an angel salutes Krishna's mother with words identical to the Bible's version; **Luke 1 : 28** *Hail thou that art highly favored, the Lord is with thee, blessed art thou among women.*

In ancient Greece, wise men and Magi attended the birth of both **Pythagoras** and **Socrates** bringing, again, gold, frankincense and myrrh. Graves tells us that this combination of gold, frankincense and myrrh were the standard gifts given to the Sun-Gods in Persia and likewise in Arabia more than three thousand years ago. Both Pliny and Aristotle record that Magi visited **Zoroaster** at his birth, which they date at 4,000 BCE. Just consider if we removed the 'borrowed' material we have encountered so far from the myth that became the Biblical story of Jesus Christ, there would be little left that is unique. It is becoming apparent that very little of the Christian message is original. We still have much more to consider.

5. Birth date of 25 December

This has been covered previously showing that this date corresponds to the European winter solstice of the sun and accordingly was a symbol of re-newal and re-birth. In times BCE, this was also the date of the New Year and it was necessary that it coincide with the re-birth of the Sun God, Sol Invictus. Thus it was celebrated as his birthday, however it didn't stop with Sol Invictus either. **Baccus** of Egypt, **Baccus** of Greece, **Adonis** of Greece, **Krishna** of India, **Chang-Ti** of China, **Chris** of Chaldea, **Mithra** of Persia, **Sakia** of India, **Jao Wapaul**, (A crucified saviour) of early Britain and the myriad of additional 'Sun Gods' were also supposedly born on 25 December according to their respective histories. In the case of Krishna his birthday was said to be midnight of the 25th of the Indian month of Savarana, which corresponds to December on our calendar. [19]

Graves also had this to say;

"Divested of all explanation, the announcement of the fact that the time of the birth of many of the incarnated Gods and Saviours of antiquity was fixed at the same period and this period the twenty-fifth of December, celebrated all over Christendom as the birthday of Jesus Christ, would sound marvelously strange, especially when it is noticed that this period formerly dated the birth of a New Year – the birth of King Sol. And when we find that the ancient pagans were in the habit of celebrating this venerated twenty-fifth of December as the birthday of their Gods in the same manner Christians now celebrate it as the birthday of Christ, we are driven to admit that something more than just a fortuitous accident must be adduced to account for the coincidence". [20]

The coincidence is easily dismissed when one studies that the Roman Emperor Constantine quite deliberately changed the birthday celebration of Jesus to the 25 December to coincide with that of Sol Invictus when he adopted Christianity as the Byzantine State religion. This was done to appease the Sun worshippers who were loath to change their age old celebration and feast days from the 25th. December. Worth noting too is that this change along with the deification of Jesus did not take place until 325 A D, when the new birth date was applied.

> *"The birthday of Horus was annually celebrated in the (Egyptian) temples, about 25 December. A figure of Horus as a baby was laid in a manger, in a scenic reconstruction of a stable, and a statue of (his mother) Isis was placed beside it. In the catacombs at Rome are pictures of the baby Horus being held by the virgin mother Isis—the original Madonna and Child... He was the daily saviour of mankind, saving us from perpetual darkness."* [21]

6. Of Royal Descent but Humble Birth

This seems a strange requirement since it would be unusual if not contradictory for someone of Royal descent to have a humble birth and upbringing or in fact to be born in a stable, cave or other inauspicious location. I believe it speaks more about the psychological needs of the populous than the requirement of an Almighty God. This is about having a saviour that the congregation could relate to, because he too (like us) has suffered. Being meek and poor made him 'one of us', and even more so because he was in fact, the rightful King.

It can be shown that the Indian God **Krishna** although humble and poor was actually of the royal house of Kousa when his linage was traced back many generations. Likewise the mother of **Buddha Sakia** was betrothed to a Rajah, placing her son in the ruling caste. Humble birth was also associated with **Mohammad**, the prophet of Islam, who showed his humility when he slept on a cloak spread on the ground, using a bag of leaves for a pillow because he had nowhere else to lay his head. [22] We may also note the many tales of the 'Fisher Kings' around the time of the Arthurian legends. These characters were found in the guise of humble but wise fishermen and were eventually shown to be of Royal descent only in the final chapter. The simple occupation of one who had turned his back on the pampering and prosperity that went with a Royal career was deemed a most admirable trait, as was humility and humble birth.

Perhaps the 'humble birth' of Jesus can be taken a bit too far. The Roman church was terrified of women holding any power, and 'adjusted' the scriptures to suit their stance removing any power or dignity from Hebrew women. Graves quotes Dr Alexander Walker, (a Christian writer) from his work on Women;

> *"It is remarkable that in the genealogy of Christ only four women are named: Thamar, who seduced the father of her late husband, and Rachel a common prostitute, and Ruth, who, instead of marrying one of her cousins, went to bed with another of them, and Bathsheba, an adulteress, who espoused David, the murderer of her first husband."* [23]

Add to this Jesus' wife, the priestess Mary Magdalene who has been denigrated to a harlot or prostitute and by the Holy Bible's reckoning, we have here a real bunch of tarts. Are we ready to believe all that from the Roman Church! Yeah! Right!

7. Threat to the Infant by the Incumbent Ruler

Again we see psychological implications where the birth of a God must be heralded by signs and wonders and then good must overcome evil for the vulnerable infant God to survive. There is always a jealous, wicked incumbent King who wants to destroy the baby. According to Livy, even Romulus along with his brother Remus, survived by being adopted and suckled by a she wolf. Romulus went on to achieve his destiny of founding Rome and was later deified. We noted in the case of Jesus that Joseph was warned by an angel that he must take Jesus and flee to Egypt to escape the evil King Herod. I often wondered why the wise men bothered to tell Herod if he was so wicked. If they were really wise they might have known he was sufficiently unstable that he would kill all babies two years of age and below in the 'slaughter of the innocents'.

We find precisely the same agencies in place at the birth of other saviours. **Zoroaster's** mother is said to have believed that evil spirits were trying to destroy her child before his birth, but a good spirit arrived to protect the child and to comfort her. In the case of **Krishna** we find an almost identical story to the Biblical tale, where the 'angel' not only warned the parents to flee from danger, he also informed the tyrant ruler **Cansa** that a rival had been born in his kingdom and Cansa set out to destroy him. [24] This may indicate a wish for fair play but somewhat negated the warning he gave the parents. These wise men and angels really don't seem all that wise, do they?

Throughout ancient history, we see kings usurp the throne of weaker kings and a myriad of battles where powerful kings gain the kingdoms of lesser kings. This was more or less accepted practice and in those times with no TV news to bring it forcefully into the homes of the populous, was more or less accepted behavior. Graves goes on to wonder why Herod or indeed Cansa took such a circuitous route in removing a rival, when normal procedure would be a simple and quick disposal once he became a real threat. Cansa's seek and destroy mission was really not necessary yet it was almost identical to Herod's. Note the words of his decree;

"Let active search be made for whatever young children there may be upon Earth, and let every boy in whom there may be found signs of unusual greatness, be slain without remorse." [25]

Quoted in a book called *'Oriental Memories'* volume II page 447, the author Forbes states that in the temple at Elephanta in India there is a sculptured relief of a king with drawn sword, surrounded by slaughtered infants. This is quite apparently this same 'slaughter of the innocents' and just as the parents of Jesus supposedly fled into Egypt to escape the angered Herod, so too the parents of **Krishna** fled with the young saviour into Gokul. The similarity to the Bible's 'slaughter of the innocents' story recorded in **Matthew 2 : 8 & 16**, is quite remarkable, more so because the identical Cansa story is considerably older than Christianity.

Graves summarizes thus;

1. **There was an angel warning in each case relative to the impending danger.**

2. **The governor or ruler was hostile in each case to the mission of the young saviour.**

3. **A bloody decree was issued in both cases, having for its object the destruction of these infant Messiahs.**

4. **The hurried flight of the parents takes place in each case.**

5. **In addition it is stated in "The Gospel of the Infancy of Jesus" that Jesus and his parents sojourned for a time at a place called Matarea (Mathura), which ironically was the name of the birthplace of Krishna.**

This strongly indicates that the Bible story was plagiarized from the Krishna records and not even the town name was changed. As a side note, when the parents of **Krishna** approached the River Jumna with the royal baby, it is recorded that the waters miraculously parted, allowing them to pass. This indicates that Moses parting of the Sea of Reeds (wrongly translated as the Red Sea in the King James Version) was also not original. The Egyptian 'Book of the Dead' has the God Ra parting the waters on his journey to the afterlife. Note too that threats to **Moses** caused his mother to hide him in the reed basket to escape death. In like manner the Chinese God Yu was hidden in a basket in a river, as was the previously mentioned Persian King Sargon. There is something archetypal about a future 'Saviour of the World' requiring saving in his infancy. This theme goes on with similar escape stories for **Buddha, Osiris** and **Horus**. Ironically, Horus who had to escape plotting brothers, had a secret name of *"IAHU"* and this was also a secret name of Almighty God YHWH.

Aleides the Greek God had to flee to Galem with his parents to escape threatening danger. So too did **Salvahana** of Cape Comorin, who was documented as the only begotten Son of God, with his father Taishnea actually recorded as a humble carpenter and his mother a virgin. **Osiris** as a suckling infant in his cradle, killed two snakes that came to destroy him.

The historian Josephus was related to Herod's wife, and being a Jew, never missed an opportunity to record the 'bad deeds' of the hated Herod. Ironically, he does not record the Biblical 'slaughter of the innocents'. Josephus lived in the same land and meticulously covered the precise period but was silent on this event. In fact it was not documented by any other writer outside the Bible. This alone would cast serious doubts that it ever occurred but coupled to the point that the aging Herod could not possibly have seen a threat from a baby who would be unlikely to rule until well after Herod's 'use by date', it appears non-sensical. As we have seen, if the 'slaughter' was historical fact, John the Baptist should not have escaped and from the additional evidence stated we have to draw the conclusion that the whole thing was once again, a farcical, borrowed fiction. [27]

8. Healing, Miracles and Remission of Sin

The episode portion of the Mahabaret Bible, 'The Baghavat Gita', is claimed by the Hindu's to be divinely inspired and to have an antiquity of over 6000 years. **Krishna** is claimed to be the Saviour promised to former generations who would teach his many followers in parables. Along with his disciples, Krishna showed great compassion and tenderness to his fellow man and is credited with assisting people where he could. Graves put it this way;

> *"His pathway was thickly strewn with miracles, which consisted in healing the sick, curing lepers, restoring the dumb, deaf and blind, raising the dead, aiding the weak, comforting the sorrow-stricken, relieving the oppressed, casting out devils etc."* [28]

He is said to have saved two boys who had been bitten by poisonous serpents. In like manner, it was the love and compassion felt for their fellow man that marked the other various saviours and resulted in records of their care for the sick and ailing, to finally be recorded as miracles. The miracles themselves however were not all that exclusive. Egyptian initiates of the secret 'mystery schools' also performed precisely these same feats.

Bacchus is attributed with turning water into wine. In addition both **Alcides** and **Osiris** turned water into wine and cast out devils. **Alcides** performed many magical cures and according to Ovid, miraculously cured the daughter of Archiades and the wife of Theogenes after the doctors had failed. Julius records that Alcides raised Tyndarus and Hippolytus from the dead. Strabo states that the ancient temples are full of tablets describing miraculous cures performed by various virgin born Gods of those times. He records the case of two blind men whose sight was restored by 'Alcides, the Son of God.' [29] The historian Pausanias states that **Esculapius** raised several people from the dead and confirms that the above Hippolytus was one of them. He furnishes proof in the form of an inscribed monument erected at the time of this momentous occasion. In Alexandria there were records of various miracle workers who frequently healed the sick, restored sight to the blind, caused the dumb to speak and made the lame to walk. As stated they were mostly graduates of the Egyptian 'mystery schools'. Even though they predate the birth of Christ, all these works hold no less documentation and credibility than the miracles attributed to Jesus in the Bible. Born some 550 years before Christ, **Pythagoras** astonished doctors in his youth with his amazing wisdom. Documentation declares that he was able to call down flying eagles by command and could subdue the ferocious Daunian bear. He cared for his fellow man, healing the sick, restoring sight, casting out devils and raising the dead. It is said he could appear in two places at once (bi-location), could walk on water and fly through the air. **Jamblicus** records that he could allay storms and that, *"…a thousand other wonderful things are told of him."* Pythagoras considered poverty a virtue and fervently instructed his fellow man to avoid war and to love one's enemies. These are all things later attributed to Jesus. [30] The Roman saviours **Prometheus** and **Quirinus** are both documented by Seneca and Hesiod as having healed the sick, restored the blind and crippled, raised the dead and cast out devils. Similar claims are made for **Simon Magus** who left Samaria for Rome in the time of Christ and also for **Apollonius of Tyana**, the saviour from Cappadocia from around the time of Christ. In a reversal of Christ's cursing the fig tree, we find documentation that **Zoroaster** at the request of King Gustaph commanded a gigantic tree to spring up on a certain man's land. There was said to be no rope in the land that would measure its circumference. [31]

The pagan churches were documenting miracles thousands of years before the event of Christianity. Once a successful miracle worker gained a large following he was invariably nominated as the next saviour and gained the title of the Son of God. In some cases great orators were classified as the next saviour and it followed that miracles were then attributed to them. There is nothing at all to suggest that it was in any way different in the case of Jesus except the fact that he was not deified in his lifetime; in fact not until almost 300 years later. Christians today try to attribute 'evil magic' to the pagan saviours and demi-gods and believe only Jesus achieved good, wholesome, 'genuine miracles.' Any miracle that helps people is in my estimation a 'good' miracle. We will take a giant step forward when we comprehend and acknowledge that magical or miraculous happenings are in themselves neutral, neither good nor bad. Man utilizes his free will in choosing to use his gifts for good or evil. Jesus and Satan were both supposedly 'Sons of God' and as such we can not say one was given 'evil powers' and the other 'good powers'. The mythical Satan of course had the capability of contributing evil designs to his miraculous powers.

Thessalonians 2 : 9 *Even him, whose coming is after the working of Satan with all power and signs and lying wonders.*

So if we are to blame Satan again for the various examples in this section, then we would have to consider that this 'time traveler' went back some 3000 years to plant phony miracles amongst the pagan Gods in order to hamper the work of Jesus in the future. This is obviously so out of step with logic that it will not be considered here.

The Bible says Jesus taught us to confess our sins to the Father to receive absolution, and also to confess our sins to each other. The absolution or remission of sin, as recorded in the Bible, must be an embarrassment for the Church today. Since absolution is made so easy to achieve, it virtually offers a license to crime and sin. Despite this the Roman Church has made of it a very lucrative business offering absolution for profit. If you have trouble believing that the early church commonly abused absolution or the remission of sin, note the words of Saint Cyprian, *"Thousands of reprieves were granted daily."* It didn't stop there. To finance the building of St. Peter's Cathedral in the Vatican the Roman Church was sufficiently strapped for funds that they chose to sell 'Absolution Packs' offering total absolution of the foulest crimes, and to the lowest criminals, as long as the price was right. I don't believe in my childhood anyone even stopped to consider if absolution was a solely Christian practice. We saw it as unique and just assumed it was. Graves had this to say about absolution and the confession of sins;

"There can be no question as to this rite having existed outside Christianity, or of it's being much older than Christianity. History proves both" Graves goes on, *"...the practices both of confessing and forgiving sins are very ancient pagan rites and customs.* [32]

The modern day translation of an ancient document from India, the *Anacalypsis*, states;

"The person offering sacrifices made a verbal confession of his sins, and received absolution."

Graves gives examples of the practice of confession and absolution and even baptism and the laying on of hands among the followers of both Mithraism, and Parsees of Persia. Absolution was also practiced in ancient Mexico and Rome. About absolution in China he states;

"The invocation of 'Omito' is sufficient to remit the punishment of the greatest crimes." [33]

So again we may be surprised to find that miracles and the remission of sin are in no way restricted to the Christian religion and both predate it by millennium.

9. Dualistic Involvement of a Serpent or Satan

The ancient Greek play *Orpheus and Eurydice*, tells how the bride of Orpheus, the lovely nymph Eurydice, was killed by a snake. Queen Cleopatra too supposedly ended her life with the bite of a serpent. These stories over time became pivotal in the development of modern opera and tragic theatre. There is unquestionably a connection between the substance of these plays and mans unexplainable abhorrence of snakes. We even find the device of a *Crucified Serpent* on the '*Anchor of Peace*' from the title page of, '*The Faerie Queen, Part II*' dated 1613, written by the learned Sir Francis Bacon. Since Bacon was initiated in many ancient secret societies we can assume an esoteric purpose for this depiction.

We find recorded in the Book of the Dead, from ancient Egypt, the **Serpent fiend Sebau** with further mention of the serpents **Sata,** whose years are infinite and **Sa-en-ta,** the dweller of the uppermost parts of the Earth, who was reborn (ekdysis) daily. The role Satan plays in Christianity is as the negative part of a dualist religion where good is deigned to triumph over evil. The same 'Satan' figure is however found in several heathen systems of considerably older date than Christianity and in many cases involves a dragon or serpent.

The Old Testament book of Genesis tells of a serpent that spoke to Eve in the Garden of Eden and the Church teaches that this serpent was really Satan the devil. For convenience, St. John in the **Revelation 12 : 8** lumps together, "the dragon, the serpent, the devil and Satan" as souls that deceive; however nowhere does it state in the Bible that the serpent was Satan. It was

St Augustine who first proposed, with no evidence at all, that this could be so. [34] The Hebrew word '*Satan*' that was appended to Lucifer actually means an opposer, adversary or accuser; completely detached from the frighteningly sinister, satanic nastiness with which we were indoctrinated. This was a tool of the Bishops to bind a frightened, subservient congregation. A political adversary in those times would have been a 'Satan'. [35]

> Laurence Gardner drawing on the Jewish scholar Raphael Patai states;
> *(The brother of Ba`al) Yamm was defined as a 'judge' (an accuser) and was therefore a Satan, as were all judges. In the book of Judges (3 : 31), the Satan-judge Shamgar was said to be the son of Anath. In Samaria, north of Judaea, Ba`al was known as Baal-zebul (or Baal-zebub), meaning 'Elevated Lord' (2 Kings 1:2) but this title was maliciously corrupted in the Christian New Testament so that Beelzebub became classified as the 'chief of the devils'.* [36]

Saviours and demi-Gods from **Egypt**, **India**, **Greece**, **Persia**, **Mexico** and **Etruria** all had to contend with a negative side to their dualist system, in the form of a Biblical Serpent or Devil. [37] In the same way that Satan was supposedly a creation of Almighty God, there was a prior, proto-type 'devil' called **Angra Mainyu** (Ahriman) in the Persian, Zoroastrianism religion, supposedly created by the God, Ahura Mazda (note the same initials). This 'created' being then chose to do evil and became the destructive spirit or destroyer for that religion and is likely the proto-type or model for the Biblical Satan. In fact Ahura Mazda also had a 'good' son **Spenta Mainyu** (like Jesus) who later became one with his father as a Holy Spirit. The bad son **Angra Mainyu** (like Satan) cannot help being evil, because it is his predestined fate. These were unquestionably prototypes for God, Jesus and also Satan.

It seems that ancient 'Holy Men' carried with them scraps of sometimes ancient scriptural parchment they had come across that contained the 'magical and mystic' words from any non-specific denomination. They gained prestige and support (and a good living) from their ability to translate and apply these words from God and promote them as important dogma. As an example;

In **Genesis 3 : 15** we read of the Lord's punishment of the serpent for deceiving Adam and Eve;

> *"And I will put enmity between thee and the woman, and between thy seed and her seed; it shall bruise thy head, and thou shalt bruise his heel."*

If we can get over a Harry Potter styled *'parcel tongued'* God who commands snakes, the message he is imparting to the Serpent is; *"man will walk on you and crush your head"*. I questioned this image as a young person in Sunday School and never received a satisfactory explanation. Now this would be forgotten in an instant except that **Osiris** of Egypt is recorded as having;

> *'Bruised the head of the serpent after it had bitten his heel'.*

Certainly way too close for coincidence. On the global spheres, **Hercules** is depicted in the act of contending with the serpent with its head under his heel but in the story of Hercules, this serpent guarded a tree with golden fruit in the Garden of Hesperides, obviously a facsimile of the tree in the Garden of Eden. [38] **Krishna** is depicted on very ancient sculptures with his heel on the head of a serpent and in 'Mexican Antiquities', Volume 6 we are told;

> *"A messenger from heaven announced to the first woman created, (Suchiquecul), that she should bear a son who should <u>bruise the serpents head</u>, then presented her with a rose."* [39]

Graves believes that this is the source of the Genesis story with the rose representing the knowledge of good and evil. The ancient Persians had a tradition that a virgin would give birth to a son who would, *"<u>crush the serpent's head</u>"* and deliver the world from sin. [40] In the Etrurian story it is the Virgin, not the son, who is represented *'with one foot on the head of the serpent'*, which believe it or not has an apple hanging from a twig, in its mouth. All coincidence… I don't think so. A Persian tradition names the first couple as **Meshia** and **Meshiane** (the prototype Adam and Eve) who submitted to their maker, the God **Ormuzd**. The evil one **Ahriman** (the prototype Satan mentioned before) envied their happiness and approached them in the guise of a serpent and presented fruit to them. Their natures became corrupt and infested their entire prosperity. Does this story sound familiar? It predates the Bible by around a thousand years. [41]

A Hindu legend states that the Gods maintained their immortality by once in a while eating of the fruit of the 'Tree of Life' that is the Chorcan (Paradise). Of course this tree was forbidden to man. The serpent **Cheiden** failed in guarding the tree and when taken to task, retaliated with evil against the Earth. [42] In fact he poured out venom that spread across the whole Earth and since the Hindu version dates in antiquity far beyond the time of Moses, we could reference this to the later copy;

> **Revelation 12 : 15** *"And the serpent cast out of his mouth, water as a flood after the woman that he might cause her to be carried away of the flood!"*

So we should consider the Church's cardinal doctrines in the areas of;

(i)   Original Sin

(ii)   The fall of man caused by a Serpent

(iii)   The resultant corruption of the Human race

It is certain that all three are of very ancient heathen origin and not the inerrant, original word of Jehovah God. Quite simply, they represent borrowed doctrine. [43]

In 1922 archaeologist **Sir John Marshall** investigated sites at Harappa and Mohenju-Daru in the Indus Valley and discovered traces of a highly developed civilization dating from the late third century BCE. Much of what he discovered there indicated close relations with Sumer, including fertility symbols and idols of bulls, serpents and sacred trees and groves. Adding to this, Zehren states;

> *"Other items were numerous statuettes of nude women wearing peculiar head and neck ornaments and a faience plaque depicting the figure of a squatting woman, sitting cross-legged amongst snakes and being worshipped by men.'* [44]

The Sumerian Anunnaki Gods were thought to have been immune to snake bite (perhaps they had a quick and effective antidote) and the ability to pick up, handle or control serpents was admired and even worshipped at that time. EN.KI of the Anunnaki was called the serpent. There is likely Sumerian influence depicted in the above plaque, and it is likely that it shows female Gods of the Anunnaki and men worshipping their immunity to poisonous snakebite. In fact there were Christian churches in North America in the last century whose chosen ones handled serpents within their worship program as an act of faith. Remember the test Moses and Aaron did with pharaoh's men turning their staffs into serpents. We see paranoia with snakes and serpents in most ancient literature and as we have just seen, even when not fully understood, these were proto types for the Bible's verses.

10. Sacrifice by Crucifixion as Atonement for Unworthy Man

Crucifixion is said to be one of the most excruciatingly painful deaths imaginable. It was considered that if the Gods were so vastly superior to man they must be able to endure far more in martyrdom. Accordingly, crucifixion seems to have been the specific lot of the sacrificed Gods. In other cases, a totally human ruler who bravely accepted, with resignation, his fate of crucifixion, was afterwards deified; thus we have another crucified God.

We were taught that the 'unique' sacrifice of Jesus is where Christians found their salvation and this sacrifice of their saviour put them way above other religions. Now we will see unequivocal evidence that they were fooled; there is certainly no shortage of crucified saviours, and this form of gaining redemption is in no way unique. Since the crucifixion of Jesus is so difficult to authenticate it matters little whether these are simply parts of ancient belief structures or are proven as historical fact, the result is still the same.

> *The theme of a divine or semi-divine being who is sacrificed against a tree, pole or cross and then resurrected is frequently found in pagan mythology. For instance, at the vernal equinox, pagans in northern Israel would celebrate the death and resurrection of the virgin-born Tammuz-Osiris. In Asia Minor (where the earliest Christian churches were established) a similar celebration was held for the virgin-born Attis, who was shown as dying against a tree, being buried in a cave and then being resurrected on the third day.* [45]

St. Paul, who we noted was more interested in the spiritual message than in historical fact, stated in his letter to the Corinthians;

> **Corinthians 2 : 2** *"For I determine not to know anything among you, save Jesus and him crucified."*

Here we see the crucifixion of Christ being made an important part of the Christian doctrine whereas it had not been previously, with no mention of it until the Bible was compiled, many years later. Kersey Graves had this to say about St. Paul's statement;

> *"There must have existed a very considerable scepticism in the community as to the truth of the report of the crucifixion of Jesus Christ in the country and era of its occurrence to make it necessary thus to erect it into an important dogma, and make it imperative to believe it. There must have been a large margin for distrusting its truth…The determination not to know anything but the crucifixion of Jesus Christ was narrowing down his knowledge to rather a small compass."* [46]

We can guess why St. Paul took this stance, since in the Bible he let us know that in his day there was considerable opposition to the doctrine of the resurrection found in Jesus.

Acts 23 : 8 *For the Sadducees say that there is no resurrection…*

Most religious teachers are guilty of this same narrow mindedness displayed here by Paul, limiting themselves to their own approved Holy Book with the result that they are not even aware of the ancient 'Kill the King' motif and that the crucifixion of Messiahs and saviours was far from uncommon with various cults and religions worldwide. Job had this to say about the chances of resurrection, and Paul would have had access to these passages;

> **Job 7 : 9-10** *As the cloud is consumed and vanisheth away: so he that goeth down to the grave shall come up no more. He shall return no more to his house; neither shall his place know him any more.*

> **Job 14 : 7-10** *For there is hope of a tree, if it be cut down, that it will sprout again, and that the tender branch thereof will not cease. Though the root thereof wax old in the earth, and the stock thereof die in the ground; yet through the scent of water it will bud, and bring forth boughs like a plant. But man dieth, and wasteth away: yea, man giveth up the ghost, and where is he?*

From this Old Testament passage it seems resurrection was something unknown to Job and yet resurrection as a result of atonement by a crucified saviour was certainly not a new thing in the time of Jesus. There is considerable convincing evidence available when we look to the Gods and Avatars before Jesus. Let's investigate some examples;

(i) **Krishna** - Lord Krishna's life of teaching in parables, healing the sick, curing lepers, casting out demons and raising the dead, ended when he was crucified in an act of sin atonement in 1200 BCE in India. At the time of his demise, darkness covered the land. He then rose again after three days. Krishna was the middle member of a trinity headed by his Heavenly Father Brahama. [47] Many writers including Graves quote an early work by the learned French writer Monsieur Guignant, *'Religion of the Ancients'* in which he specifically describes the crucifixion of Krishna, stating that this God-man was *"nailed to a tree"*. Christians use this same symbolic phrase repeatedly to describe the supposed crucifixion of Jesus. In drawings taken from ancient monuments, one shows Krishna hanging on a cross and others show nail holes in his hands and feet, the result of crucifixion plus a hole in his side. [48] I'm sure you will agree that this takes co-incidence way too far, since the death of Jesus is not just similar, it is a complete replication. This documented evidence of Krishna alone renders the uniqueness of the recorded Christ story virtually untenable.

A rock temple of extreme age, in the form of a cross, exists in Mathura India, dedicated to Krishna. It contains many statues and engravings depicting his sacrifice, and postulating his crucifixion. He was said to have *"poured out his lifeblood in an offering for mankind on the cross"* a very Biblesque phrase. Much information on Krishna is found in the *Baghavat Gita*, the episode portion of the *Mahabaret Bible,* and in reality much of the two religions is interchangeable. We find an amazing admission in the *Christian Examiner;*

"…the best precepts of the (Christian) Bible are contained in the Hindu Baghavat."

This is almost an admission of plagiarism that is actually so apparent that it becomes pointless to argue otherwise. It becomes even more difficult for the Christian church to overlook when admission comes from their own presses. The Danish archaeologist **Rasmus Christian Rask** (1787-1832) professor of History, Literature and Oriental languages in Copenhagen, travelled extensively in Persia and India collecting Buddhist and ancient Persian manuscripts. During this endeavour he lived for two years in Bombay and Sri Lanka and in an article written on his return, noted the close similarities of Old Persian records with those in Sanskrit. In fact, **Eugene Burnouf** (1801-1852) professor of Sanskrit at the College de France, made notable contributions to the deciphering of Old Persian cuneiform because of the similarities he noted in the writings.

We can't help but note the similarities between the names Krishna (originally **Chrishna**) and **Christ**, but note too that the original formal name of Lord Krishna; **"Chrishna Zeus"** was in ancient times shortened to **Jeseus.**

This much evidence simply must suggest that the allegoric Jesus Christ was certainly based at least in part on Krishna.

(ii) **Mithra** – We have probably adequately covered the many similarities between Mithraism and Christianity earlier in this chapter. Suffice now to assert that Mithra of Persia was recorded as having suffered crucifixion in 600 BCE to save mankind. [49] In addition Graves quotes Higgins who states that this Persian God was, *"Slain upon a cross to make atonement for mankind, and to take away the sins of the world."* This certainly sounds identical to what we were told about Jesus.

(iii) **Quexalcote** (*Quetzalcoatl*) – This Mexican God within the feathered Serpent (from *'coatl'* meaning *serpent* and *quetzal* a bird with stunning plumage) was recorded as suffering crucifixion on a cross between two thieves in 587 BCE as a propitiatory sacrifice for the sins of mankind. Earlier I challenged the records that stated Jesus was crucified between two thieves, on the grounds that crucifixion was for sedition against Rome, not for stealing. Now we see that the part about the thieves was likely borrowed in its entirety from the Quetzalcoatl record and wrongly allocated to Roman capital punishment. Further search of the records uncovers the following;

– *"Quetzalcoatl…only he, no other God, had a human body. He was 'el hombre-dios', the god made flesh, man embodied with divine spirit."* [50] We also find, *"Quexalcote is represented in the paintings of 'Codex*

Borgianus' as nailed to a cross." [51] This record further documents his death, burial, descent into hell and resurrection on the third day. Graves confirms too that two 'thieves' are shown crucified alongside this God and this fact is also asserted by Kingsborough showing this story to be 600 years old at the time of the supposed demise of Jesus Christ.

(iv) Quirinus - This deified Syrian ruler of the Holy land was crucified 506 BCE and again we see his attributed death fitting the pattern of the later Christian religion. He was born of a virgin, his life was threatened by the contemporary ruler King Amulius; despite a humble birth, he was of the ruling class with his mother being of kingly descent, at the time of his crucifixion darkness came over the land (as with Christ, Krishna and Prometheus), and finally, he was resurrected and ascended to heaven.

(v) Hersus - This God of the Druids was crucified 834 BCE with a lamb one side and an elephant the other. The elephant we are told represented the magnitude of the sins of the world while the lamb represented the innocence of the crucified God. Compare this to *'the lamb of God taking away the sins of the world.'* A representation of this crucifixion can be seen in Brechin, near Dundee in Scotland, on the stone tower called a 'cloichtheach' in Gaelic - literally a 'bell-house'. This features a wooden cross although it was also stated that the crucifixion of Hersus took place on the branches of an oak tree. The Druid's God had a virgin mother and at dawn on the 25 December the birth of the Sun God HU (Osiris) was celebrated. HU was murdered and resurrected back to life, at Easter time.

A crucified man is depicted on the door arch of the Brechin Round Tower near Dundee in Scotland. It is believed to represent the God Hersus.

(vi) Buddha Sakia - This Buddhist Holy man was crucified in 600 BCE as a sin atoning saviour. He took on the suffering of mankind for three days in hell before his resurrection and ascent into heaven. Some accounts say crucifixion was a result of picking a flower in a garden. This is simply a device to record that an innocent suffered capital punishment, when his deed was so humble and trivial. Perhaps it could also be associated with picking from the Tree of Knowledge in the Garden of Eden. Recall too that Christ was berated for picking corn on the Sabbath.

(vii) Tammuz - This God, originally from Syria and worshipped in ancient Samaria, was crucified in 1160 BCE. Documentation on the worship of Tammuz predates the Old Testament by around a thousand years. This cult, which still exists today, was centred in Bethlehem. Tammuz is recorded as being born of a virgin, dying on a cross with a wound in his side, rising from the dead leaving a vacant tomb with the stone rolled away and celebrating his birthday at the time of the winter solstice – 25 December.

(viii) Iao - We have very specific documentation that this God of Nepal, sometimes spelt Jao, was crucified to a tree in 622 BCE. [52] Iao was an incarnate God and his name with some reverence, appears in the Holy books of other Asian countries.

(viii) Wittoba - Again conclusive historical proof shows this Telingonese, heathen God crucified in 552 BCE. He is venerated in the area of Madura and the crown of Lombardy contains a nail said to be from his crucifixion.

(ix) Prometheus (Aeschylus) - This Greek, Titan God of the Caucasus is documented by such historical writers as Seneca, Hesiod and others, as being crucified in 547 BCE to an upright beam to which was attached extended arms. This occurred in the area of the Caspian Straits. He was, *"nailed to a cross with hammer and nails."* and documentation states that he *"Exposed himself to the wrath of (the Father) God in his zeal to save mankind."* Even the Catholic Encyclopaedia acknowledges the crucifixion of Prometheus.

(x) **Thule (Zulis)** – 1700 BCE is the date of crucifixion of this God of the Egyptian pantheon, who came down from heaven for the betterment of mankind. His history is recorded in sculptures made over 3700 years ago, and he was said to be, *"full of grace and truth"*. Twenty-eight lotus plants near his grave signified the 28 years he lived on Earth. After suffering crucifixion he was buried, rose again, ascended to heaven and is now the judge of the dead.

(xi) **Indra** – The God of Tibet was crucified in 725 BCE. He was the result of virgin birth and after his crucifixion was resurrected and rose to Heaven. The account of it is found in *'Thibetinum Alphabetum'* including picture plates of this God nailed to a cross. [53] Indra shows wounds in hands and feet and a wound in his side. The antiquity of the story contained in these writings is beyond dispute.

(xii) **Alcestos** – This female Goddess of Euripides was part of a trinity and was crucified around 600 BCE. The *'English Classical Journal'* vol 37 gives the report on this probably unique crucifixion of a female God for the redemption of sin.

(xiii) **Atys** – 1170 BCE saw the crucifixion of this God of Phrygia for the atonement of man's sin. (See earlier quotation as ATTIS). The *'Anacalypsis'* covers several histories attributed to this God, however all agree on his fate. He was suspended on a tree, crucified, buried and rose again.

(xiv) **Bali** – Bali of Orissa in Asia was crucified in 725 BCE, according to oriental books. Bali was the second member of a trinity and was known as "Lord Second." He was also called Baliu and sometimes Bel; however that is not to be confused with the Babylonian God Bel.

(xv) **Crite** – Crite of the Chaldeans. Some Christians claim that there is no early reference for this God outside Kersey Graves and his source Higgins. This is plainly not true as Crite of Chaldea had a sufficiently high profile to be amongst the five finalists in the ballot system of Constantine at the Council of Nicea in 325 AD and this is well documented. He would have needed outstanding support to be in the top five of 60 nominated 'God candidates'. Higgins records that Crite was crucified around 1200 BCE amidst violent displays of God's wrath, with Heaven and Earth shaken to their foundations. He was called *"The Redeemer"* and *"The Ever Blessed Son of God"* and is yet another proto-type for the Biblical stories of Christianity. The phonetic similarity of Crite and Christ cannot be discounted along with documentation that his crucifixion was *"the atoning offering to an Angry (Father) God."*

(xvi) **Orpheus** - We can look too at Orpheus who was the Greek God of Music, crucified on a cross around 400 BCE. A stone cylinder seal now in the Berlin Museum clearly depicts this crucifixion, showing the God nailed to a cross, and could easily be mistaken for the crucifixion of Jesus. On the seal the words "Orpheus Bakkikos" indicate the association of Orpheus with the Mysteries of Bacchus, the Greek God of wine.

A very ancient depiction of the crucifixion of the God Orpheus with a reference to Baccus in the script.

We previously noted four crucifixions documented by Josephus and should now add these to the record of Jewish Saviours crucified by the Romans in the Holy Land.

(xvii) **Yehuda of Galilee** (6 AD)

(xviii) **Theudas** (44 AD)

(xix) **Benjamin the Egyptian** (60 AD)

(xx) **Antigonus** - The Messiah, Antigonus, the rightful Hasmonean 'King of the Jews' was crucified in 34 BCE by Marc Antony and the Romans after being scourged. We saw his story in a previous chapter and the documentation of Dio Cassius.

(xxi) **Devatat** of Siam. Graves also records the crucifixion of this God of Thailand.

(xxii) **Ixion** of Rome, another God crucified in 400 BCE. According to Nimrod this God was crucified on a wagon wheel, and it was claimed, "He bore the burden (sins) of the World."

(xxiii) **Apollonius of Tyana** of Cappadocia, Turkey, who was performing miracles in the Holy Land at the very same time attributed to Jesus Christ. It is likely the Jesus story is at least partly based on this demi-God. Graves makes the point that Christian writers will record the many similarities of this God with their saviour but always fail to mention his crucifixion that occurred in the first century AD. It is possibly this same character referred to in **Acts 19 : 1** *"And it came to pass, that, while Apollos was at Corinth, Paul having passed through the upper coasts came to Ephesus"*.

Graves also quotes Mackey's *'Lexicon of Freemasonry'* which makes it clear that Freemasons secretly taught the doctrine of crucifixion, atonement and resurrection from very ancient times and that the early 'mystery schools' had very similar doctrine. [54]

So we have a plethora of heathen, pagan Gods, sharing the identical main criteria of the Christian message, most with traceable antiquity far beyond the birth of Christ. It matters not whether we have one other, or five, or ten, or the above twenty-three, or if we take the time to search for more, the facts are that the stories of Jesus from virgin birth to crucifixion and resurrection are simply the continuation of a pagan theme. To now promote this theme as unique and peculiar to Jesus Christ and record it as if it were historical fact on which to base an 'inerrant' Christian religion is at best quite naïve but at worst becomes plainly laughable.

11. Descent into Hell and Miraculous Resurrection

Probably the story with the most antiquity comes from very ancient Egyptian sources when it describes the death of Osiris and how he was resurrected in three and a half days. The Bible always states regarding the resurrection of Jesus that it occurred *"on the third day"* and this could still be an attempt to maintain the fidelity to the Egyptian original. Note too that just as Christ supposedly had his side pierced by a spear and blood and water flowed, we can read a similar story pertaining to Osiris in the Egyptian coffin texts;

> *Come that we may make a dam in his side... and there drips the efflux which has issued from his spirit.* [55]

The Apostle's Creed states;

> *"Jesus... was crucified and buried, He descended into Hell; on the third day he rose again from the dead."*

Regarding that sojourn we can read in **1 Peter 3 : 18** that Jesus *"went and preached unto the spirits in prison."* Today we can wonder what 'spirits' may be doing in 'prison' and take this to mean, the Christian hell, and this prior to the judgment. So why did the scripture writers document it this way. It seems a strange way of saying that Jesus descended into hell. This gave me a lot of trouble so I took a good look at it. Some study showed that this too is in no way an original record. The Hindu sacred books show that a millennium before Christ it was recorded that Krishna;

> *"Went down to hell to preach to the inmates of that dark and dreary prison"* [56]

Also stated about Krishna was that;

> *"So great was his tenderness, that he even descended into hell to teach souls in bondage."* [57]

The similarity of the Bible version makes it fairly apparent that it was simply borrowed from the Krishna story with no attempt to adjust its context. So Jesus 'preached to spirits in prison' even though the Bible record then makes little sense. The illogical concept of 'hell' as a place of fire where souls live in perpetual torment comes from obscure antiquity. The ancient Egyptians believed that their God Amon dispensed justice throughout the land appointing the unjust to the 'Place of Fire', but the just man to the west. An ancient Egyptian papyrus states;

> *"Her soul passed through the Lake of Fire and was devoured by Ammit, devourer of the souls of those who fail before the balance".* [58]

This concept too was adapted with little thought for its context to give the Bishops a bigger stick with which to serve the laity another dose of fire and brimstone. The *'Codex Borgianus'* records the ancient story of **Quexalcote**, the saviour of Mexico, another saviour God who was crucified, raised from the dead, descended into hell and was subsequently resurrected around 300

BCE. **Adonis** of Greece also rose again to immortality after his descent into hell. **Prometheus** of Caucasus is documented as suffering and descending into hell, rising again and ascending into heaven in 600 BCE. The Egyptian God, **Horus** supposedly reigned for a thousand years before he died, was buried then rose again to everlasting life. Homer and Virgil also have their hero's conquering hell. **Hercules, Ulysses** and **Aeneas** are all recorded as descending into the pit of hell for three and a half days on benevolent missions.

There is a valid reason that most of these Saviour Gods (including Jesus) were raised on the third day of a timeframe that corresponded to Easter. The ancients believed that the sun was idle for three days at the vernal epoch from 22nd to the 24th March before its revival to a new life cycle on the 25th. **Note that this would actually take three and a half days before the sun was due to rise again.** It is this same belief that was transferred to the later Gods, who thus lay idle for three and a half days in their graves before their resurrection.

Mithra of Persia, **Chris** of Chaldea, **Quirinus** of Rome, **Promethus** of Caucasus, **Osiris** of Egypt, **Atys** of Phrygia and **Quexalcote** of Mexico, according to their individual histories, were all raised from the dead after three and a half days and in almost every documented case it was on the 25th March, the time of Easter. It is therefore almost certain that this was associated with the ceremony of the symbolic death and resurrection of the sun. [57] If there is any doubt it can be removed by considering that the early almanacs recorded the birth of **John the Baptist** as 25th March in line with the start of the Sun's 'decrease' and had John indicate, regarding Jesus, *"I shall decrease, but he shall increase."*

Graves states,

"With respect to the physical resurrection of the Christian Saviour, it may be observed that, aside from the physical impossibility of such an occurrence, the account, as reported by the four "inspired" gospels biographers, are so palpably at variance with each other, so entirely contradictory in their reports, as to render their testimony as infallible writers utterly unworthy of credence, and impels us to the conclusion that the event is both physically and historically incredible. [59]

12. The Eucharist of the Body and Blood

In the previous chapter we read the quotation from *Annals* that outlined the abominations of Chrestus and the religion he promoted with the specific quotations, *'hated for their abominations,'* *'first source of the evil'* and *'things hideous and shameful'* which refer to a widely held belief at the time that the Christian Eucharist, was a cannibalistic feast that actually involved eating the flesh and drinking the blood of a sacrificed human, usually an innocent infant. We covered too, that in more ancient times of catastrophe, the King (being the most prestigious person available) was ritually sacrificed to appease the Gods. His body was then eaten and his blood drunk as a libation. There is little doubt that this was the prototype of the Christian Eucharist which, (thankfully) was watered down to the ritual conducted in churches today.

In the Bible, **Matthew 26 : 26** has Jesus introducing this sacrament to his disciples as something new and quite unique to his pending sacrifice and this is certainly believed by Christians today. Yet in the same Bible, we find this event noted far earlier in the Old Testament;

> **Genesis 14 : 18** *And Melchizedek, king of Salem brought forth bread and wine; and he was the priest of the most high God.*

There is no question the pagan priest Melchizedek performed the same ceremony with bread and wine for Abraham, several hundred years before Christ. This makes a mockery of it's symbolizing the sacrifice of Jesus Christ. Well before the time of Christianity, a sacred meal of bread and wine was also a sacrament of **Mithraism**, of the **Pythagoreans, Gnostics, Brahmins** and **Mexicans** but we find that it was also practised by the **Essenes** and this is no doubt where Jesus learned the practice.

Few Christians today when celebrating the Eucharist or Communion would realise that it is a very ancient pagan ritual, with a pretty nasty pedigree, originating with Regent sacrifice. They would be unlikely to accept or believe that the ceremony was practised in many denominations of pagan churches. They would be horrified to learn that in the early church it is said to have involved the cannibalistic devouring of infants after ritualistic sacrifice.

Conclusions

It seems that across the world great orators, magi or learned men who were initiated to perform miracles were either deified themselves or given the title the 'Son of God'. Obviously since most often heathen or pagan Gods were worshipped in these areas, the title 'Son of God' was used in regard to pagan Gods in almost every ancient country; the actual frequency of its usage negating any chance of it being literally correct for any one Saviour. From Thor to Krishna we find religious figures documented as the Son of God. There is no reason to believe that Jesus Christ did anything new or different from an almost endless string of 'messiahs', 'saviours', 'Gods', 'Sons of Gods' and initiated masters. Saint Basil actually states;

> *"Every uncommonly good man was called 'the Son of God'."* [60]

Although in his preaching Saint Paul made every attempt to promote a miraculous message, we saw earlier that Jesus himself was not actually deified until 325 AD. Surely if he was a *bona fide* saviour his 'Heavenly father' could have achieved much better promotion than this; at least sufficient to see him deified in his own lifetime. In addition we find that the very best precepts of the Christian religion can also be found recorded in a myriad of religious documents from Mithraism to the pages of the Hindu Baghavat. This chapter has served to indicate that in reality Jesus brought nothing new to the World's religions and achieved nothing more than a myriad of other Sons of God. His Biblical record now appears to be a mythical, allegoric, religious composite based on the common attributes of a plethora of earlier pagan, saviour Gods. His message was plagiarised from a dozen or more, earlier sources that follow a plainly pagan theme that made these Gods close to identical.

If space permitted we could continue on more minor points almost *ad infinitum*, and indicate with equal clarity that these too, are duplicate precepts from ancient pagan religions. While Christians can claim a period of 2000 years since the birth of their religion and the incarnation of their saviour, most of the heathen religions and their divine incarnations are assigned a date hundreds if not thousands of years earlier. The inference is that if there has been any borrowing, Christianity has certainly been the borrower.

In reality, if a genuine one and only God walked on this Earth in the form of Jesus Christ, that would be a unique and momentous occasion. There would be something very wrong if every part of that walk was not noted, documented and held in awe. In direct contradiction we find that from the Christian Bible, Jesus as a saviour and figure of a Godhead, had no original thoughts, brought no enlightenment from his Father God, left no great moral codes and differed so little from his pagan predecessors and contemporaries as to be almost interchangeable. It is plainly not plausible to claim that the ancient, heathen, pagan and oriental Saviour Gods were counterfeits, while Jesus Christ was the authentic and genuine Son of God. That is simply not where the evidence points.

The last point to consider here is that the sameness and continual repeats of the archetypal criteria we used above, across many religions and in many lands, must now lead us to ask if this is simply the makeup of an inbuilt desire within man? Is this simply a formula for creating a generic religion and belief system so man has something consistent to believe in? Is it of necessity a fairly standard belief, so that the real truths of our existence are never considered or broached; so that the controlling factors of our religions are never questioned? Religion is in fact a barrier that often prevents the lateral thinker from questioning or from voicing their concerns, as this just might be construed as lack of faith. Therefore it is the perfect tool to prevent alternative arguments from even being formulated. Mankind however is now on the brink of change. We are living in an enlightened age. We are becoming educated and investigative with information tools at hand, and in reality, the religious 'package' offered to date does not stand up to much scrutiny. It would seem that only clergy who enjoy their lifestyle and prestige more than the cause of truth or who are deplorably ignorant of history have the effrontery to continue with this circus as they have been.

"It is the nature of all religions based on fear and unchangeable dogmas, to deter and thus exclude its disciples from all knowledge adverse to their own creeds. And sometimes their own religious systems are magnified to such a magnified appreciation above all others as to lead them to destroy the evidence of the existence of the latter for fear of their ultimate rivalry". [61]
Kersey Graves.

CHAPTER SEVEN

THE CHICKEN OR THE EGG

"Deifying a political or spiritual leader is not a new phenomenon. We can study this occurrence right from the ancient Greeks and Incas to the Japanese who at the end of World War II, still believed their Emperor was God. Consider for a moment the irony that today we readily accept that ignorance caused the Egyptians to deify their Pharaohs, the Romans to deify their Emperors, and yet when the Hebrew king was deified, millions still believe it true, today." *Ian Ross Vayro*

Eeny, Meeny, Miney, Mo

The books of the Bible's Old Testament changed and developed over a long period of time, being translated into other languages, expanded, censored and altered along the way. We have found that several of its books consist of a poorly meshed integration of the works of two or more authors. An example of this is graphically displayed in the first book, Genesis. The Jews insist that Moses c. 1350 BCE, was the author of Genesis and the following four books (the Pentateuch). This is taught despite the fact that the Hebrew alphabet did not exist for another 400 years, and the fifth book, Deuteronomy, describes the death of its author. Further, it is claimed that Moses was recording dictation directly from God. Against this assertion is the obvious fact that a single composer whether Moses or Almighty God, would surely have got the recorded facts together in a more succinct report, and have them meshing in a more cogent manner, unless he suffered from the most acute amnesia. Josephus more lucidly indicates that these five books were written later and are considered to have been inspired by the teachings of Moses. [1] We will see now that Genesis and other Books of the Bible are an obvious composite work of various writers and timeframes. Let's have a logical look at Genesis and start with the creation that took six days;

Genesis 1 : 3-4 *On the first day, God said, "Let there be light," then divided the light from the darkness.*

Genesis 1 : 14-18 *The sun wasn't created until the <u>fourth day</u> to provide any light to divide from the darkness.*

At that time man didn't realize that light came from the sun and believed it was a separate phenomenon. Note this theme is also in the New Testament:

Matthew 24 : 29-30 *Immediately after the distress of those days the sun will be darkened, and the moon will not give its light; the stars will fall from the sky, and the heavenly bodies will be shaken. At that time the sign of the Son of Man <u>will appear</u> in the sky, and all the nations of the earth will mourn. They <u>will see</u> the Son of Man coming on the clouds of the sky, with power and great glory.*

Although the sun and the moon have gone leaving no light (or reflected light) and the stars have fallen from the sky, there is sufficient light to illuminate the Son arriving with great glory. That particular writer obviously didn't think this one through. Now Bible students might say we are being too literal, however the average person picking up a Bible to find fulfilment would look at the passages literally and would find instead utter confusion with verses like the following;

Isaiah 24 : 1 *Behold, the Lord maketh the Earth empty, and maketh it waste, and turneth it upside down, and scattereth abroad the inhabitants thereof.* This certainly sounds like a vertical gravity, flat earth!

Isaiah 30 : 26 *The moon will shine like the sun, and the sunlight will be seven times brighter, like the light of seven full days...* Yeah OK!

Daniel 4 : 11 Daniel dreams of *a tree so tall that it can be seen to the ends of the earth.*

Amos 8 : 9 The Sun will be made to set *at noon on a clear day, making the Earth dark.*

Matthew 4 : 8 There was a high mountain *from which all the kingdoms of the world can be seen.* Sounds like a flat Earth again and can we ask, where is this mountain now? Did they need oxygen breathing equipment and a full support crew to climb it to look out on the World?

In the time of the scribes who wrote the Bible, people had no idea of the orbits of planets and the positioning of stars. They believed that God could have turned over a flat Earth tipping off the inhabitants and also that the Moon gave off its own light. Education and enlightenment haven't been good for the Bible. Accordingly these passages don't have much relevance for us today, and don't help this religion at all. Continuing with Genesis:

Genesis 1 : 11-12 *Trees were created;* **Genesis 1 : 26-27** *followed by man.*

Genesis 2 : 7-9 *Man was created before the trees.*

Genesis 1 : 20-21 *God created birds;* **Genesis 1 : 26-27** *followed by man.*

Genesis 2 : 7 *God created man;* **Genesis 2 : 19** *followed by birds.*

Genesis 1 : 24-25 *Animals were created;* **Genesis 1 : 26** *before man.*

Genesis 2 : 7 *Man was created;* **Genesis 2 :19** *before animals.*

Genesis 1 : 29 *Then God said, I give you <u>every</u> seed-bearing plant on the face of the whole earth and every tree that has fruit with seed in it. They will be yours for food.*

It states *'every seed bearing plant'* so does God include in this poisonous plants such as hemlock, buckeye pod, gidgee bean, nightshade, oleander and devils claw? The contradictions continue;

Genesis 1 : 31 God's creations were good.

Genesis 6 : 5-6 God's creations were not good.

Genesis 10 : 5 *By these were the isles of the Gentiles divided in their lands; <u>every one after his tongue</u>, after their families, in their nations.*

Verse 20; *These are the sons of Ham, after their families, <u>after their tongues</u>, in their countries, and in their nations.*

Verse 31; *These are the sons of Shem, after their families, <u>after their tongues</u>, in their lands, after their nations.*

These verses stress the different languages among the tribes, yet in the very next chapter we find;

Genesis 11 : 1 *And the whole earth was of <u>one language</u>, and of one speech. There* *was only one language among the tribes.*

Then we encounter:

> **Genesis 36 : 11** *The sons of Eliphaz were Teman, Omar, Zepho, Gatam, and Kenaz.* **(Total of 5)**

> **Genesis 36 : 15-17** *Teman, Omar, Zepho, Kenaz.* **(Total of 4)**

> **1 Chronicles 1 : 35-36** *Teman, Omar, Zephi, Gatam, Kenaz, Timna, and Amalek.* **(Total of 7)**

The Wrestling Match

This next story from Genesis is quite unusual; Almighty God actually takes part in a wrestling match. We are not talking about a spiritual battle here but an actual physical wrestling match where Jacob becomes hurt. God wins by injuring Jacob's thigh. Could you picture him in a tag team event with Goliath the Giant of Gath? That would be quite a draw-card. I can see no reason for these strange verses to be in the Bible and fail to see how people could be enlightened by their inclusion. God here is shown to be a physical being and I can't help but wonder what this passage is trying to teach us. We might also ask why it commences with Jacob being alone, when it states clearly that he is with a physical God?

> **Genesis 32 : 24 – 30** *And Jacob was left alone; and <u>there wrestled a man with him</u> until the breaking of the day. And when he saw that he prevailed not against him, he touched the hollow of his thigh; and the hollow of Jacob's thigh was out of joint, as he wrestled with him.* (There is no thigh joint, unless it means his hip or his knee) *And he said, let me go, for the day breaketh. And he said, I will not let thee go, except thou bless me. And he said unto him, what is thy name? And he said, Jacob. And He said, Thy name shall be called no more Jacob, but Israel: for as a prince hast thou power with God and with men, and hast prevailed. And Jacob asked him, and said; tell me, I pray thee, thy name. And he said, wherefore is it that thou dost ask after my name? And he blessed him there. And Jacob called the name of the place Peniel: for I have seen God face to face and my life is preserved.*

This begs the questions; why did God wrestle with Jacob, particularly if he didn't know him sufficiently well to even know his name? Is it normal to wrestle God in order to receive a blessing? Why did he need to dislocate

THE CHICKEN OR THE EGG

Jacob's hip to beat him and how did seeing God, face to face, preserve Jacob's life? I thought no man could look on the face of Almighty God and live. If this story is not strange enough, God says here and then repeats it in **Genesis 35 : 10** that Jacob is not to be called **Jacob** any longer; he is now to be called **Israel**. Yet just a bit later in **Genesis 46 : 2;** God continues to speak to **Israel** and calls him **Jacob**. Weird! Most parishioners would surely agree that this is really weird!

Some study will reveal that a possible explanation is that this passage introduces a very ancient ritual 'laming' of the "Smith God". The name of the ancient God-King Dionysus actually means *"Lame God of Light"* and he is associated with the mysteries of a metal working tin-smith as opposed to the "carpenters" and "master masons" we have previously seen. From Stuart Nettleton we discover;

> *"Ancient religions all over Africa and Europe have a hobbling Smith-God. In their erotic spring beer-orgy called Pesach the smiths wore wings and performed a hobbling spiral partridge dance. This ritual celebrated the marriage of the Smith-God Hephaestus to the patron Athene."* [2]

The Jewish Talmud records Jesus the Nazarene as both Y'shu ha Notzri and as 'Balaam the Lame' and this is a remarkable association of Jesus with the lamed Smith-God. [3]

We Know Where You Live

The place where God dwells is quite strange too; how many people have noted this before?

1 Kings 8 : 12 *The Lord said that he would dwell in the <u>thick darkness</u>.*

1 Timothy 6 : 16 *God only, hath immortality, dwelling in the <u>light</u> which no man can approach.*

2 Chronicles 6 : 1 *The Lord hath said that he would dwell in the <u>thick darkness</u>.*

Peter 4 : 19 *The way of the wicked is as <u>darkness</u>.*

Psalm 18 : 11 *He made <u>darkness</u> his secret place; his pavilion round about him were dark waters and thick clouds of the skies.* God must live in Melbourne!

1 John 1 : 5 *This then is the message which we have heard of him, and declare unto*

233

you, that God is <u>light</u>, and in him is <u>no darkness</u> at all.

1 Peter 2 : 9 *that ye should shew forth the praises of him who hath called you out of <u>darkness</u> into his marvellous <u>light</u>.*

Isaiah 45 : 3 *And I will give thee the treasures of <u>darkness</u>, and hidden riches of secret places, that thou mayest know that I, the Lord, which call thee by thy name, am the God of Israel.*

Lamentations 3 : 2 *He hath led me, and brought me <u>into darkness</u>, but <u>not into light</u>.*

Exodus 20 : 21 *And the people stood afar off, and Moses drew near unto <u>the thick darkness</u> where God was.*

Psalm 104 : 1-2 *Bless the Lord, O my soul. O Lord my God, thou art very great; thou art clothed with honour and majesty. Who coverest thyself <u>with light</u> as with a garment: who stretchest out the heavens like a curtain:*

1 Kings 8 : 12 *Then spake Solomon, the Lord said that he would dwell in the <u>thick darkness</u>.*

Amos 5 : 18 *Woe unto you that desire the day of the Lord! To what end is it for you? The day of the Lord is <u>darkness</u>, and <u>not light</u>.*

John 8 : 12 *Then spake Jesus again unto them, saying, I am the <u>light</u> of the world: he that followeth me <u>shall not walk in darkness</u>, but shall have the <u>light of life</u>.*

We have all heard the Devil called the Prince of darkness and in;

2 Corinthians 11 : 14 *The Devil appears as an angel of <u>light</u>.*

God does not vary, according to the following passage yet we have just seen him vary from light to dark and back many times;

James 1 : 17 *Every good gift and every perfect gift is from above, and cometh down from the <u>Father of lights</u>, with whom is no variableness, neither shadow of turning.*

In addition to this;

Matthew 3 : 12 & 13 : 42 *Hell is a furnace of unquenchable fire and must therefore be <u>light</u>.*

Matthew 8 : 12 & 22 : 13 & 25 : 30 *Hell is an outer darkness and must therefore* be _dark_.

The only reason we will dwell on this contradictory nonsense here is that at times a main rival to Christianity was **Alchemy** which was an important part of the associated mystery schools and Gnosticism. Now the word Alchemy comes from the Arabic _'Al-khame'_ meaning 'the blackness' because it was considered to be the 'science' that would 'enlighten' its adepts and overcome the blackness or darkness of ignorance in the World.

So Where Does God Live?

Light or dark, the concepts we formed in our minds from our Bible teaching in childhood are not valid and won't stand up to the simplest scrutiny. We really don't have a clue do we? So let's try further to establish just where God lives;

> **Psalm 10 : 1** _Why, O Lord, do you stand far off? Why do you hide yourself in times of trouble?_ (God cannot be found in time of trouble. He is hiding or far off.)

> **Psalm 145 : 18** _The Lord is nigh unto all them that call upon him, to all that call upon him in truth._ (If you call on the Lord in truth, say in times of trouble, he is near.)

Christians say God lives within their hearts, and maybe that is true. Here are yet more ideas from the Bible on where God lives;

> **Matthew 7 : 21** _God resides in heaven_

> **2 Samuel 7 : 5** _Go and tell my servant David, Thus saith the Lord, thou shalt build an house for me to dwell in?_

> **1 Kings 8 : 13** _Solomon built a house for the Lord to dwell in forever_

> **Acts 7 : 47 – 48** _Solomon built him a house, howbeit the most High dwelleth not in temples made with hands._

> **Acts 7 : 49** _Heaven is my throne, and earth is my footstool: what house will ye build me? Saith the Lord: or what is the place of my rest?_ (That's precisely what we're trying to ascertain.)

There are several non canonical scriptures that seem to indicate that God lives in Mt Sinai the Lord's Holy Mountain. Here's one from the Bible;

Judges 5 : 5 *The mountains quaked before <u>the Lord , the One of Sinai</u>, before the Lord , the God of Israel.* (NIV)

This passage refers to Moses' father in law, the High Priest of Sinai, Lord Jethro the Midianite, who claimed he was also the God, El Shaddai. From the following we see that the children of Israel believed that the Lord lived <u>inside the Ark of the Covenant</u>.

1 Samuel 6 : 19 *"But God struck down some of the men of Beth Shemesh, putting seventy of them to death because they had looked into the ark of the Lord."*

This story is confirmed in **Isaiah 6 : 19** however here, it records that precisely **50,070 men** are slaughtered by the Lord for looking in at him. Modern King James Bibles now state **70** (as above in Samuel) trying desperately to inject some credibility into this silly passage; yet the Hebrew manuscripts and the Septuagint as well as early Bibles, clearly state the quite unbelievable figure of **50,070** men.

To see how ridiculous this is, imagine for a minute that you had an object to put on display to the public. Since Ark is from the Latin '*Arca*' meaning a chest, box or coffer, let's say for example it was an old chest, at an antique fair. Imagine the preparation and catering if an enormous crowd of 50,070 people were to look into that chest in just one day. Logistically that would be a huge day out. Yet that is exactly what is claimed here. The situation is plainly ludicrous if in fact all dropped dead as stated. No more than say 10 people could look in at one time. In addition do you seriously believe a continuing throng would climb over the piled up bodies of those already struck dead, be it 70 or 50,070 to also look in. The bottom line is that this last suggestion and the Bible passage above are both demonstrably wrong about God's living inside the Ark; and we are still left with a total muddle with no definitive answer to where God lives. This is however not the silliest suggestion we have. The founder of the Mormon, Church of Jesus Christ of Latter Day Saints, Joseph Smith, claims that the sun gets its light from God's home planet, a world he called **Kolob**. Though totally untrained in archaeology and linguistics, Smith claims he translated this from an Egyptian papyrus called the Book of Abraham. Leading Egyptologists **Professor Lutz** and **Professor Lesko** of the University of California agree that the original papyrus claimed by Joseph Smith to be the Book of Abraham was in fact an Egyptian funerary text called *'The Book of Breathings'* and this document made no mention whatever of Abraham or the Planet Kolob.

Has Anyone Ever Seen God?

The belief in an anthropomorphic God appears to be a carryover from pagan times. Abraham met with him and tried to talk him out of destroying Sodom and Gomorrah, Moses met with him and received the Ten Commandments. Hey, I was taught that mortal man couldn't look on Almighty God and live. We saw above that Jacob/Israel stated that he had seen the face of God and it actually preserved his life. This is 180 degrees out of phase. Is this possible? Yes? No? Maybe?

Exodus 33 : 2 0 *Thou canst not see my face: for there shall no man see me, and live.*

Exodus 33 : 11 *And the Lord spake unto Moses face to face, as a man speaketh unto his friend.*

Exodus 24 : 9-12 *Moses, Aaron, Nadab, Abihu & 70 elders meet with God and have food and drink with him.*

Numbers 11 : 24-25 *And Moses went out, and told the people the words of the Lord, and gathered the seventy men of the elders of the people, and set them round about the tabernacle. And the Lord came down in a cloud, and spake unto him, and took of the spirit that was upon him, and gave it unto the seventy elders:*

Numbers 12 : 4-5 *And the Lord spake suddenly unto Moses, and unto Aaron, and unto Miriam, Come out ye three unto the tabernacle of the congregation. And they three came out and the Lord came down in the pillar of the cloud, and stood in the door of the tabernacle, and called Aaron and Miriam: and they both came forth.*

Genesis 17 : 1 *the Lord appeared to Abram*

Genesis 18 : 1 *And the Lord appeared unto him* (Abraham)

Genesis 26 : 2 *And the Lord appeared unto him* (Isaac)

John 1 : 18 *No man hath seen God at any time.*

Job 42 : 5 *I have heard of thee by the hearing of the ear: but now mine eye seeth thee.*

Exodus 6 : 2 & 3 *And God spake unto Moses and said unto him I am the Lord. And I appeared unto Abraham, unto Isaac, and unto Jacob,*

2 Samuel 7 : 18 *Then went king David in, and sat before the Lord, and he said, Who am I, O Lord God? and what is my house that thou hast brought me hitherto?*

I John 4 : 12 *No man hath seen God at any time.*

Isaiah 6 : 1 *I saw also the Lord sitting upon a throne, high and lifted up, and his train filled the temple*

1Kings 22 : 19 *I saw the Lord sitting on his throne, and all the host of heaven standing by him on his right hand and on his left.*

Numbers 12 :8 *With him (Moses) will I speak mouth to mouth, even apparently, and not in dark speeches; and the similitude of the Lord shall he behold*

Numbers 14 :14 *thou Lord art seen face to face*

Kings 11 : 11 *And the Lord was angry with Solomon, because his heart was turned from the Lord God of Israel, which had appeared unto him twice.*

Amos 9 : 1 *I saw the Lord standing upon the altar*

Well, what a contradictory mess. Were the scribes that wrote this really inspired of God? Which verses are true and which are false? For goodness sake, someone has it wrong.

An odd addition comes from **Deuteronomy 23 : 12-14.** It states that the Lord must not be allowed to see human excrement or any unclean thing within the Hebrew camp as that is unholy. What has made God so precious about this? We thought excrement resulted from a normal bodily function of a human being, designed by God, created by God in the image of God.

The Chicken has it

Amidst all this confusion there is however one point of real value we can glean from Genesis. Have you ever really wanted to know which came first, the chicken or the egg. Well at least we can finally lay that one to rest. Read: **Genesis 1 : 20-22** *The chicken came before the egg.* But then can we be confident that the Bible really has this one right?

More Contradictions

Genesis is obviously not the only example of Biblical errors. We can assume that since God designed and made the animals he would know a little about them. In the dietary restrictions of Leviticus basic zoology and biology are thrown out the window;

> **Leviticus 11 : 4** *says the camel is not to be eaten because it chews its cud but does not have a divided hoof.* Untrue!

> **Leviticus 11: 6** *states that hares chew their cud.* Untrue! They don't.

> After mentioning several species of bird, **Leviticus 11: 20–21** *states that there are fowls that creep; that go around on all fours.* Untrue! There are no fowls or birds that walk on all fours, and if this can be construed as insects, insects have six legs.

> **Numbers 21 : 6** *Fiery serpents, sent by the Lord, kill many Israelites.*

Are these fiery serpents, really snakes or actually dragons! I guess they must all be extinct by now! The book of Revelation contains several references to dragons. Losing his usual title of 'Serpent', Satan is called a 'Dragon' in **Revelation 20 : 2**. The word 'dragon' comes from the Greek '*drakon*', and indicates a scaly skinned monster. In the Greek version of the Book of Revelation the word 'drakon' is used 12 times. We are talking again about the writings of uneducated scribes of ancient times.

When the ancient Chinese first encountered dinosaur bones they were sure they had found evidence of dragons, and apparently the scribes who wrote these passages thought dragons were just as real. In translating the Bible's Old Testament from Hebrew, the scribes encountered the word **tannim**, which could mean 'jackals', since tannim comes from the root **tan** meaning 'to howl.' If **tannin** was the intended word it could mean 'sea monsters' because despite the similarity, tannin comes from the quite different root **tanan** meaning 'to smoke'. The spouting of whales was initially thought to be smoke. It would be difficult to see how smoking 'sea monster' could replace 'jackal', however this just might account for the initial idea of fire-breathing dragons. Even in the Middle Ages when fossil tusks or horns were found they were said to come from unicorns. [4]

Unicorns are mentioned nine times in the KJV: In the early Bibles, **Deuteronomy 33 : 17** states the unicorn has 'horns' (plural) so the KJV solved this problem by translating 'unicorn' as plural 'unicorns'. In reality the unicorns result from the unfortunate translation of the Hebrew word *'reem'* that really means 'wild ox'. The initial idea of a unicorn probably came from seeing a rhinoceros skull. Despite these possible explanations, the following erroneous passages are still in the Bible and today must be considered pretty strange or should we forget the 'word of God' thing, and just write them off as quaint myth:

> **Numbers 24 : 8**; *God brought him forth out of Egypt; he hath as it were the strength of an unicorn: he shall eat up the nations his enemies, and shall break their bones, and pierce them through with his arrows.* (Nice guy!)

> **Job 39 : 9-10;** *Will the unicorn be willing to serve thee, or abide by thy crib? Canst thou bind the unicorn with his band in the furrow? Or will he harrow the valleys after thee?*

> **Isaiah 34 : 7** *And the unicorns shall come down with them, and the bullocks with the bulls; and their land shall be soaked with blood, and their dust made fat with fatness.*

The Bible also records **Seraph** that are now taught as angels. In fact a 'seraph' was a mythical all seeing beast complete with six wings that were covered with eyes. Certainly most unusual messengers!

The **Satyr** is another mythical creature that was half-man and half-goat and has several mentions in the Bible and in the Hebrew Torah. This was a real no-brainer for the Church to explain but explain it they did. A dictionary of the Old Testament explains that the Satyr depicts a particular type of demon that exhibited the likeness of a goat and was closely associated with idolatry and the high places. [5] Saint Jerome who wrote the Catholic Vulgate Bible tried hard to convince us that Satyrs were actually real phenomena;

> *"Let no man scruple to believe this incident, its truth is supported by what took place when Constantine was on the throne (died 337 AD) a matter of which the whole world was witness. For a man of that kind (a Satyr) was brought alive to Alexandria and shown as a wonderful sight to the people. Afterwards his lifeless body, to preserve*

its decay through the summer heat, was preserved in salt and brought to Antioch that the Emperor might see it." [6]

In a case of outstanding solidarity, the Bible agrees with St. Jerome;

Isaiah 13 : 21 *But wild beasts of the desert shall lie there; and their houses shall be full of doleful creatures; and owls shall dwell there, and satyrs shall dance there.*

The above passage needs additional consideration because original Bibles stated, *"...and Lilith shall dwell there."* Lilith was supposedly the first wife of Adam before Eve and the name Lilith actually means *'owl'*. Her connection with satyrs can only be guessed at.

Isaiah 34 : 14 *The wild beasts of the desert shall also meet with the wild beasts of the island, and the satyr shall cry to his fellow; the screech owl also shall rest there, and find for herself a place of rest.* Again we see the association of Satyrs with owls.

Leviticus 17 : 7 *And they shall no more offer their sacrifices unto satyrs, after whom they have gone a whoring. This shall be a statute forever unto them throughout their generations.* (Would you care to re-phrase that?)

2 Chronicles 11 : 15 *And he appointed his own priests for the high places and for the satyrs and calf idols he had made.*

The Hebrew people had a long history of calf and bull worship and many examples of these idols have been uncovered.

Finally amongst God's exotic pets we find considerable mention of the **cockatrice** in **Isaiah 11 : 8**, **Isaiah 14 : 29**, **Isaiah 59 : 5** and **Jeremiah 8 : 17**. I confess I have no idea what a cockatrice is, but Isaiah states that its fruit (offspring) are fiery serpents and if you eat its eggs, you die. (Nice pet!) Whatever it is we see also an **arrowsnake** recorded in **Genesis 49 : 17.** The relevance escapes me. How this would support a person's religious walk or promote Almighty God and a goodly lifestyle, I simply have no idea. The reason for their inclusion can only be guessed at.

Job 40 : 16 *Here we learn that behemoth's strength is in his loins, and his force is in the navel of his belly.*

Now a Behemoth is said to be a mythological beast that has been translated as everything from Dinosaurs and Rhinoceros to Elephants and Hippopotami. The Hebrew word 'behemoth' is apparently the plural of 'behemah', meaning 'a beast', however there is a possibility that the word is of Egyptian origin signifying a 'water ox' or buffalo. There are at least six mentions of this creature in the KJV and nobody knows what it is. Next we find Rehab.

Psalm 89 : 10 *Thou hast broken Rahab in pieces, as one that is slain; thou hast scattered thine enemies with thy strong arm.*

Before we ask who or what is Rehab, some translations say a "sea monster" and others a "dragon."

Isaiah 51 : 9 *Awake, awake, put on strength, O arm of the Lord; awake, as in the ancient days, in the generations of old. Art thou not it that hath cut Rahab, and wounded the dragon?*

Moving on, would you believe that when entering a Holy place you simply must wear bells and pomegranates or it can result in death? The Bible is quite definite about this;

Exodus 28 : 34 – 35 *The gold bells and the pomegranates are to alternate around the hem of the robe. Aaron must wear it when he ministers. The sound of the bells will be heard when he enters the Holy Place before the Lord and when he comes out, so that he will not die.*

We saw before that the Bible is recognizably racist but it seems particularly down on the residents of ancient Crete:

Titus 1 : 12 *Even one of their own prophets has said, "Cretans are always liars, evil brutes, lazy gluttons."*

My limited experience with people from Crete showed them to be pleasant and quite charming people with a lovely country and delicious seafood. I am yet to observe those traits described here; maybe the Bible's fierce criticism woke them up and they have all improved since those times. How do the Christians of Crete feel about this passage in their Bibles today? In like manner God apparently doesn't like Asians very much.

Acts 16 : 6 The Holy Spirit specifically forbids preaching in Asia.

Acts 19 : 8-10 Paul preaches in Asia anyway, so what of his converts?

> **2 Esdras 15 : 46-49** *And you, Asia, who share in the glamour of Babylon and the glory of her person — woe to you, miserable wretch! I will send evils upon you, widowhood, poverty, famine, sword, and pestilence, to lay waste your houses and bring you to destruction and death.*

I have traveled extensively in Asia and have met many fine people who were nice and friendly, socially and most ethical in business. On my many visits I observed that many Asians are practicing Christians. Does this weird passage actually mean that God prohibits them from his church; it certainly sounds like it. Has anyone told the Christian missionaries working in Asia? Also what about all the threats of evil God wishes on the folk of Asia? Is that still to come? If this petulant little speech came from anyone but Almighty God, people would band together in support of those he plans to harm saying, *"what a sick and bigoted megalomaniac you are."* It goes still further;

> **Exodus 33 : 4-5** *I will send an angel before you and drive out the Canaanites, Amorites, Hittites, Perizzites, Hivites and Jebusites.*

> **Nehemiah 13 : 1** *On that day they read in the book of Moses in the audience of the people; and therein was found written, that the Ammonite and the Moabite should not come into the congregation of God for ever.*

So, according to the Bible, this lot are actually banned from his church, forever. Surely this has to mean that this prejudiced God, YHWH is not the God of the **Cretans, all Asians, Canaanites, Amorites, Hittites, Perizzites, Hivites or Jebusites**. He also showed he is not the God of the **Egyptians, the Moabites, Ammonites** or the **Philistines.** Have you checked out your ancestry? YHWH may not want you! Focusing for a minute on all this bigotry that we are seeing in the Bible, we are then blown away when Peter in total contradiction states that God is wholly impartial.

> **Acts 10 : 34** *"For a certainty I perceive that God is not partial …"*

Some things are obviously wrong and totally inexcusable and I believe that a stand must be taken. It honestly bothers me why people would keep praising and worshipping this particular bigoted God. If his audience dried up he would lose all power and we could get on with business without all his particularly nasty traits. It is not reasonable or healthy to allow your children to read this racial drivel, let alone teach it to them. We don't need leaders to explain to us that these passages are WRONG. Only a Christian indoctrinated beyond a level that is healthy, would ever try to excuse away these traits in a person. Now since it is a God, well I think the answer is obvious even to a simple soul.

Heaven

For Christians who aspire to Heaven; according to the Bible there are in fact at least three heavens and likely seven. Also an 'out of body experience' is recognized in the New Testament and documented by St. Paul.

> **2 Corinthians 12 : 2 – 4** *I know a man in Christ who fourteen years ago was caught up to the third heaven. Whether it was in the body or out of the body I do not know - God knows. He was caught up to paradise. He heard inexpressible things; things that man is not permitted to tell.* I wish somebody would tell me!

I always wondered how almost every religion seemed to have a sky God who dwelt in a "Heaven" that just happened to be 'up' from any particular location on the surface of this Earth. The Sumerians claimed that the abode of the Sky-God **Anu** was a 'heaven' on the planet **Nibiru**, and this is in fact the 'Heaven in the Sky' that anyone on this Earth locates as 'up'. Being an outer planet from our sun, the supposed 3 600 year comet like orbit of this planet also takes care of the idea that Jesus has left our Earth but has promised he will return again. Otherwise what sense is there in the Saviour establishing a relationship with his people and then leaving for two thousand years? It also explains why God has not made contact for a couple of thousand years. Recently, an additional planet has been located in our solar system past Pluto and has been tentatively named **'Sedna'** after the Inuit Goddess of the ocean, and this tiny world has been wrongly referred to as Planet 'X' and Nibiru. The Anunnaki planet Nibiru is massively big, approaching the size of Jupiter, and with its comet like orbit passes between Mars and Jupiter according to the Sumerian documentation. What makes this scenario so interesting is that recently another planet 'X' fitting this description has been tentatively located and many professionals are watching the skies. More on that later.

In Heaven, the Biblical city of New Jerusalem is a particularly strange example of city planning. It is a cube about 2,200 kilometres square. Read it in your Bible.

> **Revelation 21 : 16** *The city was laid out like a square, as long as it was wide. He measured the city with the rod and found it to be 12,000 stadia in length, and <u>as wide and high as it is long</u>.*

That's one strange City! I have studied enough Civil Engineering to be extremely concerned about the foundations of these 2,200 Klm. high buildings; they would contain around 74,000 floors and at the very least would require an incredibly fast elevator. If one left for work on Monday morning it would be Friday before they arrived there.

The Bible also states:

> **John 14 : 2** *In my Father's house are many mansions: if it were not so, I would have told you. I go to prepare a place for you.*

This doesn't exactly fit with the above description but could mean many mansions spread throughout the universe or gathered together in one place. There is just not enough information available to judge.

The Scriptures According to Jesus

We were taught that the old time prophets were mighty men of God and we were led to conclude that they were fairly infallible. This is simply not true. In reality they were very much alone and held pretty accountable, often with death threats if their prophecy didn't come off, and it seems they didn't have a great success rate at all.

> **Ezekiel 14 : 9** *And if the prophet is enticed to utter a prophecy, I the Lord have enticed that prophet, and I will stretch out my hand against him and destroy him from among my people Israel.*

This doesn't sound like a God who encouraged prophecy. We can see that on many occasions, statements are made in the New Testament with reference to Old Testament scriptures or prophecy and several times Jesus himself states that he is doing certain things in order to fulfill a particular prophecy. He also on occasions makes a statement then quotes that supporting prophecies were written in the Old Testament. A thorough check often reveals that there are in fact no such records in the Old Testament.

Examples:

Romans 10 : 11 *For the scripture saith, "Whosoever believeth on him shall not be ashamed".*

There is no such quote in the Old Testament.

Matthew 2 : 23 *And he came and dwelt in a city called Nazareth: that it might be fulfilled which was spoken by the prophets, He shall be called a Nazarene.*

Jesus was a Nazarene but this had nothing whatever to do with living in Nazareth. This confused prophecy is not even found in the Old Testament. At least this next passage confirms that Jesus is recognized as a Nazarene in the Bible.

Acts 24 : 5 *For we have found this man a pestilent fellow, and a mover of sedition among all the Jews throughout the world, and a ringleader of the sect of the Nazarenes:*

Let us continue:

Mark 10 : 19 *Thou knowest the commandments, Do not commit adultery, Do not kill, Do not steal, Do not bear false witness, <u>Defraud not</u>, Honour thy father and mother.*

All of the Ten Commandments are listed in **Exodus 20 : 3-17** and *'Defraud not'* is not one of them even though this concept is of course encompassed in the laws.

Matthew 1 : 23 *Behold a <u>virgin</u> shall be with child, and shall bring forth a son, and they shall call his name <u>Emmanuel</u>, which being interpreted is, God with us.*

The New Testament lists this like the fulfillment of Isaiah's Old Testament prophesy, which is crazy because how could it, when the Jews who wrote the Old Testament did not accept Jesus as the Messiah. Ironically the word 'virgin' was not used in the originals either. In addition, Emmanuel, doesn't mean 'God with us"; it means "the hidden one is God". Note too the differing spelling of the New and Old Testament;

Isaiah 7 : 14 *Therefore the Lord himself shall give you a sign; Behold, a young* *woman shall conceive, and bear a son, and shall call his name __Immanuel__.*

It seems that 'they' didn't call him Emmanuel or Immanuel; 'they' called him Yahshua, which was altered to Yehoshua however he was mostly known by the Greek name of Jesus.

> **Matthew 27 : 9-10** *Then was fulfilled that which was spoken by __Jeremy__ the prophet, saying, 'and they took the __thirty pieces of silver__, the price of him that was valued, whom they of the children of Israel did value; and gave them for the potter's field, as the Lord appointed me'.*

'Jeremy' is the Greek name for Jeremiah; however no prophecy relating to this can be found in the book of __Jeremiah__. We can however find the following passage in __Zechariah__:

> **Zechariah 11 : 12-13** *And I said unto them, If ye think good, give me my price; and if not, forbear. So they weighed for my price __thirty pieces of silver__. And the Lord said unto me, __Cast it unto the potter__: a goodly price that I was priced at of them. And I took the __thirty pieces of silver__, and __cast them to the potter__ in the house of the Lord.*

If we were intent on meshing these passages from Matthew and Zechariah, we would have to explain why one is talking about a potter, being a maker of clay vessels in the Temple and the other a potter's field where paupers are buried. There seems no doubt that they are related but only in that the writer of Matthew got his cross-reference wrong and didn't understand the context of Zechariah or really what he was writing about. Otherwise we must believe that a chunk of the original scripture of Jeremiah found its way into the Book of Zechariah. We could also note confusion like the following, where quoted Bible passages are meshed together;

> **Mark 1 : 2-3** *It is written by Isaiah the prophet: 'Behold, I send my messenger before thy face, which shall prepare thy ways before thee. The voice of one crying in the wilderness, Prepare ye the way of the Lord, make his paths straight.'*

The author of Mark incorrectly attributes the entire quote to **Isaiah** whereas in fact it is a composite of two scriptures. The first part is actually from **Malachi** and the passage that follows is from **Isaiah**.

> **Malachi 3 : 1** *I will send my messenger, who will prepare the way before me...*
>
> **Isaiah 40 : 3** *The voice of him that crieth in the wilderness, Prepare ye the way of the*

Lord, make straight in the desert a highway for our God.

Moving on,

Acts 20 : 35 *I have shewed you all things, how that so laboring ye ought to support the weak, and to remember the words of the Lord Jesus, how he said, It is more blessed to give than to receive.*

Paul attributes this saying to Jesus however nowhere is it recorded that Jesus said this. Recall too that the letters of Paul were actually written before the Gospels so Paul could not have referenced the Gospels which supposedly record the words of Jesus.

John 17 : 12 *While I was with them in the world, I kept them in thy name: those that thou gavest me I have kept, and none of them is lost, but the <u>son of perdition</u>; that the scripture might be fulfilled.*

What scripture? There is no 'son of perdition' recorded in the Old Testament.

Matthew 12 : 5 *Or have ye not read in the law, how that on the Sabbath days the priests in the temple profane the Sabbath, and are blameless?*

Now this is an odd one. It claims an Old Testament law allows the priests to profane the Sabbath with immunity. Firstly we must ask why on Earth would a priest desire to profane the Sabbath? Obviously no such statement is found in the Old Testament and it certainly doesn't sound like part of the Biblical disciplined, harsh and austere doctrine.

John 20 : 9 *For as yet they knew not the scripture, that he must rise again from the dead.*

The disciples were supposed to know a passage that appears in scripture but again nothing like this appears in the Old Testament.

John 7 : 38-39 *He that believeth on me, as the scripture hath said, "out of his belly shall flow rivers of living water". But this spake he of the Spirit, which they that believe on him should receive: for the Holy Ghost was not yet given.*

It is not likely that an Old Testament prophet would be able to predict the coming of the Holy Spirit in this manner and hence it is not surprising that nothing like this quote appears in the Old Testament. Either we have a different Bible that does not include these passages or the above mentioned

Biblical scriptures somehow went missing. The only other alternative is that Jesus and the New Testament scribes were not familiar with the Old Testament scriptures and just 'winged it'. Christians often quote fulfillment of prophecy as the 'proof' of their doctrine; however it seems that in these instances, their proof may be generated by these non-existent scriptural prophecies.

*A painting by NICOLAES VAN HELT STOCADE (1614 - 1669)
Amsterdam, called "King Tarquin and the Sibyl of Cumae".*

Of some interest is the fact that the 'Sibyl' or prophetess was a pagan figure found in ancient times at various locations; the five major ones included the famous '**Oracle of Delphi**' in Greece, plus one at each of Rome, Egypt, Persia and Turkey. Kings and leaders regularly consulted the Sibyls for fortune telling, advice, and to predict the outcome of planned battles. There was considerable sibylline literature circulating at the time of Christ and much of it was indistinguishable from 'orthodox' scripture. Is it possible that Jesus' quotes came from these 'books'. At Delphi the most famous Sibyl was the pythoness who chewed laurel leaves over a steaming pot which put her into a trance-like state where she uttered unintelligible sounds that were 'translated' by an accompanying priest, into prophecy. The Sibyls feature strongly in early religious art and in fact Michelangelo adorned the supposedly Christian, Sistine Chapel with no less than five frescos featuring the Sibyls, indicating their early acceptance by the Church. This alone indicates that although they were the very 'soothsayers' and pagans outlawed by the Bible, they must have been sufficiently revered by the early church and considered sufficiently 'Christian' by the Vatican, to include in the Sistine Chapel. One of the Books of the New Testament was actually written by the Roman Sibyl pictured above. Can you guess which one? It will be discussed in the final chapter of this book.

Who – What – Where?

How would a Christian get around these following contradictions?

Genesis 7 : 1 *The Lord then said to Noah, "Go into the ark, you and your whole family, because I have found you righteous in this generation".* (Noah is righteous)

Job 1 : 1 *In the land of Uz there lived a man whose name was Job. This man was blameless and upright; he feared God and shunned evil.* (Job is righteous)

Job 1 : 8 *And the Lord said unto Satan, Hast thou considered my servant Job, that there is none like him in the earth, a perfect and an upright man, one that feareth God, and escheweth evil?* (OK Job is righteous)

Job 2 : 3 *And the Lord said unto Satan, Hast thou considered my servant Job, that there is none like him in the earth, a perfect and an upright man, one that feareth God, and escheweth evil? And still he holdeth fast his integrity, although thou movedst me against him, to destroy him without cause.* (Job is righteous and Satan incited God to ruin him for no reason)

Luke 1 : 28 *And the angel came in unto her, and said, Hail, thou that art highly favoured, the Lord is with thee: blessed art thou among women.* Luke 1 : 42 *And she spake out with a loud voice, and said, Blessed art thou among women, and blessed is the fruit of thy womb.* (The 'virgin' Mary was found to be righteous and blessed above all other women.)

Luke 1 : 6 *Both of them were upright in the sight of God, observing all the Lord's commandments and regulations blamelessly.* (The parents of John the Baptist, Zechariah and Elizabeth were righteous)

James 5 : 16 *The prayer of a righteous man is powerful and effective.*

1 John 3 : 7-8 *He who does what is right is righteous, just as He is righteous.*

Romans 3 : 10 *As it is written: There is no one righteous, not even one;*

Well sorry, that is not written in the Old Testament and does not concur with what is written in the rest of the Bible. In addition consider this; David was **righteous** and he had a man murdered in order to steal his wife; Moses was **righteous** and he murdered an Egyptian man; Solomon was **righteous** and he departed to follow pagan Gods; Noah was **righteous** even though he had sexual relations with his daughters. The definition of 'righteous' must be pretty flexible! Actually the Pharisees took pleasure in the fact that several Biblical (Torah) characters had seriously flawed personalities;

"Awkward Moses relied upon Aaron for strong leadership...Lecherous David coveted his neighbor's wife...so stained with war and death was David that Yahweh prevented him from building the Temple of Peace. Solomon tolerated many foreign wives sacrificing to false gods. Fratricidal Cain, fraudulently misleading Jacob, cowardly Jonah, inept Rehoboam, the list goes on." [7]

God's Punishment

Does God impart unfair punishment on the children of the offender, and even on generations to come?

Jeremiah 32 : 18 *Thou shewest loving kindness unto thousands, and recompensest the iniquity of the fathers into the bosom of their children after them:* God brings punishment for the sins of their fathers to their children.

Ezekiel 18 : 19-20 *Yet you ask, Why does the son <u>not</u> share the guilt of his father? Since the son has done what is just and right and has been careful to keep all my decrees, he will surely live. The soul who sins is the one who will die. The son <u>will not</u> share the guilt of the father, nor will the father share the guilt of the son. The righteousness of the righteous man will be credited to him, and the wickedness of the wicked will be charged against him.*

Genesis 17 : 14 *And the uncircumcised man child whose flesh of his foreskin is not circumcised, that soul shall be cut off from his people; he hath broken my covenant.* A child is to be outcast if his parents neglect to have him circumcised at 8 days old. The child is seen to have broken the covenant - weird.

Exodus 20 : 5 *You shall not bow down to them or worship them; for I, the Lord your*

God, am a jealous God, punishing the children for the sin of the fathers to the third and fourth generation of those who hate me. That's pretty definite and pretty specific.

This is simply crazy! If I am an extremely pious person, who does good works and loves God, yet am having problems in my Christian walk today, it just may be because my Great Grandfather or even his father, who was from another country and whom I never even met, offended in some way. I would then be held responsible and never even know why. Is this for real? Seriously, this creator God might be better off with an ant farm; he displays quite an odd personality the way he plays with the life of his creations.

Romans 5 : 19 *For just as through the disobedience of the one man the many were made sinners, so also through the obedience of the one man the many will be made righteous.*

The second part of this quote could mean, alternatively, that you can do as you like and remain righteous as long as your forebears did the right thing. This is madness!

2 Kings 14 : 6 *Yet he did not put the sons of the assassins to death, in accordance with what is written in the Book of the Law of Moses where the Lord commanded: "Fathers shall not be put to death for their children, nor children put to death for their fathers; each is to die for his own sins."* A direct contradiction of the above.

Exodus 34 : 7 *Maintaining love to thousands, and forgiving wickedness, rebellion and sin. Yet he does not leave the guilty unpunished; he punishes the children and their children for the sin of the fathers to the third and fourth generation.* Your actions will affect your Great Grandchildren or their children whom you may never see!

Numbers 14 : 18 *The Lord is slow to anger, abounding in love and forgiving sin and rebellion. Yet he does not leave the guilty unpunished; he punishes the children for the sin of the fathers to the third and fourth generation.* How is it that the children are called "the guilty" if they have not transgressed?

Deuteronomy 5 : 9 *You shall not bow down to them or worship them; for I, the Lord your God, am a jealous God, punishing the children for the sin of the fathers to the third and fourth generation of those who hate me.* This is not a lone passage; this theme is repeated and just as often contradicted.

2 Chronicles 25 : 4 *Yet he did not put their sons to death, but acted in accordance with what is written in the Law, in the Book of Moses, where the Lord commanded: "Fathers <u>shall not be put to death for their children, nor children put to death for their fathers</u>; each is to die for his own sins."* Yes – No – Yes – No. With all this contradiction, which do we follow, which do we believe?

Isaiah 14 : 21-22 *Prepare a place <u>to slaughter his sons for the sins of their forefathers</u>.* Yet another example of contradiction and departure from the Law of Moses.

Deuteronomy 24 : 16 *Fathers shall not be put to death for their children, nor children put to death for their fathers; <u>each is to die for his own sin</u>.* This again totally contradicts the passages above.

Just a few more to consider:

Romans 5 : 12 *Therefore, just as sin entered the world through one man, and death through sin, and in this way death came to all men, because all sinned.*

Romans 5 : 14 *Death is passed to all men by the sin of Adam.*

Ezekiel 18 : 2 *What mean ye, that ye use this proverb concerning the land of Israel, saying, The fathers have eaten sour grapes, and the children's teeth are set on edge?*

These Bible passages give us no idea whether God inflicts punishment to the third or fourth generation, or not. It says he does; it says he doesn't. So what can we make of it all? Absolutely nothing; because contrary to any successful law code, it is just a contradictory mess of threats with no consistency or motif that makes any sense. It would take a lot to please this inconsistent God.

The Resurrection of Dry Bones

The Jews believe that this following passage is an analogy of the survival of the Hebrew nation, but reading verbatim, it could cause some concern. How do you feel about dry bones coming to life? I can admire people who believe donkeys and snakes can talk or virgins can have babies, but long dead bones acquiring skin, tendons and flesh then coming to life, possibly with regenerated clothes on – no, I have trouble with that one.

Ezekiel 37 : 1-10 *The hand of the Lord was upon me, and he brought me out by the Spirit of the Lord and set me in the middle of a valley; it was full of bones. He led* *me back and forth among them, and I saw a great many bones on the floor of the valley, bones that were very dry. He asked me, "Son of man, can these bones live?" I said, "O Sovereign Lord, you alone know." Then he said to me, "Prophesy to these bones and say to them, Dry bones, hear the word of the Lord! This is what the Sovereign Lord says to these bones: I will make breath enter you, and you will come to life. I will attach tendons to you and make flesh come upon you and cover you with skin; I will put breath in you, and you will come to life. Then you will know that I am the Lord." So I prophesied as I was commanded. And as I was prophesying, there was a noise; a rattling sound, and the bones came together, bone to bone. I looked, and tendons and flesh appeared on them and skin covered them, but there was no breath in them. Then he said to me, "Prophesy to the breath; prophesy, son of man, and say to it, This is what the Sovereign Lord says: Come from the four winds, O breath, and breathe into these slain, that they may live." So I prophesied as he commanded me, and breath entered them; they came to life and stood up on their feet—a vast army.*

Yeah – Right!! There is no hidden meaning - this is just nonsense.

What can we make of these non-sensical passages and the contradictions we have seen? Is it possible in spite of these errors and contradictions to still view the Bible as the 'Word of God'? I really fail to see how. It is simply an un-edited, chaotic mess, and has little value as prose and even less as a religious work; particularly when parishioners are seeking truth and consistency.

Acts 26 : 9 *I verily thought with myself, that I ought to do many things contrary to the name of Jesus of Nazareth.*
The words of St Paul, Holy Bible, KJV.

CHAPTER EIGHT

THE SUMERIAN INFLUENCE

"For I desired … the Knowledge of God more than burnt offerings."

Hosea 6 : 6

Clay Tablets

It was the Sumerians who first gave us written records from their early hieroglyphs, which evolved into the cuneiform system, of which we have vast libraries today. After the decline of the city-states of Sumer, the Sumerian language continued to be spoken and written by the priesthood in a similar way to Latin in Catholic churches today. The Sumerian priests and learned men became the teachers of the Babylonians, Assyrians and other cuneiform writing peoples. Assyrian and Babylonian are variant dialects of the same Semitic tongue. This language is called Akkadian after Akkad, the first Semitic City-state of any consequence, dating from the third millennium BCE. [1]

Many Akkadian words are directly derived from ancient Sumerian. It is an interesting undertaking indeed to study what precisely the ancient Sumerians believed and recorded because these were the very things the Hebrew people were exposed to in Babylon, just prior to writing the books of the Bible. When studying the Bible we must also consider carefully the records that these advanced Sumerian people left us. They were spiritual people who had no incentive to invent or deceive and no percentage in recording fiction. I believe the scribes had no axe to grind, they simply tried to record the wonders they were seeing from the Gods they called **Anunnaki**, personal, living, flesh and blood, Sky Gods who came down in their land, Gods with whom they interacted in their daily lives. Global research today shows that like the Sumerians, virtually all early civilizations had important features in common;

- Their civilization seemed to emerge from nowhere, suddenly and without precedence.
- There is considerable evidence that early civilizations commenced at a peak.
- They all had legends of Sky-Gods who descended to Earth to teach them about agriculture, civilization and writing.
- They usually built pyramids, step pyramids, ziggurats or other massive monuments.
- They documented the Sky-Gods not as myth, but as flesh and blood entities who interacted with very human traits within family units.
- They were proud of their achievements and openly boasted of wins and gains and yet took no credit for the acts of the Gods which could have been the case if they were not recording truthfully.

The amazing Sumerian society is certainly one that seemed to come from nowhere. The Sumerians claimed they originally came from Tilmun or Dilmun, which many scholars believe corresponds to the island off the East coast of the Arab Emirates in the Persian Gulf where the city of Bahrain is located today. Some archaeologists prefer to locate their homeland in the mountains of Pamir and have noted that metals used in unearthed Sumerian jewelry are ores not actually found in Sumer. This of course could be the result of trade, even though we are looking at a time before the third millennium BCE. Sitchin makes a good argument that there was a Tilmun city and a Tilmun land, the latter being in the area of Sinai [2] Actually there was also a Dilmun city in the Commagene in Anatolia at the headwaters of the Tigris River. It is wondered however what would have caused this race to leave their original homeland to settle in what was essentially a mosquito ridden, in-hospitable land between the Tigress and the Euphrates Rivers where extensive draining of the swamps and canal digging was required before the land would reasonably yield crops. Nevertheless, their new home of Sumer became a civilized community from at least 5,500 years ago;

situated in the area called "The Land Between Two Rivers" (the Tigris and the Euphrates). It was later called Babylon, Assyria and Mesopotamia and equates geographically to present day Iraq.

The Biblical 'Garden of Eden' lay in this approximate area and 'Paradise', from the Hebrew word *"pardes"* meaning an orchard, was likely one and the same location. The Bible tells us that the 'Garden of Eden' was washed by The Tigris and the Euphrates and their tributaries, clearly locating the home of Adam and Eve in the land of Sumer. Who can guess why the Gods or the Sumerians chose this location? What it means however is that the people of the 19 generations of Man, from Adam to Abraham, as shown in the Bible, must be considered to have dwelled in the land of Sumer. Now the patriarch, father of the Jews, Abraham, left from the Sumerian City of Ur and migrated to the land of Canaan supposedly around 1900 BCE. He was a Sumerian prince, who became the first Jew through his covenant with his God. We will see soon however that he had strong Egyptian connections. Twentieth century archaeologists were aware, from Sumerian cuneiform texts, that a people called the Kaldu migrated from the South to the North of Babylonia and thought initially that Abraham might have led this migration. It turned out however that this was not so, because this migration occurred much later around 1000 BCE and the Kaldu were actually Chaldeans, not original Sumerians. The great early archaeologist Sir Leonard Woolley had this to say;

> *"There is nothing to show to what race the first inhabitants of Mesopotamia belonged… at a date which we cannot fix, people of a new race made their way into the valley, coming whence we do not know, and settling down side by side with the old inhabitants. These were the Sumerians. The Sumerians believed that they came into the country with their civilization already formed, bringing with them the knowledge of agriculture, of working in metal, of the art of writing - 'since then' said they, 'no new inventions have been made' – and if as our excavations seem to show, there is a good deal of truth in that tradition… later research may well discover, where the ancestors of our Sumerians developed the first real civilization".* [3]

In his work, *'Sumerian Mythology'*, Professor Samuel Noah Kramer, an informed Sumerian scholar stated, *"Their original home is quite uncertain."*

Kramer also conducted studies of the Sumerian language and noted that this language; *"...stands alone and unrelated to any known language living or dead."* [4]

The Sumerians recorded that the form of the language and the ability to write it was taught to them by the Anunnaki Gods. Their early pictographic language is today called Elamite and is the forerunner of the later cuneiform (wedge shaped) writings that was unique and unrelated to any other language of the time. The black skinned Dravidian speaking Elamites apparently moved into Ur in about 2004 BCE and exerted influence over Babylon for the next 200 years. [5] Today we find some similarities of Elamite characters with ancient Chinese, and this indicates that the Chinese may have originally descended from the land of Sumer or at least based their writing on things learned there.

Many Sumerian stories were translated into Akkadian and other Semitic languages and as such, survive today. We have a fairly good understanding of Sumerian recording, thanks to literally thousands and thousands of clay cuneiform tablets that have survived in ancient libraries. These tablets tell us some pretty amazing things if we care to listen. Most people exposed to their message however simply say no, it couldn't be so and proceed to pass them off as myth. I say let the ancients be heard. Is it easier to believe that these Sumerian people, noted for their precise language, mathematics, writing, astronomy and record keeping, suddenly went far out of character on the most important records of their own religious beliefs and historical genesis, and suddenly recorded fantasy? Laurence Gardner put it this way:

> *"What actually transpired was that the original Mesopotamian writings were recorded as history. The history was later rewritten to form a base for foreign cults - first Judaism and then Christianity. The corrupted dogma of the religions then became established as 'history' and because the contrived dogma (the new approved history) was so different from the original writings, the early first-hand records were labeled 'mythology'."* [6]

If we are to better understand the religions of today it is extremely important for us to examine what the Sumerians recorded, particularly since it is unquestionably the source of much that is included in our scriptures today.

The Enuma Elish

The Babylonian creation epic, the **Enuma elish** (meaning, 'when on high') is the Babylonian genesis, a poem consisting of seven baked clay tablets of cuneiform writing with most of the tablets containing about 150 lines each. It has survived since the time of King Ashurbanipal in the ruins of the Nineveh Library, and most scholars believe the epic is extremely old, probably dating to the Old Babylonian Period (early part of the second millennium BCE) and likely being copied from a Sumerian original. The actual 'creation' in the Ziusudra legend was when the 'Sky-Gods' EN.KI and Ninharsag fashioned the 'Black-headed people' to populate the Earth and assist the Anunnaki with gold mining operations.

Enuma Elish Tablet

Sir Austen Henry Layard unearthed these tablets in an archaeological expedition of 1848 –1876. It certainly appears, at least in part, to be the original model for the Bibles' Genesis record, being basically similar yet predating it by all of one thousand years. This is confirmed by the initial publication of an English translation by George Smith of the British Museum under the title, *'The Chaldean Account of Genesis'*. Ironically six tablets contain the Sumerian story and the seventh tells of recreation and celebration. This no doubt led the Hebrews to document; *'in six days God created the World and on the seventh he rested.'* Here from the Enuma elish is how the Babylonian primordial picture began;

> *When on high, Heaven had not been named*
> *And below Earth had not been called,*
> *Naught had but primordial Apsu* (the sun) *their begetter,*
> *Mummu* (Mercury) *and Tiamat* (original larger proto-Earth) *she who bore them all.*
> *Their waters were mingled together.*
> *No reed had yet been formed,*
> *No marshland had appeared.* [7]

There is a loose protocol by archaeologists to identify a tablet by it's opening lines. The Enuma elish commences with "When on high …" and in like manner the early Hebrews called their creation story Beresheet, *(B'rei-sheeth, literally; "At the head of things")* which refers to its opening lines that we translate in the Bible as *"In the beginning …"* The name 'Genesis' that we use today came from the Greek, and was not added until the third century. The Enuma elish states that firstly nothing existed except the chaos of salt and fresh water and the God Apsu and Mother Tiamat. In the creation story these Gods produced divine beings one of whom, EN.KI (Ea) subjugated the God Apsu. Tiamat quickly created still more divine ones to fight against the unruly and rebellious ones. These chose EN.KI's son Marduk as their leader and in the ensuing fight with Tiamat they opened her up like a shellfish and utilized the parts to create the canopy of the heavens and the dry land of Earth.

The prolific writer, **Zechariah Sitchin** takes a slightly different view from most academics in unraveling what is recorded here and explains that Tiamat was the name for an original, larger planet Earth and there is no delineating between divine beings and planets here. This is quite believable with all planets apart from Earth in our solar system today, named after Gods. These are Mercury, Venus, Mars, Jupiter, Saturn, Neptune, Uranus, Mercury and even Vulcan if it exists. Sitchin says, what is described in this part of Enuma elish is a Moon of the tenth planet Nibiru (actually called Marduk) colliding with Tiamat (the original oversized Earth) and breaking off a part from the current Pacific Ocean, leaving our present smaller Earth knocked into a new orbit and the remaining smashed part as debris forming the canopy known as the asteroid belt. The craters on our moon were caused by the flying debris. A small part of this description from the Enuma elish follows;

> *"Sir, who heaped up a mountain over Tiamat,*
>
> *Who carried off the body of Tiamat with his weapon…?*
>
> *Who crossed the wide and turbulent sea…?"* [8]

For many years, scientists believed that the Earth's moon broke off from the Pacific Ocean, however that theory is now proved to be incorrect. They probably were correct all along in their belief that something broke off from the area of the Pacific Ocean where the Earths' crust is measurably much thinner. The Sumerians said all along it was the asteroid belt that was formed from the debris of the broken off part, caused by the collision and not the Moon. Also our moon is considerably oversized for the current size of Earth, and it would be more appropriate if it originally orbited the much bigger planet Tiamat *(maiden of life)*. This makes perfect sense and is quite believable; it would help explain a lot of anomalies in our solar system and particularly the origins of the asteroid belt which baffles scientists today. Our moon also has a unique orbit with one face constantly towards the Earth, and is the exact distance from earth to be subtended as a very similar size to the much larger sun that is of course much further away. This is not only unique within our solar system but also appears to be without precedent elsewhere in the galaxy.

Many of today's scholars are trying to account for non-linear discrepancies in the orbits of Pluto, Uranus and Neptune, and believe an approaching unknown giant planet on a distant orbit within our solar system could account for this. They have begun the search for this mysterious celestial body that is affecting the outer planets in our solar system. Sitchin believes that it will turn out to be the tenth planet; the Anunnaki planet Nibiru that was documented by the Sumerians.

This is not some crackpot theory. Zechariah Sitchin has a lot of credibility. He was born in Russia and raised in Palestine, where he acquired a profound knowledge of modern and ancient Hebrew, other Semitic and European languages, the Old Testament, and the history and archeology of the Near East. He is a very informed scholar and one of the few who are able to read and understand Sumerian. He is an authority on the subject and the author of many books and papers.

The Anunnaki Sky-Gods

The Sumerian records go on to tell how the **Anunnaki** (meaning *'they came down from ANU'*) were the inhabitants of the planet Nibiru (meaning roughly, 'planet that crosses the skies'.) This planet is said to be of our own solar system with an orbit track that passes between Mars and Jupiter and is supposedly in an elongated elliptical orbit like a comet that takes it away from Earth for centuries. In fact there have been many headlines in newspapers that the Tenth Planet has already been discovered. We previously mentioned a recent discovery was the small planet outside Pluto and it has been tentatively given the name of **'Sedna'** which corresponds to the Inuit goddess of the ocean waters. This however, is not the planet X we are seeking. It would take a massive planet in our outer Solar System to account for the orbital discrepancies noted in the other planets, particularly Uranus and Pluto. There are in fact many informed articles on the existence of this planet and many noted mathematicians, astronomers and historians support its existence. Many however are still skeptical and others totally discount it. This author is a member of an Astronomical Society and can report huge controversy amongst astronomers about the existence of Planet X; however with further study of perturbences in the orbits of our outer planets, many are forced to become believers in the general hypothesis.

It is of course very easy to remain a total skeptic but by this we will certainly learn absolutely nothing and retain the enigmas of our solar system forever. Imagine for instance if Halley's Comet was on a 3600 year cycle and accordingly seen by just one in approximately every 800 generations; would we even believe in its existence? Almost certainly not.

The Sumerian Atra-hasis document tells us that the Anunnaki dug canals around the Tigris and Euphrates Rivers for 3600 years before man was created to take over the load. This by default gives credence to the 3600 year orbit calculated by Sitchin, since those left behind to prepare things had to wait for the next complete orbit to obtain relief;

"The Gods load was too great

The work too hard, the trouble too much…

When ANU had gone up to the sky,

And the Gods of the Apsu had stayed below

The Great Sky-Gods made the Igigi bear the workload,

The Anunnaki had to dig out canals,

Had to clear channels, the lifelines of the land…

The Anunnaki dug out the Tigris River,

And then dug out the Euphrates…

They were counting the years of loads,
For 3600 years they bore the excess…
They groaned and blamed each other,
Grumbled over the masses of excavated soil." [9]

The Washington Post's influential, astronomical writers had this to say about Planet X;

> *Could there be a tenth planet in our solar system? The idea is not as bizarre as it seems. For years, scientists have been scanning the skies for evidence of "Planet X," as it is called, in the hopes that it might explain such diverse phenomena as the irregular motion of the outer planets, the sudden demise of the dinosaurs and the influence of comets. So far, the object — if there is one — has eluded them. But the hypothesis remains enticing, as do the celestial mysteries that prompted the search.* [10]

Zecharia Sitchin tells us that not only were the Pioneer spacecraft utilized in an attempt to locate 'Planet X' as early as 1982, but also the 'Infrared Astronomical Satellite,' **IRAS** from 1983, as part of their planned objectives. The New York Times of 30 Jan 1983 headlined, *"Clues Get Warm in the Search for Planet X".* In this article astronomer Ray T. Reynolds of the Ames Research Centre was quoted as saying, *"Astronomers are so sure of the existence of the Tenth Planet that they think there's nothing left but to name it."* [11] As Sitchin also pointed out, it is already named; the Sumerians called it **'Nibiru'** and the Babylonians called it **'Marduk'**.

The Sumerian story tells that the Anunnaki Sky-Gods of the planet Nibiru came to Earth near Sumer and mined gold they discovered in areas of Africa. Their leader was **ANU** (God the Father) and he sent his sons **EN.KI** (Prince of the earth) to look after things of the Earth (mining) and **ENLIL** (Prince of the air) to look after things in the air (transporting the gold). ENLIL is said to have been responsible for **"the ME"**, a magic box that produced a set of universal laws governing all existence. This description could record something similar to how primitive tribesmen would respond to the information available from a palm pilot or laptop computer today. To indicate the truth of this we can read the famous quotation from Arthur C. Clark;

> *"Any sufficiently advanced technology is indistinguishable from magic."*

Just consider for a moment if this scenario is even partly true and the ancient Sumerians interacted with these Gods as they recorded. They would be absolutely staggered and way out of their depth attempting to record precisely what they were seeing and what was occurring. This is precisely how the records they left us read.

Hybrid Creation

Perhaps the Anunnaki were accustomed to cooler lands, but as we saw above in the Atra-hasis document the two lots of 300 Anunnaki miners working with EN.KI found the work so strenuous, draining marsh lands in Mesopotamia and mining in the African heat, that they revolted and refused to work. ENLIL was sent to check on the lack of production and soon conflict resulted between the brothers. The Great Father ANU arrived to check on the situation and surprisingly sided with the workers. Despite strong objection from ENLIL, it was eventually decided that EN.KI should train the (Homo erectus) hominids present on Earth to handle these chores for them. These beings, they thought, could handle the hard work; however, they had a low learning capacity and lacked the power of speech and it seems they lacked the intelligence required for the tasks.

It was then decided to improve these hominids with the Anunnaki DNA; to genetically engineer a race of workers; hybrids of the hominids and the Anunnaki themselves. After a few false starts a 'worker' was created using EN.KI's own sperm. This resulted in the first, (Homo sapiens sapiens) 'clever' or 'thinking' man; a created hybrid species. Note that 'sapiens' comes from the Latin 'sapienta' meaning knowledge or wisdom and we will look soon at how our scientists remain 'boggled' by the incredible rate of modern man's gaining knowledge and wisdom. This is the question the evolutionists cannot answer today. Why is it that early man lived for millennium basically unchanged, then quite recently, in the scale of things, displayed this amazing burst of brilliance with an almost exponential growth in knowledge?

Actual documentation is found in the Sumerian texts where the Dragon Queen requests EN.KI to create beings to assist with the mining;

"Fashion servants of the Gods and may they (then) produce doubles." [12] In other words, 'produce workers with the capacity to procreate.' EN.KI's

reply was an exclamation; *"Oh my mother! The creature whose name you uttered; it exists! Bind upon it the image of the Gods… It is Man!"* (13)

This indicates that the Anunnaki commenced with primitive man and added their own DNA to manipulate or evolve the existing Hominid into a more intelligent being after the image of these Anunnaki Gods themselves. The Sumerian texts from the Nineveh library contained this story of the creation of the first Earth Man by the Sky-God EN.KI. He named him **Adapa** and his race was called the **Adama** (Earth Man). Amazingly the Egyptian archives of Pharaoh Amenhotep III (around 1400 BCE) contain an almost identical record of this same creation story. (14) In other words the Sumerians and the Egyptians suggest that modern man was created in the image of the Gods. There is no escaping this situation; it is more than adequately confirmed in the Bible. The fact that the Bible calls the first man **Adam** indicates that it was almost certainly based on the story of the **Adama** from these much older records. Since many people accept the Bible story and it can be shown to be based on much older records, then obviously the older records must hold even more credibility.

It is truly amazing how much these writings could explain today, satisfying the mystery of the decline of the hominids and also the lightning fast advancement of our Homo sapiens race. As well as being used as workers, the Anunnaki taught selected leaders of this new Adama race; astronomy, mathematics, agriculture and things to generally impart knowl-edge and soften manners. Is this scenario really less believable than the Bible's 'zappo' creation story that uses the 'magic' finger of Almighty God? The global documentation of the creation myth makes it even more plausible and amazingly it satisfactorily explains the Bibles plurality of the Godhead. There was no trinity at this point, before the introduction of Jesus and the Holy Ghost; yet Gods (plural) are mentioned throughout Genesis. Soon we will see more evidence that the Bible seems to support much of the Sumerian version increasing the likelihood that it was originally plagiarized from Sumerian culture and records. Other clues are found in our Bibles, for example;

Genesis 5 : 2 *"Male and Female created Him them and blessed them and called <u>their</u> name Adam"* (or Adama!)

THEY LIED TO US IN SUNDAY SCHOOL

Note too that in;

Genesis 1 : 26, *"Let us make man in our image after our likeness."*

We should note that the Genesis record does not record Almighty God making the statement, in this case the Bible reads **Eloheem.** Now the plural word **Eloheem** means, "these beings" or with 'Eloh' being the singular word for God … "these Gods". If the intended word was **Elohim** the plural of Eloh (God) this alters nothing. The word "Elohim" is pronounced *Eloheem* and is likely the same word. We still know that the scribe was trying to communicate that either "These Beings" or that "Gods plural" actually made man. The point is that this is what is recorded in the early Bible and is something we must really digest. We were not given that information to consider as young people and this message was never taught in Church. Surely parts of the Bible including the early plural Gods, are not there to embarrass Christians, it either is, or isn't the word of God.

As stated the Jewish scribes were obviously sourcing information in Babylon during the captivity, and their intrinsic writings became contaminated with some of their interpretations of the Babylonian legends, which dated directly to the earlier Sumerians. Today we have Sumerian cylinder seals depicting EN.KI working with what looks like test tubes in a room the Sumerians called "the place where life is breathed in." Note some additional thoughts on this process from the Bible;

Daniel 5 : 23 *"the God in who's hand thy breath is"*

Acts 17 : 24 *" He giveth to all; life and breath".*

The Babylonian language was new to the Jewish scribes. Sometimes they got it wrong. The Bible writers apparently misunderstood the Sumerian record of the Anunnaki creation of **Earthman** and said he was actually made by God **out of earth,** hence ashes to ashes, dust to dust. It is interesting that the Biblical pronunciation of Adam is documented as *Ar-dam* supporting further that it derives from Adama. It is worth noting too that a Greek word "Adamas" came to mean "invincible man". The curious story of Eve being created from Adams rib is found in the Sumerian records perhaps by default. The *"Garden of the Gods"* found within the Enuma elish, parallels the Bible's Garden of Eden story with plants growing that are sacred to the Gods and must not be touched. When their Adam equivalent, Adapa, attempted to eat from these plants in the garden he was forcibly stopped by the Gods and sustained injuries in the scuffle. A female deity called Ninti (Eve) was created to nurse him back to health. Ironically Ninti could mean "**lady of the rib**" but is much more likely translated as "**lady who gives life**" because as if by some cosmic joke, the Sumerian pictograph for "lady who gives life" is the same as for "lady of the rib". The Hebrews writing the Bible being fairly new to the Sumerian language may have failed to see this literary pun and may have got it quite wrong, perpetuating to this day that Eve was created from Adam's rib.

The Captivity in Babylon

King Nebuchadnezzar of Babylon sacked Jerusalem and destroyed the Temple in 587 BCE, then took the learned amongst the Hebrew people back to his country. The Hebrew scribes in captivity in Babylon did some soul searching to ascertain precisely just how they had upset their God sufficiently to cause him to forsake them. They couldn't accept that this was simply a course of events; it had to be the will of their God. Their entire homeland, both Samaria and Judah were laid waste and the Jerusalem temple (the home of YHWH built by Solomon) had been desecrated and destroyed. They recount their confusion and laments in the book of Jeremiah, and their sadness and regret are quite palpable. To make sense of it they had to believe that their God, who hated heathens so badly that he had the Hebrew warriors slaughter them to gain the Promised Land, now somehow felt he should instead support Nebuchadnezzar and his heathen, Marduk worshipers. Even against his own chosen people. Of course this is nonsense but believing that things had occurred outside the will of their God was not an option to their psyche.

In Babylon, Marduk the son of EN.KI of the Anunnaki was the chief deity, worshipped as Bel. The Babylonians had their own sophisticated, fully formed religion, with an historical component largely inherited from the Sumerians. The name 'Babylon' even meant *"Gateway of the Gods"*. The Babylonian scribes were quite familiar with the long history of this area, as their predecessors the Sumerians and Akkadians had recorded it, for more than 2,000 years. As the Hebrew mingled with these learned men of Babylon over the next few decades of their captivity, as they visited their libraries, and absorbed their culture, ideas were obviously exchanged, documents studied, and portions of these religious discussions came to be written down in Hebrew. The difference was however that the Sumerians had left very specific and precise writings of their 'flesh-and-blood' Anunnaki Gods complete with their pedigrees and the way they had enacted the creation of man and then interacted with him. Their Gods showed traits identical to humans with a full spectrum of emotions and one cannot help but notice the interwoven relationships and personalities that give credence to the Sumerian records.

Before the commencement of the written scriptures, the Hebrew had the verbal folklore traditions surrounding their initial patriarch Abraham (also from Sumer) and of the exodus attributed to Moses plus the stories of Joshua and the conquest of the Promised Land. Most of their genesis was not at all specific and the God of their fathers did not even have a definite name at that stage. In fact it appears that the many names documented throughout the early period indicates that it wasn't always the same God recorded in these stories. Any written documentation of the Hebrew history, creation or religious beliefs would have been very scant indeed. Really it would have been most likely dedicated patriarchs like Abraham who preserved and passed on any stories of the God of the Fathers and an El Elyon creation and the monotheistic Moses; who preserved the stories of his new God who went by the mysterious name of YHWH and was so full of anger that he couldn't go with them on the Exodus (Exodus 33:1-5), and instead communicated through the 'Ark of the Covenant'. The point we are coming to is that when the Hebrew scribes commenced to compose and compile the books that were to become the Old Testament, it was right after their years of captivity in Babylon and their exposure to the Sumerian records. Their Temple in Jerusalem was destroyed; they were an ascetic, shattered people whose God had forsaken them for their transgressions. They were ground-down, anonymous, orphaned, lowly sinners, now incapable of greatness. The self-esteem of the Hebrew was at an all time low. In Babylon however they would have been 'boggled' by the riches, the prosperity and

The Ark of Tutankhamen (above) would be very similar to the "Ark of the Covenant" made in the same timeframe by the Hebrew of the Exodus.

the luxury on show. This would at least have left them open minded to learn how the Sumerians did it so well. Why should these heathens have such good things? The chosen race weren't getting such a good deal.

About this time the Hebrew Nation may have looked skywards and said; *"Hang on a minute God, we are supposed to be the chosen race, the Arabs get all the oil, and we get to cut off the end of our... what??"*

The content of Genesis certainly came from the Sumerian Enuma elish with parts of it almost identical. All the dialogue about Abraham and other patriarchs was information that would not have been known by Moses some 700 years after the event, unless proto Sumerian scriptures existed in Egypt even back then. Now the Jews maintain that Moses wrote the Pentateuch (the first five books of the Bible) yet our previous studies of Genesis showed that there were at least two writers whose work didn't mesh particularly well. Moses may have documented the Jewish law of Leviticus and the Ten Commandments, (things he was familiar with) however no serious scholar would accept that the Torah or the Old

Testament was written before 1300 BCE and would place this as about a millennium too early. There is evidence that the scribes from the Babylonian captivity wrote a considerable amount of the original proto-Old Testament scriptures and it is not possible to explain away this influence in the Bible. There is little doubt that the creation story of the Old Testament is a reworked version of the Sumerian creation by the Anunnaki Gods from the Enuma elish. Even though the captives by that time had become bi-lingual many held fast to their Jewish faith. So we see it was scribes, whose studies would have included the Sumerian documents and scriptures, who first wrote down the Jewish history and theology. These scribes could, no doubt, read and write the Babylonian language and had been brought up and educated in the Babylonian system.

Babylon was in turn sacked by Cyrus in 539 BCE who freed the Hebrew people who had been in captivity for varying times from 48 to 70 years. Contrary to popular belief, the majority of the Hebrew families actually stayed on in Babylon, with only those who firmly valued the Jewish faith and Jewish law returning to Jerusalem. From this time we see that many Babylonian words and customs remained with the Jewish people. For example the Jews who returned adopted the Babylonian names for the months of the year into the Hebrew language; other similar examples exist to this day.

Returning Home

The exile brought with it a new sense of alienation and separation for the Jews, as is characteristic if a 'minority group' people in another culture adopt exclusive ways to protect their identity and maintain it against the greater flux of 'foreign' ideas and genetic influences. Even though they were supposedly God's chosen people, effectively the exile cemented what was to become the separatist path for the Jews. On their return, the leader Ezra was dismayed to find those Hebrew who had remained behind in the Holy Land had intermarried with Canaanite wives. Ezra delivered a diatribe and judgement that every man should sever his ties of marriage with the Canaanite women and accept the separatist state of the Hebrew nation.

Ezra 10 : 10-12 *And Ezra the priest stood up, and said unto them, Ye have* *transgressed, and have taken strange wives, to increase the trespass of Israel. Now therefore make confession unto the Lord God of your fathers, and do his pleasure: and separate yourselves from the people of the land, and from the strange wives. Then all the congregation answered and said with a loud voice, as thou hast said, so must we do.*

All the 'strange' women and children were driven out and to this day the pure Jewish strain is maintained.

So why did their God abandon the Hebrew people and support the Babylonians? We can appreciate and understand their chagrin. Regardless of how God's chosen people might have transgressed, this simply does not make any sense. See what you think as you read the following passages remembering that they were supposedly penned by those actual scribes of that time;

Jeremiah 21 : 6 *I will strike down those who live in this city (Jerusalem) —both men and animals—and they will die of a terrible plague.* (OK God is upset. In fact he is even down on the animals.)

Jeremiah 21 : 7 *After that, declares the Lord, I will hand over Zedekiah king of Judah, his officials and the people in this city who survive the plague, sword and famine, to Nebuchadnezzar king of Babylon and to their enemies who seek their lives. He will put them to the sword; he will show them no mercy or pity or compassion.* (Zedekiah then had his sons killed in front of him then his eyes plucked out by the Babylonians. Can we ask – why?)

Jeremiah 21 : 9 *Whoever stays in this city will die by the sword, famine or plague. But whoever goes out and surrenders to the Babylonians who are besieging you will live; he will escape with his life.* (OK, I like you Hebrew people less than the heathens now.)

Jeremiah 24 : 10 *I will send the sword, famine and plague against them until they are destroyed from the land I gave to them and their fathers.* (But didn't God know everything from the beginning to the end when He gave them the land to start with.)

Jeremiah 27 : 8 *If, however, any nation or kingdom will not serve Nebuchadnezzar king of Babylon or bow its neck under his yoke, I will punish that nation with the sword, famine and plague, declares the Lord, until I destroy it by his hand.* (Why has

Almighty God now become such a strong advocate of the heathen King of Babylon?)

Jeremiah 27 : 13 *Why will you and your people die by the sword, famine and plague with which the Lord has threatened any nation that will not serve the king of Babylon?* (Well that is precisely what the scribes are trying to ascertain! What happened to, "You are my chosen people, Israel".)

Jeremiah 34 : 17 *Therefore, this is what the Lord says: You have not obeyed me; you have not proclaimed freedom for your fellow countrymen. So I now proclaim 'freedom' for you, declares the Lord – 'freedom' to fall by the sword, plague and famine. I will make you abhorrent to all the kingdoms of the earth.*

A real comedian! This punishment is for what? <u>Not proclaiming freedom for your fellow countrymen</u>. This is so very silly. A few short years earlier God was slaughtering their fellow countrymen to steal the Promised Land from them. We saw that God even sent an Angel to wipe out the inhabitants of the Promised Land in order to give it to his chosen people. Then following God's promises it seems he just changed his mind. I don't like you anymore! Go over to the Babylonians or die!

Jeremiah 38 : 2 *This is what the Lord says: 'Whoever stays in this city will die by the sword, famine or plague, but whoever <u>goes over to the Babylonians</u> will live. He will escape with his life; he will live'.*

This flies in the face of anything that is in any way cogent. It just doesn't make any sense. The only possible explanation is that the Hebrew penned these passages to try to involve their God's will in the explanation of their captivity; a happenstance occurrence that they could not accept. We know however that Babylonians were originally worshipers of Marduk the son of EN.KI. Now the brothers EN.KI and ENLIL were always at loggerheads and a family feud continued with their sons. Somehow the God Jehovah/ YHWH must fit into some form of power struggle recorded in this part of the Bible to possibly explains 'God's' changing patronage.

To indicate the reverence given to the Babylonian Marduk there are three kings, documented from Babylon before the captivity, who were obviously supporters and appended the name of this God to their own;

Marduk apal-iddina (c.1173 to 1161 BCE).

Marduk-kabit-ahhêshu (c.1156 to 1139 BCE)

Itti Marduk-balatu (ruled c.1139 to 1130 BCE)

YHWH introduced himself to the Exodus Hebrew in the fourteenth century BCE. The captivity ended in the sixth century BCE. We would have to minutely investigate the 800 years between these dates to gain some inkling of what took the Gods so long to sort out their station. This is of course assuming that somehow the Biblical record can be reconciled with the Babylonian record. Because the Hebrew in exile compiled the Biblical record in Babylon, and because so much of the Old Testament is taken from the Sumerian record, I believe it can.

Sumerian Influence in the Bible

We are now looking to show that many Old Testament stories unmistakably record and embrace stories learned from the older Sumerian or Akkadian records whilst the Hebrew were in captivity in Babylon.

> **Genesis 6 : 1-3** *And it came to pass, when men began to multiply on the face of the earth, and daughters were born unto them, That the sons of the Gods saw the daughters of men that they were fair; and they took them wives of all which they chose. And the Lord said, My spirit shall not always strive with man, for that he also is flesh: yet his days shall be an hundred and twenty years.*

This Bible passage records that man (with eternal life) began to multiply at a rapid rate causing overpopulation. The Gods decided to utilize a flood to reduce his numbers until it was found that they could remove his immortality, limiting his life to a hundred and twenty years, and have no requirement to apply genocide again. We need to recall this passage as we go forward.

How many readers know that the Biblical Noah's Ark story is not original, with Sumerian and Babylonian versions predating the Biblical story by more than a thousand years? The first is a fragmented, partly decomposed Sumerian text; the Atra-hasis Epic about a 'wise' King called Atra-hasis (*'exceedingly wise'*). This King ruled about the time when sufficient gold had been recovered, and the Anunnaki were ready to move on. In the *Atra-hasis Epic*, we can make out that the God ENLIL is angered with men and, after a few failed attempts to reduce their population, he brings great rains that flood the earth and destroy most of humanity. It could be that the pull of the planet Nibiru is the cause of this climatic anomaly effecting the earth's weather pattern and ENLIL is simply able to predict its effect. ENLIL's brother EN.KI does not want to give up on the beings he worked so hard to create and came to befriend, and warns Atra-hasis 'Noah' that the flood is coming. He gives him the design of a boat that would ride out the flood and save mankind. Remember this is written way before the Biblical story and as such must hold more credence than the later Bible epic. The Atra-hasis document records that EN.KI and his sister Nin-khursag then created an additional fourteen 'Adama' increasing the gene pool after the flood, to ensure the survival of this new species of man.

The location of the cities of the Sumerians was on a flood prone area between the Tigress and Euphrates Rivers and it would be natural to document legends of floods. We saw earlier that Ireland's Archbishop, **James Ussher** calculated from the Bible a date of 2348 BCE for the flood; although there is no evidence whatever that this is correct. Archaeological excavation and examination of the sediments of Kisch, Ur and the city of Shuruppak (which is thought to have been inundated around 2900 BCE) would suggest that this was the last massive, but nevertheless local, flood. From ancient records, there are essentially four flood legends which are identical in essence, but differ in the specific names of the hero involved. Let's compare them;

1. Atra-hasis epic; This is a Babylonian tradition where the Anunnaki Gods created the human race to take over the hard mining and agricultural activities on Earth. They were created with the power to reproduce, and were initially immortal beings. As such, the human race multiplied quickly and made so much noise that the chief Sumerian God, ENLIL, could not sleep. Accordingly he tried to reduce their numbers, first by plague, then by famine. In each case the God EN.KI, who was responsible for creating the human race, frustrated the plan. ENLIL then pressed the 'Assembly of the Gods' to co-operate in exterminating the whole human race by a huge flood. The Lamentation Texts cover the story;

"Alas all storms together have flooded the Earth.

The great flood storm of Heaven, the ever roaring storm…

The flood storm ordered in hate, which sated the land…

The flood storm that overwhelmed

The living creatures of Heaven and Earth – The Black-headed ones." [15]

We should not read too much into the fact that living creatures of Heaven and Earth were destroyed since this simply means the 'sons' of the Gods who came down to mate with Earth women. Accordingly creatures of both Heaven and Earth were destroyed. ENLIL's brother EN.KI warned his beloved Atra-hasis and gave him guidance in the manufacture of a boat to ride out the flood. This boat incidentally was like a giant cube; the same dimension in height, length and breadth. In fact it was a big box which is ironical since the Hebrew name for Noah's Ark is *'Teba'* and like the Ark of the Covenant, this means literally, a 'box'.

It seems that EN.KI showed the Council of the Gods that he could snip the DNA strands of man to *"make their days 120 years."* ENLIL also learns of other methods to control the human population like barrenness, stillbirths, and the use of sterile women who do not fall pregnant; as a result he then promises to never again bring a flood to the world. In these stories the prototype 'Noah' rode out a large local flood and 'preserved the seed of human life' from inundation. The animals taken aboard however, were clearly a food source and not for preservation of the species. This would make sense since Noah could not have done much fishing from the ark if he only had two worms!

In the Atra-hasis document there is a vivid description on alighting from the Ark, of swelled up bloated human and animal bodies that had perished in the flood. When Atra-hasis cooked meat from his livestock, the Gods swooped down on him 'like hungry flies' since their fresh meat supply had also been cut off and they were hungry.

2. Ziusudra epic; another abridged and ancient Sumerian tradition is of Ziusudra (*bearer of long life*). This story dates from about the third millennium BCE. The Assembly of the Gods decided to destroy mankind because of local overpopulation, although this appears to mean that they chose to wipe out the offspring from when the Sons of the Gods mated with Earth women. In this epic the flood failed to terminate mankind because EN.KI informed his favourite, **Ziusudra**, (a lugal or priest/king) that a flood would cover the land and that he should build a gigantic boat and so save the seed of the human race and the animals. In the Enuma elish, EN.KI spoke to Ziusudra;

> *"By our command a flood will sweep over the land (cult centres) to destroy the seed of mankind...its kingship, its rule, will come to an end."* [16]

The flood lasted seven days and seven nights. On alighting, Ziusudra cooked meat and the Gods hung around smelling the sweet savour. This was not necessarily a sacrifice as the Gods were hungry since the land had been inundated for quite some time and they 'hung around like flies' at a barbeque. ANU and ENLIL received homage from Ziusudra, who in return personally received immortality from the Gods as his name suggests.

3. Uta-napishtim epic; the hero of the Epic of Gilgamesh was the Sumerian King and demi-God, Gilgamesh (circa 2600 BCE) who sought immortality. We read from the epic;

> *"Gilgamesh, what are you doing?*
>
> *The eternal life which thou seekest thou wilt not find;*
>
> *For when the Gods created mankind,*
>
> *They allotted death to mankind."*

Gilgamesh was the offspring of a Heavenly female God who was attracted to the beauty of an Earth man. King Gilgamesh became a legendary figure in Babylon around whom many epics were later composed. Towards the end of this story, a meeting occurs between Gilgamesh and King Uta-napishtim of Shuruppak (Noah), the hero of the flood, who tells him the story of his life.

George Smith an Assyriologist with the British Museum found the story on unearthed tablets from the Nineveh library and worked on the translation. Here EN.KI informs Uta-napishtim of the 'Council of Gods' decision to cleanse the Earth with a flood and instructs him in building a boat with 7 decks to save his family and animals. This legend however states that he took 'the seed' of all living creatures, which sounds more like preservation of DNA or sperm samples, but not necessarily the animals themselves, which would be a task with overwhelming logistical problems. At the end of six days and six nights the storm stopped. One week later, Utanapishtim released a dove and a swallow, which both returned. Some time afterwards, he released a raven, which did not return. Utanapishtim came out and offered sacrifices of grain and cereals to the Gods who became reconciled with him. The Gods granted immortality to Uta–napishtim (*he found life*) after the flood, as his name indicates.

4. The Bible story of Noah; Almighty God (originally the plural, Elohim) set out to destroy the inhabitants of the Earth because they continued worshiping other Gods. He revealed this to the righteous Noah. In the apocryphal Sibylline Oracles A 127-135, 147-199 and also in the Babylonian Talmud, Sanhedrin 108a-b, Noah rebuked the evildoers over a long period of time, but his words fell on deaf ears. Eventually, Noah is given the task of saving the seed of mankind and preserving all the animals of Earth, a ludicrous task that is plainly impossible. The flood covered the earth and only the inhabitants of the ark remain alive. After the ark landed on Mount Ararat, Noah sent birds out from the ark; a raven (once) and a dove (three times). Once he was satisfied that the flood had subsided he left the ark, built an altar and raised up sacrifices to God. When God smelt the fragrant odour of the cooked meat from animal sacrifices he blessed Noah and his sons and made a promise that he will never again bring a flood to the world.

What the Bible is Telling Us?

We must acknowledge that the Sumerians and Babylonians had the above Noah's Ark stories that actually predated the Biblical record by more than 1300 years. It is now widely accepted that the Hebrew scribes plagiarized this record, relocating it within their geographical experience. Ziusudra and Atra-hasis utilized an assistant who helped them to seal up the door from the outside, while in the Biblical story this task is performed by Almighty God himself (Genesis 7 : 15). The 'Noah character' in each of these ancient stories is likely a 'Watcher' or demigod (the result of the Gods mating with Earth people) and is seeking Godly status in order to rejoin the Anunnaki Gods, and in turn to regain eternal life. It is recorded that this was actually achieved by each. Note too the various name meanings; *'exceedingly wise'*, *'bearer of long life'* and *'he found life'* each one indicating a more advanced being than man, and likely a demigod who achieved immortality. There appears considerable synergy and the three ancient stories quite apparently come from the same source. The hero's name was likely recorded as something like *'the wise man who found* (eternal) *life.* This could have been translated into the names shown, or later attributed to a favorite local hero thus accounting for the discrepancies and explaining the similarities. There is some evidence that as a real person, King Ziusudra, the son of Ubar-Tutu of Shuruppak, was also known as Uta-napishtim which was the later Akkadian variant. In fact this is actually spelled out in the Epic of Gilgamesh making them the same story. [17] In contrast, the Biblical Noah continued to live on earth until his death.

The motif is that man can gain immortality with the Gods through his beliefs and works. This entire concept is at the forefront of the Bible's message although it has become a little convoluted. Man should worship his God, endure till the end and lead a moral life in order to become 'saved' and thus gain immortality in order to spend eternity with the Gods in 'Heaven'.

Few Christians realize that two or three separate flood traditions are actually jammed together within the Biblical story, giving differing time spans for the inundation, with differing causes of rain or tidal waves stated as precipitating the catastrophe. For example;

Genesis 7 : 7 *Noah and his wife and sons enter the Ark.*

Genesis 7 : 13 *They all enter the Ark <u>again</u>.*

Genesis 7 : 17-18 *The flood waters prevailed <u>40 days</u>*

Genesis 7 : 24 *The flood waters prevailed <u>150 days</u>*

We are told that water came from both the heavens and from the earth below, whatever this means. Most creationists visualize great 'fountains of the deep' - underwater geysers of vast proportions - that contributed more water to the earth's destruction than did the forty days of rain.

Genesis 7 : 11 *the same day were all <u>the fountains of the great deep</u> broken up, and the windows of heaven were opened.*

Genesis 7 : 12 *And the <u>rain</u> was upon the earth forty days and forty nights.*

The Welsh Triads *(Trioedd Ynys Prydein)* are a mixed collection of triadic sayings that recount personages, events, or places in Welsh history. Known copies date from the 13th century but are based on considerably older writings. Included in the triads is the story that one family only of the first inhabitants of Britain survived in a great boat when all else perished in a great flood. They also saved two of every living creature carried with them. They specifically name these people as *Cymry,* a word based on the Welsh word *Cymru.* It is interesting that Assyrian texts give the Hebrew people the exact same name. [18]

In the Koran we find Noah's Ark documented as a great 'howdah' resting on Al-Judi, the City of Chanoch, the home of Thamoud, North of Medina.

> **Sura 11 : 44** *"A voice cried out: 'Earth, swallow up your waters. Heaven cease your rain!' The floods abated and Allah's will was done. The Ark came to rest upon Al-Judi, and there was heard a voice saying: 'Gone are the evil-doers.'"*

Look for a minute at the amount of water required in the Biblical version;

> **Genesis 7 : 19** *The waters rose greatly on the earth, and all the high mountains under the entire heavens were covered. The waters rose and covered the mountains to a depth of more than fifteen cubits* (about 6.9 metres).

OK. That's fairly definite but let's look at what this means. Sumer was the *'Land Between Two Rivers',* the Tigris and the Euphrates, and this is the area thought to have been the cradle of mankind. In 1920 the archaeologist Sir Leonard Woolley found evidence of a large flood in this region that seemed to correspond to a time well before the date of 2348 BCE, given by James Ussher for Noah's flood. It was admittedly a sizable flood but certainly localized to this area and certainly not global. Possibly the Sumerians were sufficiently parochial to believe that their land covered pretty much the whole known world and thus documented the flood accordingly. The Biblical concept of a global flood covering all the Earth and its mountains is quite laughable. To cover 9,000 metre, Mt Everest under 6.9 metres of water in 40 days and 40 nights, would take a continuous, 225 metres of rain per day or 9.4 metres (over 355 inches) of rain per hour, assuming no evaporation and no seepage or run-off to achieve this coverage. In addition it would have to be raining all over the entire world at this unachievable rate. This is truly absurd, but anyone who can drive a calculator can see that. How did the author possibly arrive at this ridiculous figure? Even if only local mountains were intended, (that is not what is recorded) the tallest local mountain **Agri Dagi** is 5,165 metres tall, so this equates to 5.4 metres (204 inches) of rain per hour. This is probably many hundred times what is reasonably possible.

We were always taught that Noah took two of each animal into the ark. Yet **Genesis 7 : 2 – 3** makes it clear he took <u>seven</u> of each clean beast and the fowls of the air by **sevens**. Of some other species he did take two but the common, incorrect, belief stems from the quotation that the animals went in two by two. Despite the message that the flood was because man continued worshiping other Gods, it is interesting to note that the reason given in **Genesis 6 : 13** was that the Earth was filled with **violence**. This is a bit of a double standard for the same God who justified his own violence, in promoting wholesale slaughter to gain the Promised Land.

Where is Mt Ararat?

In these earlier Babylonian records the Ark landed **on Mt Nisir.** This is a mountain located in lower Mesopotamia, now called **Pir Omar Gudrun.** The name *'Mount Nisir'* however means *'Mount of Salvation'*. This differed in the later Biblical texts where the Ark landed on **Ararat**, a generic name that simply meant, *'High Peaks'*. [19] According to Bailey the actual name Ararat comes from the kingdom of **Urartu** in present day Eastern Turkey. [20]

In truth there was no mountain named Mt. Ararat. It did not exist. There is the previously mentioned tall mountain in the Armenian part of Eastern Turkey within the province of Agri, and the Turks called it **Agri Dagi** or "the Mountain of Pain". This mountain being the tallest in the region at about **5,165** metres, was simply selected at a later time, and is now called Mt. Ararat by Christians and is even documented as such on current maps.

The Ark's landing place in the Koran is recorded as **Djebel Judi** (Al-Judi) (XI. 44) This peak of Djebel Judi is also mentioned by Josephus, the Kurdish Jews, Yeezidis and Mandaean Sabians who all hold that it is the true resting place of Noah's ark. This location appears to be the 2,114 Metre peak **Cudi Dagi**, near Sirnak. This does not alter the fact that there was no Mt. Ararat, this is simply replacement geography. It is somewhat amusing to hear of various fundamentalist groups tackling various 'manufactured' Mt Ararats looking for remnants of Noah's Ark. There have in fact been 69 separate expeditions in the past century and various reports of ancient timber, ark shaped mudslides and the like. These have always resulted in a total lack of evidence and the myriad of supposed photographs never seem to come to light. The first rule of accurate archaeology is to research back to primary sources. If in fact the Biblical Noah's Ark is not a myth then this boat will definitely not be found on Mt. Ararat (Agri Dagi). Why? The Biblical story is certainly based on the Sumerian epics thus making it absolute folly to look for it there because several much earlier sources locate it elsewhere. This alone suggests that the Bible is not an empirical source. This is very basic archaeology, and ironically the "Atra-hasis epic", "Ziusudra document" and the "Epic of Gilgamesh" are all well known and easily sourced records. Nowadays, you can find each of them on the Net.

The Pied Piper Analogy

Recall the story of the Pied Piper of Hamlin. It goes something like this. The English village of Hamlin in 1284 was over run by rats. For a bag of gold the gypsy Pied Piper agreed to rid the town of these vermin. Some folks question whether his pest control methods were un-successful and some say the townsmen went back on their word but either way, the town refused to pay him. In revenge the Pied Piper made threats to the town folk that he would take their children. He played a merry tune on his pipe and all the children of the town followed in line behind him, until the earth, on a hill outside Hamlin, swallowed them up and they were never seen again.

Sufficient records exist to prove this is based on a true story; in fact it is two true stories welded into one. When the town folk refused to pay him, the Pied Piper made threats to the superstitious townsfolk about their children, and they were taken pretty seriously. What actually happened was that about the same time men arrived to recruit unemployed young people to work in the European mines, a not so unusual practice of that time. The line of young workers followed these men to their ship, which some time later was reported wrecked off the coast of Germany. By total coincidence the name of the hill outside Hamlin was phonetically similar to the German name for the location of the shipwreck. Perhaps it was the German town of Hamelin. When the story of this tragedy and the loss of their loved ones reached the folk of Hamlin, they remembered the curse of the Pied Piper and to this day it is the distorted, incorrect story that is remembered.

Now if we went digging for the remains of the young people in the hill outside Hamlin instead of their watery grave off the coast of Germany, that would be identical to looking for Noah's Ark on the manufactured Mt Ararat. Yet vast fortunes are being raised and squandered in this pursuit. Groups of Fundamentalists promote that they are on the track to finding the ark, and fool many. Believe me no ark will be found on the 'manufactured' Mt Ararat; it is not there. Any year 12 student of classical ancient history learns of the many Noah's Ark stories embedded in various cultures, many of which considerably predate the Bible.

The Sumerian original 'Ark" story is possibly true. Firstly **Berosus**, c. 275 B.C., documented that back then, remains of it were located on the mountains of the Gordyaeans in Armenia and secondly, Flavius Josephus cites **Nicholas of Damascus** (First century AD) as a source who claimed that the Ark was located on 'Baris', however, no mountain of that name is mentioned in any other known literature. The word 'Baris' means *'freedom'* in Alfari, Azeri and Turkish. A wooden ark is unlikely to still exist today after all those years, however we may still find some artefact, someday.

Noah

There is a further consideration about the actual birth of the Biblical 'Noah'; whether this name refers to Atra-hasis, Ziusudra or King Uta-napishtim and a timeframe some thirteen centuries before the Bible. Perhaps the three are really one as we alluded to earlier, however recall that the three heroes each achieved eternal life with the Gods and may have been part God themselves. We need to consider the Sumerian records of the Anunnaki 'Sky Gods' and their creation of man followed by a continuing breeding program, as it just may also pertain to 'Noah'.

From the non-canonical Book of Enoch we find a report on the strange birth of Noah, where his father Lamech reported of his new born son that *"his body is white as snow and red as the blooming rose"*. Lamech questioned his wife who assured him that Noah was indeed his son, but Lamech remained sufficiently concerned to further request that his father Methuselah, question Enoch *(meaning initiated)*, who was staying amongst the 'Sons of the Gods', meaning the Anunnaki Watchers. Lamech is recorded as claiming;

> *"I have begotten a strange son, diverse from and unlike man, and resembling the Sons of the God of heaven; and his nature is quite different, and he is not like us…. And it seems to me that he is not sprung from me but from the angels".* [21]

We must consider that "Noah" who was chosen to preserve "the seed" of human life as well as animal life, actually had the appearance of the Sons of the Gods. His own father stated that he was diverse from and unlike man, and appeared to be the offspring of the Gods. It is believed that early man may have been black skinned and this may be recording that Noah was the first white man. It certainly seems that he was a special being with a preor-dained job to do. To take this a step further, early Bibles actually stated that Noah; *"had upon his chest, scales which he kept hidden."* This brings to mind the first records of the Anunnaki that claim they splashed down in water, and of the being 'Oannas' who was partly amphibious and was the first to make contact with man. The Book of Jasher further recorded that Noah was *"the father of those who go down into the deep and occupy themselves in much water".* [22] Methuselah was right to question Enoch, who spent much of his time with these Gods and knew their ways. Recall that the Bible tells us that Enoch did not die but was taken up to dwell with the Gods. Some of these findings just may support the work of author David Icke who believes man has reptilian origins and that the Annunaki were a reptilian, alien species. Regarding the birth of Enoch, the Book of Jubilees also tells us;

> *"In the eleventh jubilee Jared took to himself a wife; her name was Baraka (meaning Lightning Bright), the daughter of Rasujal, a daughter of his father's brother (his cousin)… and she bore him a son and he called him Enoch."*

Now why was Jared's wife, called *"Lightning Bright"?* Was there some association with the name *"Shiny Bright"* that the ancient Chinese records give to the Anunnaki Watchers?

After Noah's ordeal, God promised no more floods. Philo the Alexandrian wrote in the first century of this era;

> *"By reason of the constant and repeated destructions of (the Earth by) water and fire, the later generations did not receive from the former the memory of the order and sequence of events."* [23]

Philo understood that there had been repeated destructions of the Earth by fire and flood and this would make God's covenant in the rainbow a pretty hollow promise. In like manner the Biblical scribes had no idea how hail, snow, dew and frost are formed;

> **Job 38 : 22-23** *Hast thou entered into the treasures of the snow? Or hast thou seen the treasures of the hail, which I have reserved against the time of trouble, against the day of battle and war?*

> **Job 38 : 28** *Hath the rain a father? Or who hath begotten the drops of dew? Out of whose womb came the ice? And the hoary frost of heaven, who hath gendered it?*

Here the scribe has God telling Job that he stores up the snow and hail (like in some huge celestial freezer) and keeps them ready for times of trouble. Almighty God then goes on to ponder the great mystery of dew and frost. This may have been fine for the second century uneducated populous, however today we know that there was no God involved in generating these scriptures, just an uneducated pre-scientific scribe.

What Really Happened?

Precise reading of the Bible story of the creation and the flood leads to total confusion at the inconsistencies, impossibilities and the general departure from common sense. This is not the way a Holy Book should be, however it is the way it is. At least the Sumerian story is entirely rational if we can believe that the Anunnaki Gods were real entities. This alone should encourage us to keep an open mind on the matter as we study further. Is it really easier to believe our Bible, the result of considerable known tampering, which has shown itself to be plagiarized, inaccurate, inconsistent and demonstrably wrong? The Sumerians recorded an on-going conflict between the Anunnaki brothers ENLIL and EN.KI, in regard to the fate of the created Earthmen. From the beginning ENLIL was against the creation and then specifically against the educating of these created beings and it was EN.KI who educated them and (as the serpent) encouraged them to eat of the tree of knowledge. This is what we see in the Bible when the serpent (EN.KI) converses with Eve. A reason for his brother ENLIL's reluctance was that it "made them as Gods". This conclusion is confirmed by Professor R. Pati in *'The Hebrew Goddess'*, when he quotes Ha Qubala literature stating that EN.KI (as Sama El or Samael), along with Lilith, were personally referred to as "The Tree of Knowledge". Gardner confirms that EN.KI was the Lord (generically called El) of the land of Sama (East of Haran where Abraham moved) and accordingly was titled Sama-El or Samael. [24]

Gardner further stated;

"Since we know that El Elyon-Jehovah was synonymous with ENLIL, the garden of Eden story is a direct representation of the ongoing feud between the Anunnaki brothers. ENLIL was insistent that humankind should be kept in ignorance, and should be maintained solely to toil and to bear the yoke of the Anunnaki. But EN.KI had other ideas; he was insistent that the black-headed people should be educated." [25]

ENLIL felt that once their created Earth beings had served them and assisted in mining the gold they should be wiped out when the Anunnaki had to move on as their planet moved away from the vicinity of Earth. EN.KI felt compassion for the beings he had helped create and educate. Only the interference and 'tip-off' to 'Noah' averted the destruction of mankind. EN.KI then created the additional fourteen Adama to ensure their survival when the Anunnaki moved on.

Other Sources of the Creation Story

The sacred Book of Jubilees, not included in the Bible despite widespread usage, and supposedly dictated to Moses by an Angel, records a Creation Story with a few discrepancies. In **Jubilees 3 : 9-12** it tells how Adam is brought into The Garden of Eden 40 days after he is created, and how Eve is brought in on the 80th day. In **verse 17** it goes on that Adam and Eve spent 7 years in the garden before they ate the fruit and were sent out. These time spans cannot automatically be taken literally as 40 days (and multiples) are standard Biblical measures just as 7 years is a perfect number. This same Book also states that animals and birds could speak, up until this event;

Jubilees 3 : 28 *"And on that day was closed the mouth of all beasts, and cattle and of birds, and of whatever walks, and of whatever moves, so that they could no longer speak; for they had all spoken one with another with one lip and with one tongue."*

This is a graphic example of documents that attempt to record what supposedly happened thousands of years ago. I don't really feel that any further comment is needed on the above because animals do not have a voice box and some of this record is little more than palpable nonsense. In the same way that the first photographic cameras caused artists in fear and frustration to delve into outlandish 'modern art', it seems possible that the writers were enveloped in this esoteric drivel. Supposedly intelligent scribes must have felt a certain frustration at the slow process of the embryonic science of their time to explain life's mysteries, and as a result they adopted this surreal way of documenting and explaining things.

Adam & Eve

There is considerable confusion about the creation of Adam and Eve as one studies alternative recordings, as follows: The Gnostic scripture - **"Hypostasis of the Archons II, 4"** found in the Nag Hammadi scrolls from Egypt, states clearly that Eve was created first. Believe it or not the Bible actually hedges its bets on this subject.

Genesis 1 : 27 states that Adam and Eve were created at the same time.

Genesis 2 : 7 says that Adam was created first

Genesis 2 : 21-22 states that Eve was created sometime later;

"And the Lord God caused a deep sleep to fall on Adam, and he slept; and He took one of his ribs, and closed up the flesh in its place. Then the rib which the Lord God had taken from man He made into a woman, and He brought her to the man."

Following is an example of why we cannot take the Bible stories literally. It would be most peculiar if Adam, who had just been created, then said the following;

Genesis 2 : 23 *And Adam said: "This is now bone of my bones, And flesh of my flesh; She shall be called Woman, Because she was taken out of Man."*

This would show remarkable insight. How would Adam, who knew nothing about physiology, reproduction or surgery, know that woman was created from his rib, particularly if he was in a deep sleep at the time? In the Bible story, he continues;

Genesis 2 : 24 *Therefore a man shall leave his father and mother and be joined to his wife, and they shall become one flesh.*

If things were as we were taught, Adam would have no concept of marriage or family and wouldn't even know what a father or mother was at that stage, let alone a wife and the becoming of one flesh. He supposedly learned these things later when he ate from the tree of knowledge.

The Book of Jubilees 4 : 10-16 *tells how Adam and Eve had nine sons and at least three daughters. It also says that Cain took his sister Awan as his wife.* **This could solve an age-old Genesis mystery of how Cain found a wife with whom to have offspring in the land of Nod.**

We don't often consider this but Eve was likely the sister of Adam regardless of how they were created. In the Hindu tradition the first man Yama was married to his sister Yami. Abraham was married to his half sister Sarah and the Egyptian Pharaohs commonly married their half sisters. In fact Cleopatra was the offspring of six generations of brother sister marriages. In records left by the Sumerians we find taking a sister or half sister as wife was common among their Anunnaki Gods and this became common within pagan God relationships. Zeus was married to his sister Hera, Isis and Osiris were married, being brother and sister, as well as many, many others. This is a far cry from our present day attitudes and marriage regulations with their tabulated, prohibited degrees of consanguinity. Recent experiments however show that given a choice, monkeys will select half sisters with whom to reproduce. Perhaps we are missing something.

Cain & Able

There seems no doubt that the Old Testament writers took the records of Cain and Abel from the Sumerian records. The tablets state that the created

287

Earthman 'Adam' had a son Qayin or Carne (no doubt the Biblical Cain) apparently with his first wife, the Anunnaki, Lilitu (Lilith). The Bible records Lilith as a female demon; how else could they explain away another woman before Eve? The Sumerians said that Adam and the created hybrid female, called 'Eve of Life', then had a son called Able. According to the Sumerians, it seems that Carne was a mighty man (manifesting the traits of the Anunnaki) however Able (the progeny of two created Adama beings) proved to be a disappointment, possibly reverting to the hominid characteristics. The Bible says Cain killed Able but this is perhaps not to be taken literally. If in fact Cain was a successfully created being, whilst Able was not, it is possible that Cain (or rather Carne) was asked to destroy the unsuccessful Able. It is even possibly that the original meaning was simply that Carne outstripped Abel in every way.

Sacrifices to the Gods are documented from the most ancient times when mankind thanked and rewarded his Gods for various mercies, including protection, good harvests and fertility or as conscience atonement for wrongdoing. Originally the gifts were given directly to the Gods when they came to Earth. Since a sacrificial gift of meat or produce could not be delivered to the celestial throne of absent sky Gods, a procedure developed where the atonement or libation was burned and the enticing smoke drifted skywards to the God. It became the practice that the value of the sacrifice should be proportional to the mercy requested and accordingly fine flour, precious oil and the firstlings of the flock, lambs without blemish or spot, were considered the highest offering short of the sacrifice of one's first born son. The Biblical Cain and Abel story shows a certain inconsistency with the modus of Almighty God. There appears to be some mystery in the events recorded. Cain tilled the soil so his sacrifice was naturally produce, while Able kept the flock so he sacrificed livestock. We see in this passage that God prefers and respects Abel's sacrificial offering over Cain's. The result?

Genesis 4 : 4-6 *"Cain was very wroth, and his countenance fell. And the Lord said unto Cain, Why art thou wroth? And why is thy countenance fallen? If thou doest well, shalt thou not be accepted? And if thou doest not well, sin lieth at the door. And unto thee shall be his desire, and thou shalt rule over him."*

The Bible states;

> **Hebrews 9 : 22** *And almost all things are by the law purged with blood; and* <u>*without the shedding of blood is no remission*</u>.

Accordingly to the scribes (if not Almighty God) there would have been more value in sacrificed meat than in produce. However something seems screwy about this section of the Bible. For goodness sake with supposedly only the two sons in the entire world, why would one brother want to rule over the other, unless as stated he was a vastly superior species? If things were as we were taught from the Bible, why would the concept of 'rule' or 'kingship' even come up prior to many generations of populating? At that early stage they would have no concept of ruling over descendants. Does this make any kind of sense at all from a supposedly intelligent God?

Try to visualize the actual conversation: *"Cain, there's just the two of you, Able's sacrifice is great and yours really stinks, also your temper needs a little work but OK, you can rule over your brother."* That really is quite ridiculous! Well, what would be Abel's reaction? It seems he didn't get that far.

> **Genesis 4 : 7** *And Cain talked with Abel his brother; and it came to pass, when in the field that Cain rose up against his brother, and slew him."*

Well it seems God got that one wrong; or is it possible that this is what he actually meant all along when he said to Cain, *" and unto thee shall be his desire, and thou shall rule over him."* (Go and kill him). It started however with God's preference for Abel's sacrifice. Let's look at the Bible's contradictions to this scenario.

> **2 Corinthians 19 : 7** *God shows no partiality. He treats all alike.*

> **Acts 10 : 34** *God is no respecter of persons. He treats all alike.*

> **Romans 2 : 11** *For there is no respect of persons with God.*

After considerable research on this subject I discovered that Gardner recorded it thus;

> *"When we read (Genesis 4 : 3-5) that Abel's offerings were acceptable to the Lord, but Cain's were not, we get the impression that Cain's offerings were in some way inferior. But the original emphasis was on the premise that offerings (venerations) were acceptable from Abel as a subordinate subject, whereas for Cain to make offerings was unacceptable*

because of his kingly status." [26]

We find this 'Kingly Status" in the Bible and it seems an unusual context, however it is confirmed when the Lord then said to Cain, *"And unto thee shall be his (Abel's) desire, and thou shall rule over him.*

The acts of the Gods within our religious literature appear quite ritualistic. A connection today is that the cyclic feasts of Israel and the associated ritual seem to have been learned from the edicts of the Gods. It could be considered that Cain brought an offering from the power of his own hand and thus broke the ritual which Abel adhered to. It seems that we were on the right track, but maybe we can glean more sense from this when Gardner further states;

> *"When we move to the sequence wherein Cain is reckoned to have slain Able in the field, but the word indirectly translated to 'slew' was yaqam and the text should read that Cain (Qayin) was 'elevated' (raised or exalted) above Abel. The terminology that Cain 'rose up' against Abel is used in the English translation, but in quite the wrong context. Abel was a man conditioned according to his station, time and location. His blood was, therefore, figuratively swallowed into the ground – which is to say that he became so mundane as to be indistinguishable from his toil."* [27]

So if this is correct Cain did not slay Abel at all, he simply overshadowed him as we previously suggested. This in turn was considered Kingship for Cain and his offspring, and in his Kingly status he ruled over the more mundane descendants of Abel. Why are we taught the nonsensical and quite incorrect story? If there is a spiritual message or a moral for everyday living in this Bible section, then man just didn't get it. Nor is he likely to.

More on Cain and Able;

Proverbs 15 : 3 *God is everywhere. He sees everything. Nothing is hidden from his view.*

Jeremiah 16 : 17 *"For mine eyes are upon all their ways; they are not hid from my face, neither is their iniquity hid from mine eyes."*

Hebrews 4 : 13 *"Neither is there any creature that is not manifest in his sight; but all things are naked and opened unto the eyes of him with whom we have to do."*

And yet;

Genesis 4 : 9 *God asks Cain where his brother Able is.* (Why did he need to do this?)

Jeremiah 23 : 24-25 *"Can any hide himself in secret places that I shall not see him. Do not I fill Heaven and Earth saith the Lord."*

Next we find;

Genesis 4 : 15 *Cain goes to live in the land of Nod.*

Genesis 4 : 16 *Cain went away (or out) from the presence of the Lord.* (How did he do this?)

The old Bible chestnut is how did Cain find a wife in the land of Nod if God had only created Adam and Eve who bore only Cain and Able. The Bible doesn't tell us, however it agrees he found a wife;

Genesis 4 : 16 *Cain knew his wife and had a son.*

If we choose to believe the Book of Jubilees we see that he had previously married his sister Awan. Rutherford H. Platt however states in his book '*The Forgotten Books of Eden*' that Cain's wife was Luluwa (Pearl) a daughter of Lilith, again emphasizing his kingly status. [28] This is also supported in the Jewish Talmud where she is called Luluwa-Lilith.

Now another name for EN.KI was Nudimud, abbreviated to Nud, and it is possible that Cain went off to live in the land of Nud (the person). Of course if Cain was an intelligent Anunnaki descendant, he would be part God himself and probably welcomed there. The most logical explanation is that his wife may have been his sister (or half sister) and may have been the daughter of a full blood Anunnaki, Lilith as stated. This would be a consideration particularly if Cain was the first successfully bred hybrid and this union was essential to the on-going breeding program, or even an opportunity to reinforce the Anunnaki blood. This would suggest that rich Anunnaki blood was favorable for the continuation of the breeding program for man and may have necessitated their removal to Nod away from the plebeians. EN.KI would certainly be watching his created beings in the early part of the breeding program. The whole thing sounds like it could have been carefully staged.

Let's move on to the confusion over what later happened to Cain;

Genesis 4 : 16 *"Cain went out from the presence of the Lord and dwelt in the land of Nod on the East side of Eden."*

Jubilees 4 : 31 *"Cain was killed after him (Adam) in the same year; for his house fell upon him and he died <u>in the midst of his house</u>, and he was killed by its stones; because <u>with a stone he had killed Able</u>."* (Was this true?)

Book of Jasher 1 : 25 *"...and took the <u>iron part of his plowing instrument</u>, with which he suddenly smote his brother and he slew him."*

Book of Jasher 2 : 27-28 *And Tubal told his father (Lamech) to draw his bow, and <u>with arrows he smote Cain</u>, who was yet far off, and he slew him, for he appeared to be an animal. And the arrows entered Cain's body although he was distant from them, and he fell to the ground and died."*

Oh really! Strange too is that in **Genesis 4 : 13-15** Cain seems to be offered protection by God (with the mark of Cain) so that no harm can come to him. If so it certainly didn't work!

Reality of the Rulers

Most of us are fairly familiar with the Bible's creation story but most of us are unaware that there are a plethora of slightly varying, alternate stories in other scriptural works. These works were widely used by the early church but are amongst those scriptures not selected for inclusion in the Bible assembled some considerable time after Christ. Perhaps the strangest creation story to our conditioned thinking comes from the book we previously mentioned, the Gnostic - **"Hypostasis of the Archons II, 4"** found at Nag Hammadi. This title means 'Reality of the Rulers', and emphasizes the creation of Earthly man by *'The Rulers'*. It also documents *'The Authorities'* who are described as *'beings that came down'* and accordingly makes them identical to *'The Watchers'*. The work constitutes an esoteric interpretation of the Genesis creation and just may be a more accurate record than the one we know. This is a pretty similar concept to the Sumerian creation epic. It has the actual creators being very like the Anunnaki Sky-Gods and has beings like the Watchers interfering with women on Earth. In **Hypostasis of the Archons II, 4; Pista Sophia** (Faith Wisdom) is a 'heroine' ruler with her daughter **Zoe** (Life) (sometimes called Sophia Zoe) and the blind and arrogant 'villain' ruler God, **Samael** who we saw was most likely the Sky-God EN.KI. In this Book Pista Sophia actually says, *"Come let us make Man in the image of the God who appeared in the waters."* This then places her as a Goddess assisting in the creation.

The Gnostic Gospels are part of a library of early Christian literature discovered at Nag Hammadi in Upper Egypt in 1945. This information in 52 separate tracts was preserved in terracotta jars in similar fashion to the Dead Sea Scrolls, and despite a frustratingly protracted period of over 30 years, was finally available in English in 1977. The library makes it quite apparent that Gnostic information was strongly suppressed by the Catholic Church as heretical, although this aspect of the original Christian message predated Catholicism and was certainly closer to the message of Jesus. They also showed that Gnosticism was extremely popular and widespread and those who converted to Catholicism, in most cases, did not do so through choice.

In the widely used **Acts of Judas Thomas** too, we find a recurring image of a female element in the Godhead, sometimes identifiable as Sophia, sometimes as the Mother figure but certainly setting these writings apart from more familiar patriarchal Christian composition. We see in this work that having made Man from clay they could not get him to rise until there is some intervention. The Spirit came from the Holy Adamantine Land and made him a living soul. It goes on to describe the creation of Eve and how she (or rather a created likeness of her) was defiled, foully, by the 'Authorities.' (This is identical to the sons of the Gods mating with the daughters of men). Again Cain and Abel are born followed by Seth. Adams wife, Eve then has a daughter, Norea, and over-emphasis is made of her virginity. This daughter Norea is rescued from the 'Authorities' advances, by an 'Angel' of God.

Following this book and in a similar vein is: **On the Origins of the World II , 5** In this work Pista Sophia dwells in the 6th level of Heaven and sees the same darkness and chaos described in Genesis. (This belief in different levels of Heaven is not new; recall that St. Paul claimed he knew a man who visited the third level of Heaven; (**2 Corinthians 12 : 2 – 4.**) In

'Origins of the World' it is Pista Sophia and not God who adds light and performs the creation of beings to become 'Rulers'. There is considerable manufacturing of likenesses (cloning?) of Adam and Eve by these rulers, similar to the Sumerian version. The following quote is from **Verse 112.** The 'Authorities' said: *"Come let us create a man out of earth, according to the image of our body and according to the likeness of this being, (Adam of Light) to serve us."* Create man in our image to serve us; this is just what the Anunnaki said in the Sumerian record.

Then: **Verse 120 –123** *"Now when the rulers saw that their Adam had entered into an alien state of acquaintance they desired to test him. Now when the seven Rulers came down from Heaven to the Earth they made for themselves 'Angels' numerous to serve them."* These texts are from early Gnostic works of religious groups and their alignment with the Sumerian records is simply uncanny.

The author Vendyl Jones, in his book *"Will the Real Jesus Please Stand"*, described the making and testing of a Golem;

"In Revelation 13 : 14-15, John describes the creation of a "Golem." When a Kabbalist receives the secret of the Holy Name or "Tetragrammaton," he tests his ability to pronounce it properly by the creation of the Golem. In this procedure, an image of a man is made of clay. The word TRUTH (?ahMehT) is written on the clay forehead of the image. The Kabbalist then chants the seventy-two intonations of the Holy Name over the clay image. If the sounds are correct, the image comes alive. The soul-less beast is then destroyed by rubbing away or covering (a Hebrew character) which changes the word TRUTH to DEATH. The image of the beast of the Golem then reverts back to clay."

Don't try this at home! In line with this ritual, the whole record of the creation of mankind from clay and then the breathing in of life, in the Bible, shows considerable Kabbalistic influence. In **Verse 110;** it says that Adam loved his female counterpart and condemned *"the other alien likenesses"* and loathed them. Then in **verse 114:** *"Now Eve is the <u>first virgin</u>, the one who <u>without a husband, bore her first offspring</u>. It is she who served as her own midwife."*

This passage intrigued me not only because it pre-empted the 'virgin' birth of Jesus and maybe tells something about the Anunnaki breeding program, but because I had always wondered at a Bible passage in **Genesis 5 : 3** that seemed to be trying to say something between the lines, emphasizing Adams paternity of his third son Seth. It states: *"And Adam begat a son in his own likeness, after his image; and called his name Seth.* The Bible didn't say anything like that for his first sons, Cain or Abel. This passage, with it's over emphasis of Adams paternity of Seth, suggests that Adam may not have been the father of Cain or Able with Seth being his first son (particularly if as stated Eve remained a virgin). The reality is with so much discrepancy we can never really know which story, if any, is correct. With so many varying scriptures available, to assume that the correct ones just happened to be those selected for the Bible is to be naïve to the extreme.

Gardner seems to agree with the suggestion that Adam was not involved in the births of his first two sons, when he states;

> *"In the opening verse of Genesis 4, it is written that Hawah (Eve) said, "I have gotten a man from the Lord". Other variations are "I have got me a man with the Lord", and "I have acquired a man from the Lord." The text then continues to say that this new man (Hawah's first son) was Qayin — better known by the phonetic translation Cain. Subsequently Hawah is said to have given birth to a second son, Hevel — or as we know him, Abel."* [(29)]

This starts to sound plausible because there is evidence that Cain along with his sister wife Luluwa (or Awan) were the children of Lilith, whether or not Adapa (Adam) was involved. Then if Hawah (Eve) had a son with the Lord it would be Hevel (Abel) making Seth, the first son that Adam and Eve had together. This would perfectly explain the strange paternity statement of Adam's but of course would not account for the mundane blood of Abel. We cannot fully explain it but somehow the first-born Cain had the kingly, rulers 'pendragon' Anunnaki blood from EN.KI and/or Lilith, the second born Abel had mundane blood and according to the Gnostics, the third born son Seth was exceedingly wise and knowledgeable, displaying Anunnaki traits. No matter how we read it there is still something missing.

Returning to **On the Origins of the World II 5,** from the Nag Hammadi corpus; another anomaly of this book is that it again records that Eve was created first and a failed Adam who had no life, lay for 40 days.

When created by the Seven Rulers, he received sympathy from Sophia Zoe, who breathed life into him. He came to life but still couldn't stand up and it seems Sophia Zoe sent her 'daughter' Zoe called Eve (Eve of Zoe or Eve of Life) who nursed him and helped him. Adam was put into a deep sleep by the Archangels who lied, telling him that he was created first and that Eve came from his rib so that he could maintain dominance over her.

Lilith

It seems that the Anunnaki breeding program may have required a bit of 'wife swapping' (to prevent inbreeding) that would not look good in a Holy book, so we are not given the full details. The Hebrew legend of Lilith as the first woman (before Eve) is documented in fragments of a book of Judaic writings, from the eleventh century called *"The Alphabet of Ben Sira,"* of Persian or Arabic origin. Lilith first appears however, in the text of *'The Hullupu Tree'*, on a clay tablet dated to c. 2500 BCE. [30]

The legend tells how God created a companion for Adam named Lilith. Adam and Lilith however bickered endlessly over matters large and small, with Lilith refusing to let Adam dominate her in any way, and particularly during sex. Instead she insisted that they were equal. Eventually Lilith pronounced the 'Ineffable Name of God' and flew out of the Garden of Eden to the shore of the Red Sea. There she made her home in a cave. It is possible that this was a literary creation, using the Anunnaki Lilitu (Lilith) simply to explain away certain discrepancies in the Biblical story. This is an interesting subject and further information is available in *"Lilith's Cave"* by Howard Schwartz, *"Hebrew Goddess"* by Professor Raphael Patai and *"From the Poetry of Sumer"* by Samuel Noah Kramer.

In Sumerian literature, Lilith was recorded as the daughter of Nergal, King of the Netherworld (this may simply mean the 'down under' land of Africa where the mining was taking place). Nergal's wife and Lilith's mother was Eresh-kigal of the Anunnaki. It is fitting that **Lilith,** who the Sumerians believed, had Carne (Qayin or Cain) with Adam, wouldn't stay with Adam because he tried to dominate her. Women's lib in 11 000 BCE. Go girl!

Lilith is mentioned in the Bible in **Isaiah 14 : 21** *"...daughters of Lilith shall dwell there."* And again in **Isaiah 34 : 14** *"Lilith also shall settle there."*

Lilith in Sumerian artwork (baked clay plaque. Mesopotamia. Isin-Larsa-Old Babylonian period c 2000-1600 B.C. Paris, Louvre AO 6501). Lilith is often depicted with owls feet and is accompanied by owls in artwork.

Modern translations however, record her simply as **Owl** (the meaning of Lilith.) Early depictions of Lilith show her with accompanying pet owls or herself with owl's feet. The reason for this is to do with a Sumerian custom for preserving the Anunnaki blood by the consumption of a white powder form of gold, which was also used to heighten awareness. A side effect of this was extreme light sensitivity of the eyes or 'day-blindness' and the appropriate symbol for these people, who only came out at night, was the owl. This was also practiced by the Egyptians and will be covered further in a later chapter.

As a side note, on 15 July, 2000, radio talkshow host and documentary filmmaker Alex Jones infiltrated the 2,700 acre compound at Bohemian Grove near Monte Rio in Sonoma County, Northern California where the infamous 'Illuminati' (including names like Henry Kissinger and George Bush) meet each year under a giant stone owl. We mentioned previously that David Icke and others confirm that the 'illuminati' are associated with the Anunnaki and this establishes a link. Ceremonies apparently coincide with the alignment of the Sirius star system with the Earth on 23rd July each year, and are said to involve human sacrifice officiated by 'Priests' in red and black robes. Every Republican president since Coolidge, including Nixon and Regan, as well as a host of other huge names in business and politics are members of this 'boy's club' and are said to have witnessed the ritualistic, *'killing of conscience'* sacrificial ceremonies at the alter at the base of this 'Owl God'. I wonder if there is a connection.

Gnostic Information

In the Nag Hammadi scrolls there are some interesting lesser-known Gnostic documents we should touch on. **The Second Treatise of the Great Seth** follows a Christian theme but is clearly Gnostic (<u>where knowledge not faith, is the means of salvation</u>). The God of this world (like the previously mentioned Samael) is clearly '**ignorant, arrogant and somewhat evil**' yet can be satisfactorily identified as the God of the Old Testament. The words "counterfeit" and "laughing-stock" are liberally applied to all his minions, particularly the old patriarchs from Adam to Noah. The Gnostic theme of the crucifixion is re visited where Simon of Cyrene was crucified in his place. This is not a new theme and is recorded and believed in many Gnostic and other circles usually with Jesus laughing from afar at his executor's blindness.

There is something intrinsically wrong with the crucifixion story. I must confess that the whole story of the atonement is something that gives me trouble. How does a father requiring blood as an atonement for the inadequacies of the beings he himself created (complete with those intrinsic inadequacies) then set out to make the sacrifice of his only son and have him butchered as a blood sacrifice in order to satisfy his own demand for retribution. That is nonsensical! It is not logical. And how can he suggest that it is done because he "so loved the world'. The Bible outlines the sacrifice of a blameless Jesus dying for the sins of mankind and this is really no different to the perfect lamb or dove being slaughtered for someone's sin. The similarity of this scapegoat theme with the innocent bystander (the substitute Simon of Cyrene) being sacrificed in lieu of Jesus cannot be discounted as it adopts the very same theme.

Sethian Gnostics had a very strong following in these ancient times and wrote of the outstanding wisdom of **Seth** the son of Adam and Eve, holding both he and his sister wife **Norea** in particularly high esteem. There is even evidence that some thought he was one and the same with the Egyptian God '**Set**', also known as **Seth**, and this is possibly true. This next quote from the Sethian Gnostics found amongst the Nag Hammadi documents is simply amazing; as you read it, imagine the difference to Christianity if this document had been selected for inclusion in the Bible.

The Three Steles of Seth. (vii, 5) in verse **119** talking to the Almighty it states, *"Thou hast appeared in order that thou mightest reveal the Eternal Ones. Therefore thou hast revealed those who really are."* Because of their extreme longevity, the Anunnaki are called the 'Eternal Ones' by the Sumerians and I don't believe the Biblical angels (again) will cover it. Particularly when it goes on: **120;** *and thou art from another race for thou art not similar* but their place is over *other races* for their place is in (eternal) life.

These are ancient religious works that were hidden in Egypt for some considerable time preserving their purity and allowing far less chance of tampering; this is particularly hard documentation to overlook. We must realize that with slightly different circumstances, these scriptures might easily have ended up in the Old Testament, and had that happened, how would the clergy explain this away. Most readers would have to agree that these records are almost certainly talking about the Anunnaki.

Lastly from the Nag Hammadi scrolls, a verse from a short book, **"The Thought of Norea."** *"It is Norea who cries out to them. They heard and they received her into her place. They gave it to her in the father of nous* **(Gnostic knowledge)** *Adamas as well as the voice of the Holy Ones.* This sounds like Adamas (created beings) as well as Anunnaki (eternal, Holy ones). This Gnostic writing certainly sounds closer to the Sumerian version than the Biblical Genesis version that we were taught. There is no doubt Kabalistic thought among these Gnostic works we have just looked at, however it does not start to address precisely who these contemporaries of Adam might be. We need to further confirm who were the Rulers, the Authorities, the Holy Ones and the Eternal Ones?

Back to the **Book of Jubilees** and the offspring of Adam. Mahalalel a great grandson of Seth married his cousin Dinah and had a son **Jared.** This same Jared or *Yeh-rad* (meaning descend) an Old Testament patriarch from **Genesis 5 : 18,** was so named according to both Genesis and Jubilees, because it was in his time that '**the Watchers**' descended upon the earth to instruct man. Look it up, it's in your Bible! It is also interesting to note that 'Jordan' comes from that same root word as Jared, denoting 'descent, coming down or falling' – *Yar-dane* (the place of the descent). The book of Jubilees states;

"In the eleventh jubilee Jared took to himself a wife; her name was Baraka (meaning Lightning Bright), the daughter of Rasujal, a daughter of his father's brother... and she bore him a son and he called him Enoch."

We noted earlier that the Chinese name for the Anunnaki was the **'Sons of Light'** and they were said to wear clothing that was **'shiny bright'** which just may indicate that Jared took a wife who was at least part Anunnaki. We could note too that descriptions of the arch angels often include shiny clothing or faces and bodies that shone like sapphire. **Enoch** the son of Jared was supposedly the first Earthman who could write. Let's look at that:

Jubilees 4 : 17 *"And he was the first among men who learnt writing, knowledge and wisdom and who wrote down the signs of heaven, according to the order of their months."* (Astronomy-astrology & timekeeping). We don't know when this was but it was certainly before 4000 BCE. The likelihood of discovering writing dating prior to 3000 BCE is fairly remote.

2 Enoch 10 *The Lord said to the angel take a book from the deposit and give a pen to Enoch and explain to him and dictate the books to him, so the Angel taught Enoch all the works of Heaven and the earth and the sea and all elements and all time periods and commandments and instructions. So he wrote the 360 books of creation.*

2 Enoch 12 *Take thou the books which thou hast written thyself . . . and go down to earth and tell thy sons all that I have told thee.... And give them the books of thy handwriting, and they will read them and will know me the creator of all; and let them distribute the books of thy handwriting children to children, generation to generation, nation to nations.... Thy handwriting and the handwriting of thy fathers Adam and Seth shall not be destroyed till the end of time, as I have commanded my angels . . . that it be preserved, and that the handwriting of thy fathers. . . perish not.*

First question; if Enoch was the first man who was taught writing, how could handwriting of Adam and Seth exist? This can only mean that Adam and Seth are not classed as Earthmen in this passage but as Gods. Next question; where are the 360 books today if in fact they are to be preserved to the end of time and will not perish?

1 Enoch 81 : 1, 2 *Observe, Enoch, these heavenly tablets, says the angel, and read what is written thereon....And I observed the heavenly tablets, and read everything .*

. . and understood everything, and read the book of all the deeds of mankind . . . to the remotest generations.

1 Enoch 93 : 2-3 *I Enoch will declare unto you, my sons, according to that which appeared to me in the heavenly vision, and which I have known through the word of the holy angels, and have learnt from the heavenly tablets. And Enoch began to recount from the books.*

1 Enoch 68 : 1 *After . . . Enoch gave me the teachings of all the secrets in the book and in the Parables which had been given to him, he . . . put them together for me in the words of the Book of Parables.*

To water down the Enoch story just a little, we find that a minimalist summary of the *Corpus Hermeticum* was supposedly set down on the *Emerald Tablet* which is part of the *Lost Wisdom of Lamech*. The Biblical Lamech's sons were **Jabal**, **Jubal** and **Tubal-Cain**, respectively a mathematician, a mason and a metalworker. These sons supposedly preserved the ancient wisdom on two pillars called the *Antediluvian Pillars*. The Master of Alchemy, **Hermes Trismegistus** apparently discovered one of these pillars and transcribed it into the *Emerald Tablet*. Greek legend claims that **Pythagoras** inherited the tablet and went on to discover the other pillar and its sacred geometry. [31]

The 1st century historian, Josephus, confirms that Enoch left astronomical data recorded on two pillars. This too was in order for it to survive the predicted, coming flood. According to the Bible generations in **Genesis 5 : 21-24,** Enoch lived on Earth for 365 years, considerably fewer years than other Biblical patriarchs, for example we are told that Adam lived 930 years. The KJV Bible reports however that Enoch did not die but *"was no more, he walked with God and was taken up."* Note that early Bibles did not record 'God', they said, "...walked with **Elohim.**" Recall this is plural and means 'these beings' or 'these Gods'. This indicates that like Gilgamesh and the various 'Noah's', Enoch had gained immortality and his right to join the Anunnaki Gods. We noted above that his parents or his mother at least could have been from the Anunnaki Gods. A TV special seen by the author claimed that sourced documentation recorded that Enoch was actually taken up by two Giants; however I cannot find any original source for this. The Bible is not a reliable source either as in **Genesis 4 : 16-23** Enoch is the son of

Chanoch and the grandson of Cain; yet in **Genesis 5 : 6 – 18** Enoch is the son of Jared and great, great, great grandson of Seth (Cain's younger brother). It doesn't end there, in **Luke 3 : 37–38** it agrees with Genesis Chapter 5 that Enoch was the 6th from Adam but **Jude 1 : 14** says Enoch was the 7th from Adam. At the very least, the Bible's editors were asleep again.

The Book of Enoch

The Book of Enoch that we have today is an apocryphal work of the Gnostic Gospels found in Abyssinia (now Ethiopia) in 1773 by Scottish explorer James Bruce and contains "**The Book of the Watchers**" (written in Ethiopic). Later fragments were found in Egypt written in Greek and finally more fragments in Hebrew were found with the Dead Sea Scrolls in Cave 4. In fact a total of nine copies were found with the Dead Sea corpus indicating that it was probably widely used at Qumran. It is thought to have been written perhaps even before 300 BCE, and is considered to be possibly the first of the early Scriptural works. There is a practice where Biblical scribes attributed their work to a known patriarch or Biblical character. This practice in religious literature is quite common and is called "pseudoepigraphal" and accordingly we can be pretty certain that the book was not based on anything actually written by Enoch, who lived before the flood. Although well known, widely used and actually referred to in **Jude 14-15** of the Bible, the **Book of Enoch** was not selected, in 325 AD, by the Council of Nicea for inclusion in the Bible. Again, just imagine if it had been included. This book explains at great length that the Sons of the Gods (*Watchers or Anunnaki*) descended to Earth in the days of his father Jared to the summit of Mt Hermon, and taught him everything about writing and knowledge and revealed the "eternal secrets, which were preserved in Heaven." This theme keeps re-occurring.

Here we must pause for a moment and consider our own scepticism. This whole 'Sky-God' story all sounds a bit 'far fetched' and yet we are seeing quote after quote from ancient manuscripts which make it apparent that the ancients must have believed these things to devote so many of their valuable manuscripts and tablets to this subject. In reality though, is this genesis of man less plausible than the one selected for inclusion in the Bible, that has proved to be so erroneous. Now human nature dictates that one would be proud of one's achievements and learning and would delight in the telling or the recording. It is not likely that a person would volunteer that the Anunnaki Gods had taught him and helped him if this isn't what occurred. There is no doubt that we have seen serious errors and shortcomings in the Bible's message. Now we are seeing evidence of something quite amazing. Scepticism of something different from what we were taught, and led to believe most of our lives, cannot be overturned in an instant. As we see these things consistently making sense however, we must begin to ponder.

Enoch was so adamant that his information must not be lost, that we are told he preserved it on two pillars. This shows a definite link to the secrets of Freemasonry, which uses two identical pillars called Jachin and Boaz in its craft. There are also recorded higher degrees of the Masonic Craft that involve the *'Wisdom of Enoch'*. In the entrance of the Jerusalem temple built by King Solomon (and dedicated to YHWH) were two pillars Jachin and Boaz, said to stand for the sun and moon.

> **1 Kings 2 : 21** *And he set up the pillars in the porch of the temple: and he set up the right pillar, and called the name thereof Jachin: and he set up the left pillar, and called the name thereof Boaz.*

The Book of Enoch goes on to tell us that the Holy Gods (plural) did not approve of the Watchers mating with Earth women, probably upsetting the structured breeding program orchestrated by EN.KI. Members of the Watchers, who had married Earth women, eventually sent Enoch, who must have enjoyed some strong rapport, to plead their case before the Gods. Enoch returned with a message from the Gods and strongly reprimanded the Watchers, who had gone native, that they now couldn't go back up to Heaven (to their original homes). To add credibility, Watchers are entirely scriptural and are mentioned often in the Bible. It seems in **Enoch 14 : 5** that the writer of the document understands 'original sin' to be the failure to observe the correct breeding protocol, and hence those who sin in this way (or are accordingly not the right pedigree) will not go up to Heaven (or back to their planet Nibiru).

Is it possible that this is the root of the whole belief in sin stopping mankind from going up to Heaven? (This comes from a time well before the law of Moses, and contrary to popular belief, the New Testament says only that the rejection of Jesus Christ will prevent one going to Heaven; not sin itself.) Recall how ENLIL objected to EN.KI's breeding program, and yet ENLIL could have been the very one who saw to Enoch's education in order to give him this mission to reprimand the Anunnaki Watchers. It seems that Enoch went "up" to live with the Anunnaki, possibly as a reward for undertaking these duties. Remember the Bible states that he did not die but *"he walked with Elohim and was taken up."*

Enoch himself supposedly reports in **Enoch 39 : 3** *"And in those days a whirlwind carried me off from the Earth, and set me down at the end of the Heavens."*

For comparison, let's look at how the accepted, orthodox Biblical account goes;

> **Genesis 6 : 1-4** *"Now it came to pass, when men began to multiply on the face of the Earth, and daughters were born to them, that the sons of God saw the daughters of men, that they were fair; and they took wives for themselves of all whom they chose. There were Giants in the Earth in those days, and also afterwards, when the sons of God came in to the daughters of men and they bore children to them. Those were the mighty men who were of old, men of renown."*

Did they teach this passage in Sunday School? No they did not, and they had no understanding of it either. This certainly appears to be Sumerian doctrine included in the Hebrew Bible. If you would prefer to still believe that the sons of the Gods were 'fallen angels', the learned Rabbi ben Jochai after careful consideration and a lifetime of study, stated that they were not. It is only fair to caution that the original word used and translated here as "Giants" was the same word used by the historian Flavius Josephus to depict *"big, strong men as the mighty Titans."* The actual translation as *"giants"* is not entirely accurate although they are elsewhere described as being close to 3 metres tall. Note also that in Greek mythology there are two types of Giants called *"Gigantes"* and *"Megistanes"*. The Megistanes were documented as a bigger species of Giant and ironically 'Megistanes' in Greek also means

'Titans'.

'Men of renown' is not a correct notation either. Sitchin disputes this translation and documents it as *'men of the shem'*. The Bible translators didn't know what a 'shem' was so wrote, *'men of renown.'* Sitchen explains his reasoning that a 'shem', in the ancient Sumerian time, was depicted as a cone shaped vehicle, spouting flames that were shown in records left for our perusal. If we didn't know better, looking at the depictions we would have to say they were the Anunnaki transport vehicles or in other words, spacecraft or fiery rockets. So men of the 'Shem' are apparently 'men of the spacecraft' or most likely Anunnaki Gods. In support of Sitchen's translation, a *'Shem Priest'* is referred to in the Egyptian, 'Book of the Dead' which makes it clear that this priest is from the Sky-Gods, the beings that used these vehicles. [(32)]

We should also look at the following somewhat incredible story written or modified at a much later time and contained in a Gnostic piece called **The Acts of Andrew and Matthias** (a pseudoepigraphal piece attributed to Jesus' disciples Andrew and Matthew). This can at best be described as weird! Here the Devil is taken to task for all sorts of misdemeanors, including causing the Nephilim, "fallen angels" to be defiled with Earth women and also for causing their savage Giant offspring to devour men;

> *"Andrew looked at the victims, who were naked and eating grass, and smote his breast and reproached the devil: How long warest thou with men? Thou didst cause Adam to be cast out of paradise: thou didst cause his bread that was on the table to be turned to stones. Again, thou didst enter into the mind of the angels and cause them to be defiled with women and madest their savage sons the giants to devour men on the earth, so that God had to send the flood."* [(33)] This piece revisits the notion that the flood was to remove these breeding errors.

The Watchers

We need to learn more about the Watchers that Enoch reprimanded. The Sumerians tell us that supervising groups of the Anunnaki were commonly called "**Watchers**". The Sumerians recorded that the Anunnaki created workers to mine the gold while a group of them **watched** and supervised.

The connotation was watchers and workers. We will see later that this connotation is supported by the Egyptian scribes who spoke of the **Neteru**, who were Gods from the sky and were accompanied by intermediary God-men called **Urshu**. It is profoundly interesting that the Egyptian *'Urshu'* translates precisely as *'Watchers'*. I would think that this is way beyond any chance of coincidence. Not surprisingly, clergy today tend to pass Watchers off as fallen angels. This subject caused me trouble aplenty in Sunday School because it is quite apparent that we are not discussing angels. The Bible has several mentions of "Watchers" and like angels, the connotation certainly remains that "they came down to earth from Heaven".

> **Daniel 4 : 13** *...and there was a Watcher, a holy one coming down from Heaven.*

> **Daniel 4 : 17** *This decision* (to punish a man) *is by decree of the Watchers and the demand by the word of the Holy Ones.*

> **Daniel 4 : 23** *...the King saw a Watcher, a holy one, coming down from Heaven.*

The pseudoepigraphal Enoch made it clear in **Enoch 10 : 16** that the Watchers were the same Godlike beings who mated with Earth women and these were not angels. In the same context the Bible calls them *'the Sons of the Gods'*. This gives us a pretty good indication who they were and adds credibility to the Sumerian record. The above quoted passage from Daniel also makes it apparent that Watchers and Nephilim are one and the same.

In *'From Ashes to Angels'*, Andrew Collins tells that **Julius Africanus** of Edessa (200-245 AD) stated that the Elohim were certainly Gods but to be fair Elohim are also found recorded in some non-canonical scriptures as 'foreign rulers' and 'Judges'. If we believe Watchers are the same as Elohim, then this further supports the Biblical passage;

> **Jeremiah 4 : 16** *'Watchers come from a far country.'*

It seems they come from a far country at the end of Heaven (Nibiru); look what Isaiah records;

> **Isaiah 13 : 3-5** *"...I have commanded my sanctified ones; I have also called my mighty ones... They come from a far country, from the end of heaven..."*

Remember that Enoch verbalized this location in exactly the same way when he described where he was taken to join the Anunnaki;

Enoch 39 : 3 *"And in those days a whirlwind carried me off from the Earth, and set me down at the end of the Heavens."*

Our skepticism must fade as we see this documentation. If one is not indoctrinated with the Biblical hosts of angels, this becomes very hard documentation to refute and if it holds no credence, we must explain why remnants are in our Bibles. It becomes fairly apparent that the Biblical Watchers were one and the same as the Sons of the (Anunnaki) Gods and these are also referred to as Nephilim. Regarding Nephilim, Zecharia Sitchin stated;

> *'The term literally means "Those who from Heaven to Earth came"They are spoken of in the Bible as the Anakim, and in Chapter 6 of Genesis are also called Nephilim, which in Hebrew means the same thing; "Those who have come down from the Heavens to Earth".* [(34)]

The recordings in the Bible make it clear that the Watchers were thought of as Holy Ones who came down from heaven and that they came from a far country; in fact *"from the end of heaven"*. These are also apparently the men of the 'Shem' we saw earlier; the men of the 'space vehicles'.

Look back now to **Genesis 2 : 5** *"…and there was no man to till the ground"* (or in fact to dig the gold) and also **Genesis 1 : 26** *"Then Elohim said, "Let Us make man in Our image, according to Our likeness…"*

Remember Elohim means "these beings" (plural). Are we to conclude that the Bible refers to the Anunnaki, because if not, we are left with a lot of unusual beings not accounted for, and we would need to ask, if not the Anunnaki, then who? We must recall that the singular God we worship today was translated from original plural documentation as ELOHIM (ELOHEEM). We should now renew our search for this God.

Perversion is the keynote of all the debased forms of Gnosticism. According to Eliphas Lévi, certain of the Gnostics introduced into their rites that profanation of Christian mysteries which was to form the basis of black magic in the Middle Ages. The glorification of evil, which plays so important a part in the modern revolutionary movement, constituted the creed of the Ophites, who worshipped the Serpent.
Nesta Webster in the book *'Secret Societies and Subversive Movements'*

CHAPTER NINE

WHO IS THIS GOD?

And that which was said out of the bush to Moses, "I am that I am, the God
of Abraham, and the God of Isaac, and the God of Jacob, and the God of
your fathers," this signified that they, even though dead, are yet in existence,
and are men belonging to Christ Himself. For they were the first of all men
to busy themselves in the search after God;

Justin Martyr, First Apology

Gods Of The Early Hebrew

This chapter is of paramount importance because here we will attempt to
discover precisely who the God of many names; the God of the Hebrew
Nation was (or is) and it may come as a surprise to many. This is not esoteric
supposition it is actual recorded fact and though somewhat hidden, it is
mostly found in our Bibles. Firstly however, there is the considerable
metamorphosis of this God to uncover and appreciate. Recall that the
Jewish, Christian and Moslem religions all more or less worship this same
entity today and not one can precisely identify their mysterious God, where
he resides or where he came from. We must understand how this entity
became the Storm God of the Hebrew people; then evolved into a God of
war and finally a God of love in the New Testament. We will follow his
metamorphosis from the angry, wrathful, bigoted God of the Old
Testament, into the loving, peaceful and merciful God of the New
Testament. Jesus said that he was 'one with God' and if Jesus was in reality
the kind, gentle and peaceful man we were taught to believe, then it was
quite apparently not this same God of the Old Testament about whom he
was preaching. For example;

- Old Testament: **Nahum 1 : 2** *God is jealous, and the Lord revengeth; the Lord revengeth, and is furious; the Lord will take vengeance on his adversaries, and he reserveth wrath for his enemies.*

Despite this we were requested (ordered) to love him. **Deuteronomy 6 : 5** *And thou shalt love the Lord thy God with all thine heart, and with all thy soul, and with all thy might.* (Love is an emotion we simply can't force and it is patently stupid to try to force people to love you – it just won't happen.)

- New Testament: *"God is Love".* Jesus taught; **John 16 : 27** *For the Father himself loveth you, because ye have loved me, and have believed that I came out from God.*

Paul told us;

> **2 Corinthians 13 : 11** *Finally, brethren, farewell. Be perfect, be of good comfort, be of one mind, live in peace; and the God of love and peace shall be with you.*

Christians don't seem to even notice the metamorphosis of angry into loving, yet the scriptures make it quite obvious and apparent. Here we will attempt to ascertain God's identity. We will discover (to the chagrin of some) that despite all the nonsense regurgitated from pulpits each Sunday, this particular God can no more save us or judge us in this 21st. Century, than other "Gods" like the deified Augustus Caesar, 'Simon Magus the Holy God' or the deified World War II Emperor of Japan.

Some considerable time after the Biblical flood, around 1900 BCE, the 'Shepherd King' Abram left Sumer and with his new name 'Abraham', dwelt near Mt. Hebron in the land of Canaan, that later was to become Judah. Now the name Abram means something like *"beloved of the father"* and a name change to Abraham, meaning *"father of a nation"* was required following his covenant with God. Abraham is regarded as the initial patriarch of the Jewish people and it was he who made a covenant with the 'God of his fathers', at that time called **El Shaddai, El Elyon** or **Adonai.** The word *Shad* meant 'breast' so El Shaddai was called, "God of my heart" and yet the name also had a definite connotation to do with 'mountains' and meant something like *'God of the Mountains'.* It appears El Shaddai became a mixed identity and is often documented as one and the same with **El Elyon.** The name El Shaddai was retained in the Vulgate Bible and is used <u>48 times</u> in the canon. [1] We find other names of Almighty God recorded in early Bibles and the ongoing mixing of the Hebrew and Canaanite Gods is what is actually recorded there. According to the Bible, God (El Elyon) spoke often with Abraham and later spoke personally with Moses and Jacob/Israel.

By the time of Moses, we are told, either God evolved to a stage where he wanted to now be called YHWH meaning *"I am that I am"*; or a totally new God had arrived. The translation of this secret name of God has always been a puzzle to scholars, so much so that the Jewish Publication Society leaves the name untranslated with the footnote, *"Meaning of the Hebrew uncertain"*. [2] The meaning of *"ehyeh asher ehyeh"* is however not at all obscure and means precisely *"I am that I am"* This is even spelt out in the King James Bible when we see Moses asking God to his face, to identify himself;

> **Exodus 3 : 13-14** *And Moses said unto God, Behold, when I come unto the children of Israel, and shall say unto them, The God of your Fathers hath sent me unto you; and they shall say to me, What is his name? What shall I say unto them? And God said unto Moses, I am that I am: and he said, Thus shalt thou say unto the children of Israel, I am hath sent me unto you.*

Laurence Gardner had this to say;

> *"In early tradition, Jehovah (just like ENLIL and El Elyon) had a wife and family, but the essential difference between the ENLIL and Jehovah portrayals was that ENLIL was seen to have identifiable parents and grandparents, as detailed in the Enuma elish and other ancient documents."* [3]

The author David Rohl in his influential book 'Legend' mentions that YHWH and its cryptic meaning 'I am that I am' was recorded as the Hebrew 'eahyeh asher eahyeh'. Rohl maintains that the second eahyeh should have been recorded as 'Eya' (phonetically the same). The Akkadian name for the Anunnaki Sky-God EN.KI (the brother of ENLIL) was in fact Ea and pronounced 'Eya'. In other words in a straight phonetic translation of the question, the answer to Moses may have simply been, *"I am EN.KI"*. Now wouldn't that throw a spanner in the works? The problems with this however are firstly that YHWH is more likely associated with ENLIL and likely not his brother EN.KI, and secondly, one would reasonably expect a God to be able to communicate in such a manner that he would be understood. Karen Armstrong commented that *'I am that I am'* in common parlance could have simply meant, *"Mind your own business!"* [4]

It certainly seems that there was something secretive about this God YHWH who didn't want to readily disclose his identity. In the Hebrew characters, **YHWH** was originally documented as **YHVH** by the Hebrew and it is actually an abbreviation for a longer 72 triplet (or 216 character) name. This name was known to the Hebrew from the very ancient times and is discussed in both the *Bachir* and the *Zohar* which outline the process of constructing the name. It is recorded as the name for the God who does not respond to logic but only to faith. In the eleventh century it was recorded in Rashi's commentaries;

> *"The Name of seventy-two triplets is derived from three Biblical verses;* **Exodus Chapter 14 : Verses 19, 20 & 21.** *Whether by coincidence or design, each of these verses contains exactly seventy-two Hebrew letters. These verses then form the basis for the seventy-two triplets in the name."*

(i)   Take the letters of the first verse in <u>direct</u> order

(ii)   Those of the second verse in <u>reverse</u> order

(iii)   Those of the third verse in <u>direct</u> order

Begin with the first letter of the first verse, which is **W** (Vav). Then take the last letter of the second verse, which is **H** (He), and finally, the first letter of the third verse, which is **W** (Vav). The first triplet is, **WHW.**

In order to construct the second triplet, one proceeds in the same manner. Take the second letter of the first verse, **Y** (Yod) the second last letter of the second verse, **L** (Lamed), and the second letter of the third verse, **Y** (Yod). The second triplet is, **YLY.** This method is continued until all seventy-two triplets are recorded.

Exodus 14 : 19

WYSO MLAK HALHYM HHLK LPhNY MChNH YShRAL WYLK MAChRYHM WYSO OMWD HONN MPhNYHM WYOMD MAChRYHM:

"And the angel of God, who went before the camp of Israel, moved, and went behind them, and the pillar of cloud moved from before them and went behind them."

Exodus 14 : 20

WYBA BYN MChNH MTzRYM WBYN MChNH YShRAL WYHY HONN WHChShK WYAR ATh HLYLH WLA QRB ZH AL ZH KL HLYLH:

"And it came between the camp of Egypt and the camp of Israel, and cloud and darkness were there, yet it gave light in the night, and one did not come near the other all that night."

Exodus 14 : 21

WYT MShH ATh YDW OL HYM WYWLK YHWH ATh HYM BRWCh QDYM OZH KL HLYLH WYShM ATh HYM LChRBH WYBQOW HMYM:

"And Moses stretched out his hand over the sea, and God caused the sea to go back with a strong East wind all the night, and it made the sea into dry land, and the waters were parted."

This is Gods complete name of 72 triplets:

WHW YLY SYT OLM MHSh LLH AKH KHTh HZY ALK LAW HHO YZL MBH HRY HQM LAW KLY LWW PhHL NLK YYY MLH ChHW NThH HAA YRTh ShAH RYY AWM LKB WShR YChW LHCh KWQ MND ANY HOS RHO YYZ HHH MYK WWL YLH SAL ORY OShL MYH WHW DNY HChSh OMM NNA NYTh MBH PhWY NMM YYL HRCh MTzR WMB YHH ONW MchY DMB MNQ AYO ChBW RAH YBM HYY MWM

This is the actual ineffable, unpronounceable, sacred name of this new God that is shortened to YHWH. In his brilliant book, *"Will the Real Jesus Please Stand?"* author and archaeologist Vendyl Jones (who inspired the Indiana Jones, 'Raiders of the Lost Ark' series), states;

> *"In Revelation 13 : 14-15, John describes the creation of a "Golem." When a Cabbalist receives the secret of the Holy Name or "Tetragrammaton," he tests his ability to pronounce it properly by the creation of the Golem. In this procedure, an image of a man is made of clay. The word TRUTH (?ahMehT) is written on the clay forehead of the image. The Cabbalist then chants the seventy-two intonations of the Holy Name over the clay image. If the sounds are correct, the image comes alive."*

The soul-less beast is then destroyed by rubbing away or covering a Hebrew character, which changes the word TRUTH to DEATH. The image of the beast of the Golem then goes back to clay. Now Tetragrammaton is from the Greek and simply means "four letters" however its usage is not restricted to the Hebrew. In fact in a great number of tongues the divine name of their deity was expressed in four letters. We find the Greek - Zeus and Theo, the Latin - Deus, the Spanish - Dios the Scandinavian - Odin, the German - Gott, and the English - Lord.

It is interesting in **Revelation 13 : 18** that St. John states that *"the number of the name of the image of the Golem shall be 666"*. This is the number of 'the beast' however it is not some sinister mystery as is often claimed; it is a direct statement of one of the principles of the forty-two laws of the Kabbalah. This principle is called Gematria. It bears thinking about that this Kabalistic procedure is so closely related to the creation of Adam (mankind) out of clay.

One of the twelve-letter names of YHWH:
AHYH   YHWH   ADNY

Kabbalah teaches that there are three (four letter) names, one above the other.

AHYH (Ehiyeh: *Great I am*) **is on top**
YHWH (Yahweh: *I am that I am*) **in the middle**
ADNY (Adonai: *Lord God*) **is on the bottom.**

Many other Gods were proscribed by YHWH; the same God we call Jehovah or Almighty God today, who first came on the scene when he introduced himself to Moses as YHWH. The Yahvist scribes are responsible for changing the original names of the Biblical deities, willy-nilly from the early writings, so that in reading a current Bible it is all but impossible to ascertain what was originally recorded. As a result of their vandalism, much is now credited to Almighty God under the name of YHWH that occurred before he even arrived on the Biblical scene or before he commenced using that name. In addition, I find it hard to reconcile God introducing Himself as YHWH, more than a thousand years before Exodus was written. Without Exodus, how did the Hebrew (or God for that matter) generate the 72-triplet name of which YHWH is a diminutive?

A couple of interesting side notes are that the ancient *Beth-Luis-Noin* calendar of 364 plus 1 days (based on 52 weeks X 7 days) was actually replaced by the *Boibel-Loth* calendar of 360 plus 5 days (based on 45 weeks X 8 days). Eight is the symbol of rejuvenation and corresponds to the eight-fold name of the *God of Light*. This name is **JEHUOVAQ**.[5] The similarity to Jehovah is obvious. In Greek Mythology, **Palamedes** was the son of the Euboian king Nauplius and queen Clymene and was also the grandson of Poseidon and Amymone and was the personification of time-honoured wisdom. From the contents of Pallas Athena's bag came the Mysteries of the triple Goddess and the great secret of alchemy, Palamedes' secret letters of the alphabet and the disc with the spirally engraved nine letter name of the Goddess of Wisdom. This almost identical name was **JIEHUOVAQ**.[6] Again we note the similarity to the name of God JEHOVAH and ask ourselves which came first.

We must acknowledge that Abraham was a Sumerian Prince and although he is regularly called the first Jew he came from Sumer and worshipped a Sumerian God. With his travels to Haran, into the land of Canaan and then to Egypt, there was some mingling of the Sumerian religion of Abraham with the religions of Canaan and Egypt. In addition some time later Moses (with his followers) were brought up in the Hebrew and Egyptian religions, and in time merged them with the religions of Canaan (the Promised Land), when (by God's covenant) they went to dwell in that location. We will look at that soon. Their main rivals, the Philistines, were part of a wave of maritime people from Europe who came to Syria and Cannan bringing still more pagan Gods around the 12th Century BCE. In fact it was the Philistines (Pelishtim or Philistaci) who gave Canaan its new name of Palestine. The deities became more and more intermingled since it was usual practice at that time to adopt the Gods of a new land without dropping those from one's homeland.

We are to believe from the Bible that God introduced himself to Moses as YHWH and was either a new God or for some reason choose to disregard his former aliases. By a further covenant of God the YHWH worshippers with Moses then brought their Egyptian-ized religion to the land of Canaan to further embellish that doctrine. Just try to picture yourself in the position of the Biblical patriarchs, if contact with God happened as recorded in the Bible, with the deity suddenly like a thunderclap out of a clear sky, choosing to speak to mankind and introduce Himself. These ancient Gods were however recorded as flesh-and-blood Gods, not spirit entities. According to Bible verses, God not only spoke face to face with Abraham and Moses, but also sat down to meals with them.

Genesis 18 : 1-8 *Abraham washed their feet and had roast beef, cakes and milk with God and His entourage.* In **Genesis 18 : 2** of a current KJV; Abraham gives us an eyewitness account of running out to meet Gods party, and guess what; he clearly states: *there were three men*.

So is this the Trinity? Does God have an entourage? Does he travel with a couple of friends? This is in the Bible but it still boggles every Christian I show it to, and there is really no need. We were created in the image of God and this makes perfect sense that in looks, the Gods were pretty much indistinguishable from man. Genesis has many reports of plural Gods so there should be no surprise that there were at least three Gods. The fact that the description comes from a person of the calibre of Abraham makes me believe it is not fabricated and he tells what actually occurred. There would be something wrong if it were otherwise!

Exodus 24 : 9-12 *Moses, Aaron, Nadab, Abihu and 70 elders met with God and had food and drink with him.*

For some this may be a bit hard to reconcile, eating with a physical God and mistaking Him for a man, when the God of the Hebrews (and our modified God today) is supposedly Spirit. The only real surprise however is that we were taught: '*no man can gaze upon Almighty God and live*'? I believe that both Abraham and Moses told the truth and did meet with physical "God Men" who originally came from the sky and made us in their image. These are the flesh-and-blood Gods referred to by the Sumerian 'fathers' who called them 'Anunnaki.' They described many centuries of interaction with these entities as did the Egyptians, the Chinese, the early inhabitants of India, the Australian Aborigines and in fact most ancient peoples on Earth. As we have said before, if this evidence does not fit our 'mind picture', then guess which one is wrong. We should consider something strange in the Bible for a moment and it is this; could the Sky-God who brought the children of Israel out of Egypt have actually used a form of flying machine to achieve this rescue. "No way", I hear you say. OK, then consider this;

Exodus 19 : 4 *Ye have seen what I did unto the Egyptians, and how I bare you on eagles' wings, and brought you unto myself.*

The earliest Hebrew coin (inset) showing Jehovah seated on a winged chariot that closely rembles the chariot of Triptolemus on the Greek vase. (bottom)

This could be just another nonsensical Bible passage except for two things;

(i)   The first Hebrew coin minted in the 'Promised Land' depicts the God YHWH seated in a winged chair or flying chariot.

(ii)   The Jewish <u>Zohar</u> contains a passage that draws on a third century mystical work by Rabbi Eleazar ben Pedath that states;

"As Pharaoh came out of Egypt, to follow the Israelites, he raised his eyes to Heaven,

and saw the Prince of the Egyptian Angels flying in the air. [7]

Now in addition we read in the apocryphal Book of Adam and Eve how the angels of the Lord descended to the Gates of Paradise, where Eve was mourning the death of Adam. At this point the Sun, Moon and stars grew dark, the Heavens opened and the Eagles appeared. [8]

There is another passage in the Bible that disturbs my 'mind picture' of an omnipresent God. Here it tells us that to commute, God hitches a ride with a passing cherub;

2 Samuel 22 : 11 *And he (the Lord) rode upon a cherub, and did fly: and he was seen upon the wings of the wind.*

We can speculate forever on what is recorded here but it seems there is simply insufficient documentation to arrive at a firm conclusion. What is recorded however is fairly strange!

Abraham was a Sumerian prince from Ur and he would have been familiar with the *Enuma elish* records of the Sumerian Genesis and its Anunnaki Gods. It is far more plausible that Abraham was telling the truth and served food and refreshment to flesh-and-blood Gods (plural) and not some esoteric spirit being. The Gods were correctly documented in Sumer with human characteristics and emotions, and from the records, they certainly liked food and drink. The Hebrew later stored this information in verbal traditions. Once Hebrew writing began scribes would on occasions write down the more interesting bits as history. In this way the support of this original storm God amongst the Elohim and the slow change to monotheism can be tracked.

The Hebrew Worshiped 'Other Gods'

The early Hebrew like the Sumerians, Babylonians, Canaanites and Egyptians before them, had a plethora of Gods. War Gods, Sun Gods, Gods of Thunder, Harvest Gods and Fertility Gods were all worshipped. In the Bible we still find traces of the early 'Planting, Rain and Harvest' role;

Leviticus 26 : 3-5, *If you follow my decrees and are careful to obey my commands, I will send you rain in its season, and the ground will yield its crops and the trees of the field their fruit. Your threshing will continue until grape harvest and the grape harvest* *will continue until planting, and you will eat all the food you want and live in safety in your land.* (Revised version, Not KJV)

The main festivals of Judaism; **Pesach, Shovous, Sukkos, and Purim** certainly demonstrate that the Hebrew people experienced difficulty in breaking free from agricultural cycles, since these festivals all have themes of harvest and planting. [9] We mentioned earlier ancient Regent sacrifice rituals and this could also constitute part of a fertility ritual or harvest rite. In fact the feast of Purim was loosely modelled on the Sumerian, *Festival of Sacaea* where an ordinary citizen was dressed in royal robes and after reigning for five days (in which time he was allowed to enjoy the Kings concubines) was summarily stripped, scourged and killed. [10] Not only is this a rehearsal of the Jesus theme to come, but we can also appreciate the tenacity of the agricultural theme. We can read in the KJV Bible about King Saul's seven sons and grandsons, all being sacrificed (hanged) as part of the barley harvest sacrifice ritual. It truly is still recorded in today's Bible. We can read of many planting, harvest and rain sacrifice rituals from pagan times and the ultimate sacrifice that involved killing the most prestigious members of the community, the offspring of the regent and quite often the king himself;

> **2 Samuel 21 : 8-10** *But the king took the two sons of Rizpah the daughter of Aiah, whom she bare unto Saul, Armoni and Mephibosheth; and the five sons of Michal the daughter of Saul,* (married to David) *whom she brought up for Adriel the son of Barzillai the Meholathite: and he delivered them into the hands of the Gibeonites, and they hanged them in the hill before the Lord: and they fell all seven together, and were put to death <u>in the days of harvest, in the first days, in the beginning of barley harvest</u>. And Rizpah the daughter of Aiah took sackcloth, and spread it for her upon the rock, <u>from the beginning of harvest until water dropped upon them out of heaven</u>, and suffered neither the birds of the air to rest on them by day, nor the beasts of the field by night.*

In later times of course YHWH God demanded sacrifices of the 'first born' from the womb;

> **Exodus 22 : 29-31** *Thou shalt not delay to offer the first of thy ripe fruits, and of thy liquors: <u>the firstborn of thy sons shalt thou give unto me</u>. Likewise shalt thou do*

with thine oxen, and with thy sheep: seven days it shall be with his dam; on the eighth
day thou shalt give it me. And ye shall be holy men unto me:

Numbers 8 : 17-18 *For all the firstborn <u>of the children of Israel</u> are mine both*
man and beast; on the day that I smote every firstborn in the land of Egypt I sanctified
them for myself and I have taken the Levites for all the firstborn of the children of
Israel.

This human and animal, blood sacrifice is abhorrent to me. It is barbaric and
we cannot argue away its presence in the Bible. We are hearing it from a
God who is the same, yesterday, today and tomorrow! Since we were on the
subject of Saul, we should look at his interaction with the Lord and events
surrounding his eventual death;

1 Samuel 9 : 15-17 The Lord tells Samuel that Saul has been chosen
to lead the Israelites and will save them from the Philistines.

1 Samuel 15 : 35 The Lord is sorry that he has chosen Saul

1 Samuel 28 : 6 Saul inquired of the Lord, but received no answer.

1 Chronicles 10 : 13-14 Saul died for not inquiring of the Lord.

1 Samuel 31 : 3, 1 Chronicles 10 : 3 Saul was shot by Philistine
archers.

1 Samuel 31 : 4-6 Saul killed himself by falling on his sword.

2 Samuel 2 : 2-10 Saul, at his own request, was slain by his armour
bearer, an Amalekite.

2 Samuel 21 : 12, 1 Samuel 31 : 8 Saul was killed by the Philistines
in Gilboa.

1 Samuel 31 : 2 Saul and his three sons were killed by the Philistines.

1 Chronicles 10 : 13-14 Saul was slain by God.

2 Samuel 21:12 The Philistines slew Saul and his sons and hanged
them in the streets of Bethshan.

1 Samuel 31 : 4-7 Saul committed suicide and the Israelites were
overrun by the Philistines which makes a bit of a mockery of the above
will of God.

Very little is recorded in the Hebrew Bible regarding the religious development of the first patriarchs for quite a time after the creation, because by the
time it was recorded the tenure was simply too long for verbal tradition to

last. It seems they had little personal relationship with the creator and that God did little to really promote himself with the descendants of Adam. If we consider Anunnaki Sky-Gods, who left the Earth until the next orbit of Nibiru, this would make perfect sense, and explain these long lapses in the relationship with God. Taking this further wouldn't one think that God would choose to make contact and communicate regularly with modern man who has achieved so much and advanced so quickly? Why after creating man would he not continue to follow up with meetings as he did with Abraham and Moses? I believe that this helps support that God is not able to make contact until his home planet Nibiru approaches to a point closer to the Earth.

There is a passage that claimed men began calling on the Lord in the time of Adam's grandson Enos;

Genesis 4 : 26 *And to Seth, to him also there was born a son; and he called his name Enos: then began men to call upon the name of the Lord.*

In time, the traditions that survived tell us, God talked to Noah about saving the seed of mankind in the Ark while He brought about the destruction of the world. Ironically in the Bible this was cited as being because the people had continued worshipping other Gods.

Deuteronomy 29 : 20 *For the Lord will not spare him, but then the anger of the Lord and his jealousy shall smoke against that man* (who worships other Gods) *and all the curses that are written in this book, shall lie upon him, and the Lord will blot out his name from under heaven.*

Even if in the beginning God was disappointed in Adam and Eve it seems strange that they and their descendants would choose, without cause, to abandon their own creator and worship other Gods. Human nature is to oppose change; to stay within ones own gang, or community, or race, or country or with one's own leader. I believe it would have taken some strong motivation to force them to abandon their creator and seek other Gods. How did they find these Biblical, "other Gods"? What were the other Gods doing whilst God was creating man?

What I believe we are seeing is the rulers within separate family dynasties of the Anunnaki jockeying for positions, and for the support and worship of the masses, similar to that outlined in the Sumerian records. Each one who obtained a leadership role did it with the support of their followers from among the inhabitants of Earth. Therefore it seems these passages depict the Gods quite arrogantly requesting the support and worship of mankind to achieve their leadership aspirations. We move on to another interesting passage;

> **Joshua 24 : 2** *Thus sayeth the Lord God of Israel, "Your fathers dwelt on the other side of the flood in old time, even Terah, the father of Abraham, and the father of Nachor: and they served other Gods."*

This appears to make no sense at all. The Bible categorically states here that Abraham's father Terah lived on the other side of the flood. He is known to have lived at least 2000 years after the flood with Abraham. Are we to assume he hitched a ride with Noah to survive, and then lived a couple of thousand years? The time frame is way out of wack and accordingly this passage has real credibility problems for me. Think about it, for this passage to be in any way true, Terah would have to live for over 2000 years and be virtually an immortal being. That would actually make him one of the Anunnaki Gods or at least one of the Watchers, a being with so great a longevity that the inhabitants of Earth considered them immortal. It is interesting too, to note another passage in Genesis that can not be explained

> **Genesis 6 : 3** *And the Lord said, My spirit shall not always strive with man, for that he also is flesh: yet his days shall be an hundred and twenty years.*

This sounds to me like the time when man's "immortality' (extreme longevity) was clipped by the Gods after the breeding program was out of the dangerous early stages and overpopulation of the local area was becoming a threat. Can we identify precisely when this took place assuming the Bible record is correct? I find it hard to believe the clergy never documented this or bothered to look at what is recorded here.

The Bible states the following life spans for the patriarchs:

Adam	**930 years**
Seth	**912 years**
Enosh	**905 years**
Kenan	**910 years**

Mahalalel	**895 years**
Jared	**962 years**
Enoch	**did not die. Taken up to the Gods**
Methuselah	**969 years**
Lamech	**777 years**
Noah	**950 years**
Shem	**602 years**
Arphaxad	**438 years**
Shelah	**433 years**
Eber	**464 years**
Peleg	**239 years**
Reu	**239 years**
Serug	**230 years**
Nahor	**148 years**
Terah	**205 years**
Abraham	**175 years**

We can identify a number of channels here. The first group of ten (with the exception of Enoch and Lamech) all lived consistent life spans close to or over 900 years. We see Shem at 602 followed by the next group of three in the 400's then a group of five between 148 and 239. Following on is Abraham at 175 years. Man seems to have then lived within the spans we see as reasonable today. So what does this mean? The Bible states that Terah lived before the flood then contradicts this by attributing just 205 years to him. It further states that at the time the sons of the Gods were mating with the daughters of men (around the time of Enoch) the Gods decided man should live for just 120 years, then contradicts this by quoting the above life spans. Another contradiction we must consider is that we see in the table above that Nahor and Abraham had the shortest life spans of all the early patriarchs, living only a fifth the duration of some of their forbears. Yet surprisingly, despite this, the Bible emphasises the longevity of Abraham three times in this one passage;

Genesis 25 : 8 *Then Abraham gave up the ghost, and died <u>in a good old age</u>, <u>an old man</u> and <u>full of years</u>; and was gathered to his people.*

WHO IS THIS GOD?

A plausible answer comes from Alan Alford who correctly states that the early records were Sumerian and followed the sexagesimal system based on 6 and 10. Thus numbers were written differently and it was easy to erroneously translate them as far greater numbers than were intended. This numbering system presented enormous problems to the Hebrew scribes unaccustomed to the way this system was recorded, and according to Alford they adopted methods of adjusting the figures to what they thought would sound plausible. Alford goes to great lengths with examples of how this might have occurred and it is recommended that those interested in this topic read his excellent book. [11]

From the doctrine we were taught in Sunday School, there are also problems with the structure of the following:

Deuteronomy 32 : 16-17 *They made Him jealous with their foreign Gods and angered him with their detestable idols. They sacrificed to demons, which are not God - Gods they had not known, Gods that recently appeared, Gods your fathers did not fear.*

Note that it does not say "false" Gods or "make believe" Gods; just foreign Gods, other Gods and Gods that recently appeared. According to the Bible there seems to have been no shortage of these Gods. The Hebrew psyche was that they had selected a good macho, warlike God, one of many from the International pantheon, and it seems in this verse that God supports the existence of other foreign Gods and those who had recently appeared. <u>Note that no instruction was ever given to man to help him understand which God he should follow or why; just abuse when he followed the 'wrong' God.</u> The only plausible explanation is that this passage is telling of warring factions and entities within the Anunnaki Sky-Gods each struggling for support and perhaps worship. In fact in a snippet of the Bible we later see the victorious Biblical God judging these other Gods:

Psalm 82 : 1 *God standeth in the congregation of the mighty; He judgeth among the Gods.*

We cannot simply skip over this point. The Sumerians recorded how the Anunnaki did things with regular meetings to discuss plans and tactics. They had a sort of parliamentary system of rule with Anu as the 'President'.

Indeed he was also the 'Chief Justice' when a court was required to decide and rule on a situation. This Bible report sounds much more like the Anunnaki forum from the Sumerian record, than the singular God of the Christian Bible. Obviously from the Bible a monotheistic God would be hard pressed judging among the plural Gods anyway. We need to look further at this situation.

Asherah, Ashtoreth & Anath

In very early traditions, the God Jehovah (YHWH) had a wife and family.[12] **Ashtoreth** was said by some to be the consort of **Jehovah** and by others, the consort of **Ba`al**. We are about to find that these traditions could both be correct as we see evidence that Jehovah and Ba`al in those times were almost certainly one and the same God. This may astound some, considering the Bible's obvious hatred of the Ba`al worshippers, however it is certainly where the evidence points. *Ashtoreth* was mostly known as *Asherah* and over time and through many aliases these two female entities tended to merge into one. Also the ancient moon God, *Sin,* was transformed to become *Ashima,* also the wife of Jehovah. Clergy cannot overlook these Goddesses or simply dismiss them as being part of the early 'Trinity' or the 'Jehovah pantheon' since they are mentioned no less than **40 times** in the Bible. Once in Exodus, three times in Deuteronomy, five times in Judges, twice in Isaiah, once in Jeremiah, once in Micah and twenty-seven times in the books of Kings and Chronicles [13] Ashtoreth was also worshipped as a Mesopotamian deity called **Ashratu** in Babylon and **Atirat** by the Assyrians. She was also **Elath, Ashratu, Atirat, and Sud** [14]

The displacement of matriarchal rights over time played a large part in effecting the roles and records of Biblical women. This started when the somewhat patriarchal religion of YHWH eventually rejected the Mother Goddess role and in turn, that of women in general. As a result women were denigrated and lost all control over property and the control of religious celebration, being prevented from participation, and forced to simply watch from the women's gallery. This transition suited the later patriarchal Catholic hierarchy just fine because it presented more power to the Priests.

Judges 10 : 6 *And the children of Israel did evil again in the sight of the Lord, and* *served Baalim, and Ashtaroth, and the Gods of Syria, and the Gods of Zidon, and the Gods of Moab, and the Gods of the children of Ammon, and the Gods of the Philistines, and forsook the Lord, and served not him.*

Anath was an early Hebrew Goddess said to be the daughter of Jehovah and Ashtoreth. We find in the Old Testament;

> **Judges 3 : 31** *And after him was Shamgar the son of Anath, which slew of the Philistines six hundred men with an ox goad: and he also delivered Israel.*

Shamgar was supposedly a son of El Elyon and Anath and is shown here as a 'flesh and blood' God putting in a sterling performance fighting with the accursed Philistines and killing 600 of them. Anath (whether the daughter of Astarte or not) became the equivalent of Astarte as a **fertility goddess**. This is quite apparent with the word Astarte actually meaning 'womb'. Asherah (or Ashtoreth) is often referred to as the 'Queen of Heaven' and under whatever names she may have been worshipped earlier, – belonged to Jewish cult since ancient times. Later Mary (Miriam) the mother of Jesus was adapted to replace her, becoming for a time, the new 'Queen of Heaven.' For those who have never read these things in their Bibles and are having trouble believing it, here is one more item for you. The Temple of Jerusalem was simultaneously dedicated to **Yahweh** and to the **Queen of Heaven**. This is not made up, this is documented fact. Symbolic trees in quite sizable groves were planted before this Temple; called the sacred '**asherah**', that are throughout Semitic lands associated with the female aspect of the deity. We can observe the continuing popularity of the Queen of Heaven when Jeremiah made contact with her worshippers and asked them to instead worship his God:

> **Jeremiah 44 : 16 – 18** *"As for the word thou hast spoken unto us in the name of the Lord, we will not harken unto thee. But we will certainly do whatever thing goeth forth out of our own mouth, to burn incense unto the Queen of Heaven, and to pour out drink offerings unto her, as we have done, we and our fathers, our kings and our princes, in the cities of Judah, and in the streets of Jerusalem: for then we had plenty of victuals, and were well, and saw no evil. But since we left off to burn incense to the Queen of Heaven and to pour out drink offerings unto her, we have wanted all things, and have been consumed by the sword and by the famine."*

Laurence Gardner makes an interesting point:

> *"For the Israelites, the god-and-goddess concept came to an end when they dismissed Ashtoreth and pledged their allegiance to the one and only Jehovah, who was appropriated from El Elyon. But this pledge of singular allegiance was not made in the time of Abraham, nor even in the time of Moses - it occurred much later, in the time of Samuel the judge, when 'the children of Israel did put away Ba`al and Ashtoreth, and served the Lord only' (1 Samuel 7 : 4). This was about 1060 BCE."* [(15)]

We can follow the effort expended by the later priests in removing the groves (the asherah) and trying to dismiss the 'Queen of Heaven' and cement YHWH as the one true God. Here we see the actions of Josiah, the descendant of David, after finding hidden in the temple a book of the laws of Moses that promoted the monotheism of YHWH only:

> **2 Chronicles 34 : 3 - 5** *".. and in the twelfth year King Josiah began to purge Judah and Jerusalem from the high places, and the groves, and the carved images, and the molten images. And they brake down the altars of Baalim in his presence; and the images, that were on high above them, he cut down; and the groves, and the carved images, and the molten images, he brake in pieces, and made dust of them, and strowed it upon the graves of them that had sacrificed unto them. And he burnt the bones of the priests upon their altars and cleansed Judah and Jerusalem"*

If in fact it was the entire Torah that was found in the temple, it would include this text from Deuteronomy also attributed to Moses, and the cleansing would have been in response to this passage;

> **Deuteronomy 12 : 1** *"These are the statutes and judgements, which ye shall observe to do in the land, which the Lord God of thy fathers giveth thee to possess it, all the days that ye live upon the Earth. Ye shall utterly destroy all the places wherein the nations, which ye shall possess, served their Gods, upon the high mountain and on the high hills and under every green tree. And ye shall overthrow their altars and break their pillars and burn their groves with fire and ye shall hew down the graven images of their Gods, and destroy the names of them out of that place.*

No religious tolerance here, we see the commandment of God to destroy all traces of any other past Gods (or was it the successful Anunnaki candidate removing any potential threats to his leadership from his competitors). Throughout the Old Testament we find several patriarchs who seemed intent on promoting Jehovah-YHWH as the only God and accordingly justified the destruction of the images, alters, groves and high places. The previous **'thou shalt have no other Gods before me'** requirement of the laws of Moses was thus altered and instigated as the strict monotheistic **'no other Gods at all!'** Today the clergy attempt to portray the early Jewish history as having always been monotheistic when in fact nothing could be further from the truth. We just looked at a Biblical record of Jehovah judging amongst the other Gods. We can find another clue in the following Bible passage where these other Gods are told;

Psalm 82 : 7: *But ye shall die like* (mortal) *men, and fall like one of the princes.* Take the time to read the entire chapter in your Bible. Barré had this to say about it:

> *"Psalm 82 relates to the plural Elohim and shows Jehovah-El in a position where He; 'judgeth among the other Gods'. Psalm 82 is remarkable in that <u>it has El 'firing' all his sons and condemning them to mortality</u>. Although this Psalm shares the same view of El and his sons, this tradition descends from northern tradition and in this respect differs from the Jerusalem tradition found in Deut 32:8-9. In Psalm 82, Yahweh is not explicitly mentioned even though Deut 32:8-9 would place him among the "sons of Elyon" (v. 6)."*

Barré continues:

> *"One wonders what inspired such a Psalm that has El condemning his sons to death through whom he had formerly maintained his rule. The only event that could have triggered such a radical idea seems to be the establishment of the kingship of Jeroboam I. Apparently, among his reforms, intended to distance Israel from Judah and to promote national identity, Jeroboam I and his court thought it best to announce El's decision that the Gods of the other nations had been condemned to death and that El was now forced to rule alone."* [16]

This is a crucial point, because it seems that man did not appreciate or understand the way Jehovah apparently overcame the other Gods to become the sole ruler God. And why should he? Nothing was ever explained to man and he was not privy to the events like the meetings of the Gods. This apparently important information, was relegated to a couple of lines in Psalms and then made one of the *'Thou shalt nots'* of the Ten

Commandments without any explanation. Even that commandment said, *"…no other Gods before me"* and not the revised *"no other Gods at all"*. This is extremely important because this is precisely what 'ticked of' God in the first place. The Old Testament is jammed full of the wrath of God against people who worship other Gods. It is likely man did not understand or appreciate the actual documented change from polytheism to monotheism that occurred right there. He just didn't follow what was going on. There is a communication problem displayed here and it seems to be the root of all the wrath and unpleasantness from Almighty God to this day. I believe that with better communication, man would have 'got it'. Further, this could have been achieved with far less kicking and screaming, far less plagues and pestilence and much less cursing of children and children's children.

So man just couldn't figure it out! He was used to multiple Gods from birth and simply did not comprehend monotheism. The prophet Ezekiel reports huge problems later in Jerusalem with the Hebrew abominations that even involved the elders of the church. These are not just adopted Gods like Tammuz, the elders and laity alike are discovered in their involvement with idols that were recorded as being of the house of Israel and also in sun worship:

Ezekiel 8 : 10-16 *So I went in and saw; and behold every form of creeping things, and abominable beasts, and all the idols of the house of Israel, portrayed upon the wall round about. And there stood before them seventy men of the ancients of the house of Israel, and in the midst of them stood Jaazaniah the son of Shaphan, with every man his censer in his hand; and a thick cloud of incense went up. Then said he unto me, Son of man, hast thou seen what the ancients of the house of Israel do in the dark, every man in the chambers of his imagery? For they say, the Lord seeth us not; the Lord hath forsaken the earth. He said also unto me, Turn thee yet again, and thou shalt see greater abominations that they do. Then he brought me to the door of the gate of the Lord's house, which was toward the north; and, behold, there sat women weeping for Tammuz. Then said he unto me, hast thou seen this, O son of man? Turn thee yet again, and thou shalt see greater abominations than these. And he brought me into the inner court of the Lord's house, and, behold, at the door of the temple of the Lord, between the porch and the altar, were about five and twenty men, with their backs toward the temple of the Lord, and their faces toward the east; and they worshipped the* *sun toward the east.*

The *'seventy men of the ancients of the house of Israel'* is not a good translation, it simply means the 70 Elders of the Sanhedrin, or chief council of the nation, and these men in office were expected to restrain and punish idolatry and to destroy and abolish all superstitious images wherever they found them; yet here we see that they chose to endorse their worship and personally worship them in private. It is quite apparent that they had not understood that Almighty God Jehovah had judged the other Gods and condemned even his own sons to death and now was to rule alone. This also shows that monotheism was again very difficult to achieve with even the leaders of the Hebrew again reverting to polytheistic idol worship and even sun worship in the guise of Re, Aten, or possibly of Sol Invictus. Today clergy claim that what was involved here was the sun being utilized for 'time keeping' to properly align the religious feasts of YHWH. That however is not what the above Bible passage states. It is made clearer in the passages below that YHWH will not tolerate 'sun worship' or the worship of idols or graven images.

> **Deuteronomy 4 : 19** *And lest thou lift up thine eyes unto heaven, and when thou seest the sun, and the moon, and the stars, even all the host of heaven, shouldest be driven to worship them, and serve them, which the Lord thy God hath divided unto all nations under the whole heaven.*

> **Exodus 20 : 4** *Thou shalt not make unto thee any graven image, or any likeness of any thing that is in heaven above, or that is in the earth beneath, or that is in the water under the earth.*

The Hebrew Exposed to Canaanite Deities

We noted that the Hebrew God, mainly called El Elyon in the early times, had been selected by the Hebrew people for his warlike nature and ability to protect them. It was El Elyon, they believed, who had created Adam. Now as we mentioned earlier, 'Elyon' was in fact a name for the Canaanite God Ba`al. 'El' in Sumerian relates to 'Mighty One' and 'Shining One' but its usual meaning is "high or lofty" and across many languages became an early generic term for God. The Bible states that Jesus was to be called **Emmanu-**

el and this is an example of the generic use. The Canaanites however, had a supreme deity in their pantheon actually named **El**, whom they believed lived at the source of the Tigress and Euphrates Rivers. El is recorded as the God who created Lucifer and in fact in early Bibles, the passage **Isaiah 14 : 12** states that: *El was the father of Helel or Lucifer symbolized in the morning star.* The name Lucifer means literally 'Morning Star' and accordingly there was extensive reverence given to Venus and other bright stars in those ancient times. The Roman Catholic *Paschal Praeconium* of Easter Holy week, involves two candles still representing Jesus as Christ of *Wisdom* and Venus as the 'morning star' of *Knowledge*. An associated prayer goes;

> *"We beseech thee therefore O Lord, that this candle consecrated in the honour of thy Name, may continue to dispel the darkness of this night. And being accepted as a sweet savour, may it be united with the lights supernatural. May the morning star find it burning; that morning star, I pray, which knows no setting. That which being returned from the depths, shineth serene upon the human race."* (17)

Now this is odd because from the Earth, Venus is seen to rise and set. Accordingly a 'morning star' that does not set, just has to refer to Lucifer. As incongruous as it seems, that is what is apparently recorded here. This would promote a lot of heart burn within the Church if they knew but why is it still included in this Easter ceremony be it Venus or Lucifer?

The modern Bible states that Jehovah created Lucifer, so this again indicates a connection between Jehovah and El. We certainly cannot discount the incidence of El worship amongst the Hebrew. Let's document a bit of 'no place to hide' feedback for the Christians; "Israel" was the new name given to Isaac's son Jacob and from here the nation of Israel took its name. Now *Isra-el* means *'soldier of El'* and the original *Ysra-el* means *'El rules'*. (18) This must be seen to mean unequivocally that the God of the Hebrew people at that time was not YHWH at all but actually El, God of the Canaanites, the original owners of the promised land.

The Canaanites recorded that El had seven sons, the first of whom was Elyon and in most cases this certainly refers to Ba`al. When El became old and retired, Ba`al overcame challenges from his brothers Yamm *(Yham)*, Mot, Shahar and Shalem to become the principal deity. Ba`al was possibly not the real son of El as he is also recorded as the son of Dagon who, like El, is a retired deity and quite probably his uncle and part of the family dynasty. Ba`al vanquished Mot in a power struggle which cost him his life, but was resurrected by his own sister Anath (the daughter of YHWH), who cleaved Mot in half; this resurrection seems to be a common theme in many early religions. The Egyptian story of Osiris and Horace and even the resurrection of Jesus show similarities to this entire theme.

In the land of Canaan, Asherah (or Ashtoreth) the 'Queen of Heaven' was finally eclipsed by her own son, the **God Adon** (Adonai) a previously subordinate deity. Adonai started life as a metalworking 'Smith-God' called *Q're Adonai*; the word *'Q're'* meaning 'furnace' or referring to the working of metal. Asherah was usually connected with a sacred grove and certainly had agricultural connotations. The more conservative elements among the Hebrew tribes, led by Moses out of Egypt, found agricultural forms of this Semitic cult an abomination. By the time of Ezekiel however, so completely had El Elyon/Yahweh become assimilated to Adon that not only were the cults confounded, but also the very names had become inextricably blended; the hybrid God became spoken of as Adon, or **Adonai** who was also the Syrian Adonis, born from a tree. [19] As well as being recorded as the son of Asherah, Adonai was supposedly born in Bethlehem of the Virgin Myrrha, in a cave that Christians later claimed as the birthplace of Jesus. He is likely one and the same as the God, Tammuz. As a saviour God, Adonai was castrated and then finally sacrificed in redemption for unworthy man.

Canaanite Temples

We see in the Bible that the Hebrew people used stones to erect altars to accommodate their blood sacrifices;

> **Deutoronomy 27:6** *Thou shalt build the altar of the Lord thy God of whole stones: and thou shalt offer burnt offerings thereon unto the Lord thy God:*

Our 'mind picture' from Sunday School, of the Hebrew temples built in the Promised Land is all wrong. We must understand that the 'temples' taken over from the Canaanites were astronomy focused constructions more like the early Stonehenge, complete with standing stones and a ditch filled with water, rather than our vision of a conventional temple. If we doubt this it is made obvious from the Bible when Elijah repaired such a temple;

1 Kings 18 : 30 – 35 *And Elijah said unto all the people, Come near unto me. And all the people came near unto him. And he repaired the altar of the Lord that was broken down. And Elijah took twelve stones, according to the number of the tribes of the sons of Jacob, unto whom the word of the Lord came, saying, Israel shall be thy name: And with the stones he built an altar in the name of the Lord: and he made a trench about the altar, as great as would contain two measures of seed. And he put the wood in order, and cut the bullock in pieces, and laid him on the wood, and said, Fill four barrels with water, and pour it on the burnt sacrifice, and on the wood. And he said, Do it the second time. And they did it the second time. And he said, Do it the third time. And they did it the third time. And the water ran round about the altar; and he filled the trench also with water.*

In their book **'Uriel's Machine'**, Knight and Lomas note the construction of Solomon's Temple for the Lord;

"The Bible and Masonic legend tell us that Solomon then called in Hiram, King of Tyre, who was head of the Canaanites / Phoenicians, to provide the specialist workmen who could build an appropriate building for Ba`al-Yahweh, the God of the new kingdom of a united Israel and Judah." [20]

This raises two interesting points, the first confirms that a combined, Ba`al-Yahweh was worshipped in the early kingdom, and secondly that the Hebrew who's fathers had supposedly constituted the workforce that built the pyramids had insufficient knowledge and skills to construct the appropriate temples and had to call in specialist Canaanite expertise.

Ba`al of the Canaanites

In the ninth century BCE, Elijah denounced the widespread influence of the Ba`al cult. Ba`al was originally a Storm God worshiped by the Canaanites, and in agricultural forms by Hebrew peasants who sought to insure good harvests. Eighth century prophets like Hosea continued the struggles against the Ba`al cult since Ba`al worshippers were extremely tenacious. A 'Tyrian' Ba`al was introduced to the Holy Land by the royal dynasty, when Ahab married the Tyrian princess Jezebel. The cult spread from the royal centre in

Samaria to the provincial towns. Political pragmatism may have led the king to make an alliance with the local populous and this in turn resulted in the widespread idolatry noted in the Bible.

Until the 20ᵗʰ Century AD we knew very little about Ba`al or the religion of the Canaanites. In 1929 a French archaeological team led by F.A. Schaeffer and G. Chenet arrived in the North-western, Syrian, coastal town of Ras Esh Shamra (Cape Fennel) to investigate an ancient clay tablet that had been unearthed by a farmer ploughing his field. The team discovered that the entire field was a tel mound of the ancient Canaanite City of **Ugarit**. Many further discoveries were made in 1975 at nearby Tel Mardikh the ancient City of **Elba** including a virtual library of clay tablets. Many statuettes, drinking vessels and inscribed clay tablets, from around the 14ᵗʰ Century BCE, were discovered amongst the palace and temples excavated at Ugarit and the later finds at Elba. These ancient writings confirmed that Ba`al was certainly the chief deity of the Canaanite pantheon and was thought of as the ruler of the universe. In addition they detailed his female consort as **Asherah** (Anat). Having the same wife as YHWH again indicates a link between these composite deities. One tablet documented;

> "The virgin Anat turns to Ba`al as the heart of a cow goes out to her calf; as the heart of a ewe is to its lamb, so is the heart of Anat to Ba`al."

Discussing the Ugaritic tablets, **Lilinah biti-Anat** 1995-7 makes the following observations and conclusions;

> "I present here the most important of the mythological stories uncovered, the Myth of Ba`al. Seven tablets, written on both sides, five columns per side, contain the story. Unfortunately several were badly damaged during their almost 3200 years in the ground, so parts of the story are unclear. The language, however, is quite vivid, and in some cases very beautiful. Scholars now see that the writing style of the Torah is a continuity of that of the Canaanites, and certain expressions and descriptions are virtually identical, while some Canaanite Pagan vignettes have been rewritten in the Bible to support the newer religion. The language describing the deity YHWH shows that many of his characteristics are a combination of the Canaanite El and Ba`al." [21]

Because of the composite mixing and evolution of this God, Christians worshipping YHWH (as Jehovah) today are really following an altered version of past, pagan, Canaanite doctrine, just as the Hebrew patriarchs did. There is certainly sufficient evidence to support that this is the case. How many Christians do you think would feel comfortable with this situation? It seems also true that Asherah was a <u>Hebrew goddess</u> and not simply an adopted Canaanite entity as some modern Jewish commentators endeavour to make out. Many, many Bible passages relate to the destroying of the past Hebrew practice of worshipping in the high places with small shrines or tabernacles dotted throughout the countryside. Each site had its trees or sacred grove. In his book *Tempest & Exodus,* Ralph Ellis shines some new light on the goddess **Ashtoreth** (**Asherah**) and shows evidence of **Asher-t** being an Egyptian word for a burnt offering. He outlines a strange Egyptian ritual associated with the God Anubis, to which the followers of Moses would have been exposed, which involved the sacred tree of **Asher-t**, and showed the God Anubis talking through its branches. [22] Now **Aser-t** (without the 'h') actually means 'tree' in ancient Egyptian, which explains the sacred trees and groves associated with Asherah worship, but then the Egyptian word, **Asher** actually means 'fire'. Ancient Egyptian records are often recorded by way of these word puns (which was at that time thought to show the intelligence of the scribe) and in this case we have sacrifices to a God who then speaks from a sacred fire/tree. Ellis draws the obvious conclusion that this is the Biblical 'burning bush' of Moses and goes further to state that it is this practice that survived into recent times via the lights or candles on our Christmas trees. This strongly indicates that Asherah as a deity may have been originally transported from ancient Egypt by the followers of Moses.

Canaanite adulation was directed toward several Ba`al deities;

Ba`al Hammon, *Based on the Egyptian God Amon also a Carthaginian Sky-God*

**Ba`al Semed,** *Ox God of Agriculture. Separate entity from Ba`al Hammon.*

Ba`al Lebanon, *The Lord of the Cedars*

Ba`al Tsaphon, *The Lord of the North or northern districts*

Ba`al Addir, *The Lord of Help*

**Ba`al Kaneph,** *The Winged Ba`al*

Ba`al Moganim, *The Protector and Lord of the Shields*

Ba`al Marpah´a, *The Lord of Healing particularly battle wounds*

Ba`al Shamim, *The Lord of the Heavens*
In addition various forms of Ba`al were worshipped as adopted City Gods. **Ba`al-Hadad, Ba`al-Sidon, Ba`al-peor, Ba`al-Hazor** and **Ba`al-Hermon** are examples.

It is relevant to our research that in Canaan, Ba`al was originally an epithet applied to the Weather God (actually Storm God) *(Hadd or Haddu)*. The composite; **Ba`al-Hadad** mentioned above, shows that they were at times combined as one. The name *El Shaddai* also comes from the same root word as *Haddu* and we will come back to that soon. It is interesting to note in the Bible, a Syrian King named Ben Hadad, which means more or less *'Son of Ba`al Hadad'*.

2 Kings 8 : 7 *And Elisha came to Damascus; and Ben Hadad the king of Syria was sick; and it was told him, saying, The man of God is come hither.*

1 Kings 20 : 1 *And Ben Hadad the king of Syria gathered all his host together: and there were thirty and two kings with him, and horses, and chariots; and he went up and besieged Samaria, and warred against it.*

It is strange that Gideon, by Biblical accounts, a mighty man of God, was often called Jerub-ba`al for example: **Judges 8 : 35.** *Neither shewed they kindness to the house of Jerubbaal, namely, Gideon, according to all the goodness which he had shewed unto Israel.* It is also particularly strange that in the Bible we see a covenant made with Ba`al at the time of Gideon's death;

Judges 8 : 33 *And it came to pass, as soon as Gideon was dead, that the children of Israel turned again, and went a whoring after Baalim, and made Baalberith their god.*

Baalim is a plural word that covers the entire group of Ba`als and Ba`alberith means, *'God of the covenant'*, or more accurately, *'Ba`al of the covenant'* and no matter what you were taught, it becomes fairly apparent that the descendants of Gideon saw Ba`al as their God and made covenants with this deity. We read it from the Bible.

Judges 9 : 4 *And they gave him threescore and ten pieces of silver out of the house of Baalberith, wherewith Abimelech hired vain and light persons, which followed him.*

Judges 9 : 46 *And when all the men of the tower of Shechem heard that, they entered into an hold of the house of the God Berith. (This is Ba`alberith – the God* of the covenant)

Shechem is relevant here because we also find that oracles were using sacred trees, divining from bird calls or the rustling of the leaves of the 'oak of the augurs' amongst the sacred oaks and terebinth near Shechem. These trees were cut down in **Judges 9 : 48 & 49**. Way back in Genesis it is recorded that Jacob took the strange Gods of his household together with the amulet earrings and buried them under the oak or terebinth at Shechem.

Genesis 35 : 4 *And they gave unto Jacob all the strange Gods which were in their hand, and all their earrings which were in their ears; and Jacob hid them under the oak which was by Shechem.*

This continues to indicate that a very concerted effort was required over many years to wipe out polytheism, and finally arrive at the monotheistic worship of YHWH God. How YHWH actually became the dominant deity seems pretty 'hit and miss'. There appears no doubt that the practice of Ba`al worship (whether practised in Egypt or not and whether adopted from the Canaanites or not), was both widespread and of long duration amongst the early Hebrews. The following texts in the Bible substantiate this;

Jeremiah 11 : 12-14 *For according to the number of thy cities were thy Gods, O Judah; and according to the number of the streets of Jerusalem have ye set up altars to that shameful thing, even altars to burn incense unto Ba`al.*

Horsea 11 : 1-3 *As they called them, so they went from them: they sacrificed unto Baalim, and burned incense to graven images.*

Jeremiah 9 : 13-15 *But have walked after the imagination of their own heart, and after Baalim, which their fathers taught them:*

1 Samuel 12 : 10 *"We have abandoned YHWH and we have done service to the Ba`als and the Ashtorets."*

Recall that Baalim is simply the plural form of Ba`al embracing the various Ba`als that were worshipped. Ashtoreth is again confirmed as a fertility Goddess and consort of Ba`al. In addition there must have been a reason to 'abandon YHWH' *en mass* and do service to Ba`al. This is hard to ascertain when these Gods became merged in a composite deity.

2 Kings 17 : 16 : *And they left all the commandments of the Lord their God, and*

made them molten images, even two calves, and made a grove, and worshipped all the
host of heaven, and served Ba`al.

In the Ugaritic ritual texts, it becomes apparent that at that time Ba`al was considered an individual God held in opposition to YHWH. Nevertheless there was sufficient cross-over of identity to cause considerable confusion. The problems associated with this delineation are confirmed in the Bible;

1 Kings 18 : 21 *And Elijah came unto all the people, and said, How long halt ye*
between two opinions? If the Lord (YHWH) be God, follow him: but if Ba`al, then
follow him. And the people answered him not a word.

Soon after the great temple of YHWH was completed, we are told that Solomon reverted to Ba`al worship. It was said to be his foreign wives who led Solomon back to pagan worship and in **1 Kings 3 : 1**, one of these wives was the daughter of the Egyptian Pharaoh. We really must question the 'Wisdom of Solomon' in the following passages that certainly indicate that Solomon was not such a mighty man of God;

1 Kings 11 : 1-10 *But king Solomon loved many strange women, together with the*
daughter of Pharaoh, women of the Moabites, Ammonites, Edomites, Zidonians, and
Hittites: Of the nations concerning which the Lord said unto the children of Israel, Ye
shall not go in to them, neither shall they come in unto you: for surely they will turn
away your heart after their Gods: Solomon clave unto these in love. And he had seven
hundred wives, princesses, and three hundred concubines: and his wives turned away
his heart. For it came to pass, when Solomon was old, that his wives turned away his
heart after other Gods: and his heart was not perfect with the Lord his God, as was the
heart of David his father. For Solomon went after Ashtoreth the goddess of the Zidonians,
and after Milcom the abomination of the Ammonites. And Solomon did evil in the
sight of the Lord, and went not fully after the Lord, as did David his father. Then did
Solomon build a high place for Chemosh, the abomination of Moab, in the hill that is
before Jerusalem, and for Molech, the abomination of the children of Ammon. And
likewise did he for all his strange wives, which burnt incense and sacrificed unto their
Gods. And had commanded him concerning this thing that he should not go after other
Gods: but he kept not that which the Lord commanded.

Molech was a god with metal arms used for sacrificing children. A huge fire was lit within the metal god and parents threw their babies and children into the red-hot arms. This practice is mentioned in; **Leviticus 18 : 21**; **Leviticus 20 : 2-5** and **Jeremiah 32 : 35**.

As a side note, **Verse 3** above states that Solomon had 700 wives, an unspecified number of princesses and 300 concubines. If this number is correct and he spent a night with each in turn he would see each about once every three years. This is just part of the macho ancient Hebrew (more is better) psyche. The Bible also gives us an unusual insight with Solomon's son Rehoboam, King of Judah, discussing with his friends what actions he should take to ease burdens imposed on the constituents by his father. They suggested he show his strength, **1 Kings 12 : 10** and the message is repeated to make sure it is understood **2 Chronicles 10 : 10** with Rehoboam quoting to the people, *"My little finger is thicker than my father's loin"*. This traditional rendering of, "My little finger is thicker than my fathers (erect) penis" shows all the more cheek when it is remembered how renowned Solomon was for his sexual prowess.

We should note too the undertones of feminine seduction of the sons of Israel contained in the above verses. This is the way their conceptualization worked, with men 'defiling' themselves with 'unclean' women or men 'enticed' by these women who went 'whoring' after idols and false Gods. It is apparent in much of their writing and speaks volumes about their psyche. We see it in many passages;

> **Exodus 34 : 13** *"But ye shall destroy their altars, break their images, and cut down their groves: For thou shalt worship no other god: for the Lord, whose name is Jealous, is a jealous God: Lest thou make a covenant with the inhabitants of the land, and they go a whoring after their Gods, and do sacrifice unto their Gods, and one call thee, and thou eat of his sacrifice; And thou take of their daughters unto thy sons, and their daughters go a whoring after their Gods, and make thy sons go a whoring after their Gods."*

There is evidence that Solomon actually named cities and localities after Ba`al and despite the reverence of YHWH attributed to his father David, and in fact also to Solomon, it certainly appears that Solomon was a staid Ba`al worshipper and was never really committed to YHWH and only 'hedged his bets' with monotheism;

2 Chronicles : 8-6 *And Baal`ath, and all the store cities that Solomon had, and all the chariot cities, and the cities of the horsemen, and all that Solomon desired to build in Jerusalem, and in Lebanon, and throughout all the land of his dominion.*

Song of Solomon : 8-11 *Solomon had a vineyard at Ba`alhamon; he let out the vineyard unto keepers; every one for the fruit thereof was to bring a thousand pieces of silver.*

Worship of YHWH must have deteriorated quickly from the time of King David since we can see how lacklustre King Solomon's support really was. Then Rehoboam, King of Judah, the son of Solomon, actively promoted Ba`al worship;

1 Kings 12 : 28- 27 *Whereupon the king (Rehoboam) took counsel, and made two calves of gold, and said unto them (the people of Israel), It is too much for you to go up to Jerusalem: behold thy Gods, O Israel, <u>which brought thee up out of the land of Egypt</u>.*

Rehoboam clearly believed it was the plural Gods Ba`al and Ashtoreth that brought the Hebrew people out of Egypt. Jews and Christians can argue till they're blue in the face that this is not part of their past doctrine but these passages come straight from the King James Bible which is supposedly the same yesterday, today and forever. They are also backed up with archaeological and anthropological evidence and we are learning more and more about these things as more evidence comes to hand. Laurence Gardner drawing on the Jewish scholar Raphael Patai clarifies the evolution of YHWH a little in the following piece;

"In fact, all deities had at least two names - a proper name and an epithet. Just as Ashtoreth was also Asherah, so <u>El Elyon was called Jehovah</u>. Their son Hadd was generally known as Ba`al (a titular distinction meaning Lord), while his brothers Mot and Yamm were known as Gazir and Nahar, respectively. Yamm was defined as a 'judge' (an accuser) and was therefore a Satan, as were all judges. In the book of Judges (3:31), the Satan-judge Shamgar was said to be the son of Anath. In Samaria, north of Judaea, Ba`al was known as Baal-zebul (or Baal-zebub), meaning 'Elevated Lord' (2 Kings 1:2) but this title was maliciously corrupted in the Christian New Testament so that Beelzebub became classified as the 'chief of the devils'. [23]

Archaeologists tell us that in Ekron, of the Philistines, a magnificent temple was erected to Ba`al Zevuv *'God of the Fly'* and by the phonetic similarity there seems no doubt that the name Baalzebub must relate to this Philistine God, showing further that initially, the name or title had nothing whatever to do with Satan who was a later creation.

Ba`al vs. YHWH

We saw passages that showed that the son and grandson of King David certainly supported and worshipped other Gods and supported Ba`al worship. So was King David as solid in his support for YHWH as we were taught. When the holy man of God, King David, scored a decisive victory over his enemies, recorded in Chronicles, he appears to have credited his victory not to almighty God but to Ba`al. Now this is absolutely amazing but read the passage for yourself;

> **1 Chronicles 14 : 11** *Then David said, God hath broken in upon mine enemies by mine hand like the breaking forth of waters: therefore they called the name of that place Baalperazim.*

The King James Bible states that this means *" place of breaches"* however it is not difficult to believe an alternate translation as; *"place where Ba`al breaches."* It is hard for us to refute that the 'God' that King David credits with his victory, in this case, is most certainly Ba`al! Our research uncovered further interesting information about King David not being a total supporter of Almighty God and it is enlightening to find that he actually named his son **Baaliada** *(Man of Ba`al)*. This is pretty hard to overlook for a man of YHWH-God.

In David's army of 'mighties' there was a man with the similar name of **Baaliah** *(b`lyh)* which ironically translates as *'YHWH is my Ba`al'*. This is flabbergasting to think that David may not have been the mighty man of God we were led to believe but appears by the evidence to have worshipped Ba`al. In his defence it seems David must have acknowledged some connecting relationship between YHWH and Ba`al. Several locations like *Baalperazim* in his kingdom also record the patron God they were named after and it seems David made no attempt to have these names changed;

2 Samuel : 6-2 *And David arose, and went with all the people that were with him from Baale of Judah, to bring up from thence the ark of God, whose name is called by the name of the Lord of hosts that dwelleth between the cherubims.* There is an amazing parallel when the Lord instructs the Hebrew people on how he is to be addressed. Check it in your own Bible;

Hosea 2 : 16-17 *… and it shall be at that day, saith the Lord, that thou shalt call me Ishi; and shalt call me no more Baali.*

Now **Ishi** means *'My Husband'* and it becomes apparent that the Lord has previously been referred to as **Baali** which means *'My Ba`al'*. Lets get this straight, the Lord Himself is requesting that the Hebrew commence calling him 'Ishi' and no longer call him, **'my Ba`al'** which by the text, must have been their recent custom. This may be difficult to accept but it is even more difficult to dispute. The evidence is that this could only have occurred because El Elyon, Adonai and Ba`al are a composite, or in other words the very same multifaceted entity encompassing YHWH. If this is not so, then somebody better please explain to us why these passages are in the Holy Bible.

This concept also brings new meaning to the following verses;

Psalms 44 : 20-21 *If we had forgotten the name of our Elohim, or stretched out our hands to a foreign god, would not Elohim search this out? For He knows the secrets of the heart.*

Jeremiah 23 : 27 *Which think to cause my people to forget my name by their dreams which they tell every man to his neighbour, as their fathers have forgotten my name, for Ba`al.*

There has been some tampering here in Psalms since Elohim means (plural) Gods; then follows 'He' meaning (singular) God. In addition there are 'foreign Gods' additional to the Elohim Gods. In Jeremiah we again see Almighty God extremely concerned about his name being changed or forgotten, and with good reason it seems, since there are supposedly over 7,000 corruptions to God's name in the King James Bible. The real irony is, however, that the name of Ba`al has remained unchanged right to the present day.

Getting Rid of Ba`al

The ancient site of **Kuntillet `Ajrud**, in northern Sinai, contains unique drawings and inscriptions in ancient Hebrew and in Phoenician. It is a single-phase site dated archaeologically to ca. 800 BCE. This site is precisely in the path of the earlier exodus even though it is dated to some five hundred years later. Our research located the following interesting piece from Baruch Halpern about an inscription found there;

> "...a fragmentary plaster inscription at Kuntillet `Ajrud, where YHWH (and his Asherah) was the primary object of veneration, runs: "When El shines forth [from Teman?] ... the mountains are melted ... To bless Ba`al in the day of batt[le] [...] for the name of El in the day of [his] batt[le]." [24]

Halpern was from York University Toronto, and agrees with the conclusions we are drawing. He sums up the above piece with this conclusion;

> "Probably, El is the Ba`al in this text, both being identical with YHWH. Not coincidentally, the expression brk b`l (Ba`al bless) occurs at Kuntillet `Ajrud (Meshel 1978), again, given the distribution of divine names at the site, probably of YHWH, and if not, certainly of a subordinate." [25]

If we now reference the Catholic Encyclopaedia;

> "Names like Esbaal (I Par., viii, 33; ix, 39), Meribbaal (I Par., viii, 34; ix, 40), Baaliada (I Par., xiv, 7), given by Saul, Jonathan, and David to their sons, suggest that Yahweh was possibly spoken of as Ba`al. The fact has been disputed; but the existence of such a name as Baalia (i.e. "Yahweh is Ba`al", I Par., xii, 5) and the affirmation of Osee (ii, 16) are arguments that cannot be slighted. [26]

Not only is this piece enlightening it confirms our earlier conclusion that the Clergy are aware of these things but are quite selective in their teachings in line with the requirements of the Church. In the Columbia library we find the following;

> "The Ba`al cult penetrated Israel and at times led to syncretism. In the Psalms, Yahweh is depicted as Ba`al and his dwelling is on Mt. Zaphon (Zion), the locale of Ba`al in Canaanite mythology. The practice of sacred prostitution seems to have been associated with the worship of Ba`al in Palestine and the cult was vehemently denounced by the prophets, especially Hosea and Jeremiah." [27]

This is a bit close for comfort isn't it? We saw these passages earlier where YHWH is depicted as Ba`al in the Bible and now we find that his abode Mt Zaphon, is precisely the home of Ba`al in Canaanite mythology; it makes this line of evidence very credible indeed and strongly supports the conclusions we are drawing.

After the destruction of the temple in Jerusalem by the Babylonian King Nebuchadnezzar in 587 BCE, some Jews fled to Egypt and formed a colony at Ebb (Elephantine) at the first cataract of the Nile. [28] They built a temple there, which was clearly against the Hebrew law of centralization, outlined in Deuteronomy, and it is thought that their intent was to reproduce the Temple of Solomon. The extraordinary thing claimed about the Elephantine temple, however, was that this group of expatriated Jews worshiped **Yahweh** (as the great God of the sky) **and two other Gods,** one male and one female. This additional God-pair in their trinity format was actually **Ba`al** and **Ashtoreth.** In fact scholars were puzzled to find Ashtoreth recorded there as Anat-Yahu, which is the familiar name of the Canaanite goddess in a Cyprian inscription. [29] The Yahweh-ist Jews living elsewhere were apparently not happy with this development, for when the Elephantine temple was destroyed in the 5th century BCE, they would not lend any assistance to rebuild it. [30]

Our research has shown repeatedly that Yahweh and Ba`al were regularly considered to be one and the same. In our search for the monotheistic Almighty God we have uncovered several examples of the trinity. Even Strabo, who lived just before the traditional time of Christ (63-19 BCE) describes a Persian triad of Mithras, Selene (the Moon) and Aphrodite that existed within the one true God, Zeus. So here he gave us a Trinity within yet another God. The Egyptians had an early trinity of Atum, Shu and Tefnut with the latter two emanating from Atum although at a later time this God created another nine Gods (an ennead). As we saw earlier, the Christian church, post Constantine, have always insisted that there is a trinity with YHWH and over the years have included several different participants. It would seem reasonable that this alone negates the chance of any of them being correct. In the above passage, we are looking at yet another trinity of that time, on this occasion YHWH, Ba`al and Astoreth, and that probably flies in the face of all we were ever taught. Recall though that Astoreth was considered by some to be the wife of YHWH and by others to be the wife of Ba`al. In fact the entire trinity concept is hard to accept in light of another contradictory scripture that reads;

> **Deuteronomy 32 : 12**: *So the Lord alone did lead him, and there was no strange God with him.*

My investigative nature cautions however, that this passage would not be recorded this way if there had never been plural deities in this monotheistic religion. It could not have been an obvious, accepted, foregone conclusion that strange Gods did not exist at some time or the statement would be superfluous. It is outlining a situation where the Lord is alone and reinforces that on this occasion there were no strange Gods with him. So can we assume that at some time there were other strange Gods with him?

In the Psalms we find examples of an unusual composite name of **YHWH Elyon** used both adjectively and in parallel. (As previously stated, the King James Version translates YHWH as 'Lord' and Elyon as 'most high'.) This combination in early Bibles does however make it abundantly clear that YHWH and Elyon can be one and the same God as documented in the Christian Bible. The second quote shows that there were also other Gods for YHWH-Elyon to be exalted high above.

> **Psalms 47 : 2** *For YHWH Elyon is terrible; he is a great King over all the earth.*

> **Psalms 97 : 9** *For thou, YHWH Elyon art high above all the earth: thou art exalted far above all other Gods.*

> **Psalm 7 : 17** *I will praise YHWH according to his righteousness: and will sing praise to the name of Elyon.*

I think at this point the Christian monotheists may need a 'time out'. These passages are from their Bible and they certainly leave some questions to ask of the clergy and teachers of their doctrine, now don't they?

There is considerable evidence that the early Hebrew in the land of Canaan took over the indigenous pagan temples and it seems, at least for a time, they adopted much of the local religion. Even circumcision, which was also certainly practiced by the Egyptians, is believed to have been an ancient Canaanite practice that was adopted by the Hebrew. For example Abraham practiced circumcision in the land of Canaan, long before the Moses led Yahweh-ists could have brought the practice from Egypt. In his book *'The Religion of Israel'*, Professor G. W. Anderson states;

> *"Much that was borrowed from Canaanite religion was later swept away in various Yahweh-istic reform movements: but much remained as part of the religion of Israel."* [31]

There were many more serious attempts to wipe out Ba`al worship. The Bible tells us that Asa did have a partial removal of the idols, but they did not extend to the high sanctuaries;

> **1 Kings 15 : 11 – 15** *"And Asa did that which was right in the eyes of the Lord, as did David his father And he took away the sodomites out of the land, and removed all the idols that his fathers had made. And also Maachah his mother, even her he removed from being queen, because she had made an idol in a grove; and Asa destroyed her idol, and burnt it by the brook Kidron. But the high places were not removed: nevertheless Asa's heart was perfect with the Lord all his days."*

Once again the Bible is not an empirical source of historical information. On the subject of removing pagan sites of worship we find;

> **1 Kings 15 : 14**: Asa did not remove the high places.
> **2 Chronicles 14 : 2-32** He removed them.

And it doesn't stop there;

> **1 Kings 22 : 42-43** Jehoshaphat did not remove the high places.
> **2 Chronicles 17 : 42-43** He removed them.

The Yahweh-istic reforms imposed by Moses were not really successful either, since the following passage from Judges serves to indicate that the Hebrew people reverted to Ba`al worship yet again, well after the Exodus out of Egypt;

> **Judges 2 : 11-13** *And the children of Israel did evil in the site of the Lord, and served Ba`alim: and they forsook the Lord God of their fathers, which brought them out of the land of Egypt, and followed other Gods, of the Gods of the people that were around about them, and bowed themselves unto them, and provoked the Lord to anger. And they forsook the Lord, and served Ba`al and Ashtaroth.*

> **2 Kings 23 : 3** *And the king commanded Hilkiah the high priest, ... to bring forth out of the temple all the vessels that were made for Ba`al, and for the grove, and*

for all the host of heaven: and he burned them without Jerusalem in the fields of
Kidron, and carried the ashes of them unto Bethel.

After the captivity in Babylon the Hebrew returned to their homeland to discover that the Jews who had remained behind had taken 'strange' (Canaanite) wives and were worshipping Ba`al. To maintain the pure Hebrew pedigree, Ezra demanded that all non-Jewish wives and their children be cast out. Ezra wiped out the Ba`al worshippers and it seemed he used Ba`al as an excuse to separate Jewish men from wives and families. It had to be simply an excuse because we have seen repeatedly that Ba`al and YHWH were mostly considered one and the same entity or at the very least members of the same trinity and family unit. It seems that Ezra frowned on Ba`al worship but his real problem was failing to maintain the pure Jewish bloodline;

Ezra 10 : 10-12 *And Ezra the priest stood up, and said unto them, Ye have transgressed, and have taken strange wives, to increase the trespass of Israel. Now therefore make confession unto the Lord God of your fathers, and do his pleasure: and separate yourselves from the people of the land, and from the strange wives. Then all the congregation answered and said with a loud voice, as thou hast said, so must we do.*

This attitude was long lasting. The **Book of Jubilees** goes so far as to proscribe death by stoning for an Israelite who would give his daughter or sister to a Gentile, and the woman is to be burned to death. The **Testament of the Twelve** in the first century BCE concedes a stem from which *"shall grow a rod of righteousness to the Gentile to judge and save all that call upon the Lord"* suggestive both of eventual integration and Jesus' Gentile mission.

We should balance our thinking however because in the linage to King David there was Rahab the Canaanite and Ruth the Moabite. David's wife, Bathsheba, was the wife of Uriah the Hittite, and their son, Solomon, had wives from other nations round about Israel. Over time it became clear that those who joined Israel were also to be accounted as Israel, so eventually Israel ceased being exclusively the physical descendants of Jacob. These undescended Israelites were religious and political proselytes, but they became an equal partner with the physically descended Israelites. Under King David (of the tribe of Judah) the tribes were unified, and it was David

King David (of the tribe of Judah) the tribes were unified, and it was David who was able to totally subject all the previous occupants to Israel's rule. Thus Israel became defined as a kingdom. Sol Abrams presents an interesting commentary in a piece called 'Polytheism in Genesis: Ba`al and Ashtoreth vs. Yahweh';

> "Ezra's purging of Ba`al appeared to be complete. It was his wish to erase Ba`al completely from the Israelite past; however, the residuals in Genesis 1 and 3 continue to remind us not only of <u>Israel's polytheistic past</u> but the <u>Canaanite origins of Judaism</u>." [32]

This seems to be the point at which Ba`al became 'despised and hated' by the Hebrew nation. Formerly he and YHWH were one; however, from here on the records were changed to indicate a separation, and to reflect very poorly on Ba`al.

Sun Worship

We have previously looked at the 'heavenly host' who praise God and are mistakenly thought by many to be angels. Interestingly in the next passage we consider, the heavenly host are seen as competitors of YHWH and seem to indicate worship of the heavenly bodies. To understand the concern with timekeeping, astronomy and astrology the next passages make it clear that this involved worship of the sun, moon, planets and even the stars;

> **2 Kings 23 : 5** And he put down the idolatrous priests, whom the kings of Judah had ordained to burn incense in the high places in the cities of Judah, and in the places round about Jerusalem; them also that burned incense unto Ba`al, to the sun, and to the moon, and to the planets, and to all the host of heaven.

> **2 Kings 23 : 11-12**. And he took away the horses that the kings of Judah had given to the sun ... and burned the chariots of the sun with fire. And the altars that were on the top of the upper chamber of Ahaz, which the kings of Judah and Manasseh had made, did the king beat down, and cast the dust of them into the brook Kidron.

It is amazing what we find in the Bible when we dig for it! Regardless of how the Hebrew people sorted and recorded their early religious beliefs and pantheon of Gods, all this information was eventually filtered through the re-writing of Ezra, the manipulation of Rome, and then subjected to the editing of the Yahvists and other fanatical groups, before it went to

English translation and was made available for study in our Bibles. Although it is well documented fact that in the time of Constantine, Rome changed from Sol Invictus sun worship to Christianity as a state religion, it is not fully appreciated just how many concessions were made to these pagan sun worshippers. We have seen that the Hebrew themselves had much earlier certainly embraced Sun worship and this exposure would have aided this cause;

> **Ezekiel 8 : 16** *And he brought me into the inner court of the Lord's house, and, behold, at the door of the temple of the Lord, between the porch and the altar, were about five and twenty men, with their backs toward the temple of the Lord, and their faces toward the east; and they worshipped the sun toward the east.*

> **Jeremiah 8 : 2** *And they shall spread them before the sun, and the moon, and all the host of heaven, whom they have loved, and whom they have served, and after whom they have walked, and whom they have sought, and whom they have worshipped: they shall not be gathered, nor be buried; they shall be for dung upon the face of the earth.*

Most Christians would have a lot of trouble believing that many of the early Christian Church fathers actually worshipped Jesus as a 'Sun God'. Jesus was said to walk in the light and stated that he was the 'light of the world' and this appears to have been taken literally where he was conceptualized as a Sun-God. There is certainly sufficient evidence to support this;

- Mani a leader of the third century Christian sect called Manicheans was eventually put to death and flayed as a heretic by the Roman Church. His doctrine for many years taught a huge band of followers, *"Krist is the glorious intelligence which the Persians call Mithras.... His residence is on the sun."* [33]

- Saint Augustine a stalwart of the Catholic faith was formerly a Manichean for many years, and throughout his life believed that *"Jesus Christ resided in the Sun"*. [34]

- Many of the early presbyters taught that the sun was *'Jesus Christ driving his chariot across the sky'*. [35]

- The Christian Bishop of Troy stated that he had always secretly prayed to *"Jesus Christ, in the Sun"*. [36]

- The Sabbath was changed from Saturday (Sabato the Sabbath) to Sunday (the Sun's Day) to appease the Roman, Mithras, **Sol Invictus** sun worshippers who adopted the Christian faith.
- The Christmas feast celebrating Jesus' birth was changed from its likely **1st March** and aligned with the winter solstice of the sun, the pagan - Mithras feast date of **25th December**.

The Egyptians on the other hand were known sun worshippers with Ra (Re) and later 'The Aten'. The Hebrew tribes were sun worshippers as shown above from the Christian Bible, and the Romans were known Sol Invictus sun worshippers. From the evidence, Jesus Christ is considered by many scholars to this day to have been a 'Sun-God' deity and somehow from this the Christian religion evolved.

"What has occurred over the centuries is that, irrespective of the Bible texts, Jehovah has been sidestepped into a wholly singular identity, the thoroughly non-historical identity of the 'One God', which prevails today. In this context (outside the more traditional esoteric circles) Jehovah has been divested of his wife, his family and fellow Gods, to be left alone in a wilderness of enigma that no one has ever truly understood. There are numerous references in the Old Testament to the 'Gods' (the Elohim) and to the 'sons of the Gods' (the bene ha-elohim), and these seemingly anomalous entries have caused their own confusion through the years because of Jehovah's perceived isolation."

Laurence Gardner.

CHAPTER TEN

"GOD" IS NOT GOD'S NAME

"God is ineffable; all the rest is man's cleverness."

A Rabbinical Expression.

"God" is not God's name

A King James commentary states, *"The actual name that God is called, holds an important key to the understanding of the doctrine of God."* Despite this, modern Bibles including the King James have gone ahead and substituted the words "God", "Lord" or "Almighty" for almost every variation of Gods name, effectively obliterating the original message of multiple Gods. This acts to contradict the commentary above and only a very flexible doctrine could possibly accommodate the many names used for God. The Yahvists are guilty too, as we have seen, of openly and deliberately vandalizing the original scriptures by substituting YHWH (now Jehovah) for any name of God mentioned.

Origen (*Origenes Adamantius*) one of the most distinguished of the fathers of the early Church, was born, probably at Alexandria, about 185 AD, and died at Caesarea around 251 AD. He was one of the most learned men of his time and received from his father, Leonides, a most complete teaching of the Bible, and was schooled in other elementary studies. From the writings of Origen we find mention of various known names of God from the Bible plus Gnostic names coupled to the names of Gods of ancient Egypt. Origen insists that they are all one and the same God;

> *"For we too, desired both to learn and set forth these things, in order that sorcerers might not, under pretext of knowing more than we, delude those who are easily carried away by the glitter of names. And I could have given many more illustrations to show that we are acquainted with the opinions of these deluders, and that we disown them,*

as being alien to ours, and impious, and not in harmony with the doctrines of true Christians, of which we are ready to make confession even to the death. It must be noticed, too, that those who have drawn up this array of fictions, have, from neither understanding magic, nor discriminating the meaning of holy Scripture, thrown everything into confusion; seeing that they have borrowed from magic the names of Ialdabaoth, and Astaphaeus, and Horaeus, and from the Hebrew Scriptures him who is termed in Hebrew Iao or Jah, and Sabaoth, and Adonaeus, and Eloaeus. Now the names taken from the Scriptures are names of one and the same God; which, not being understood by the enemies of God, as even themselves acknowledge, led to their imagining that Iao was a different God, and Sabaoth another, and Adonaeus, whom the Scriptures term Adonai, a third besides, and that Eloaeus, whom the prophets name in Hebrew Eloi, was also different." [1]

It may come as a surprise to find the Egyptian God Horus (Horaeus) and the Gnostic Ialdabaoth also represented here alongside the Biblical names of God. This just may support the Lord's statement in the Bible that he is one God alone and "there is none else". But doesn't this mess up the concept of the trinity?

Corruption

Now that we have some appreciation that Almighty God evolved as a composite of a number of pagan entities, and was included in a plethora of different trinities, we should look at the way the records were documented in the books that became included in the Bible. It may be surprising to note that the name YHWH, supposedly dating from the time of Moses, was not utilized at all in Genesis in original Bibles; recall that Moses supposedly wrote Genesis and also that this name for God was derived by a letter game from passages in Exodus 14. As we encountered earlier, the Biblical scriptures are divided by scholars into the sectarian groups of the various writers. 'Yahvism' was but one of three major Jewish sects of the day. Each had a different agenda and different views about God (something like denominations do today). The delineation was;

    1. **Priestly**   2. **Elohist**   3. **Yahvist.**

Neither the Priestly scribes nor the Elohist scribes used the name "YHWH" anywhere in their writings. The Yahvist group however, quite incorrectly, inserted "YHWH" into their scriptures as early as **Genesis 2 : 4** and we must contend with this vandalism today. As we have seen, the Bible has been altered repeatedly by various groups and no longer holds its original information. Blindly following it as the unchanging 'Word of God' is folly in the extreme and this attitude doesn't help anyone. The original names of Elohim, God of the Fathers, El, El Elyon, El Shaddai, Adonai, and others, were deliberately replaced with the concocted name YHWH, by the Yahvist scribes as they copied the ancient texts. They were firmly on a mission, since they believed it was the will of their God to promote the newly devised name, and hence they proudly and openly corrupted the original manuscripts. The name YHWH, they felt, would maintain a mystery about God as well as being a device to hide the previous pagan worship of the Hebrew people recorded in the scriptures. This they openly admitted. Today it is very difficult to know how many verses were changed and precisely which ones; and to determine what original name it replaced. The King James Bible too is notorious for its translation of God's name to "Lord" or "God Almighty" or the incorrect "Jehovah", and we lose much informa-tion in this mistranslation. This of course exacerbated the prior damage done by the Yahvists. As a result the following passage tends to lose all meaning;

> **Exodus 6 : 2-3** *"And God spake unto Moses, and said unto him, I am the Lord. And I appeared unto Abraham, unto Isaac and unto Jacob, by the name of God Almighty, but by my name Jehovah was I not known to them."*

A more correct translation should read; *"And God spake unto Moses, and said unto him, I am your God. And I appeared unto Abraham, unto Isaac and unto Jacob by the name of El Elyon, but by my new name YHWH was I not known to them."*

This Bible passage goes all the way towards supporting the notion that Almighty God **YHWH** (Jehovah) certainly developed from **El Elyon** (Ba`al). Now once they commenced promoting the wrathful YHWH, the Yahvists worked hard to have the Hebrew people totally scorn Ba`al. These were the same folks who had previously, vehemently adored him. The scribes showed their abhorrence of that name in the use of the pejorative name Baalzebub

(Beelzebub) for Satan. They are scathing in their denouncement of the pagan Ba`al and the passages **2 Kings 10 : 18-28** show a totally treacherous, unscrupulous and ruthless Jehu, involved in the final massacre of the Ba`al worshippers. Thus Jehu finally destroyed Ba`al out of Israel.

It seems that in the Christian Bible, all traces of foolishness and evil in the Godhead were eventually transposed onto Ba`al and Mastema and later to Satan. Thus Ba`al went from widespread early acceptance, to be finally recorded in the Bible as the epitome of evil. Are we to believe that he was so despised by the scribes because, like Mastema, he was considered an evil characteristic that YHWH was trying to control, subdue or exorcise?

The New Wrathful God

The Exodus occurred many years after the time of Abraham when the new God YHWH approached Moses and asked him to lead the people out of Egypt. Moses was noted as a staunch supporter of monotheism, and worked hard with the Hebrew people he led, to constrain them to worship YHWH only. Now YHWH represented a new era of rule by a secretive God who wished to remain anonymous for the time being. In fact he explained that because of his uncontrollable wrath he could not travel with the followers of Moses on the Exodus as he would probably end up killing them. This sounds like a psychopathic entity who could not possibly be the loving God of the New Testament; he is totally out of control. In fact we could visualize him consuming copious quantities of black coffee, eating valium like minties and badly in need of professional help. He probably could have benefited from yoga training or at least some anger suppression techniques! Read it and see;

> **Exodus 33 : 1-5** *Then the Lord said to Moses, "Leave this place, you and the people you brought up out of Egypt, and go up to the land I promised on oath to Abraham, Isaac and Jacob, saying, 'I will give it to your descendants.' I will send an angel before you and drive out the Canaanites, Amorites, Hittites, Perizzites, Hivites and Jebusites. Go up to the land flowing with milk and honey. <u>But I will not go with you, because... I might destroy you on the way</u>." When the people heard these distressing words, they began to mourn and no one put on any ornaments. For the Lord had said to Moses, Tell the Israelites, 'You are a stiff-necked people. <u>If I were to go with you even</u>*

for a moment, I might destroy you.'

Clergy never mention it but Moses' first question would have to have been, *"Well who on Earth are Abraham, Isaac and Jacob?"* The only way he would have heard of them is if they were in fact Hyksos Pharaohs based in Egypt as we speculated. Next Moses might have questioned just why this God had chosen the Hebrew and why he was so down on Canaanites, Amorites, Hittites, Perizzites, Hivites and Jebusites sufficiently to want to kill them and steal their land. At this point Moses and his followers just might have decided that they weren't bloodthirsty and racist warmongers and didn't want to play God's nasty little game. At the very least I feel sure Moses would have told YHWH;

> *"Well to be perfectly honest; with your attitude and personality disorder, we are sort of glad you aren't coming along with us. Actually, you're were never even invited".*

The Exodus is believed to have taken place not long after the Egyptian Pharaoh *Akhenaten* had introduced the monotheism of his God, 'The Aten' in that country. This was a radical change after some 3,000 years of Egyptian polytheism. Re (Ra) was the **Sun God** and along with Amun and Horace were main deities of devotion. To differentiate from Re and to explain the

Nefertiti (on the left) the wife of Akhenaten (right) was the High Priestess of the Aten.

omnipresence of his invisible God to the unlearned among his subjects, Pharaoh Akhenaten showed 'The Aten' as the actual **rays of the sun** ending in tiny hands that embraced all. He made his wife Nefertiti the High Priest of Aten and devoted much of his time to the monotheistic worship of this God. It is hard to accept that the monotheism of Akhenaten and the monotheism of Moses just happened to take place at the same time and in the same place; there simply has to be a link. It would appear likely that it was the Egyptian God, 'The Aten' who became the newly created YHWH. Reading the following Biblical passage, it would seem logical, due to the huge numbers of people involved in the exodus, and because of the time frame, that the main Egyptian God that was relocated to the Holy Land just had to be 'The Aten' with the relocating done by the followers of Moses.

One of the charges of Ezra was that Egyptian ways were still followed in the holy land after the captivity;

Ezra 9 : 1 *Now when these things were done, the princes came to me, saying, The people of Israel, and the priests, and the Levites, have not separated themselves from the people of the lands, doing according to their abominations, even of the Canaanites, the Hittites, the Perizzites, the Jebusites, the Ammonites, the Moabites, the Egyptians, and the Amorites.*

This spells out pretty clearly that the confusion and convolution of various religions was very real for these Hebrew people. We were led to believe that they had seen so much evidence for the existence and support of their God that a choice would be easy for them. Not so, they probably had seen very little and relied on charismatic leaders like Moses who told them what he had supposedly seen. This is why they found it so difficult to pledge total allegiance to this strange and angry new God YHWH.

An amazing fact to consider is that the Egyptians had a special sacred name for their moon God **Thoth;** the 'three times great' that was in fact **Yaheweh**. [2] The Egyptian and Hebrew languages are both recorded without the vowels so both this Egyptian name Yaheweh and the Biblical Yahweh would be recorded YHWH. With such an obvious similarity to the God they brought from Egypt in that precise timeframe it seems entirely plausible to assume a connection even without the supporting evidence. This may well be the prototype of the name YHWH and would go a long way towards explaining the new name of God that came out of Egypt.

Now these things are a part of history, they are real; even the Bible records these events as happening, yet the laity of the Church today have trouble appreciating the evolution of the doctrine they now hold as unchanging and irrefutable. We must remove the 'magic wand' theory and observe the formation of the Christian religion to see how happenstance it really was. We should further observe aspects of the various pagan deities that added to the make up and evolution of the Christian God worshipped today.

Making Sense of it all

There are more than sufficient verses quoted above to indicate that Ba`al worship was not easy for the Hebrew people to give up and we also noted the merging of deities plus several composites in addition to the different trinities. Thus it seems strange that we were told only of a trinity of God the Father, Jesus the Son and the Holy Spirit. No one ever told us of this triple personality of El Elyon/Ba`al/Adonai. The Church cannot argue because right from **Genesis 1 : 26** *And God said, 'Let us make man in our image…"* we saw indications of a plural Godhead, long before the trinity existed. Jesus and the Holy Ghost were not known in the Old Testament; in fact the concept of the Trinity was only established at the Council of Nicaea in **325 AD** and this was also the time when Jesus was deified. The fact that in the early Bible the plural word 'Elohim' (Gods) was frequently used, the only plausible solution is that this early nomenclature referred to the same flesh and blood 'Sky-Gods' documented by the Sumerians and Egyptians. These were the Anunnaki, and ENLIL the son of their leader Anu became known as El Elyon as seen above. There had to be various rival dynasties and allegiances within the Anunnaki, and these were the competing Gods.

The Sumerian and Egyptian records are further supported by similar if not identical stories from China and India. I propose that it is these Anunnaki 'Sky-Gods' who visited Earth exactly as recorded and were the original plural Gods of the Old Testament who met with Abraham and looked just exactly like men. I propose that YHWH was an Anunnaki God who introduced himself to Moses prior to challenging Marduk in Babylon for divine supremacy. I further propose that the Hebrew in Egypt learnt these things; then during the captivity in Babylon for 70 years absorbed the Sumerian records and adopted this message into their own religion and scriptures. Each of these Anunnaki sons of the great father God Anu had many aliases and showed very human-like qualities as they jockeyed for ruling positions and were involved in various family feuds.

Recall that Ashtoreth is mentioned 40 times in the Bible. Now Ashtoreth was also a documented member of the Anunnaki. The Assyrians recorded ENLIL as *Ashur*, stating that he was the consort of *Atirat* which was their name for the 'Queen of Heaven' Ashtoreth. Now ENLIL's wife was the great lady Ninlil so accordingly Ashtoreth became associated with her. It seems that ENLIL was called Ilu Kur-gal, Ashur, Amurru and El Elyon. [3] Similarly his brother EN.KI was called Ea and 'the Serpent' and was very likely the serpent who spoke to Eve, trying to help his creations in the Garden of Eden, and was of course nothing to do with Satan who did not exist at that time. EN.KI's symbol was the entwined serpents still used by our medical profession today. This in part represents the helical spiral of DNA that he utilized to bind the essence of the Anunnaki onto primitive man to create the hybrid Homo Sapiens Sapiens race precisely as recorded by the Sumerians.

So – Who is Almighty God?

After reading earlier, Professor Anderson's statements about the Hebrew borrowing from the Canaanite religion and these parts being later partially swept away in Yahweh-istic reform, we need to now read a bit further. In the same passage we studied earlier;

> Exodus 6 : 2 *"And God spake unto Moses, and said unto him, I am your God. 3. And I appeared unto Abraham, unto Isaac, and unto Jacob, by the name of El Elyon, but by my new name YHWH was I not known to them. 4. And I have also established my covenant with them, to give them the land of Canaan, the land of their pilgrimage, wherein they were strangers.*

> *5. And I have also heard the groaning of the children of Israel, whom the Egyptians keep in bondage; and I have remembered my covenant. 6. Wherefore say unto the children of Israel, I am the Lord, and I will bring you out from under the burdens of the Egyptians, and I will rid you out of their bondage, and I will redeem you with a stretched out arm, and with great judgments. 7. And I will take you to me for a people and I will be to you a God."*

These passages show fairly clearly that the original proto-Jews; Abraham, Isaac and Joseph (and obviously their descendants) had been given the land of Canaan by ENLIL, El Elyon (Ba`al). The second part, from verse 5, then shows that a new God entity (now as YHWH) is going to take the next step and now lead the children of Israel out of Egypt and become their God. There are no arguments here; it makes perfect sense that the ENLIL, El

Elyon (Ba`al) worshipping recipients of the land of Canaan are to be joined at some future time by the YHWH worshippers that Moses is to lead out of Egypt. This is a new entity introducing himself, certainly aligned to, but not exactly, a previously worshipped entity. We can identify something unusual hidden in the last part of the above passage. There is something different about this God or he would have no reason to say, "*And I will take you to me for a people <u>and I will be to you a God</u>.*" We saw earlier that he is a wrathful God to the extent that he cannot accompany them in the Exodus for fear he will kill them. So how do we identify this cranky YHWH, the same Almighty God worshipped to this day?

Let's look at something truly amazing. From the Sumerian texts, ENLIL had a son named **ISH.KUR,** also known as **Adad** or in Hebrew, **Hadad**. [4] Now the name ISH.KUR translates as *'God of the Mountain Lands'* thought by Alford to represent the Andes Mountains in Central America where those ancient records indicate a similar God had been dwelling. I maintain that the translation 'the mountain lands' could also apply to the same word used for the pyramids of Egypt where they were thought of and recorded as mountains. The exploits of ISH.KUR youngest son of ENLIL, recorded by the Sumerians, show him to be a somewhat rebellious and erratic Storm God and there are examples of his displays of wrath, utilizing storms and tempests to wreak havoc. In fact he was actually noted as an emotional God with a violent streak. [5] If this is starting to sound familiar it is because the Genesis record names God as El Shaddai, which means *'God of the Mountains'.* This God we saw earlier was actually one and the same with Ba`al. We also saw earlier that Ba`al was shown to have the name *Hadad* and in places was worshipped as Ba`al-Hadad. Now going full circle, this name Hadad is the Hebrew version of ISH.KUR and the name this same God was called.

This means father and son Gods ENLIL (El Elyon) and ISH.KUR (El Shaddai) were respectively the God of Abraham and the God of Moses; a father and son dynasty within the same Godhead. The consort of ENLIL and mother of ISH.KUR was Ashtoreth the 'Queen of Heaven', fully explaining this early trinity. This is not easy to refute; recall this Queen of Heaven is documented in your Bible a full 40 times and is shown as a

358

member of the Trinity. She is in fact the mother of the God ISH.KUR, the son of El Elyon. El Elyon and El Shaddai are likewise recorded in the Bible.

The Anunnaki were said to be based in the areas of Palestine and Sumer so this seems to further prove that YHWH was the identity of ENLIL's son ISH.KUR who wished to remain secretive about his identity until he returned home, possibly from exile, with a support group consisting of the followers of Moses, to challenge his cousin Marduk, the son of EN.KI who was the ruling God in this area at that time. There was a change of God within the same trinity and the Bible and the Sumerian records both spell it out, however we were never told about it and never understood what had happened, even when the changed personality made it apparent.

Note too that 'KUR' was a Sumerian term for a cone shape, precisely in line with the cone shaped depictions of Anunnaki transport vehicles, although they also appear to be 'mountains'. 'KUR' also depicts an iron furnace, indicating that ISH.KUR was initially recorded as a metalworking 'Smith-God'. This is identical to the traits of Adonai who was known as Q're Adonai; the 'Q're' meaning 'furnace' or referring to the working of metal. Now we saw that the traits of Adonai were taken on by Yahweh who was similarly seen as a 'Smith-God'. We can find further confirmation in the fact that Yahweh was also known as *Elath-Iahu* the Kenite 'Smith-God'. In fact the Bible gave us a clue to this in the following passage;

1 Kings 4 : 29-34 *And God gave Solomon wisdom and understanding exceeding much… and he spake three thousand proverbs: and his songs were a thousand and five. And he spake of trees, from the cedar tree that is in Lebanon even unto the hyssop that springeth out of the wall: he spake also of beasts, and of fowl, and of creeping things, and of fishes. And there came of all people to hear the wisdom of Solomon, from all kings of the earth, which had heard of his wisdom.*

Why would the wise Solomon speak about trees? Well the hyssop was the tree of the Winter solstice known as **'IA'**. The cedar was the tree of the Summer solstice known as **'HU'**. Together they form the divine name **IAHU**. This was another secret name of YHWH, yet it somehow existed from more ancient times in Egypt where around 2630 BCE it referred to the God Set. Horus the son of Osiris who overcame his uncle Set was called the *Calf Iahu.* [6]

This provides further confirmation and if we have not discovered that **ISH.KUR** the son of ENLIL is actually **YHWH**, the Almighty God still worshipped today, then coincidence has certainly been stretched to a most abnormal degree.

"The foolish, thinking in their heart that if they confess, 'We are Christians', in word only but not in power, while giving themselves over to ignorance, to a human death, not knowing where they are going nor who Christ is, thinking that they will live, when they are really in error - hasten towards the principalities and the authorities. They fall into their clutches because of the ignorance that is in them. For if only words which bear testimony were affecting salvation, the whole world would endure this thing and would be saved."

"The Testimony of Truth" from the Nag Hammadi corpus.

CHAPTER ELEVEN

WHERE DO WE GO FROM HERE?

Proverbs 14 : 15-16 "The simple believe everything and acquire folly;
the prudent look where they are going and are crowned with knowledge."

Holy Bible KJV.

Secrets

With the turbulent years that followed in the Promised Land after the death of Moses, we saw the Hebrew people involved in the worship of a multitude of Gods (particularly Ba`al). Much later they found an ancient book containing the Law of Moses. This book certainly showed how far their doctrine had departed from the original;

> **2 Chronicles 34 : 14** *And when they brought out the money that was brought into the house of the Lord, Hilkiah the priest <u>found a book of the law</u> of the Lord given by Moses.*

> **2 Kings 22 : 8** *And Hilkiah the high priest said unto Shaphan the scribe, I have found the book of the law in the house of the Lord. And Hilkiah gave the book to Shaphan, and he read it.*

> **2 Kings 22 : 13** *Go ye, enquire of the Lord for me, and for the people, and for all Judah, concerning the words of this book that is found: for great is the wrath of the Lord that is kindled against us, <u>because our fathers have not hearkened unto the words of this book</u>, to do according unto all that which is written concerning us.*

All were amazed at the mysterious things it contained. This means they had deviated far from the things Moses brought out of Egypt or they would not have been in awe of the teachings in the newly discovered ancient book.

Later during the captivity, the Hebrew were exposed to all the wonders of Babylon and ancient Sumerian records like the epic of Gilgamesh and the Enuma elish. Many worked as scribes in the libraries and must have passed on what they read and discovered, to the other Hebrew households. This continued for around 70 years. After their return from the captivity, when they discovered that their scriptures had been burned, the leader and priest Ezra took five scribes and re-wrote the Old Testament's 24 Books for the general populous and an additional 70 secret books for the 'worthy and the initiated'. We aren't told if the Hebrew still had the ancient work of Moses or if Ezra actually worked from scratch. It is likely that some secrets were lost in that burning or became changed and in fact new ones substituted. This could well have included the adding of some of the amazing things recently learned in Babylon. We don't know if Ezra was writing entirely new material or trying to preserve the fidelity of the Moses work. We might also wonder; where are those seventy secret books now? It is unlikely that they simply disappeared and it seems more likely that they became part of the Gnostic works or the scriptures held by the Essenes or even were amongst those works later claimed to be heretical. Are some of them in the Vatican library still?

In a much later time at the formation of the Roman Church, Constantine concentrated hard on ridding the world of all scriptural works that did not fit his new proto-orthodoxy; in like manner the Muslims wanted to destroy all scripture but the Koran. The Christians, the Romans and the Muslims all took a hand in destroying the greatest receptacle of human learning in the Great Library of Alexandria, precisely where most 'mystery schools' existed. Later during the Inquisition all books considered 'heretical' were burned or seized by the Vatican. We even find a record of the burning of magical books in New Testament times;

Acts 19 : 19 *Many of them also which used curious arts brought their books together, and burned them before all men: and they counted the price of them, and found it fifty thousand pieces of silver.*

The likelihood of the genuine message left for us by the Gods; actually filtering through to us today, after all this turbulence, is pretty remote and man has worked hard to destroy any traces of that original message. Even if we were to find the actual original message we would not be in a position to recognise it because it is so far outside our twisted thoughts of pseudo-orthodoxy. Like the Cinderella 'glass slippers' we prefer to hear about virgins having babies and men walking on water and raising the dead. We have not pushed our clergy and our teachers to tell us the truth. We were lied to and have accommodated it; we lapped it up and went back for more.

To this day Christians try to gain everlasting life out of their Bibles and we discovered earlier that there is no clear scriptural format to achieve this within the Bible. In fact it is a convoluted mess, and parishioners have only the method of individual clergy's personal choice, to lead the way. The original method of gaining eternal life is no longer recorded in our English Bibles, they have been edited, watered down and vandalised, re-written and changed to the point of being virtually useless. The Egyptian 'Book of the Dead' makes it clear that many secrets and mysteries were passed to man by the Sky-Gods who had the power of resurrection and these secrets became the basis for all the ancient mystery schools. Watered down versions are found today in the ceremonies of groups like the Masonic order who readily admit that the original secrets were lost and they are operating on alternate secrets. The Masonic literature also makes it clear that their doctrine originated in ancient Egypt. The awe of the Egyptian mystics is still documented in the Bible;

Exodus 7 : 11 *Then Pharaoh called in his wise men and magicians and they did the same thing with their secret arts.*

Exodus 7 : 22 *But again the magicians of Egypt used their secret arts, and they, too, turned water into blood.*

Exodus 8 : 7 *But the magicians were able to do the same thing with their secret arts. They, too, caused frogs to come up on the land.*

Exodus 8 : 18 *Pharaoh's magicians tried to do the same thing with their secret arts, but this time they failed.*

It seems that a compelling reason why Moses initiated the early Jewish religion, was as a vehicle to preserve the secret information of the mystery schools of Egypt. These secrets were documented within the pages of the Hebrew Holy Books claimed to have been written by Moses. The Torah was of course later hi-jacked to become part of the Old Testament in the

Christian Bible. The proof of these secrets is that much of our Bible's message comes from the pages of the Egyptian 'Book of the Dead' and from the records of the Sky-Gods in the 'Enuma elish' of ancient Sumer. The secrets and the message were real but became so muddled and convoluted that now there is little relevance at all. Man no longer knows who the plural Gods of the Old Testament were (or are). He doesn't know for certain when Jesus lived and it certainly looks like he was not the Son of God and was likely never crucified. It seems probable that the capital punishment of Antigonus the last King of the Jews, who was scouged and then crucified was allegorically credited to Jesus. Since we have lost the keys, we can no longer unlock the meanings and the purpose for the requirements, ceremonies and procedures of the Christian Religion and the attaining of everlasting life has become a fairly hollow promise. The spiritual master G. I. Gurdjieff (1877-1949) documented;

> *"The Christian Church is a school, concerning which people have forgotten it is a school. Imagine a school where the teachers give lectures and perform explanatory demonstrations without knowing that these are lectures and demonstrations; and where the pupils or simply the people who come to the school take these lectures and demonstrations for ceremonies, or rites or 'sacraments', or for magic. This would approximate to the Christian Church of our times."* [1]

The secrets are virtually lost, the message is virtually lost and the procedure for gaining eternal life is also virtually lost for the church-going public. We no longer understand the words and the requirements as the religion has become a 'watered down' 'play acting' attempt to replicate what once was. If we believe otherwise we are ignoring the facts; the vandalism of the scriptures, the documented evolution of the Godhead, the history of God's people and we are actually kidding ourselves. The only way left to step beyond the myth and rediscover the secrets is through education and re-evaluating what the ancient Sumerians and ancient Egyptians left us, because that is where the message originated. We must return to the source.

Worth noting too is that doctrines of empowerment are among the very things that have been removed from our modern Bibles; karma, reincarnation, astrology and the use of white powder gold. They were all there and tragically these have been replaced with doctrines of fear; God's wrath, the Devil, eternal damnation and hellfire, deliberately substituted with only one purpose in mind; to give power to the Bishops and ultimately to the Church. There is no reference in the original Greek New Testament scriptures that can be truly translated "eternal damnation" or "hell". If hell was such an important part of God's eternal doctrine surely it would have heavy mention in the original scriptures. In its absence we can assume nothing less than the fact that it was an introduced threat for no other purpose than controlling man. It is literally a man-made hell. The true question arising for humanity today is one of empowerment. **"Knowledge is power"** and until recent times the masses have quite effectively been kept in the dark.

What About Jesus?

Of major concern to us in this work is the fact that the life of Jesus is pretty much a blank canvas, allegoric certainly, with virtually no documentation outside of the New Testament. We saw that Jesus went to Egypt and there learned mysteries, most likely in Alexandria and he possibly even attended ceremonies in the Great Pyramid.

The Bible would have us believe that he went there to escape Herod's 'slaughter of the innocents'; an event that history says never even happened. We cannot reasonably assume that he just happened to get caught up in a mystery school and it is far more likely Jesus travelled to Egypt specifically to gain knowledge in such a school and gain the 'panther' level or to exercise his 'Pendragon' status.

Why Doesn't God make Contact?

We were told that the Godhead of Genesis created the World in 6 days then rested on the 7th. When Jesus left he went to prepare a place for us and promised to return. So what is a reasonable time to wait, another 7 days? Let's assume he is preparing something really spectacular; that will take him maybe ten times as long as creating the entire World, say 70 days. Hang on; he's been gone for 2000 years. Hasn't somebody twigged that something is wrong.

God visited Abraham, Moses and Solomon. Jesus spent at least 33 years on Earth and now we see total absence for almost 2000 years. If God is no respecter of persons why doesn't he visit us today to at least give the Bible an update? Why did he lavish so much time and effort on his chosen Semitic race, around 1350 – 500 BCE and we have not heard from him since. He visited the ancients, wouldn't it make sense to drop in now and again, just to confirm he is still with us, and has things under control. Instead, we have been totally abandoned. This is likely the longest gap ever without a visit in history. I'm sure you will agree this is a fairly strange way to rule or to conduct a relationship with his people.

So why did God have to depart at all? If in fact the Gods abide on the planet Nibiru (Planet X) and if it is on a 3600 year orbit as calculated by Sitchin, then at least it could be credible in this situation that the Gods have left and have promised to 'return again'. It seems the only possible reason 'God' would need to depart with the promise to 'come again'. It just may take 3600 years!

Putting it all together

It seems apparent that following his initiation Jesus believed (out of compassion for his fellow man) that all men deserved the right to share in the knowledge about eternal life left for us by the Sky-Gods; knowledge that could lead to immortality. Not just the initiated but also the common man.

He always supported the meek and saw it as his destiny to help the poor and oppressed, the meek and the downtrodden. Because of their circumstance, they had little chance of ever attaining access to the secrets of the mystery schools and learning the mysteries of the Sky-Gods. We are told that later in Jerusalem, Jesus borrowed a handwritten copy of the Hebrew Scriptures from the Tabernacle in Jerusalem. The reason he required this is because he had the secret information smuggled out of Egypt, but now he needed to locate these secrets hidden in the Torah in order to explain them and make them known to all men. This is the very act that annoyed the Priests who wanted him crucified. Ancient documentation states that this led to the stoning of Jesus after which his body was 'hanged' on a tree. The priests wished to preserve the mysteries even if they didn't fully appreciate their magnitude or fully understand them. Jesus chose to make 'all things known to all men'. He even said in the Bible that this was his intent;

Luke 12 : 2-3 *For there is nothing covered, that shall not be revealed; neither hid, that shall not be known. Therefore whatsoever ye have spoken in darkness shall be heard in the light; and that which ye have spoken in the ear in closets shall be proclaimed upon the housetops.*

John 18 : 20 *Jesus answered him, I spake openly to the world; I ever taught in the synagogue, and in the temple, whither the Jews always resort; and in secret have I said nothing.*

Despite the attitude of Jesus on total disclosure, there are several references to secrets and mysteries within the Bible and how they will be revealed only to the elect. The other Rabbi's secured a power base by withholding this information to which they were privy. Jesus however had received far deeper initiation and chose to reveal all. There is no shortage of Biblical quotes about secrets and mysteries in the scriptures;

Isaiah 29 : 11 *"I cannot for it is sealed"*

Psalm 25 : 14 *Friendship with the Lord is reserved for those who fear him. With them he shares the secrets of his covenant.*

Romans 16 : 25-26 *Now to him that is of power to stablish you according to my gospel, and the preaching of Jesus Christ, according to the revelation of the mystery, which was kept secret since the world began, but now is made manifest, and by the scriptures of the prophets, according to the commandment of the everlasting God, made known to all nations.*

Matthew 13 : 11 *He answered and said unto them, Because it is given unto you to know the mysteries of the kingdom of heaven, but to them it is not given.*

1 Corinthians 2 : 7 *But we speak the wisdom of God in a mystery, even the hidden wisdom, which God ordained before the world unto our glory:*

Mark 4 : 11 *And he said unto them, Unto you it is given to know the mystery of the kingdom of God: but unto them that are without, all these things are done in parables:*

Ephesians 6 : 19 *And for me, that utterance may be given unto me, that I may* *open my mouth boldly, to make known the mystery of the gospel,*

In the Bible, Jesus tells us in **Matthew 13 : 44** that the kingdom of heaven is *"like unto a treasure hid in a field."*

This is a universal truth that has been carried through the ages. The ancients before Christ expressed it in the form of 'mystery religions' with a secret message for the initiated. We don't know precisely what went on for example in the Eleusinian and Dionysian mysteries but we do know that they too were about death and resurrection. St. Paul records in his letter to the Colossians that he has a mission to reveal and announce something hidden;

> *'The secret hidden for long ages and through many generations that he can now reveal to the very elect'*

When the reader finally gets to it, guess what? The secret is this;

Colossians 1 : 27, *"Christ is in you!"*

This is not so different to the cry of the Children of Israel in the desert; (Exodus 32 : 23) *"make us Gods"* - You are created precisely in the image of the Sky-Gods with their blood and their DNA; *"You are Gods now ... Christ is already in you."* That is the message!

Right and Wrong

Most of us are gentle folk and still hold considerable respect for things of God even as we query those things about religion that we find to be spurious. As we saw above, even non-believers are moved by religious ritual. When we consider those souls we encounter in our daily lives, who promote their religion, many of us think that provided their heart is in the right place and they do no real harm we really should leave them be and not object. Certainly there has been damage done to primitive cultures by zealous missionaries indoctrinated with the arrogance to believe that they have the correct answers and are somehow helping the inferior heathens. Unfortunately religious differences have been the catalyst for many problems and most wars down through the ages. Even terrorism today is all too often a result of fanatics believing it is the requirement of their God to remove the infidels. Religion writer and ex nun, Karen Armstrong wrote;

"At the very least, the Holocaust showed that the secularist ideology can be just as lethal as any religious crusade." [(2)]

Whilst most of us would have no real problem with the ethical teachings of the world's great religions, we would now have to be less than convinced about their effectiveness, inerrancy or divine origins. We have seen the proven pagan and mythical basis of the Christian religion and that a sizable part was 'borrowed' from the Sumerians, Egyptians and Hebrew. This religion today professes to be both inerrant and divinely inspired, and our information makes such a stand, plainly laughable. This book has given indications of the magnitude of the deception within the Christian religion to which we have been subjected. Now it is decision time; we are becoming educated.

Do we continue 'play-acting' and teaching our children this concocted 'fairytale' religion or do we admit we were all 'sold a pup' and expose the religion for what it is? Do we continue giving our respect and support to the Roman Church that has perpetrated such blatant crimes against humanity, or do we expose those within its engine room for what they are? Do we continue to follow, the Christian religion when we now know that its doctrine was borrowed from pagan sources and its genesis hijacked from the Hebrew religion, which in turn had learned it from the Sumerians and Egyptians? Man is still a spiritual being and has a requirement to seek fulfilment for the spiritual side of his make up. I fully appreciate this having long been a member of ROTARY and on the board of a local hospital as well as participating in other local service and fund raising organizations. I personally choose to devote considerable effort and resources to assist people in many and various ways, and part of the proceeds from this book will be employed to help feed the hungry. I take considerable time to count my many blessings and hold the spiritual belief that the 'Temple' is actually within all of us, and that our bodies should be treated accordingly without substance abuse, or excessive eating or drinking. I also agree that the Buddhist belief of seeking happiness and fulfilment whilst, where possible, supporting the fellow travellers that share this planet, is sound philosophy. I believe in telling the truth.

The Taoist doctrine teaches that left alone, man will usually do the right thing. This is of course contrary to the opinion of the Christian community who would see total chaos occurring the moment God removed his Almighty, restraining hand. The fact is that history has graphically shown that it is the introduction of the arts and sciences that impact most on reducing corruption and crime and on raising the morals and integrity of third world countries and not the introduction of religion at all, as the supporters would have us believe. This has become proven fact from long term sociological observations. [3]

Since the renaissance we have seen a burst of creative brilliance that has led man from the 'Dark Ages' to the Moon and beyond. I believe that man is a pretty amazing creature. I fail to see that he is a 'fallen' being in dire need of redemption. It is this kind of negative thought that allowed the Church to hold back progress through the 'dark ages' and even to this very day and for what? Obviously to maintain a power base over a subservient congregation. Here is the rub; their entire motif is negative, austere, counterproductive and harmful to the self-esteem of their constituents. Unfortunately 'control' has always been the aim. The scare tactic encompassed in the 'Devil', 'Hell' and 'fire and brimstone' rubbish that indoctrinated the laity, was created specifically to promote loyalty to the Bishops and bind people to the Church. It has been an effective tactic for centuries. It was also found to be quite successful in feathering the Vatican nest at the expense of the laity. Did it solve world poverty? No it didn't. Did it solve the world's wars? No religion was the cause of many of the wars. Did it assist or benefit mankind? No, it held him back with outdated thinking on things like bigotry, equality, technology and birth control. Look at the big picture; the Church has really done very little to assist mankind. Mankind on the other hand has provided the obscene quantity of tax-free wealth and power that the Church enjoys to this day, with prime real estate holdings that are many times those of McDonalds, and every cent gained from donations and ultimately tax free. It's a frightening thought.

As I stated in the introduction of this book, this is not meant to be a tearing down exercise and I am not out to crucify anybody. In my long and often arduous research process, it became more and more apparent that we had been hoodwinked in the entire spectrum of our spiritual life, and this deception came with a price tag. This realization of deception when we were trying hard to do the right thing, stirs up ones anti-church feelings, and destroys one's faith in the theological system and in the clergy who promoted it. The sense of betrayal is very real. This however does not mean that it contributes to the denigrating of a nations morals and ethics. Religion is not a guarantor of social order. Although Jesus was in all likelihood an astute and compassionate Rabbi initiated in the Egyptian mysteries; he indeed offers us no salvation. People, who now realize this fact don't just go out and commence murdering people and robbing banks. They must channel their energies elsewhere and alter the diet on which they feed their spirit.

Something that bears thinking about; in the Bible, man is actually asked to behave better, to suppress his anger and to act more nobly than his God. If man was to display the wrath, the angry little 'dummy-spits' and do the bloodthirsty things attributed to God in the Bible, out would come the threats of stoning, excommunication, fire, brimstone and eternal damnation. Throughout this work we saw that the vengeful and unpredictable behaviour attributed to Almighty God was far less than exemplary, and actually at times was quite shabby. Could it be that man has a mission to advance and improve the nasty Godlike nature he was given? Any documentation of reincarnation was removed from the scriptures in 325 AD so could it also be that the belief of the Indian religions, of improving oneself in each reincarnation to eventually attain a Nirvana, is in fact true and correct?

Carl Jung wrote that he could not dismiss the *"absence of human morality"* in YHWH's commands to the Hebrew people, as recorded in the Bible. He states that YHWH displays a gross deficiency of reason and of morality, the very two characteristics of a mature and balanced human mind. This in turn speaks volumes, not necessarily about YHWH-God, but rather about the psyche of the Hebrew scribes. We have discovered that the Christian message will no longer hold water in our generation and 'big stick' threats of 'fire and brimstone' and the devices of the 'Devil' no longer work at shackling people in an educated environment. Add to that, the feeling of betrayal each individual must feel when it becomes obvious that we were lied to from Sunday School right up to the present, and that Jesus can no more save us than any twenty or so of the plethora of virgin born saviours who came before him or for that matter those who came after him.

It is fairly apparent that this is not news to the clergy or many of our civic leaders. In fact over 100 years ago, because of this knowledge, the British Parliament dispatched a team to India to make a study of the documents and monuments in that country and to record and compare the similarities between the Christian religion and the much older Indian religion of the God Krishna. Their extensive and diligent work resulted in a massive collection of documents that reflected this 'sameness', that were left for shipping with the Christian Bishop of Calcutta. When copies of these priceless artefacts finally arrived in London, the records were so badly mutilated and vandalised that they were unrecognisable and unusable. The account of the crucifixion of Krishna had been completely removed. [4] The inference is patently obvious.

No matter how much of a hatchet job this book has done on organised or institutionalized religion, I simply cannot view this as a tearing down exercise, even as the last remnants of the belief structure I was taught are torn away. I cannot forget that when I was seeking truth; the church was giving me lies. When I wanted education they tried to tighten the shackles. I am not the sort of 'lemming' who can take that for the long term. To believe that publishing this book documenting what my research has discovered is actually counterproductive, I would have to also view the removal of a malignant tumour as a tearing down exercise, and counterproductive. Sometimes we must back up a little before we can go forward. No matter how magnificent our plans and architectural drawings, we must demolish the old building before we can begin building the new.

A huge problem is that we subliminally inherited the formula that is hard to shake:

Belief in God = Good person

No belief of God = Bad person.

One may believe that they lead an honest life, have considerable integrity and try hard to offer support and kindness to all men. They are scrupulously honest and fair in all dealings, care for their family and do their best to assist others. It is possible that they have attained fairly lofty goals of integrity and spirituality yet they simply cannot believe literally that virgins have babies, and the dead are raised and men walk on water. They cannot accept that the expensive, pomp and ceremony of the Church are warranted at the expense of the poor. Even in this situation it is still difficult to remove that last shred of baggage and let go of an indoctrinated religion no matter how silly its dogma. We are social creatures and it is made easy for members of a congregation to overlook the obvious flaws of some doctrine, forget the past atrocities, and put aside the passages that are offensive and instead simply enjoy the fellowship with acquaintances and friends, and focus on the 'nice' Bible passages. You may well ask, where do we go from here?

The first point is that a natural progression is occurring anyway and I am but one of the pioneers. The next is that education has throughout history, disclosed 'flat earths', 'sacred cows' and other nonsensical myths and obliterated them and today this process is occurring at a rapidly increasing rate. It is absolutely pointless to prolong the deceit by play-acting at a religion, trying to maintain integrity, no matter how elevated its ideals, when it can so easily be proved faulty and inherently flawed. Even if some of our study in this book could in time be shown to be in error, we got enough right to see that this is so. The Earth remained round no matter how long it was promoted as flat. Aircraft still commute in our skies despite those who were adamant that heavier than air craft could never get off the ground. We must learn the truth and act in accordance with that truth to build a better self and accordingly a better world. We need to advance, to move forward in the areas that have been held back for so many years by the Church. We must question all those things that should be questioned. We must find a better way. If we simply sold up the real estate owned by the established churches of the world and put the capital into appropriate, well-managed business ventures, it would go a long way towards funding programs to assist and ultimately cure world poverty, hunger and disease. We would no longer need to wrestle with the conflict of the hypocritical Church that preaches its heartfelt concern for the poor, sick and hungry whilst continuing to flaunt its pomp and wealth. More particularly since documents researched in this book, leave no doubt that the part of that wealth that wasn't donated was in fact stolen. Individually we certainly can't help the poor by joining them, but we can do far more by seeking a better way.

As a student of classical ancient history I studied the wars fought in the name of religion that could have and should have been avoided. I uncovered unspeakable deception by the early church and the inhumane treatment of branded heretics who did no more than question obvious fraud as I have done. I feel for the many thousands of young women brutally slain as witches when in all probability not even one was actually guilty of anything. In fact the scripture that drives the church wild against witches is really quite paranoid; it gives no detail whatever on who, is or isn't a witch and precisely what the problem is and in many cases was aimed at the pioneers of science who threatened the Church, by offering educated explanations;

Exodus 22 : 18 *Thou shalt not suffer a witch to live.*

Micah 5 : 12 *And I will cut off witchcrafts out of thine hand; and thou shalt have no more soothsayers:*

I particularly feel for the Gnostic Cathars (pure ones) involved in the Albigensian slaughter started in 1208 in the Languedoc by **Pope Innocent III** of Rome. I am appalled at the arrogance of the various Popes down the ages who despite displaying very earthly traits considered themselves infallible, '*Vicars of Christ*', generating hypocritical commands via papal bulls, protected by a church that claimed its false doctrine to be the irrefutable Word of God and used its massive power to ensure its orthodoxy, by removing the competition. I am stunned to discover that so much uncertainty surrounded the birth and ministry of Jesus that he was not even deified in his own lifetime; in fact not until 325 AD and then he achieved his Godhood and the title 'Son of God' by a vote! This makes a mockery of all the Bibles verses that say he was the Son of God as they are quite obviously later additions.

It does however still take fortitude to step away from the entire belief structure we were taught. The realization though, of just how corrupt, bigoted and totally rotten the regime we are leaving has been for hundreds of years, should make our departure easier. For example; the Rotary organization has no ethnic boundaries; no "us" and "them". In a global society it is 'us' and 'us'. I don't believe in any war I could shoot another Rotarian no matter what his race or religious beliefs. What an accomplishment it would be to avert the possibility of future "Holy wars" based on hate and mistrust and fought on "religious" principles, simply by removing the 'us and them' situation from world religions. This would achieve solutions in Palestine, in Kashmir, in Afghanistan, in Iraq, in fact globally. There is no longer room for 'us and them' in a global society. Wouldn't we encounter a dramatic reduction of the 'us and them' requirement in a world without the various religious factions?

We must go forward ...that's where we can go from here! This book has shown that much of what we leave behind is far better left behind as we go forward, perhaps as new age **"Jedi Knights"** utilizing 'The Force' on a more compassionate, altruistic and fulfilling mission for the betterment of self and our neighbours. Now an amazing fact is that the writers of the 'Star Wars' stories coined 'Jedi Knights' as being the disciplined and dedicated followers and protectors of 'The Force.' These characters were respected and admired much as would be, a martial arts master or Yogi 'wise man'. Whether they were aware or not, the 'Jedi' root actually comes from an ancient Egyptian word '*Djedi*' (*Djeheuti*) the name attributed to an early Egyptian God with those identical humanitarian characteristics and bound by similar heritage and discipline. [5]

Thinking Straight

It was stated in the introduction that if this book caused you to stop and think even for a moment then all the research and effort was worth it to me. We must identify that a person can only become informed and enlightened after they consider new possibilities. If one is afraid to let go in order to grow, then they are destined to peruse the real estate document, more closely than the articles of their religious faith, which are supposed to be of such monumental proportions that their lives will change forever. They will place their entire spiritual life in the hands of clergy who just may not have their best interests at heart or be sufficiently educated to warrant that trust. This act alone further empowers the clergy and church as the blind continue to lead the blind.

We noted earlier that a work entitled '*The Life of Apollonius of Tyana*', written by Flavius Philostratus was among the few works saved from the fire in the Alexandrian Library. Had it not been saved we would have no knowledge of the amazing deeds of **Apollonius of Tyana,** the universally acclaimed religious teacher of the First Century, revered from one end of the Roman Empire to the other by everyone, from the lowest slave to the Emperor himself. [6] Dr. Raymond W. Bernard, B.A., M.A., Ph.D. discusses Apollonius of Tyana in his book '*The Secret Life of Jesus the Essene,*' and goes on to state;

> "*For Philostratus in his book described a character born in the very year of the birth of Christ who, in every respect, was the equal, if not the superior, of the Christian messiah.*"
> [7]

Almost all available records about Apollonius of Tyana were destroyed by Constantine soon after the Council of Nicea, as these certainly threatened the Christian message. [8] Because of the suppression of this literature by the Church, many would have no inkling of the magnitude of this demi-God and with slightly different events his record could have been totally lost forever. This graphically shows how very simple it has been for the Roman Church to steer things in the direction they chose.

Final truth is a product of interaction with all the information that comes in our direction and involves the informed acceptance or rejection. Christians in particular need to get to the point where they are willing to question things. This is however a remarkably big hurdle. To assist in this endeavour recall that the Bible states, "*Come as little children*". It does not say "*Stay as little children*". How many times have you been deceived in this life through simple acceptance of what others labelled 'truth'? We can be sure that we have advanced on the journey however if we are questioning the things that need to be questioned and asking the right questions of those who claim to know the way. We can not rest, we must overcome the inertia; we need to consider the options, take stock of what we are being told and to finally stop and think!

Getting Over it

Earlier I shared my belief that our body is the Temple and that our God is within each and every one of us. Christ supposedly taught that our body is the Temple of the Holy Ghost and the secret disclosed by Paul is that "Christ is in you". We saw how the Taoists believe that man will ultimately do the right thing. We are superior to the animals, we are the highest intelligence we currently know of and we are as Gods, right now!

Timothy Freke and Peter Gandy remark, that;

> 'this is the perennial mysticism of Gnosticism and the Pagan Mysteries — that within each one of us is the one Soul of the Universe, the Logos, the Universal Daemon, the Mind of God' … The purpose of our evolutionary pilgrimage is to bring this inner Christ or Buddha nature to full expression over the course of numberless lives. [9]

Whether we 'got' the message or not, it was there for us. The Bible actually states;

Genesis 3 : 5 *"Ye shall be as Gods".*

Genesis 3 : 22 *"Behold, the man is become as one of us".*

Psalm 82 *"You too are Gods".*

Helena Petrovna Blavatsky (1831-91), the founder of modern Theosophy put it this way;

> "Christ — the true esoteric Saviour — is not man, but the <u>Divine Principle in every human being</u>. He who strives to resurrect the Spirit crucified in him by his own terrestrial passions, and buried deep in the 'sepulchre' of his sinful flesh; he who has the strength to roll back the stone of matter from the door of his own inner sanctuary, <u>he has the risen Christ in him</u>. The 'Son of Man' is no child of the bondwoman — flesh, but verily of the free-woman — Spirit, the child of man's own deeds, and the fruit of his own spiritual labour. [10]

This indicates that we have the answers within ourselves and don't require the aid of the Clergy, the Bible, Jesus or the Church. There is considerable doubt following the research within this book, that these alternate devices can offer any assistance anyway. We have seen that at times when we seek God's will in our poor vandalized Bible; it offers us gems of wisdom and instruction that are not only inane but fully contradictory and confusing;

Matthew 26 : 52 *Dispose of swords. All who take the sword will perish by it.*
Luke 22 : 36–38 *Buy swords.*

When we seek Jesus in the Bible we find a fairly blank canvass. Let's look at it in reality; perhaps ninety-five percent of happenings during the timeframe of Jesus' life are not documented; at least ninety percent of the life of Jesus is left unrecorded. Add to that, a large proportion of the words attributed to Jesus have proved to be allegoric rhetoric; words never said by Jesus. These were the findings of the 'Jesus Seminar' who sought the real Jesus and found only myth and veiled allegory. Christian teachers of divinity are forced to admit the truth of this statement. Rev. Kythera Ann Grunge got it correct when she cogently observed;

> *"Allegorical interpretations arise spontaneously whenever a conflict between new ideas and those expressed in a sacred book necessitate some form of compromise."* [11]

Consider this; there is something very wrong if Almighty God actually walked on this Earth in the form of his only begotten son, and left us virtually no trace. The traces of the Bible are most definitely man made. In the momentous event of a God walking on the Earth we could reasonably expect far more. This was conveyed by Kersey Graves thus;

> *"The fact that no history, sacred or profane, - that not one of the three hundred histories of that age, makes the slightest allusion to Christ, of any of the miraculous incidents engrafted into his life, certainly proves, with a cogency that no logic can overthrow, no sophistry can contradict, and no honest scepticism can resist, that there never was such a miraculously endowed being as his many orthodox disciples claim him to have been. The fact that Christ finds no place in the history of the era in which he lived, that not one event of his life is recorded by anybody but his own interested and prejudiced biographers, settles the conclusion beyond cavil or criticism, that the godlike achievements ascribed to him are naught but fable or fiction. It not only proves he was not miraculously endowed, but proves he was not even naturally endowed to such an extraordinary degree as to make him an object of general attention. It would be a historical anomaly without precedent, that Christ should have performed any of the extraordinary acts attributed to him in the Gospels, and no Roman or Grecian historian, and neither Philo or Josephus, both writing in that age, and both living almost on the spot where they are said to have been witnessed, and both recording minutely all the*

religious events of that age and country, make the slightest mention of one of them, nor their reputed authors. Such a historical fact banishes the last shadow of faith in their reality." [12]

The God of the Bible was always promoted as a God of love, yet actually delivered his message with a very big stick. His frequent outbursts of jealousy and wrath include ongoing threats, intimidation, genocide, plagues and pestilence and are way outside world's best practise for a management style. Empathy was never shown in this doctrine and self esteem was hard to maintain under the eyes of a God who was such a hard taskmaster who simply hated everything and everyone outside his chosen Hebrew race. Sacrifice was an integral part of receiving forgiveness or blessings demanded by this God who was alpha and omega and yet today, blood sacrifice is considered offensive, unnecessary and totally barbaric. In modern society it is no longer acceptable under any guise. Further, if the people of Earth continue to worship a dedicated, loving God who promised, "I will be your God"; why has this God now broken off all communication with man? With no contact for almost 2000 years something is seriously amiss.

The reality is that we were taught from an early age the concept of our parent's religion by unqualified and unsuitable people. We were sold a pup and it took an amazingly long time before we realized it. Until very recently the Bible has exercised a profound and powerful grip on Western conscious-ness, so much so that one is almost forbidden from questioning its veracity. There are no doubt those who believe that for daring to question the Bible and convey my findings in this book, I may be destined to burn in Hell. I actually now find it hard to take the Biblical threats too seriously and I'll show you why. You may like to get out your Bible and follow this one. Let's just think straight for a minute and use some common sense. I feel sure you will agree that although supposedly an inerrant and unimpeachable source (the words of Almighty God) there is something quite amiss with a Holy Book that contains a ludicrous sequence of events like the following:

(i) Exodus 9 : 3 *God <u>totally destroys</u> all the horses, donkeys, camels, cattle, sheep and goats belonging to the Egyptians.* (OK so they are <u>ALL</u> dead.)

(ii) Exodus 9 : 9 *The people and the <u>livestock</u> (although all destroyed) are then*

379

afflicted with boils.

(iii) Exodus 12 : 12 *All the <u>first-born of the livestock</u> of the Egyptians are then destroyed.* (What Again? And with or without boils?)

(iv) Exodus 12 : 29 *At midnight God struck dead all the first-born of men <u>and</u> <u>animals</u>.* (Clobbered yet again, they must be getting sick and tired of this?)

So after having all their livestock destroyed, then afflicted with boils, and then the first-born of their livestock destroyed twice, what could possibly happen next?

(v) Exodus 14 : 9 *the Egyptians now pursue Moses <u>with chariots and on horseback</u>.* You see my point? I know Christians who have not found the peace they seek in following Jesus. Whilst they enjoy the social fellowship and sense of belonging offered by their church, some live with concern about their own unbelief of this convoluted message. Others actually live in dread and fear of the holocaust mentioned in the Bible's final Book of Revelation without realizing it is not even a scriptural work but was actually written by one of the pagan Sibyls. A document re-discovered in the Vatican in 1925 and called *'The Mysteries of Osiris and Isis'* was first thought to originate in Egypt but when traced, was found to be a modified version of an original written by the *'Sibyl of Cumae'* a woman called **Herophile** who lived in a cave in Cumae, Campania - Rome (Italy) around 500 BCE who was thought by the local populous to be immortal as she appeared to age very slowly. This work is the original **Book of Revelation** that appears in our Bibles today as the ineffable Word of God. So in fact a pagan Sibyl wrote a work that was included in the Christian Bible; how does the Church get around that? The fact that it was discovered in the Vatican lends credence to the fact that somebody within the Catholic Church must have known about its original confiscation and the ongoing deception or it would not have been there in the first place. This Book finally gained entry to the New Testament at the ecumenical councils and still gives trouble to clergy and parishioners alike. The fact that it holds 22 chapters (corresponding to the 22 letters in the Hebrew alphabet and the 22 Tarot cards) makes many scholars believe it holds the secrets from the ancient Egyptian mystery schools and includes the words of the Gods. [13] The Book of Revelation is not satisfactorily transparent or sufficiently understood to be of much spiritual use anyway and has even been interpreted as the life of Jesus after the crucifixion. [14] It very nearly didn't make it into the Bible and neither it should. Despite this, the church insists on teaching it as the final holocaust. They see it as **'Annihilation'** and not **'Revelation.'** That is not an obvious conclusion to draw at all, yet the power brokers within the Church have only one *modus operandi* and scare tactics and threats of fire and brimstone that worked for the Bishops of old must still work to some extent today. The church should surely be anticipating a <u>revelation</u> from their God and yet they insist that Christians anticipate <u>annihilation</u>. Actually this annihilation supposedly predicted for the last days should really concern us, however with education, it does not.

The unveiling of God's wrath against Ancient Egypt that we just read described in the Book of Exodus above, becomes really almost laughable, and in like manner, the sting is somewhat removed from his threats in the final Book of Revelation, leaving it instead as a tragic comedy. The remnants of my concern seem to disappear as I look at the display of Gods wrath predicted in this final Book from the Word of God;

Revelation 8 : 7 *All of the grass on earth is burned up,*

And then right after that...

Revelation 9 : 4 *An army of locusts, which is about to be turned loose on the earth, is instructed by the Almighty not to harm the grass.*

We must gain education. We can not trust the Church with the hidden agenda that has orchestrated for us to be misled and lied to. We can not trust all that we learn in school and Sunday School. We must free ourselves. We should overlook the inane threats that have been added to the Bible and are counterproductive to our wellbeing. We must look to other sources and increase our knowledge and gain confidence in our own decisions. We should eliminate "us" and "them" within the global society, feel more compassion and better care for each other. We must be gentle with ourselves and stand in awe of our enormous potential because we are as Gods - right now. We must recognise that the Church has ulterior motives and doesn't always have it right. We can no longer blindly follow their faulty dogma. They lied to us in Sunday School!

"The whole religious complexion of the modern world is due to the absence from Jerusalem of a Lunatic Asylum."
Havelock Ellis (1859-1939); *Impressions and Comments*, 1914.

ANSWERS TO PARTY TRICKS

Q1. *Was Adam the first man and Eve then created to be his mate? Were they created as babies and cared for, or created fully grown? Was Eve the only wife of Adam?*

A. (i) The entire story is likely veiled allegory however if we treat it as real, the Bible says **Adam** was the first man and **Eve** was then created to be his mate however various records do not agree on who was created first. Their race was Adama (not their names) and indications are that they shared a birth date but then we find Eve was created from Adam's rib indicating he was born first. The man we call Adam, the Sumerians called **Adappa of the Adama**. In **Jubilees 3 : 9–12** it tells how Adam is brought into The Garden of Eden, 40 days after he is created and how Eve is brought in on the 80th day. In **verse 17** it goes on that Adam and Eve spent **7 years** in the garden before they ate the fruit and were sent out. – **"Hypostasis of the Archons II, 4"** found in the Nag Hammadi scrolls from Egypt, states clearly that Eve was created first. The Bible actually hedges its bets on this subject.

(ii) It is assumed in the Bible that Adam and Eve were not nursed, so accordingly they must have been created fully grown however the earlier Sumerian records describe nurse mothers who raise them which is of course more believable.

(iii) It was thought in olden times that Lilith was the first wife of Adappa (Adam) and she left him when he tried to dominate her. Women's Lib over 6000 years ago!

Q2. *Does the Bible say that Adam, Eve or both of them ate the forbidden apple? Who sinned, Adam or Eve? In the Garden of Eden, what did Adam and Eve use to cover their nakedness?*

A. (i) The apple as we know it today was not in existence when the creation is supposed to have taken place. When Eve approached the tree, the Bible simply states: **Genesis 3 : 6** "took of the fruit thereof" nowhere does it state 'apple'. We are told that 'figs' grew in the garden but likely not apples. The fruit was probably a symbolic representation of either 'life' or 'knowledge'.

(ii) Eve has been blamed throughout the ages however it is an unfair rap. How does one account for the actions of Adam if he was not himself, deceived and why in **Genesis 3 : 17 – 24** does it detail the punishments metered out by God, specifically to Adam for his sin.

(iii) Adam and Eve did not cover themselves with a fig leaf. In fact **Genesis 3 : 7** tells us they sewed <u>aprons</u> from fig leaves. These were to cover them until in **Genesis 3 : 21** The Lord made <u>coats of skins</u> for them.

Q3. *According to Genesis, how many of each animal did Noah take into the ark? Was he rescuing them to preserve the species or were they a food source for his family?*

A. (i) We were always taught that Noah took two of each animal into the ark. Yet **Genesis 7 : 2 – 3** makes it clear he took seven of each clean beast and the fowls of the air by sevens. Of some other species he did take two but the common, incorrect belief stems from the quotation that the animals went in two by two.

(ii) The Sumerians and Babylonians had their own Noah's Ark stories that well and truly predate the Bible. The Atra–hasis and Ziusudra (Noah) stories from about the third millennium BCE and the Epic of Gilgamesh with its King Uta–napishtim of Shuruppak (Noah) who actually ruled around 4000 BCE; were written on clay tablets stored in the library of Nineveh (Ninua) about 1900 BCE, and actually predated the Biblical record by more than 1300 years. In these stories the prototype 'Noah' rode out a large local flood and 'preserved the seed of (human) life' from inundation. In the former, the animals taken aboard were clearly a food source and not for preservation of the species. The King

Uta-napishtim legend however states that he took 'the seed' of all living creatures which sounds more like preservation of DNA or sperm samples but not necessarily the animals themselves which would be a task with overwhelming logistical problems. Of course the current Bible resulted from these writings commenced by the Hebrew scribes in Babylon.

Q4. *How long did the waters prevail? What birds did Noah release to see if there was dry land? Where did the ark land?*

A. (i) It is obvious that a number of differing stories were meshed into one and that becomes apparent with the following;

Genesis 7 : 17–18 The flood waters prevailed 40 days

Genesis 7 : 24 The flood waters prevailed 150 days

(ii) Noah sent birds out from the ark; a raven (once) and a dove (three times). The earlier Utanapishtim however released a dove and a swallow, which both returned. Some time afterwards, he released a raven, which did not return.

(iii) In the earlier Babylonian records the Ark landed on **Mt Nisir.** This is a mountain located in lower Mesopotamia, now called **Pir Omar Gudrun;** the Bible changed this to Mt Ararat *(high peaks)* which was never the name of a mountain. A mountain called **Agri Dagi** is now called Ararat to fit with the Bible story. Ararat is named in the Koran as **Djebel Judi** (Al-Judi).

Q5. *Was Jesus born in a stable in Bethlehem? Was Jesus' birthday 25 December 0001?*

A. (i) Dr. Barbara Theiring claims Jesus was born in the Queen's House at Qumran and if he was of a Royal linage this makes sense. (ii) The Bible tells us that Jesus was born while Herod the Great was still alive. Herod died in 4 BCE so we can easily dismiss dates after this time. Some confusion comes from the tax census that we can prove actually happened at the time when Joseph and Mary were said to travel to

Bethlehem. The Syrian governor Quirinius (Cyrenius) was appointed by Rome to oversee the Holy Land and immediately ordered this census in 6 AD. Jesus at this time was ready for the Jewish "Born Again" ceremony, the forerunner of the Bar Mitzvah, which occurred at age 12, so it was in fact the "second birth" and not the actual birth that was celebrated at this time. Thus 12 years prior would put his actual birth at 7 BCE and this likely occurred at Qumran. This meets all criteria and it appears that Jesus was actually born in March 7 BCE.

Q6. *What is a manger? How many Wise men visited the baby Jesus?*

A. (i) A *'manger'* was a kind of feed basket or frame to hold hay or straw for livestock. The word *'manger'* in French means *'to eat'* and there is likely a connection. It was quite common practice in those times to place one inside a house to use as a baby crib.

(ii) We were always taught that there were three wise men but this is not scriptural. These men brought Gold, Frankincense and Myrrh, so the clergy must have just decided one gift apiece so there must have been three men. The Bible covers the visit of the wise men in Matthew and in Luke, but not once mentions the number as three. The Persian version of this story is more specific. It clearly states that there were five Wise Men and coincidently this is the same number who attended the birth of Confucius according to the ancient Chinese texts. Still our Nativity scenes and our Christmas cards always show three wise men from the East. Perhaps there were five, perhaps ten, perhaps twenty, but the number is not recorded in the Bible.

Q7. *Was Jesus' mother Mary described in the Bible as a 'virgin'? How is it that she had a sister also called Mary?*

A. (i) The concept that Mary was a virgin, is not original Christian dogma at all, and stems from the beliefs of various pagan cults, where a mother figure produces a God, in each case born of a virgin. Nowhere, in the original Hebrew Bible or in the original New Testament does it state that Mary was a virgin. This was mistranslated in the English versions. It is actually easy to see how this happened. In the Latin translations of the Roman church, Mary was described as "**virgo**" but in Latin this simply means a young woman. To describe a virgin they would have to use "**virgo intacta**" which they did not. Now the Latin translation "virgo" came from the Hebrew "**almah**" which again meant a young woman. To denote "virgo intacta" they would have to use, "**bethula**" which they did not. The concept of the "immaculate conception" and that Mary was "ever virgin" (and this despite having a number of children after Jesus) came some 700 years later, from the Catholic, Council of Trullo in AD 692. Almost 700 years after the birth of Christ. The Catholic hierarchy 'decided' that Mary was "ever virgin" then claimed contrary to the Bible, that the brothers and sisters of Jesus were really his cousins. We should note too that the Nazarene sect, at one stage led by Jesus' brothers James and likely Joses, denied the virgin birth.

(ii) In **John 19 : 25** Mary had a sister Mary. To explain this Jesus' mother was actually **Miriam** called Mary. The name "**Mary**" by which Miriam is known in the Bible was actually more a Royal title related to her Davidian descendency, than a name but it was also a title of servitude. This title was gained when she became betrothed to "the Joseph" who was of the tribe of Judah and the kingly descendent of King David. Likewise her sister also became called Mary by joining the dynasty of Cleophas, by marriage.

Q8. *Was Mary in fact the "Queen of Heaven"? Was it the same 'virgin' Mary who made contact with the shepherd children at Fatima, Portugal in 1917, the event classed as a miracle by the Vatican?*

A.   (i) We can find recorded in **Jeremiah 7 : 18** and **Jeremiah 44 : 17–25** examples of the Hebrew worshipping **Ashtoreth** as the Queen of Heaven some five centuries before Christ and it is not surprising to find this Goddess included in early trinities. Later Mary (Miriam) the mother of Jesus was adapted to replace her by the Roman church, becoming the new 'Queen of Heaven'. The temple of Jerusalem was simultaneously dedicated to **Yahweh** and to the **Queen of Heaven** but this was Ashtoreth and not Mary (Miriam).

(ii) Although the Vatican classed the appearance of Mary at Fatima as a miracle the departure from scripture and the inane dialogue recorded makes it very suspect indeed. The researchers Andrew Newberg and Eugene D'Aquili state; *"The human brain has been genetically wired to encourage religious beliefs."* In their book "Why God won't go away" they explain that the desire to find a higher being is inherent in our psyche. This goes a long way to explaining what these impressionable young children supposedly saw.

Q9. *What is a 'messiah'; does this title mean 'Saviour'; 'Son of God'; King of the Jews or something else? Was Jesus actually the King of the Holy land, the so called "King of the Jews"? Why did the scriptures say he was to be called Immanuel, yet we call him Jesus?*

A. (i) The word 'messiah' meant 'anointed one' and most kings and priests were anointed with oil as was recorded happening to Jesus in the Bible.

(ii) Any ancient 'king list' did not include Jesus as a historical King of the Jews and this despite claims that the anointing by Mary Magdalene and the triumphant entry into Jerusalem was after he was made king. In addition the signs on the cross are listed as reading, "Jesus of Nazareth – King of the Jews'. It is hard to reconcile this as fact if Jesus was never made the historical king. Before the birth of Jesus the popular Hasmonean leader **Antigonus** ruled the Holy Land as the rightful **King of the Jews** and is seems this rule and the crucifixion of Antigonus was transferred to the personage of Jesus as veiled allegory.

(iii) It is strange too that the Old Testament prophet stated the messiah was to be called <u>Emmanuel</u> and the New Testament <u>Immanuel</u>. However they called him **Yahshua** which means **'YHWH gives salvation'** but because this name included God's name (Yah) which was not to be pronounced, he was instead called **Yehoshua.** Jesus was called **Y'shua ben Yoseph** in Hebrew and a close English translation would be Joshua. Instead the later Greek translation was romanticised so the Greek name **'Jesus'** is most commonly used today.

Q10. *What is an angel? Are they white robed sons of God, flying with magnificent wings from the 'Heavenly Host' of God to assist mankind and intercede, on his behalf? Who comprise the Heavenly Host? If Lucifer was a son of God and Jesus was a son of God does this mean they were brothers?*

A. (i) In reality the word "angel" simply means **messenger.** Where confusion came in, was when early writers felt that persons undertaking a journey or a religious work were led by God. Accordingly they wrote, "And God caused an angel to be sent unto Gideon" and this was immediately seen as a winged creature flying down to Earth from Heaven. All it really meant was that a messenger was dispatched from somewhere near, with a message for Gideon. The word used for messengers (now called angels) in the original Hebrew Scriptures was **Mal'ark** (Hebrew for messenger). This was translated into Greek as **"Aggelos"** (Greek for messenger). The Latin, **"Angelus"** (meaning messenger) was the first to give this ridiculous connotation of heavenly flying men. Then of course English translations instead of translating Angelus to the appropriate English word 'messenger' created the new word **"Angels"** and carried on the fallacy.

(ii) At times the Heavenly Host can mean the stars and planets; however it was a previously non-existent word coined because the Bible translators were not comfortable with the correct translation of 'Heavenly Army'. They may have wondered why a peaceful loving God would require an Army and who they might fight.

(iii) The story of Jesus becomes silly when we see that both Lucifer and Jesus were 'Sons of God' but could not possibly be considered brothers. Satan was a Bible addition, added after 325 AD.

Q11. *What is it that the Bible says will send us to Hell?*
    (a)   *The rejection of Jesus*
    (b)   *Lack of faith*
    (c)   *Sin*
    (d)   *Lying*
    (e)   *Breaking the Ten Commandments*
    (f)   *Not doing good deeds*
    (g)   *All the above*

A.   The aim of every Christian is to become "born again" or "saved" and achieve eternal life of perpetual bliss with their Lord. This is of prime importance to Christ's followers and its achievement has become the keystone to all Christian dogma. So, what does it take to be saved? We were taught that according to the Bible it is the <u>rejection of Christ</u> alone that will send one to hell. For example the Jews and the Islam followers reject Christ. The Bible is not at all clear on what it takes to be saved with differing versions throughout the New Testament.

Q12. *Did both Joseph and Jesus work as carpenters? What was the occupation of Mary Magdalene? What was the occupation of Jesus' mother Mary?*

A.   (i) Despite recordings to the contrary, Joseph and Jesus were certainly not carpenters, this fallacy coming from a blatantly incorrect Greek to English translation, of *'ho-tekton'* as 'carpenter', when in reality a rough translation from the Hebrew documentation might be "*learned in the craft*". The original Semitic was *'naggar'* which meant something like "*Master Craftsman*". This certainly refers to something like the Masonic Craft in line with the Egyptian Mysteries.
(ii) Mary of Bethany or Mary the Magdalene was born in 3 AD. Her mother was Eucharia of the Royal House of Israel and her Father was Syrus (the Jairus) of Capernaum. Syrus was the Chief Priest subordinate to the High Priest. Mary was of Royalty and herself a <u>priestess</u>. She was a very high profile person, held in the highest esteem and as such was the person selected from all the Holy Land to anoint Jesus the

future King of Israel.

(iii) 'It is recorded "*His mother was Miriam, <u>a dresser of woman's hair</u>?*"

Q13. *When God gave his only begotten Son to die as atonement for the sins of mankind; was this sacrifice of Jesus the 'Son of God' a totally unique event that sets Christianity apart from other religions? Had this sort of sacrifice ever occurred before? Do other religions follow a similar theme or is this what makes Christianity unique? Why does Christianity require the sacrifice of the 'innocent' to redeem the 'guilty'?*

A. (i) It seems that across the world great orators, magi or learned men who were initiated to perform miracles were either deified themselves or given the title the 'Son of God'. Obviously since most often heathen or pagan gods were worshipped in these areas, the title 'Son of God' was used in regard to pagan Gods in almost every ancient country; the actual frequency of its usage negating any chance of it being literally correct for any one Saviour. There is no reason to believe that Jesus Christ did anything new or different from an almost endless string of 'messiahs', 'saviours', 'Gods', 'Sons of Gods' and initiated masters. Saint Basil actually states; *"Every uncommonly good man was called 'the Son of God."* Although in his preaching, Saint Paul made every attempt to promote a miraculous message, we saw earlier that Jesus himself was not actually deified until 325 AD. Surely if he was a *bona fide* saviour his 'Heavenly father' could have achieved much better promotion than this; at least sufficient to see him deified in his own lifetime.

(ii) In addition we find that the very best precepts of the Christian religion can also be found recorded in a myriad of religious documents from Mithraism to the pages of the Hindu Baghavat. In reality Jesus brought nothing new to the Worlds religions and achieved nothing more than a myriad of other Sons of God. His Biblical record now appears to be a mythical, allegoric, religious composite based on the common attributes of a plethora of earlier pagan, saviour Gods. His message was plagiarised from a dozen or more identical earlier sources and we looked at more than 20 'Saviours' who were crucified.

(iii) The need for the 'innocent' to redeem the guilty is non-sensical and a totally unfair concept. It comes from the Hebrew fixation with virginity and sacrifice of 'first-born' children and livestock however the Anunnaki Gods also used 'innocent' scapegoats to redeem them from wrongdoing.

Q14. *Where does God reside and is it 'off limits to mankind'? Can a man gaze on the face of God and live?*

A. (i) Christians say God lives within their hearts, and maybe that is true. Here are yet more ideas from the Bible on where God lives.

Matthew 7 : 21 *God resides in <u>heaven</u>*

1 Kings 8 : 13 *Solomon built a <u>house</u> for the Lord to dwell in forever*

2 Samuel 7 : 5 *Go and tell my servant David, Thus saith the Lord, thou shalt build an <u>house</u> for me to dwell in?*

Acts 7 : 47 – 48 *Solomon built him a <u>house</u>, howbeit the most High dwelleth not in temples made with hands.*

Acts 7 : 49 *<u>Heaven</u> is my throne, and earth is my footstool: what house will ye build me? Saith the Lord: or what is the place of my rest?*

Judges 5 : 5 *The mountains quaked before the Lord , <u>the One of Sinai</u>, before the Lord , the God of Israel.* (NIV)

1 Samuel 6 : 19 *"But God struck down some of the men of Beth Shemesh, putting seventy of them to death because they had looked into the <u>ark of the Lord</u>.*

(ii) The belief in an anthropomorphic God appears to be a carryover from pagan times. Abraham met with him and tried to talk him out of destroying Sodom and Gomorra; Moses met with him and received the Ten Commandments. Hey, I was taught that mortal man couldn't look on Almighty God and live. This is stated then contradicted again and again in the Bible.

Q15. *Could we someday locate God, perhaps on another planet? From the Bible, does he dwell in darkness or in the light? Is he accessible, or hidden?*

A. (i) The Book of Abraham is claimed by the Mormon Church to have been translated by the totally unqualified Joseph Smith, from a papyrus at least in part penned by Abraham himself. According to Joseph Smith's translation of the Book of Abraham, the sun gets its light from <u>God's home planet</u>, a world he called **Kolob**. The Bible's Elohim (Gods) seem to correspond to the Anunnaki Gods of the planet Nibiru (Planet X) in our solar system.

(ii) Light or dark - we have no idea!

1 Kings 8 : 12 *The Lord said that he would dwell in the thick <u>darkness.</u>*

1 Timothy 6 : 16 *God only, hath immortality, dwelling in the <u>light</u> which no man can approach.*

It is contradicted again and again. You decide, it could be either!

(iii) **Psalm 10 : 1** *Why, O Lord, do you stand far off? Why do you <u>hide</u> yourself in times of trouble?* God cannot be found in time of trouble. He is inaccessible hiding or far off.

Q16. *The Catholic Church gave specific, stern warnings about one of the following describing it as 'dangerous'; which do you think? (a) rock & roll music (b) motor racing (c) eating chocolate (d) martial arts.*

A. We saw in the introduction, it was eating chocolate. The early Bishops saw it as a 'dangerous' food they said however, the real reason was that the early inhabitants of Central America had dedicated the chocolate plant to their pagan Gods. They ceremoniously fed massive amounts of chocolate to persons selected for sacrifice so the blood would be enriched by chocolate and thus more appealing to the Gods. The Bishops of the early church knew about the dedication of chocolate to pagan Gods, and accordingly still had a problem with this food, until quite recent times.

Q17. *What can you recall about the god Ba`al? Was he a 'pagan' entity? Why was he so hated by the Old Testament Hebrew scribes? Was he ever worshipped by the Hebrew people?*

A. The Hebrew certainly engaged in Ba`al worship over a very long period of time. We saw considerable evidence that they reverted to Ba`al worship again and again. We saw a mountain of evidence that Ba`al and YHWH were originally considered one and the same God or at the very least members of the same trinity and family unit. Ezra finally wiped out the Ba`al worshippers and it seemed he used Ba`al as an excuse after the captivity, to separate Jewish men from wives and families. Ba`al worship was simply an excuse because we have seen repeatedly that Ezra frowned on Ba`al worship but his real problem was failing to maintain the pure Jewish bloodline:

Q18. *Why was Jesus called, 'Jesus of Nazareth' if he was born in Bethlehem, sojourned in Egypt and lived in various parts of Galilee? Did Jesus ever marry?*

A. (i) There is considerable information available that strongly suggests that **Nazareth** was not even a town at the time of Christ and when it finally became a town it was called **Natzrat**. A person from Natzrat was called a **Natzrati**. First settlement here was believed to have taken place around 60 AD, some 67 years after the birth of Christ. It then took at least another 30 years to become a sizeable town. Jesus and his brothers were associated with a Jewish sect called the Essenes and within this group was a sub group called the **Nazarenes**, which meant '*keepers*' or in full, '*keepers of the covenant*'. Accordingly Jesus the Nazarene was wrongly thought to indicate he came from the town of Nazareth.
(ii) The Roman Church had a reason to hide the fact that Jesus left a bloodline of Jewish descendants and the Vatican worked feverishly to eradicate the Desposyni. All documentation of his specific relationship and marriage was excised from the scriptures. This is because the Vatican usurped the dynasty of Jesus and replaced it with its own dynasty of Popes fraudulently said to be based on St Peter.
(iii) In the Bible, Jesus is referred to as Rabbi some 16 times. These titles are not to be taken lightly and if Jesus was called Rabbi then he certainly was a Jewish Rabbi. A requirement of this title was to be over 30 years of age and <u>to be married</u> in line with Jewish practice and law

that instructs the Hebrew to be fruitful and multiply.

Q19. *Since the <u>Jewish</u> religion rejects Jesus Christ as the Messiah, how is it that the <u>Christian</u> religion still embraces the Jewish Torah and Talmud in the form of the Old Testament and retains the early Jewish history and its patriarchs like Adam, Noah, Abraham, Moses, and King David as its own? Are the Christians telling the <u>Jews</u> who wrote the Bible that they got it wrong?*

A. (i) It is well accepted fact that the Christian (Catholic) church 'hijacked' the pedigree and genesis of the older Jewish religion. The Jewish religion however, does not accept Jesus as its messiah; and yet the Christian Church (based on Jesus Christ being the only son of God) traces its linage back to Abraham and Moses, King David and Solomon and the other patriarchs of the Jewish Church. Christians today utilize the New Testament certainly, but back it up with the Old Testament simply borrowed from the Jews. What makes this really weird is that the Jewish Torah on which the Old Testament is based was not written for the Gentiles and most of its covenants are plainly only for the Jew.

(ii) Right from the time of Constantine, to prop up its fraudulent position, the Catholic Church began removing the competition with a war on descendants of Jesus, on heresy, magic and learning. From this time until around 1500 AD the Catholics specifically targeted not only Manicheans, Cathars and Bogomils but also Knights Templar, Jews (particularly Desposyni), Muslims and Gypsies. Fr. Malachi Martin relates that in 318 AD a delegation of Desposyni journeyed to Rome where they were given an audience with Bishop Silvester in the Lateran Palace. Their spokesman called Joses; argued that the Church should be rightfully centered in Jerusalem not in Rome and that a member of their Desposyni and genuine descendant of the Saviour should be the rightful Bishop of Jerusalem. They were actually told that the teachings of Christ had now been superceded by a doctrine that was more amenable to the requirements of Imperial Rome and that the power of salvation no longer rested in Jesus Christ but in fact with the Emperor

(Constantine).

Q.20. *How many Disciples did Jesus recruit and how were they selected? Did Jesus previously know them or did he select them at random? Who replaced Judas Iscariot?*

A. This must give clergy pretty severe heart burn. Firstly the primary source the Jewish Talmud on which the Old Testament is based, stated there were only <u>five</u> disciples as was fairly normal for Jewish Rabbi's, and then actually names them. Next the Bible gives three totally unrelated versions of how Jesus found his disciples making us wonder if any version is true, particularly when we find that Jesus actually knew these folks and they were mostly related to him. One of two disciples chosen to replace Judas Iscariot, was named <u>Joseph called Barsabas,</u> surnamed Justus and the other was <u>Matthias.</u> They finally cast lots and the choice went to Matthias.

That's the twenty questions.

Hope you enjoyed them and are pleased with your results. If you didn't do so well, be happy that you may have learned something from this exercise.

BIBLIOGRAPHY

Johann Mosheim, *'Institutes of Christian History'*, Ecclesiastical Historian 1755.

Higgins, Ana. Volume 1 page 143 as quoted by Kersey Graves in *'The Worlds Sixteen Crucified Saviours'*, 1875.

Moore, *'The Hindoo Pantheon'*, as quoted by Kersey Graves, *'The Worlds Sixteen Crucified Saviours'*.

Kersey Graves, *'The World's Sixteen Crucified Saviours, (Christianity Before Christ)'*. First Published 1875.

Martin Luther *'D'Aubigne'*, book. 5.

Martin Luther *D'Aubigne'*, book. 6.

Bart D. Ehrman, *'The Orthodox Corruption of Scripture'*,

Rudolf Karl Bultmann, *'Jesus Christ and Mythology'*, New York, Scribner 1958.

Martin Buber, *'I and Thou'; (Ich und Du*, 1923) translated by Ronald Gregor Smith (New York: Charles Scribner's Sons, 1958).

Martin Buber, *'Two Types of Faith'* translated by Norman P. Goldhawk. New York: Harper and Row. Pub. Torchbooks 1961.

Alister McGrath, *'In the Beginning, the Story of the King James Bible'*.

Vendyl Jones *'Will The Real Jesus Please Stand'*.

Dr. Barbara Theiring, *'Jesus, The Man'* Doubleday 1992.

Dr Barbara Thiering, *'Jesus of the Apocalypse; The Life of Jesus After the Crucifixion'* Doubleday 1995.

Dr. Barbara Thiering's report on Scroll: IQS 6 : 24-7: 25.

Jack P. Lewis, *'The English Bible from KJV to NIV: A History and Evaluation'*, published by Baker, 1981.

Francis X. King, *'Mind and Magic'*; (London: Dorling Kindersley Ltd., 1991) commenting on the statement by Tertullian.

Laurence Gardner, *'Genesis of the Grail Kings'*, Transworld London 1999.

Laurence Gardner, *'Lost Secrets of the Sacred Ark'*, Harper Collins London 2003.

Otto Scott, *'James I: The Fool As King'*, (Ross House: 1976).

Melvyn Bragg, *'Two Thousand Years - The First Millennium: The Birth of Christianity to the Crusades'*, Foreword.

Henri Frankfort, *'Kingship and the Gods: A Study of Ancient Near Eastern Religion as the Integration of Society and Nature.'* Distributed for the Oriental Institute of the University of Chicago. 1948 Series: (OIE) Oriental Institute Essays

Rev. Kythera Ann Grunge, *'The Festival of Unification'* http://www.geocities.com/~kabbalah/harmony.html

Immanuel Velikovsky, *'Worlds in Collision'*.

Joseph Fielding Smith, Jr., *'History of the Church'*, 6: 474

Brigham Young, *'Journal of Discourses'* 7: 333

Stephan A. Hoeller, *'The Genesis Factor'*. This article was also published in Quest, September 1997.

Christopher Knight and Robert Lomas, *'The Hiram Key'*, Arrow Books 1997.

Christopher Lomas & Robert Knight *'Uriel's Machine - The Ancient Origins of Science'*.

David Pratt, *'Who Was The Real Jesus? Jesus in the Talmud'* September 2001.

Tony Bushby, *'The Bible Fraud'*, Joshua Books Australia 2001.

Tony Bushby, *'The Secret in The Bible'*, Joshua Books Australia 2003.

Margaret Starbird, *'Magdalene's Lost Legacy: Symbolic Numbers and the Sacred Union of Christianity'*, 2003.

Alan F. Alford, *'When the Gods Came Down'*.

Alan F. Alford, *'Gods of The New Millenium'*, Hodder & Stoughton 2000.

James A. Sauer, *'The River Runs Dry'*, Biblical Archaeology Review, July/August, 1996.

Stuart Nettleton, *'The Alchemy Key'*.

Harold Bloom author of, *'American Religion'* (1992) and *'Omens of Millennium'* (1996).

G. A. Wells, *'The Jesus Myth'*, Chicago, IL: Open Court, 1999.

Earl Doherty, *'The Jesus Puzzle: Did Christianity begin with a Mythical Christ?'* Ottawa: Canadian Humanist Publications, 1999, pp. 26, 149, 294-5, 331. (http://www.magi.com/~oblio/jesus).

Michael Wood, *'Legacy-A Search for the Origins of Civilization'*.

Alvin Boyd Kuhn, *'The Great Myth of the Sun-Gods'*,

Professor Thomas S. Khun; *The Structure of Scientific Revolutions*, The University of Chicago Press, 1970 (1962).

Margaret Starbird, *'Magdalene's Lost Legacy: Symbolic Numbers and the Sacred Union of Christianity'*, 2003.

Gustav Dalman, *'Jesus Christ in the Talmud, Midrash, and the Zohar'* - <u>*1894*</u>.

T. Herford, *'Christianity in the Talmud'*,

Alvar Ellegard, *'Jesus: One Hundred Years Before Christ: A Study in Creative Mythology'*, (1999)

Josh McDowell and Bill Wilson, *'He Walked Among Us'*.

John Lightfoot, *'Commentary On the New Testament from the Talmud and Hebraica'*, Oxford University Press, 1859; with a second printing from Hendrickson Publishers Inc., 1995, vol. 1, p. v; vol. 3.

Sam Shamoun *'Jesus in the Rabbinic Traditions'*.

C. W. Leadbeater, *'Glimpses of Masonic History'*, The Theosophical Publishing House, Madras.

Dr Franz Hartmann, *'The Life of Jehoshua'*.

Dr. Raymond W. Bernard, B.A., M.A., Ph.D. (1964) '*The Secret Life of Jesus the Essene'*, *(Essene-Jesus-Apollonius Series Vol. 2)*

David Flusser Prof. Emeritus of Religion, Hebrew University; *'Jesus'*; translated by Ronald Walls, New York: Herder and Herder, 1969

Robert J. Gillooly, *'All About Adam & Eve'*, *Prometheus Books New york* 14228-2197

Robert Eisenman, *'James the Brother of Jesus: The Key to Unlocking the Secrets of Early Christianity and the Dead Sea Scrolls'*, Viking, Penguin, 1997.

Frank R. Zindler, *'How Jesus Got a Life'* vol. 34, no. 6 1992), .

Werner Keller, '*The Bible as History'*, 2nd revised edition (US: Bantam, 1988) 2nd revised edition (US: Bantam, 1988; translation by William Neil Hodder & Stroughton, London.

David L. Kent quoting from, *'Did Jesus Exist?'* vol. 36, no. 3 (1998), and *'American Atheist'*; same author,

H. P. Blavatsky, *'The Secret Doctrine'* (1888), Pasadena, CA: Theosophical University Press, 1977, 2:504fn. (http://www.truthbeknown.com);

H. P. Blavatsky, *'Collected Writings'*, Wheaton, IL: Theosophical Publishing House, 1950-91, 8:373, 11:495.

H. P. Blavatsky, *'Collected Writings'*, 8:374. Wheaton, IL: Theosophical Publishing House, 1950-91, 9:225;

'The New Testament Commentaries of H. P. Blavatsky', San Diego, CA: Point Loma Publications, 1987.

H.J. Spierenburg (comp.), *'The New Testament Commentaries of H. P. Blavatsky'*, San Diego, CA: Point Loma Publications, 1987.

H. P. Blavatsky, *'Collected Writings';* Vol 2.

Nesta Webster, *'Secret Societies and Subversive Movements'*, Boswell Publishing Co., Ltd., London, 1924.

S. Acharya, *'Did Jesus Live 100 BC?'*

S. Acharya, *'The Christ Conspiracy: The Greatest Story Ever Sold'*, Kempton, IL: Adventures Unlimited, 1999.

G. de Purucker, *'Fundamentals of the Esoteric Philosophy'*, Pasadena, CA: Theosophical University Press, 2nd ed.,

G. de Purucker, *'Fountain-Source of Occultism'*, Pasadena, CA: Theosophical University Press, 1974.

G. de Purucker, *'Studies in Occult Philosophy'*, Pasadena, CA: Theosophical University Press, 1973, p. 679; see also *'Dialogues of G. de Purucker'*, Pasadena, CA: Theosophical University Press, 1948, 2:425.

Fr. Raymond E. Brown, *'The Death of the Messiah'*, Vol. 2, Anchor/Doubleday: 1994

S. Dalley, *'Myths from Mesopotamia',*.

Bagient, Leigh & Lincoln, *'The Messianic Legacy'* Arrow Books 1996.

Mark Mason, *'In Search of the Loving God',* - Copyright © 1997.

John Allegro, *'The Sacred Mushroom and the Cross'*.

John M. Allegro, letter to Father Roland de Vaux, 16 September 1956.

Erich Zehren, *'The Crescent and the Bull',*; 1962, Sidwick & Jackson, London, translated from the German by James Cleugh, Hawthorn, NY.

Immanuel Velekovski, *'Worlds in Collision';*

Dr. M D Magee, 'Christmas - Sun Gods', 2001.

Karen Armstrong, 'In the Beginning', Harper Collins, London, 1997.

Karen Armstrong, 'A History of God',

Karen Armstrong, 'The Battle for God - Fundamentalism in Judaism, Christianity and Islam'.

Yvette Gayrard-Valy, 'The Story of Fossils'.

Zecharia Sitchin, 'Genesis Revisited', Avon Books.

Zecharia Sitchin, 'The Stairway to Heaven', Avon Books.

Sir Leonard Woolley, 'Ur of the Chaldees, Seven Years of Excavation'.

Professor Samuel Noah Kramer, 'Sumerian Mythology'

The Sumerian clay tablets 'Inanna's Descent to the Underworld.' According to Samuel Noah Kramer, "Inanna's Descent" was available in fourteen tablets and fragments (1972:84). He "reconstructed and deciphered" the poem over a six year (1972:83).

S. N. Kramer, Mythologies of The Ancient World.

Diane Wolkstein, Samuel Noah Kramer, 'Inanna, Queen of Heaven and Earth: Her Stories and Hymns from Sumer', Harper Collins, August 1983.

A. Heidel, 'The Babylonian Genesis'.

Stephanie Dalley, 'Myths from Mesopotamia: Creation, The Flood, Gilgamesh and Others'.

R.S. Harrington & P.K. Seidelmann; 'In Search of the Mystery Planet', Washington Post, Column: Space Outposts, November 8, 1987; Page c3.

Piotr Michalowski, 'The Lamentation over the Destruction of Sumer and Ur', (Mesopotamian Civilizations, 2).

Rachel Bromwich, editor and translator. 'Trioedd Ynys Prydein: The Welsh Triads'. Cardiff: University of Wales Press, 1978. ISBN 0-7083-0690-X.

LaHaye, Tim & Morris, John, 'The Ark on Ararat', 1976; Thomas Nelson Inc. and Creation Life Publishers, Nashville/New York.

Lloyd Bailey, 1989. 'Noah: The Person and the Story in History and Tradition', University of South Carolina Press.

Rutherford H. Platt, 'The Forgotten Books of Eden', New York 1974.

W. L. Reed, 'The Asherah in the Old Testament'.

Richard Elliott Friedman - 'Who Wrote the Bible'?.

L. Michael Barré PhD. *'El, God of Israel —Yahweh, God of Judah'*.

Robert Briffault, *'The Mothers'*, Vol. 3.

Ralph Ellis, *'Tempest & Exodus'*, Edfu Books 2000.

Baruch Halpern, *'The Baal (and the Asherah?) in Seventh - Century Judah'*, York University, Toronto.

G. W. Anderson, *'The History and Religion of Israel'*, Oxford UP, 1971.

Sol Abrams, *'Polytheism in Genesis: Baal and Ashtoreth vs. Yahweh'*.

http://www.infidels.org/library/magazines/tsr/1994/1/1poly94.hmtl

J. L. C. Lugo, *'Sungods in Mythology'*, Vienna, c 1870.

George Ivanovitch Gurdjieff, from the websites.

Timothy Freke and Peter Gandy, *'The Jesus Mysteries'*.

Library: Magazines: *The Skeptical Review.* 1990: Number 3. 'The Flat-Earth: Still an Embarassment to Bible Inerrantists' by Adrian Swindler, P. O. Box 695, Elmwood, IL 61529.

Excerpts from Global Insights.

J. W. Seregereus, *'St. Augustine, Secrets of the Christian Fathers'* - 1685.

Lilinah biti-Anat, *'Synopsis of the Ugaritic Myth of Baal'* (Six Incomplete Tablets & Some Fragments) 1995-7, code refined 28 July 1999.

Theosophical Society in America 1926 North Main Street, Wheaton, IL 60187 website, Article, 'Problems of a literal reading of the Bible and some solutions' Chapter 2 -The Testimony of Early Authorities

'From Jesus to Christ; A Story of the Storytellers', from The Gnostic Gospels by Elaine H. Pagels. Published by Vintage Books.

'Galileo', reported by De Genesi ad literam, end of book. ii.

Hans Kung, *'Infallible? An Inquiry'*; 1972.

Flavius Josephus, *'Antiquities of the Jews'*, Book I : 2.

Josephus, *'Antiquities of the Jews'* - Book XVII .

Flavius Josephus *'Antiquities of the Jews'*, Jud. xiii.

Bishop Eusebius (260-339 AD) (Eccl. Hist. lib.)

'Eusebius of Caesarea, Church History': Book II; First Apology, Mosheim volume 1, The Mar Saba monastery letter, found in 1958 by Morton Smith. Translation by Professor Morton Smith of Columbia University.

'Holman's Bible Dictionary', The New Unger's Bible Dictionary.

The writings of St Epiphanies, the Bishop of Salamis (315-403)

Babylonian Shabbath, 104b; also Babylonian Sanhedrin, 67a.

Wasiutynsky om Bibelen ... Utdrag av bind 2, side 287 - 296. 'Mennesket Og
Geniet', av Jeremi Wasiutynski, Nasjonalforlaget, 1944.

The Sepher Toldoth Jeshu (pp. 317-8, 415)

Origen: 'Contra Celsus'; Chapter XXXII.

The Acts of Thomas, Translation into English by M. R. James.

Jackson Snyder on the "Acta Thomae" (Acts of Thomas).

The Safed or Mehgheehlla Scroll discovered near Lake Tiberius in 1882 by a Jewish,
Russian physician Dayve Boris de Waltoff (b. 1865).

Photius' Bibliothecam code 33.

Dio Cassius book xlix.

"The Narrative of Joseph of Arimathea"

Christian Origins website. 'The Talmud Ben Stada Jesus Stories' Chapter 10.
167 - 169. Christian Origins is copyright © 2003-2004 Peter Kirby.
http://www.christianorigins.com/mead/ch10.htm."

Babylonian Shabbath, 104b.

Dr. Khalifa's translation of the Koran (Quran).

Yusuf Ali, 'The Holy Qur'an'.

Abdul-Haqq, 'Sharing Your Faith with a Muslim'.

Gospel of Nicodemus.

Catholic Encyclopaedia vol II 1907.

Gnostic Society Library's online translation of 'Against Heresies' by Irenaeus.

Gospel of Philip.

Tacitus, 'Annal's 16:54.

Tacitus report of 115 AD, (Book 15) in the 'Annals' (109) (Translated by Alfred John
Church and William Jackson Brodribb).

Justin Martyr, 'First Apology', 26 : 5.

Justin Martyr, 'First Apology', 26 : 1

Gaius Suetonius Tranquillus; 'Lives of the Caesars', which included (Divas Claudius)
'Life of Claudius'.

The Acts of Pilate, Chapter 9 : 32-33.

'The Catholic Encyclopaedia', Volume XI. Copyright © 1911 by Robert Appleton Company, Online Edition Copyright © 1999 by Kevin Knight.

L: Adventures Unlimited, 1999.

'Mexican Antiquities', Volume 6.

Georgius 'Thibetinum Alphabetum'

Egyptian - Coffin Texts, Spell 74.

'The Greyhound and the Bluebird': An Ancient Egyptian Love Story, freely translated from the hieroglyphs by John Anthony West.

'Lexicon Talmudicum', sub "Abanarbel" and Talmud Babli Sanhedrin 106b, 43a, 51a; New International Dictionary of Old Testament Theology & Exegesis Vol.3, 1260.

Saint Jerome, 'Life of Paulis', The First Hermit; Chapter VIII.

Sumerian 'Enuma elish' from Tablet 1 lines 1-6, translation by E. A. Speiser found on pages 60-72 of 'Ancient Near Eastern Texts Relating to the Old Testament', edited by James B. Pritchard (Princeton: Princeton University Press, 1969, 3rd edition with supplement). This source provides the full epic. Compare to Genesis 1:1-2.

'Epic of Gilgamesh', Tablet XL.

Eisenbrauns: Winona Lake, IN, 1989.

Egyptian - 'Book of the Dead', Chapter 114.

Book of Enoch.

Book of Jasher.

Plato, 'Timaeus' 23 100.

'The Apocryphal New Testament' M. R. James-Translation and Notes. Oxford: Clarendon Press, 1924.

The Catholic Encyclopaedia, Volume II Copyright © 1907 by Robert Appleton Company Online Edition Copyright © 1999 by Kevin Knight Imprimatur. +John M. Farley, Archbishop of New York.

The Columbia Electronic Encyclopaedia, Sixth Edition Copyright © 2000, Columbia University Press. Licensed from Lernout & Hauspie Speech Products N.V.

E. Sachau, 'Aramaische Papyrus and Ostraka aus einer judischen Militarkolonie zu Elephantine', (1911).

Origen (Origenes Adamantius), From the work 'Against Celsus' Chapter XXXII.

REFERENCES & ENDNOTES

All Bible references are from the King James Bible unless stated otherwise. All highlighting and underlining particularly in quotations is for emphasis of a point, and is <u>not</u> from the original. Note the meanings and differentiations of the following;

Kabbalah:

Defines practices based on Rabbinic tradition and primarily utilizes Hebrew and the Old Testament, though can expand to include the New Testament and Greek if using the same principles and techniques.

Cabala:

Defines practices based on Roman Catholic Catholicism and primarily utilizes Latin and the New Testament, though can expand to include the Old Testament and Hebrew if using the same principles and base assumptions.

Qabbalah:

Defines 'magical' ritual and ceremonial practices that can draw for authority from Kabbalah or Cabala. A form of practice that developed from Alchemical traditions of the Middle Ages. Has evolved very differently than its sources and often is in conflict as a result.

CHAPTER 1: THEY LIED TO US

(1) Professor Thomas S. Khun, 'The Structure of Scientific Revolutions', The University of Chicago Press, 1970 (1962)

(2) Bishop Eusebius (260-339 AD) (Eccl. Hist. lib. 2, cp. 12)

(3) Mosheim volume 1, page 198.

(4) Higgins, Ana. Volume 1 page 143 as quoted by Kersey Graves in 'The Worlds Sixteen Crucified Saviours', 1875, Page 336. Both Graves and Higgins acknowledge the outstanding original work of esteemed Christian author Sir William Jones, President of the Asiatic Researches society whose publications from the late 18th century pioneered the study of Eastern culture and religion with its comparison and correspondence to that of the West.

(5) Martin Luther, 'D'Aubigne', book. 5- Ch.1

(6) Martin Luther, 'D'Aubigne', book. 6- Ch.9

(7) Bart D. Ehrman, 'The Orthodox Corruption of Scripture', Page 10 referencing 'Clement', Strom VI, 9 and Origen, Ser Mt 100.

(8) Bart D. Ehrman, 'The Orthodox Corruption of Scripture', Page 4.

(9) J.W. Seregereus, 'St. Augustine Secrets of the Christian Fathers' - 1685).

(10) Reported by Kersey Graves, 'The World's Sixteen Crucified Saviours' Page 131.

(11) Rudolf Karl Bultmann, 'Jesus Christ and Mythology', Page 15, New York, Scribner 1958.

(12) Professor Martin Buber, 'I and Thou'; (Ich und Du, 1923) translated by Ronald Gregor Smith (New York: Charles Scribner's Sons, 1958).

(13) Alister McGrath, 'In the Beginning, the Story of the King James Bible'.

(14) Vendyl Jones, 'Will The Real Jesus Please Stand'.

(15) Dr. Barbara Theiring, 'Jesus, The Man', page 69

(16) Library: Magazines: 'The Skeptical Review': 1990: Number 3. "The Flat-Earth: Still an Embarassment to Bible Inerrantists" by Adrian Swindler, P. O. Box 695, Elmwood, IL 61529.

(17) Otto Scott, 'James I: The Fool As King', Pages 108, 111, 120, 194, 200, 224, 311, 353, 382 (Ross House: 1976).

(18) Excerpts from Global Insights

(19) Jack P. Lewis, 'The English Bible from KJV to NIV: A History and

Evaluation', published by Baker, 1981.

(20) Theosophical Society in America 1926 North Main Street, Wheaton, IL 60187website, Article, "*Problems of a literal reading of the Bible and some solutions*" Chapter 2 - *The Testimony of Early Authorities.*

(21) Francis X. King, *'Mind and Magic', Page 100; (London: Dorling Kindersley Ltd., 1991) commenting on the statement by Tertullian.*

(22) Laurence Gardner, *'Genesis of the Grail Kings',* Page 60.

(23) *'Galileo',* reported by De Genesi ad literam, end of book. ii.

(24) Hans Kung, *'Infallible? An Inquiry';* 1972.

CHAPTER 2 :
SOMETHING IS WRONG HERE

(1) Melvyn Bragg, *'Two Thousand Years - The First Millennium: The Birth of Christianity to the Crusades',* Foreword.

(2) Henri Frankfort, *'Kingship and the Gods: A Study of Ancient Near Eastern Religion as the Integration of Society and Nature.'* Distributed for the Oriental Institute of the University of Chicago. 1948 Series: (OIE) Oriental Institute Essays

(3) Dr. Barbara Thiering's report on Scroll: IQS 6 : 24-7: 25.

(4) Rev. Kythera Ann Grunge, *'The Festival of Unification'* http://www.geocities.com/~kabbalah/harmony.html

(5) Immanuel Velikovsky, *'Worlds in Collision',* Page 175-179.

(6) Joseph Fielding Smith, Jr., *'History of the Church',* 6: 474

(7) Brigham Young, *'Journal of Discourses'* 7: 333

(8) Stephan A. Hoeller, *'The Genesis Factor'.* This article was also published in Quest, September 1997.

(9) Laurence Gardner, *'Genesis of the Grail Kings'* page 31 & 32.

(10) Laurence Gardner, *'Genesis of the Grail Kings'* page 31 & 32.

(11) Laurence Gardner, *'Genesis of the Grail Kings'* page 31 & 32.

(12) James A. Sauer, *'The River Runs Dry',* Biblical Archaeology Review, July/August, 1996.

(13) Laurence Gardner, *'Genesis of the Grail Kings',* Page 31 & 32.

(14) Flavius Josephus, *'Antiquities of the Jews'* Book 1 : 2.

(15) Dr. Barbara Theiring, *'Jesus the Man',* page 69-71.

(16) Josephus *'Antiquities'* Jud. xiii, page xv. Pliny also confirms this.

(17) Christopher Knight and Robert Lomas, *'The Hiram Key'*, Page 97.

(18) David Pratt, *'Who Was the Real Jesus'*.

(19) Christopher Knight and Robert Lomas, *'The Hiram Key'*, Page 94.

(20) Tony Bushby, *'The Bible Fraud'*, Chapter 8.

(21) Margaret Starbird, *'Magdalene's Lost Legacy: Symbolic Numbers and the Sacred Union of Christianity'*, 2003.

(22) Tony Bushby, *'The Bible Fraud'*, Page 107.

(23) Tony Bushby, *'The Bible Fraud'*. Page 107.

Chapter 3 :
LIES & DECEPTION

(1) Alan F. Alford, *'When the Gods Came Down'*, Page 336.

(2) Laurence Gardner, *'Genesis of the Grail Kings'*. Page xviii, quoting the Catholic Churches, Apostolic Constitutions.

(3) This letter was found in the Mar Saba monastery, southeast of Jerusalem, in 1958, by Morton Smith. Translation by Professor Morton Smith of Columbia University.

(4) Stuart Nettleton, *'The Alchemy Key'*, Page 315.

(5) Harold Bloom author of, *'American Religion'* (1992) and *'Omens of Millennium'* (1996).

CHAPTER 4 :
THE JESUS PEDIGREE

(1) G. A. Wells, *'The Jesus Myth'*, Chicago, IL: Open Court, 1999, pp. ix–x.

(2) David Pratt, *'Who Was The Real Jesus'*, quoting Earl Doherty, *'The Jesus Puzzle: Did Christianity begin with a mythical Christ?'* Ottawa: Canadian Humanist Publications, 1999, pp. 26, 149, 294–5, 331. (http://www.magi.com/~oblio/jesus).

(3) Michael Wood, *'Legacy-A Search for the Origins of Civilization'* page 34 & 35.

(4) Alvin Boyd Kuhn, *'The Great Myth of the Sun-Gods'*,

(5) *Holman's Bible Dictionary*; The New Unger's Bible Dictionary.

(6) Josephus, *'Antiquities of the Jews'* - Book XVII . *"Now Herod the king had at this time nine wives; one of them Antipater's mother, and another the high priest's daughter, by whom he had a son of his own name. He had also one who was his brother's daughter, and another his sister's daughter; which two had no children. One of his wives also was*

of the Samaritan nation, whose sons were Antipas and Archelaus, and whose daughter was Olympias; which daughter was afterward married to Joseph, the king's brother's son; but Archelaus and Antipas were brought up with a certain private man at Rome. Herod had also to wife Cleopatra of Jerusalem, and by her he had his sons Herod and Philip; which last was also brought up at Rome. Pallas also was one of his wives, which bare him his son Phasaelus. And besides these, he had for his wives Phedra and Elpis, by whom he had his daughters Roxana and Salome. As for his elder daughters by the same mother with Alexander and Aristobulus, and whom Pheroras neglected to marry, he gave the one in marriage to Antipater, the king's sister's son, and the other to Phasaelus, his brother's son. And this was the posterity of Herod."

Josephus, 'Antiquities of the Jews' – Book XVII –

"He also allotted one of Aristobulus's daughters to Antipater's son, and Aristobulus's other daughter to Herod, a son of his own, who was born to him by the high priest's daughter; for it is the ancient practice among us to have many wives at the same time..... So Herod yielded to him, and changed his resolution at his entreaty; and the determination now was, that Antipater himself should marry Aristobulus' daughter, and Antipater's son should marry Pheroras's daughter. So the espousals for the marriages were changed after this manner, even without the king's real approbation."

(7) Flavius Josephus, 'Antiquities of the Jews' – Book XVII – chapter 3; verse 2,.

(8) Gustav Dalman, 'Jesus Christ in the Talmud, Midrash, and the Zohar' - _1894_.

(9) T. Herford, Christianity in the Talmud', pp. 37 seqq, 344 seqq."

(10) Stuart Nettleton, 'The Alchemy Key', Page 151& 241.

(11) Stuart Nettleton, 'The Alchemy Key', Page 150.

(12) Stuart Nettleton, 'The Alchemy Key', Page 318; H.P. Blavatsky, 'Isis Unveiled',Vol 2 Page 382.

(13) Alvar Ellegard, 'Jesus: One Hundred Years Before Christ: A Study in Creative Mythology' (1999) p. 158. Professor Ellegard was until recently Dean of the Faculty of Arts at the University of Goteburg, Sweden.

(14) David Pratt, 'Who Was the Real

Jesus', drawing on the work of Michael Wise.

(15) This is found in the writings of St Epiphanies, the Bishop of Salamis (315-403)

(16) Babylonian Shabbath, 104b; also Babylonian Sanhedrin, 67a.

(17) Wasiutynsky om Bibelen ... Utdrag av bind 2, side 287 - 296. "Mennesket og geniet", av Jeremi Wasiutynski, Nasjonalforlaget, 1944.

(18) Sam Shamoun, *Jesus in the Rabbinic Traditions'*.

(19) David Pratt, *'Who Was The Real Jesus, Jesus in the Talmud'*.

(20) The *'Sepher Toldoth Jeshu'* (pp. 317-8, 415)

(21) Josh McDowell and Bill Wilson, *'He Walked Among Us'*, Page 69.

(22) Tony Bushby, *'The Bible Fraud'*, Page 30.

(23) John Lightfoot, *'Commentary On the New Testament from the Talmud and Hebraica'*, Oxford University Press, 1859; with a second printing from Hendrickson Publishers Inc., 1995, vol. 1, p. v; vol. 3, Page 55.

(24) Origen: *'Contra Celsus'*; Chapter XXXII.

(25) Sam Shamoun *'Jesus in the Rabbinic Traditions'*.

(26) Tony Bushby *'The Bible Fraud'*-Page 30.

(27) Stuart Nettleton, *'The Alchemy Key'*, Page 150.

(28) Tony Bushby *'The Bible Fraud'*-Page 155.

(29) C.W. Leadbeater, *'Glimpses of Masonic History'*, The Theosophical Publishing House, Madras.

(30) Tony Bushby, *'The Secret in the Bible'*, Page 35.

(31) Tony Bushby, *'The Secret in the Bible'*, Page 35.

(32) Kersey Graves, *'The World's Sixteen Crucified Saviours, (Christianity Before Christ)'* Page 56. First Published 1875.

(33) Dr Franz Hartmann, *'The Life of Jehoshua'*.

(34) Dr. Barbara Theiring, *'Jesus the Man'*, Page 110.

(35) Reported in *'From Jesus to Christ; A Story of the Storytellers'*, from *'The Gnostic Gospels'* by Elaine H. Pagels. Published by Vintage Books.

(36) *'The Acts of Thomas'*, Translation into English by M. R. James.

(37) Tony Bushby, *'The Bible Fraud'*, Page 91.

(38) The God of Ancient Mexico, Quetzalcoatl was a twin, and so was Judas Thomas. The Buddha's soul-twin was Vajrapani. The

twin motif recurs throughout *'The Acts of Judas Thomas'*, where Thomas is repeatedly recognized as the twin of Jesus. Some Gnostics thought that each soul imprisoned in a human body has a counterpart angel in the heavenly realm to which it is joined at death — if its possessor is an enlightened one. The roles of the favrashi in Zoroastrianism and Vajrapani in Buddhism are not entirely unlike the twin motif of Judas Thomas and Jesus.

(39) Jackson Snyder on the *'Acta Thomae'* (Acts of Thomas).

(40) *'The Acts of Thomas'*

(41) Tony Bushby *'The Bible Fraud'*, Page 84.

(42) Tony Bushby, *'The Bible Fraud'*, Page 31-2 reports on The Safed or Mehgheehlla Scroll. This document was discovered near Lake Tiberius in 1882 by a Jewish, Russian physician Dayve Boris de Waltoff (b. 1865).

(43) Dr. Raymond W. Bernard, B.A., M.A., Ph.D. (1964) *'The Secret Life of Jesus the Essene'*, (Essene-Jesus-Apollonius Series Vol. 2).

(44) Tony Bushby, *'The Bible Fraud'*, Page 31-2.

(45) Barbara Theiring, *'Jesus the Man'*, page 76 & 77.

(46) Martin Buber, *'Two Types of Faith'* translated by Norman P. Goldhawk. New York: Harper and Row. Pub. Torchbooks 1961.

(47) David Flusser Prof. Emeritus of Religion, Hebrew University; *'Jesus'*; translated by Ronald Walls, New York: Herder and Herder, 1969

(48) Vendyl Jones, *'Will the Real Jesus Please Stand?'* page 2-9.

(49) Robert J. Gillooly, *'All About Adam & Eve'*.

(50) Sanhedrin 43a.

(51) Josh McDowell and Bill Wilson, *'He Walked Among Us'*, Page 65.

(52) Laurence Gardner, *'Lost Secrets of the Sacred Ark'*. Page 208.

(53) Robert Eisenman, *'James the Brother of Jesus: The Key to Unlocking the Secrets of Early Christianity and the Dead Sea Scrolls'*, Page 119. Viking, Penguin, 1997.

(54) Laurence Gardner, *'Lost Secrets of the Sacred Ark'* Page 208-9.

CHAPTER 5 : THE CRUCIFIXION

(1) David L. Kent quoting from, *'Did Jesus Exist?'* vol. 36, no. 3 (1998).

(2)   Tony Bushby, *'The Bible Fraud'*
       Page 87.

(3)   Photius' Bibliothecam code 33.

(4)   David L. Kent quoting from, *'Did
       Jesus Exist?'* vol. 36, no. 3 (1998),
       and *'American Atheist'*; same
       author, *"How Jesus Got a Life"*
       vol. 34, no. 6 1992), Frank R.
       Zindler.

(5)   Werner Keller, *'The Bible as
       History'*, 2nd revised edition (US:
       Bantam, 1988) Page 434; 2nd
       revised edition (US: Bantam,
       1988; translation by William Neil
       Hodder & Stroughton, London.

(6)   Dio Cassius book xlix, page 405.

(7)   Dr. Raymond W. Bernard, B.A.,
       M.A., Ph.D. (1964) *'The Secret
       Life of Jesus the Essene'*, (Essene-
       Jesus-Apollonius Series Vol. 2).

(8)   Dr. Raymond W. Bernard, B.A.,
       M.A., Ph.D. (1964) *'The Secret
       Life of Jesus the Essene'*, (Essene-
       Jesus-Apollonius Series Vol. 2).

(9)   (http:/www.truthbeknown.com);
       H. P. Blavatsky, *'The Secret
       Doctrine'* (1888), Pasadena, CA:
       Theosophical University Press,
       1977, 2:504fn.

(10) S. Acharya, *'Did Jesus Live 100
       BC?'* pp. 138-9; S. Acharya, *'The
       Christ Conspiracy: The Greatest
       Story Ever Sold'*, Kempton, IL:
       Adventures Unlimited, 1999,
       Page 326

(11) Vendyl Jones *'Will The Real
       Jesus Please Stand'* Page 3-15.

(12) Tony Bushby, *'The Secret in the
       Bible'*, quoting from the
       Egyptian, *'Book of the Dead'*.

(13) *'The Narrative of Joseph of
       Arimathea'* quoted by Tony
       Bushby, *'The Secret in the Bible'*,
       Page 102.

(14) *'The Narrative of Joseph of
       Arimathea'*

(15) *'The Narrative of Joseph of
       Arimathea'*

(16) *'The Narrative of Joseph of
       Arimathea.'*

(17) *'The Narrative of Joseph of
       Arimathea'*

(18) Tony Bushby, *'The Secret in The
       Bible'* also see Christian Origins
       website. *'The Talmud Ben Stada
       Jesus Stories'* Chapter 10. 167 -
       169. Christian Origins is
       copyright © 2003-2004 Peter
       Kirby.
       http://www.christianorigins
       .com/mead/ch10.htm."

(19) Christian Origins Website. *'The
       Talmud Ben Stada Jesus Stories'*
       Chapter 10. 167 - 169.
       Christian Origins http://
       www.christianorigins.com/ is
       copyright © 2003-2004 Peter
       Kirby.

http://www.christianorigins
.com/mead/ch10.html

(20) Ibid plus Babylonian Shabbath, 104b.

(21) H. P. Blavatsky, 'Collected Writings'; Vol 2; Page 386.

(22) G. de Purucker, 'Fundamentals of the Esoteric Philosophy', Pasadena, CA: Theosophical University Press, 2nd ed., 1979, p. 320; G. de Purucker, 'Fountain-Source of Occultism', Pasadena, CA: Theosophical University Press, 1974, pp. 484, 496, 522.

(23) Fr. Raymond E. Brown, 'The Death of the Messiah', Vol. 2, Anchor/Doubleday: 1994

(24) Dr. Khalifa's translation of the Koran (Quran).

(25) Yusuf Ali, 'The Holy Qur'an', Page 230.

(26) Abdul-Haqq, 'Sharing Your Faith with a Muslim', Page 133.

(27) From the Sumerian clay tablets 'Inanna's Descent to the Underworld.' According to Samuel Noah Kramer, "Inanna's Descent" was available in fourteen tablets and fragments (1972:84). He "reconstructed and deciphered" the poem over a six year period. (1972:83).

(28) S. Dalley, 'Myths from Mesopotamia', Page 13.

(29) Stuart Nettleton, 'The Alchemy Key', Page 36.

(30) Dr. Barbara Thiering, 'Jesus of the Apocalypse', Page vii.

(31) Bagient, Leigh & Lincoln, 'The Messianic Legacy', Page 76.

(32) Johann Mosheim, 'Institutes of Christian History', Ecclesiastical Historian 1755.

(33) Acts 1 : 21-26 "And they appointed two, Joseph called Barsabas, who was surnamed Justus."

(34) Gospel of Nicodemus. 9 : 5 "and let Dysmas and Gestas the two malefactors be crucified with thee." and Gospel of Nicodemus 10 : 2 "And one of the malefactors that were hanged [by name Gestas] spake unto him, saying: If thou be the Christ, save thyself, and us. But Dysmas answering rebuked him."

(35) Catholic Encyclopaedia vol II 1907 Page 582.

(36) Gnostic Society Library's online translation of 'Against Heresies' by Irenaeus.

(37) Gospel of Philip.

(38) Dr Barbara Thiering, 'Jesus of the Apocalypse; The Life of Jesus After the Crucifixion', Page 11.

(39) Dr. Barbara Thiering, 'Jesus the Man', Page 343.

(40) Mark Mason, 'In Search of the

Loving God', – Copyright © 1997.

(41) Ibid.

(42) Tacitus, *'Annals'* 16:54.

(43) Ibid.

(44) H. P. Blavatsky *'Collected Writings'*, 8:374. Wheaton, IL: Theosophical Publishing House, 1950-91, 9:225; see also 8:373, 11:495. See H.J. Spierenburg (comp.), *'The New Testament Commentaries of H. P. Blavatsky'*, San Diego, CA: Point Loma Publications, 1987.

(45) Tacitus report of 115 AD, (Book 15) in *'The Annals'* (109) (Translated by Alfred John Church and William Jackson Brodribb).

(46) Tony Bushby, *'The Bible Fraud'* - page 94 & 95.

(47) Justin Martyr, *'First Apology'*, 26 : 5.

(48) Ibid.

(49) Gaius Suetonius Tranquillus; *'Lives of the Caesars'*, which included (Divas Claudius) Life of Claudius.

(50) The Acts of Pilate Chapter 9 : 32-33.

(51) The Catholic Encyclopaedia, Volume XI. Copyright © 1911 by Robert Appleton Company, Online Edition Copyright © 1999 by Kevin Knight.

(52) Justin Martyr, *'First Apology'*, 26 : 1.

(53) Nesta Webster, *'Secret Societies and Subversive Movements'*, Boswell Publishing Co., Ltd., London, 1924.

(54) Eusebius of Caesarea, *'Church History'*: Book II; First Apology, 26.

(55) Dr Barbara Thiering, *'Jesus the Man'*, Pages 106-7.

(56) Stuart Nettleton, *'The Alchemy Key'*, Page 145.

(57) John Allegro, *'The Sacred Mushroom and the Cross'*.

CHAPTER 6 : ALL THE OTHER SAVIOURS

(1) John M. Allegro to Father Roland de Vaux, 16 September 1956.

(2) Erich Zehren, *'The Crescent and the Bull'*, Page 114; 1962, Sidwick & Jackson, London.

(3) Erich Zehren, *'The Crescent and the Bull'*, Page 126 & 127; 1962, Sidwick & Jackson, London.

(4) Reeves, Justin, page 86, referred to by Kersey Graves, *'The World's Sixteenth Crucified Saviours'*, page 201.

(5) Alvin Boyd Kuhn, *'The Great Myth of the Sun-Gods'*.

(6) David Pratt, *'Who Was The Real Jesus?'* September 2001.

(7) Stuart Nettlefold, *'The Alchemy Key'*, Page 33.

(8) Christopher Knight and Robert Lomas, *'The Hiram Key'*.

(9) Immanuel Velekovski, *'Worlds in Collision';*

(10) H. P. Blavatsky, *'Collected Writings'*, Wheaton, IL: Theosophical Publishing House, 1950-91, 9:225; see also 8:373, 11:495. See H.J. Spierenburg (comp.), *'The New Testament Commentaries of H.P. Blavatsky'*, San Diego, CA: Point Loma Publications, 1987.

(11) G. de Purucker, *'Studies in Occult Philosophy'*, Pasadena, CA: Theosophical University Press, 1973, p. 679; see also *'Dialogues of G. de Purucker'*, Pasadena, CA: Theosophical University Press, 1948, 2:425.

(12) Kersey Graves, *'The Worlds Sixteen Crucified Saviours'*, Foreword.

(13) Kersey Graves, *'The Worlds Sixteen Crucified Saviours'*.

(14) Kersey Graves, *'The Worlds Sixteen Crucified Saviours'*. Page 35 & 36.

(15) Kersey Graves, *'The Worlds Sixteen Crucified Saviours'*. Page 61.

(16) Kersey Graves, *'The Worlds Sixteen Crucified Saviours'*; Page 59.

(17) Kersey Graves, *'The Worlds Sixteen Crucified Saviours'*; Page 59.

(18) Kersey Graves, *'The Worlds Sixteen Crucified Saviours'*. Page 64- 65.

(19) Kersey Graves, *'The Worlds Sixteen Crucified Saviours'*. Page 69.

(20) Kersey Graves, *'The Worlds Sixteen Crucified Saviours'*. Page 68.

(21) Dr. M D Magee, *'Christmas - Sun Gods'*, 2001.

(22) Kersey Graves, *'The Worlds Sixteen Crucified Saviours'*. Page 78.

(23) Kersey Graves, *'The Worlds Sixteen Crucified Saviours'*. Page 82.

(24) Kersey Graves, *'The Worlds Sixteen Crucified Saviours'*. Page 84.

(25) Kersey Graves, *'The Worlds Sixteen Crucified Saviours'*. Page 84 & 85.

(26) Ibid

(27) Kersey Graves, *'The Worlds Sixteen Crucified Saviours'*.

Page 90.

(28) Kersey Graves, 'The Worlds
Sixteen Crucified Saviours'.

(29) Kersey Graves, 'The Worlds
Sixteen Crucified Saviours'.
Page 301 and 315.

(30) Kersey Graves, 'The Worlds
Sixteen Crucified Saviours'.
Page 302

(31) Kersey Graves, 'The Worlds
Sixteen Crucified Saviours'.
Page 314.

(32) Kersey Graves, 'The Worlds
Sixteen Crucified Saviours'.
Page 189.

(33) Kersey Graves, 'The Worlds
Sixteen Crucified Saviours'.
Page 190.

(34) Karen Armstrong, 'In the
Beginning', Harper Collins,
London, 1997, Page 21.

(35) Laurence Gardner, 'Genesis of the
Grail Kings', Page 96.

(36) Laurence Gardner, 'Genesis of
the Grail Kings', Page 112.

(37) Kersey Graves, 'The Worlds
Sixteen Crucified Saviours';
Page 38.

(38) Kersey Graves, 'The Worlds
Sixteen Crucified Saviours'.
Page 38-39

(39) Kersey Graves, 'The Worlds
Sixteen Crucified Saviours';
Page 39, referencing 'Ruin of the

Empire' by Volney, Page 169.

(40) Kersey Graves, 'The Worlds
Sixteen Crucified Saviours'.
Page 39, referencing 'Ruin of The
Empire' by Volney, Page 169.

(41) Kersey Graves, 'The Worlds
Sixteen Crucified Saviours'.
Page 39; as quoted from the
'Vandidatsade of the Persians',
page 305 & 428.

(42) Kersey Graves, 'The Worlds
Sixteen Crucified Saviours'.
Page 39, referencing 'Ruin of The
Empire' by Volney, Page 169.

(43) Kersey Graves, 'The Worlds
Sixteen Crucified Saviours'.
Page 45.

(44) Erich Zehren, 'The Crescent and
the Bull', Page 135,1962,
Sidwick & Jackson, London.

(45) S. Acharya, 'Did Jesus Live 100
B.C.?' Pages 140-1, 188, 199-
201. IL: Adventures Unlimited,
1999.

(46) Kersey Graves, 'The Worlds
Sixteen Crucified Saviours'.
Page 102.

(47) Kersey Graves, 'The Worlds
Sixteen Crucified Saviours'.
Page 104-111 & 152.

(48) Moore, 'The Hindoo Pantheon', as
quoted by Kersey Graves, 'The
Worlds Sixteen Crucified Saviours'.

(49) Kersey Graves, 'The Worlds

Sixteen Crucified Saviours,
Page 128.

(50) *'Mexican Antiquities'*, Volume 6.

(51) *'Mexican Antiquities'*, Volume 6,
page 166.

(52) Georgius *'Thibetinum
Alphabetum'* page 202, Also
Kersey Graves, *'The Worlds
Sixteen Crucified Saviours'*.
Page 121.

(53) Georgius, *'Thibetinum
Alphabetum'*, Page 230.

(54) Kersey Graves, *'The Worlds
Sixteen Crucified Saviours'*.
Page 129.

(55) Coffin Texts, Spell 74.

(56) Kersey Graves, *'The Worlds
Sixteen Crucified Saviours'*.
Page 141.

(57) Ibid.

(58) *'The Greyhound and the Bluebird'*:
An Ancient Egyptian Love Story,
freely translated from the
hieroglyphs by John Anthony
West.

(59) Kersey Graves, *'The Worlds
Sixteen Crucified Saviours'*.
Page 144.

(60) Kersey Graves, *'The Worlds
Sixteen Crucified Saviours'*,
Page 146.

(61) Kersey Graves, *'The World's
Sixteen Crucified Saviors'*,
Page 72.

CHAPTER 7 : THE CHICKEN OR THE EGG

(1) Flavius Josephus, *'Antiquities of
the Jews'*, Chapter 1.

(2) Stuart Nettleton, *'The Alchemy
Key'*, Page 37.

(3) *Lexicon Talmudicum*, sub
"Abanarbel" and *Talmud Babli*
Sanhedrin 106b, 43a, 51a; see
Kersey Graves, *'The World's
Sixteen Crucified Saviours'*,
Page vii.

(4) Yvette Gayrard-Valy, *'The Story
of Fossils'*, Page 22.

(5) New International Dictionary
of Old Testament Theology &
Exegesis Vol.3, 1260.

(6) Saint Jerome, *'Life of Paulis, The
First Hermit'*; Chapter VIII, as
quoted by Tony Bushby, *'The
Secret in the Bible'*, Page 65.

(7) Stuart Nettleton, *'The Alchemy
Key'*, Page 146.

CHAPTER 8 : THE SUMERIAN INFLUENCE

(1) Erich Zehren, *'The Crescent and
the Bull'*, Page 41, translated
from the German by James
Cleugh, Hawthorn, NY.

(2) Zecharia Sitchin, *'The Stairway
to Heaven'*. Chapter X, Pages
197-207.

(3) Sir Leonard Woolley, *'Ur of the

Chaldees, Seven Years of Excavation'.

(4) Professor Samuel Noah Kramer, *'Sumerian Mythology'*

(5) Stuart Nettleton, *'The Alchemy Key'*, Page 64.

(6) Laurence Gardner, *'Genesis of the Grail Kings'*, Page 60.

(7) Sumerian *'Enuma elish'* from Tablet 1 lines 1–6, translation by E. A. Speiser found on pages 60–72 of *'Ancient Near Eastern Texts Relating to the Old Testament'*, edited by James B. Pritchard (Princeton: Princeton University Press, 1969, 3rd edition with supplement). This source provides the full epic. Compare to Genesis 1:1–2.

(8) A. Heidel, *'The Babylonian Genesis'*, Page 57.

(9) Stephanie Dalley, *'Myths from Mesopotamia: Creation, The Flood, Gilgamesh and Others'*, Page 9–10.

(10) R.S. Harrington & P.K. Seidelmann; *'In Search of the Mystery Planet'*, Washington Post, Column: Space Outposts, November 8, 1987; Page c3.

(11) Zecharia Sitchin, *'Genesis Revisited'*, Page 319.

(12) S. N. Kramer, *'Mythologies of The Ancient World'*, Page 103.

(13) Laurence Gardner, *'Genesis of*

(14) Laurence Gardner, *'Genesis of The Grail Kings'*, Page 79.

(15) Piotr Michalowski, *'The Lamentation over the Destruction of Sumer and Ur'*, (Mesopotamian Civilizations, 2). Eisenbrauns: Winona Lake, IN, 1989.

(16) Sumerian *'Enuma elish'*, translation by E. A. Speiser.

(17) *Epic of Gilgamesh*, Tablet XL.

(18) Rachel Bromwich, editor and translator. *'Trioedd Ynys Prydein: The Welsh Triads'*. Cardiff: University of Wales Press, 1978. ISBN 0-7083-0690-X.

(19) LaHaye, Tim & Morris, John, *'The Ark on Ararat'*, 1976; Thomas Nelson Inc. and Creation Life Publishers, Nashville/New York.

(20) Lloyd Bailey, *'Noah: The Person and the Story in History and Tradition'*, University of South Carolina Press. 1989.

(21) Book of Enoch as cited by Z. Sitchen in *'Stairway to Heaven'* Page 110.

(22) Book of Jasher 2 : 3.

(23) Plato, *'Timaeus'* 23 100.

(24) Laurence Gardner, *'Genesis of The Grail Kings'*, Page 101 & 123.

(25) Laurence Gardner, *'Genesis of*

The Grail Kings', Page 94.

(26) Laurence Gardner, *'Genesis of The Grail Kings'* Page 102;

(27) Laurence Gardner, *'Genesis of The Grail Kings'* Page 102; referencing Carlo Suares, *'The Cipher of Genesis'*, Page 137.

(28) Rutherford H. Platt, *'The Forgotten Books of Eden'*, New York 1974, Page 53.

(29) Laurence Gardner, *'Genesis of The Grail Kings,* Page 101.

(30) Diane Wolkstein Samuel Noah Kramer, *'Inanna, Queen of Heaven and Earth: Her Stories and Hymns from Sumer'*, Pages 4-9, Harper Collins, August 1983.

(31) Stuart Nettleton, *'The Alchemy Key'*, Page 196.

(32) *'Book of the Dead',* Chapter 114.

(33) *'The Apocryphal New Testament'* M. R. James-Translation and Notes. Oxford: Clarendon Press, 1924.

(34) Zecharia Sitchin, *'Genesis Revisited'*, Page 19.

CHAPTER 9 :
WHO IS THIS GOD?

(1) Laurence Gardner, *'Lost Secrets of the Sacred Ark'*, Page 42.

(2) Alan F. Alford, *'Gods of the New Millennium'*.

(3) Laurence Gardner, *'Genesis of the Grail Kings'*.

(4) Karen Armstrong, *'A History of God'*, Page 30.

(5) Stuart Nettleton, *'The Alchemy Key'*, Page 214, referencing Kersey Graves.

(6) Stuart Nettleton, *'The Alchemy Key'*, Page 246-7.

(7) Alan F. Ashford, *'When the Gods Came Down'*, Page 259.

(8) Alan F. Ashford, *'When the Gods Came Down'*, Page 259-260.

(9) Stuart Nettleton, *'The Alchemy Key'*, Page 92.

(10) Stuart Nettleton, *'The Alchemy Key'*, Page 92.

(11) Alan F. Alford, *'Gods of the New Millennium'*.

(12) Laurence Gardner, *Genesis of the Grail Kings*; Pages 64 & 85.

(13) Laurence Gardner, *'Genesis of the Grail Kings'*; Pages 64 & 85 plus W. L. Reed, *'The Asherah in the Old Testament'*.

(14) Richard Elliott Friedman - *'Who Wrote the Bible'? Page 153.*

(15) Laurence Gardner, *'Genesis of the Grail Kings'*; Pages 25 referencing; Judges 2 : 13 & 1 Kings 11 : 5, 32 .

(16) L. Michael Barré PhD. *'El, God of Israel —Yahweh, God of Judah'*.

(17) Reported by Stuart Nettleton,

'The Alchemy Key'.

(18) Laurence Gardner, 'Genesis of the Grail Kings', Page 26.

(19) Robert Briffault, 'The Mothers', Vol. 3, Page 109).

(20) Christopher Lomas & Robert Knight 'Uriel's Machine - The Ancient Origins of Science" Page 375.

(21) Lilinah biti-Anat, 'Synopsis of the Ugaritic Myth of Baal' (Six Incomplete Tablets & Some Fragments) 1995-7, code refined 28 July 1999.

(22) Ralph Ellis, 'Tempest & Exodus', Page 161.

(23) Laurence Gardner, 'Genesis of the Grail Kings' drawing on the work of Jewish scholar Raphael Patai.

(24) Baruch Halpern, 'The Baal (and the Asherah?) in Seventh - Century Judah', York University, Toronto.

(25) Baruch Halpern, 'The Baal (and the Asherah?) in Seventh - Century Judah', York University, Toronto.

(26) The Catholic Encyclopaedia, Volume II Copyright © 1907 by Robert Appleton Company Online Edition Copyright © 1999 by Kevin Knight Imprimatur. +John M. Farley, Archbishop of New York.

(27) The Columbia Electronic Encyclopaedia, Sixth Edition Copyright © 2000, Columbia University Press. Licensed from Lernout & Hauspie Speech Products N.V.

(28) Richard Elliott Friedman, 'Who Wrote the Bible?' Page 153.

(29) E. Sachau, Aramaische Papyrus and Ostraka aus einer judischen Militarkolonie zu Elephantine, (1911) page 25.

(30) Richard Elliott Friedman - 'Who Wrote the Bible?' Page 154.

(31) G. W. Anderson, 'The History and Religion of Israel', Oxford UP, 1971.

(32) Sol Abrams, 'Polytheism in Genesis: Baal and Ashtoreth vs. Yahweh'. http://www. infidels.org/library/magazines/ tsr/1994/1/1poly94.hmtl

(33) Johann Mosheim, 'Institutes of Christian History', Book 2, Ecclesiastical Historian 1755.

(34) J. L. C. Lugo, 'Sungods in Mythology', Vienna, c 1870.

(35) J. L. C. Lugo, 'Sungods in Mythology', Vienna, c 1870.

(36) Tony Bushby, 'The Bible Fraud'.

CHAPTER 10 : "GOD" IS NOT GOD'S NAME

(1) Origen (Origenes Adamantius), From the work 'Against Celsus'

Chapter XXXII.

(2) Ralph Ellis, *'Tempest & Exodus'*, Page 132.

(3) Laurence Gardner, *'Genesis of the Grail Kings'*; Page 64.

(4) Alan Alford, *'Gods of the New Millennium'*.

(5) Alan F. Alford, *'Gods of the New Millennium'*, Page 525.

(6) Stuart Nettleton, *'The Alchemy Key'*, Page 71-72.

CHAPTER 11 : WHERE DO WE GO FROM HERE?

(1) George Ivanovitch Gurdjieff.

(2) Karen Armstrong, *'The Battle for God - Fundamentalism in Judaism, Christianity and Islam'*.

(3) Kersey Graves, *'The Worlds Sixteen Crucified Saviours'*, Page 427-433.

(4) Kersey Graves, *'The Worlds Sixteen Crucified Saviours'*, Page 107.

(5) Ralph Ellis, *'Tempest & Exodus'*, Page 191.

(6) Dr. Raymond W. Bernard, B.A., M.A., Ph.D. (1964) *'The Secret Life of Jesus the Essene'*, (Essene-Jesus-Apollonius Series Vol. 2).

(7) Ibid

(8) Dr. Raymond W. Bernard, B.A., M.A., Ph.D. (1964) *'The Secret Life of Jesus the Essene'*, (Essene-Jesus-Apollonius Series Vol. 2).

(9) Timothy Freke and Peter Gandy, *'The Jesus Mysteries'*, Page 205.

(10) H. P. Blavatsky, *'Collected Writings'*, 8:173.

(11) Rev. Kythera Ann Grunge, *'The Festival of Unification'* http://www.geocities.com/~kabbalah/harmony.html

(12) Kersey Graves, *'The Worlds Sixteen Crucified Saviours'*.

(13) Tony Bushby, *'The Secret in the Bible'*, Page 298-9.

(14) Dr. Barbara Theiring, *'Jesus of the Apocalypse - The Life of Jesus after the Crucifixion'*.

INDEX

From the publisher

As publishers Joshua Books believe in freedom of speech and your right to have access to all points of view. The controversy created by Author Ian Ross Vayro will continue as more and more people seek the Truth. Ian's second book is presently in the early stages of editing.

Joshua Books is also the publisher for the internationally acclaimed author Tony Bushby.

If you have enjoyed reading *'They Lied to us in Sunday School'* then please take time to look at the titles by Tony Bushby featured over the following pages.

We also invite you to log on to www.joshuabooks.com and subscribe to our **free newsletter.** That way you will be kept right up to date with all that is happening at Joshua Books.

Joshua Books
JoshuaBooks.com

BOOKS BY TONY BUSHBY

To purchase visit www.joshuabooks.com

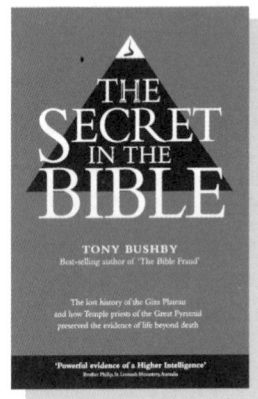  

What others have said about Tony Bushby's books...

I thoroughly enjoyed Tony Bushby's **The Bible Fraud**. *Its tale ended my own research into the origins and source material of the Bible (not for a book! Just my own curious hunger to know!). This author has done in a careful and extremely well researched book, far better than most in this genre. The attention to detail, which I have confirmed myself over the past twenty years from various sources, is validated and more accurate than many academic papers found in our universities.*

It is undoubtedly the most important book on Christianity and the Roman legacy ever written, and most likely will have the least impact because it explodes the mythology and power basis for a religion which will be impossible for most to swallow. It opens eyes to the true wonders and we finally put away the destructive toy of over simplified pacification tripe that exists in political, commercial establishment religions.

MAE, Isle of Sanday, Orkney, Scotland

Thank you for your huge contribution to unravelling millennia of obscuration.

Andrew Yates, International

A real truth seeker will realise that a guy who brings his bedroll to a library so he can research night and day would be an infinitely more reliable source than a writer whose main focus is fame and ego enhancement. Congratulations Tony Bushby.

Claudia, USA

ALSO FROM TONY BUSHBY